Teacher

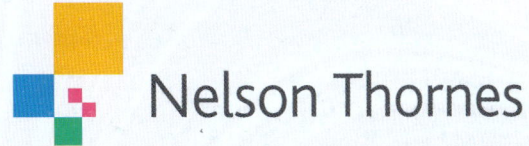

fusion

Science 11–14

Geoff Carr
Darren Forbes
Ruth Miller
Nick Pollock

Series Editor:
Lawrie Ryan

2

Nelson Thornes

Acknowledgements:

The authors wish to express their special thanks to the following people:

Neil Roscoe	David Sang
John Payne	Sam Holyman
Sarah Ryan	Phil Routledge
Amanda Wilson	Paddy Carr
Annie Hamblin	Harry Carr
Hazel Banfield	Pip Carr
Jane Taylor	Wilf Carr
Judy Ryan	Enid Carr
Paul Lister	

Text © Lawrie Ryan, Geoff Carr, Ruth Miller, Nick Pollock and Darren Forbes 2008

Original illustrations © Nelson Thornes Ltd 2008

The right of Lawrie Ryan, Geoff Carr, Ruth Miller, Nick Pollock and Darren Forbes to be identified as author of this work has been asserted by him/her in accordance with the Copyright, Designs and Patents Act 1988.

All rights reserved. The copyright holders authorise ONLY users of Fusion 2 Year 8 Teacher's Book to make photocopies for their own or their students' immediate use within the teaching context. No other rights are granted without permission in writing from the publishers or under licence from the Copyright Licensing Agency Limited. Further details of such licences (for reprographic reproduction) may be obtained from the Copyright Licensing Agency Limited, of Saffron House, 6–10 Kirby Street, London EC1N 8TS.

Copy by any other means or for any other purpose is strictly prohibited without prior written consent from the copyright holders. Application for such permission should be addressed to the publishers.

Any person who commits any unauthorised act in relation to this publication may be liable to criminal prosecution and civil claims for damages.

Published in 2008 by:
Nelson Thornes Ltd
Delta Place
27 Bath Road
CHELTENHAM
GL53 7TH
United Kingdom

10 11 12 / 10 9 8 7 6 5 4 3 2

A catalogue record for this book is available from the British Library

ISBN 978 0 7487 9837 7

Illustrations by GreenGate Publishing, Barking Dog Art, Harry Venning and Roger Penwill

Cover photograph: Photo Library

Page make-up by GreenGate Publishing Services, Tonbridge, Kent

Printed in China

Contents

Introduction · · · iv

B1	**Body Systems**	2
B1.1	Body Systems	2
B1.2	The Digestive System	4
B1.3	Digesting Food	6
B1.4	Food and a Balanced Diet	8
B1.5	Breathing	10
B1.6	Lungs	12
B1.7	Inhaled and Exhaled Air	14
B1.8	The Heart and Circulation	16
B1.9	Supplying the Cells	18
B1.10	Exercise	20
B1.11	Excretion and Homeostasis	22
B1.12	The Nervous System	24
Answers to End of Topic Questions		26

B2	**Ecology**	28
B2.1	Ecology	28
B2.2	Making Food	30
B2.3	Photosynthesis	32
B2.4	Leaves and Photosynthesis	34
B2.5	Food Chains	36
B2.6	Food Webs	38
B2.7	Food Pyramids and Energy Flow	40
B2.8	Predators and Prey	42
B2.9	Habitats and Adaptation	44
B2.10	Habitats Changing	46
B2.11	Investigating a Habitat (1)	48
B2.12	Investigating a Habitat (2)	50
Answers to End of Topic Questions		52

C1	**Elements and Compounds**	54
C1.1	Elements and Compounds	54
C1.2	Building Blocks	56
C1.3	Elements and their Properties	58
C1.4	Symbols	60
C1.5	Compounds and their Elements	62
C1.6	Compound Names	64
C1.7	Compound Formulas	66
C1.8	Properties of Compounds	68
C1.9	Word Equations	70
C1.10	Symbol Equations	72
C1.11	Mixtures	74
C1.12	Discovering Oxygen	76
Answers to End of Topic Questions		78

C2	**Our Planet**	80
C2.1	Our Planet	80
C2.2	Igneous Rocks	82
C2.3	Sedimentary Rocks	84
C2.4	Metamorphic Rocks	86
C2.5	Which Rock?	88
C2.6	Weathering	90
C2.7	Chemical Weathering	92
C2.8	Acid Rain	94
C2.9	Physical Weathering	96
C2.10	Erosion	98
C2.11	Rock Cycle	100
C2.12	Rocks in the Universe	102
Answers to End of Topic Questions		104

P1	**Light and Space**	106
P1.1	Light from Space	106
P1.2	Straight-line Light	108
P1.3	Materials and Light	110
P1.4	Mirror, Mirror on the Wall . . .	112
P1.5	Rays that Bend	114
P1.6	Colours of the Rainbow	116
P1.7	Sources of Light	118
P1.8	Solar System	120
P1.9	Phases of the Moon	122
P1.10	The Seasons	124
P1.11	Eclipses	126
Answers to End of Topic Questions		128

P2	**Heat and Sound**	130
P2.1	Heat and Sound	130
P2.2	Taking Temperatures	132
P2.3	Warming up, Cooling down	134
P2.4	Thermal Conduction and Insulation	136
P2.5	Expansion and Contraction	138
P2.6	Radiation and Convection	140
P2.7	Seeing Sounds	142
P2.8	How Sound Travels	144
P2.9	Noise Annoys	146
Answers to End of Topic Questions		148

How Science Works	150
Carrying out Project Work	150
Communicating New Science	152
The Application of Science	154
Glossary	156
Acknowledgements	160

Welcome to Fusion

About the course

Motivate, Improve, Progress …

Fusion has been written specifically to help you to deliver the new Programme of Study for Key Stage 3 Science from 2008. With its fully blended approach including the Pupil Book, Teacher Book and online electronic resources, you have the tools in place to deliver your science lessons in a stimulating and engaging way, with differentiation included throughout. The electronic resources are located in our online environment, Nelson Thornes learning space, and provide you with the facility to assign differentiated resources to individual pupils making **personalising learning** easy. **Assessment for learning** is built in throughout the course.

The Pupil Book

Fusion Pupil Book is structured into six teaching topics per year each with How Science Works (HSW) integrated throughout. Each topic has an Introduction lesson enabling you to establish prior learning, usually through the means of a practical activity. The Introduction lesson is also used to experiment and formulate ideas about the forthcoming topic. All this is done in a context that pupils are familiar with, either in their everyday lives or that they have previously visited relevant topics in science lessons.

The topic itself has a very practical approach to motivate and engage pupils. Context-led throughout, the text is highly accessible to ensure that there are no barriers to learning and understanding about science.

At the end of each topic is a spread of questions – one page assesses knowledge and understanding of the range and content whilst the other page assesses application of ideas and the How Science Works approach.

In addition to How Science Works being integrated throughout, there is also additional support for How Science Works at the back of the Pupil Book and Teacher Book. This additional section incorporates a skills-based approach and can be used separately or integrated within the teaching of the rest of the topics.

How to use the Teacher Book

This Teacher Book is designed to help you to plan and deliver motivating and engaging science lessons. It contains a reduced size replica of the Pupil Book page, and the curriculum references, objectives, opportunities to incorporate How Science Works, Functional Skills, Teaching Notes, Practical Support Notes, Support for SEN and Extension and potential homeworks to support the delivery of the lesson.

Questions: In-text questions support the learning from the page and build confidence. The Summary Questions reflect the Learning Objectives for the spread and are listed hierarchically. Answers are provided in the Teacher Book to support the teacher.

Functional skills: Opportunities have been identified to help you to deliver Functional skills throughout your teaching of science. Functional skills are practical skills in English, mathematics, and ICT. These equip individuals to work confidently, effectively and independently in their every day lives, be it in school, at home or in the workplace. Other opportunities for linking up to other subjects are explored in both the Teacher Book and Pupil Book.

Introduction double-page spread: These two pages provide the information to help you teach the topic ahead. It provides details of how the new Programme of Study will be covered by the topic. It also covers Level Descriptors for the topic as well as Learning Objectives and learning outcomes for the Introduction lesson including How Science Works opportunities.

The Lesson: Every page of the Pupil Book and Teacher Book has electronic support located in the online environment, Nelson Thornes learning space. With two starter and two plenary suggestions tailored to the teaching time, the lesson has a suggested route through with lots of teaching ideas based around each Pupil Book double-page spread. For every practical within the Pupil Book you will find the corresponding Practical Support feature in the Teacher Book that gives a list of the equipment needed, safety references and further guidance to carry out the practical. Differentiated Practical Support sheets, Teacher Notes and Technician Notes are located in the Nelson Thornes online learning environment.

Differentiation: Ideas to support pupils with SEN and to extend those who have successfully completed other activities in the lesson are provided to help you tailor your lessons to individuals.

Homework suggestions: Based around the lesson, potential stimuli for homework are identified, and there is additional support for homework activities in the online resources.

Online Resources

Animations, simulations, interactive activities and non-interactive worksheets are located in the Nelson Thornes learning space to fully support the delivery of the Fusion course. These are linked to the Pupil Book and help deliver the ideas suggested within the Teacher Book as indicated by icons.

A wealth of resources is included in the online environment including differentiated practical support sheets, Teacher Notes and Technician Notes, differentiated Level Assessed Tasks, Webquests, resources to support starters and plenaries, interactive activities to support teaching and learning, Lesson Objectives (including WALT and WILF objectives), Revision Quizzes, Progress Checks, differentiated homeworks and much more!

To help you identify the electronic resources that have been created to specifically support the lesson, icons have been placed in the Teacher Book next to the area that they support. All topics additionally have Revision Quizzes and Progress Checks in both an interactive and non-interactive format, a Level Assessed Task and a Webquest. The assessment resources provide you with an opportunity to monitor and record pupil progress and tailor your lessons accordingly.

To help you to determine the type of electronic resources available to support the lesson, the following icons have been used:

Video – Exciting and relevant video taken from a variety of sources to enhance the learning of certain topics

Worksheets – to include practicals, Teacher Notes, Technician Notes, some homeworks and specific materials to support lower attainers and extend higher attainers.

Interactives – simulations, animations, Webquests, interactive activities and PowerPoints.

Learning Objectives PowerPoint – for each lesson to include WALT (We Are Learning To) and WILF (What I am Looking For)

We hope that this course will provide you with everything you need to engage your pupils in their science lessons and that its flexible approach will help you to motivate all pupils to progress and achieve their best. Good luck!

B1.1 Body Systems

NC links for the topic
- Organisms, behaviour and health.
- Life processes are supported by the organisation of cells into tissues, organs and body systems.
- Use a range of scientific methods and techniques to develop and test ideas and explanations.
- Plan and carry out practical investigations both individually and in groups.
- Assess risk and work safely in the laboratory.
- Obtain, record and analyse data from a wide range of primary and secondary sources, including ICT sources, and use their findings to provide evidence for scientific explanations.
- Evaluate scientific evidence and working methods.
- Use appropriate methods, including ICT, to communicate scientific information and contribute to presentations and discussions about scientific issues.

Level descriptors for the topic
- **AT2 level 4:** Pupils describe improvements, processes and phenomena related to organisms, their behaviour and the environment. They recognise that evidence can support or refute scientific ideas. They recognise some applications and implications of science.
- **AT2 level 5:** Pupils describe processes and phenomena related to organisms, their behaviour and the environment, drawing on abstract ideas and using appropriate terminology. They explain processes in more than one step or using a model. They apply and use knowledge and understanding in familiar contexts. They describe applications and implications of science.
- **AT2 level 6:** Pupils use appropriate terminology. They apply and use their knowledge in unfamiliar contexts. They describe some evidence for some accepted scientific ideas. They explain the importance of some applications and implications of science.

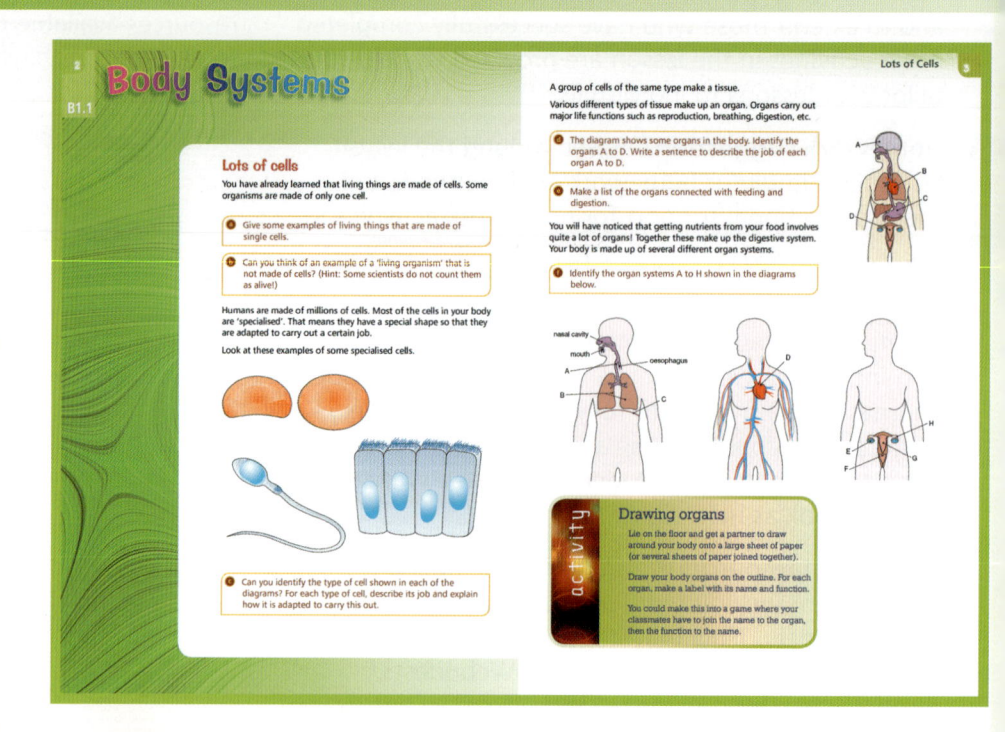

Learning Objectives
Pupils should learn:
- That cells are organised into tissues, organs and body systems.
- The structure and functions of body organs.
- The organisation and functions of body systems.

Learning Outcomes
- All pupils should be able to understand that cells are organised into tissues, organs and body systems.
- Most pupils should be able to describe the structure and functions of the body organs and body systems.
- Some pupils should also be able to describe the relationship between different body systems.

Learning styles
Visual: Observing the PowerPoint presentation.
Auditory: Listening to the explanations.
Kinaesthetic: Taking part in the body parts activity.
Interpersonal: Working in pairs or groups on the body parts activity.
Intrapersonal: Completing the word search.

The Lesson

Starter Suggestions

Locked up in a cell

Working in groups, tell the pupils to imagine that they are locked up in a prison cell. Get them to work out what they would need to be supplied with and what they would need to get rid of in order to be able to survive. Ask a group for their ideas and then discuss how this can be related to the needs of body cells. Widen the discussion to include plants and ask if the conditions would be different. [This should revise the concept of the cell and the differences between plant and animal cells.] (10–15 mins)

Organ word search

Ask the pupils to complete a word search with the names of the major organs of the body in it. This can be made simple or more complex, depending on the time available and the level of attainment of the pupils. Put a time limit on it or award a small prize for the pupil who completes it first. (5–10 mins)

Main Lesson

- Let the pupils do the activity 'Drawing organs', working in pairs or in groups. One pupil in each group should lie on top of a piece of lining paper, or several pieces of paper joined together, or the back of a large poster placed on the floor. With a felt tip marker, they draw around the outline of the pupil's body. Give the pupils in each group a list of body organs which they must draw within their outline. They should aim to get the organ in the correct location and also try to get the size right, labelling each organ with its name and function. Pin the outlines up around the room and score each group for location and approximate size of the organs.

- Illustrate the specialisation of cells using a PowerPoint presentation of the different types of cells in a section of the small intestine or a blood vessel such as an artery or a vein. Give the pupils a worksheet so that they have a record of the cells and their functions. Discuss which cells are the most highly specialised and the functions that they carry out. Draw out that the most highly specialised cells have fewer functions than those that are the least specialised.

- Extend the activity above by allocating an organ to each group of pupils and allow them to research, using any sources available (reference books, Internet etc.), which types of cell are involved and what their functions are. Gather the results together in a table which the pupils can copy into their notebooks.

Plenary Suggestions

Missing links

Make a set of cards, or slips of paper, on each of which is written the name of a body system. Choose two pupils to draw a card or slip of paper. The pupils must then decide how the two body systems are linked and explain this to the rest of the class. For example, if one pupil draws 'Digestive system' and the second pupil draws 'Nervous system', then references to energy are needed for the transmission of nerve impulses, a link between the nervous system and the trigger for the secretion of digestive juices. The activity continues by selecting another pair of pupils to choose two more cards. This activity can be adapted to the level of attainment and knowledge of the pupils. (10–15 mins)

OK! Name them

In this activity, groups of pupils bid against each other to see which group can name the greatest number of specialised cells, the most body organs or organ systems (based on a popular game associated with the National Lottery!). This game can be made more exacting by ensuring that the correct terminology is used, e.g. not just blood cells, but red cells, white cells and so on. (5–10 mins)

Practical Support

Drawing organs

Equipment and materials required

Large pieces of paper (lining paper or pieces of paper stuck together or backs of posters) and felt tip pens.

Differentiation

SEN

Pupils can be supplied with pictures of the body organs to place in the correct positions on an outline of the human body.

Extension

Design a game, based on 'Happy families', where participants collect the parts of a body system.

Homework Suggestion

Pupils could choose a specialised cell, e.g. a muscle cell or a nerve cell, and write a paragraph about how it is modified to carry out its function.

Ask pupils to complete the copying of tables into their notebooks.

Answers to in-text questions

a Protozoa, *amoeba*, *paramecium*, bacteria, named bacterial species.

b Virus.

c Red blood cell – carrying oxygen – contains haemoglobin, large surface area.

Sperm – carries genetic material/fertilises egg – tail for swimming, head contains chemical to break down membrane of egg, produce lots of energy, streamlined.

Epithelial cells – remove dirt and bacteria from lungs – bacteria etc. stick to mucus, cilia remove mucus.

d A: brain – controls the body, learning, memory etc.; B: heart – pumps blood; C: stomach – digestion of food; D: uterus/womb – where foetus/baby develops.

e Stomach, intestine, liver, pancreas.

f Respiratory; circulatory; reproductive.

A: trachea/windpipe; B: lung; C: diaphragm; D: heart; E: ovary; F: vagina; G: uterus/womb; H: oviduct/egg tube/Fallopian tube.

B1.2 The Digestive System

NC links for the lesson
- Organisms, behaviour and health.
- Life processes are supported by the organisation of cells into tissues, organs and body systems.

Learning Objectives
Pupils should learn:
- About the parts of the digestive system.
- The different parts of the digestive system and describe their structure.
- The functions of the different parts of the digestive system.

Learning Outcomes
- All pupils should be able to state that food needs to be broken down so that it can be absorbed.
- Most pupils should be able to label the main parts of a digestive system diagram.
- Some pupils should also be able to give detailed and alternative names and functions of the parts of the digestive system.

Learning Styles
Visual: Observing PowerPoint presentation.
Auditory: Listening to the explanations.
Kinaesthetic: Making a model villus or demonstrating the function of digestion.
Interpersonal: Working in groups in the starter activities.
Intrapersonal: Composing mnemonic or song.

Answers to in-text questions
a) It makes it easier to swallow; enzymes help to digest it.
b) Food pushed along the intestine by muscular contractions.
c) Tiny finger-like projections in the intestine wall. They increase the surface area so food can be absorbed faster.

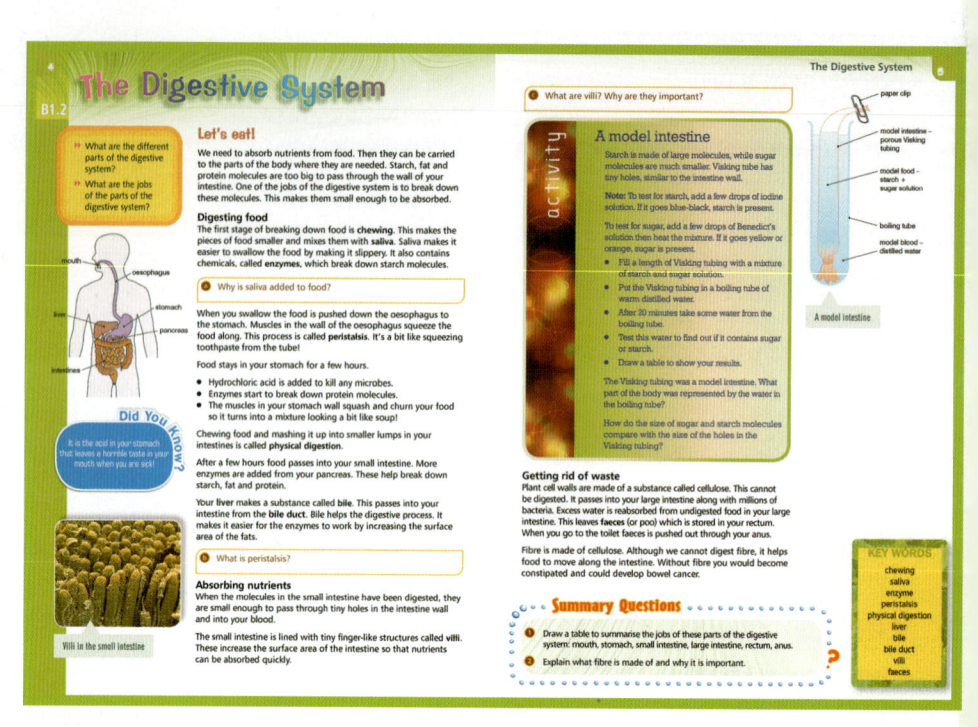

The Lesson

Starter Suggestions

Have you got the guts for it?
Working in groups, ask the pupils to write down as many names as they can for the parts of the digestive system, starting at the mouth and working downwards. They can include slang names. Get one group to read out their list and then the others to add any extra ones. Have a small reward for the group which gets the most names. (5–10 mins)

Where is food needed and how does is get there?
Pose this question and give the pupils the task of reporting their ideas on a large piece of paper in whatever manner they choose – it could be an outline diagram of the human body or a concept map. If they have mobile phones with photo facilities, get them to take a photo of the finished product. Display the results and share the responses with other groups. (10–15 mins)

Answers to Summary questions

1)

Part	Function
Mouth	Food mixed with saliva; chewed into pieces small enough to swallow; digestion of starch begins
Stomach	Acid mixed with food, kills bacteria, etc.; digestion of protein begins
Small intestine	Digestion; absorption
Large intestine	Re-absorption of water
Rectum	Storage of faeces
Anus	Removal of faeces

2) Indigestible part of plant foods/cell walls/cellulose which absorb water and help food move through the intestine.

The Digestive System

Main Lesson

- Using a human model torso or PowerPoint diagrams, take the pupils through the main parts of the digestive system. It could be useful to give each pupil a blank outline diagram to fill in as the parts are named.

- Illustrate the role of teeth in providing extra surface area by getting the pupils to consider how they eat a chocolate bar. If the whole bar is put into the mouth, which bits could the saliva get to? What happens if you cut it in two? This can be repeated several times until they get the idea that cutting things up increases the surface area. Suggest that using teeth also make things easier to swallow.

- To introduce the oesophagus and the idea of peristalsis, show the Simpson's clip featuring Itchy and Scratchy in 'Oesophagus now' (season 7, episode 3F03) or use a sock with a hard-boiled egg in it (or the leg of a pair of tights with a tennis ball) to show how it is squeezed through.

- Peristalsis at work can be demonstrated using a volunteer male pupil and getting him to do a handstand against a wall, with his head resting on a pile of sweaters and supported by two strong and trustworthy peers. Give the pupil a soft sweet, such as a flump or a marshmallow, to swallow. Ask the class how the sweet has just risen up from the mouth to the stomach. As no eating is allowed in the laboratory, do this in another room such as in the Home Economics department.

- The functions of the stomach can be illustrated by reference to the story of Alexis St Martin, who had lumps of meat dangled inside him. The functions of the small intestine in absorption can be illustrated by using pieces of rolled up carpet to convey the idea of the villi increasing the surface area. A model villus can be made from the finger of a rubber glove and felt tip pens. This can either be done as a demonstration or the pupils could make their own. Now is a good time to do the activity from the pupil book: 'A model intestine' (see 'Practical support'). The standard tests for a reducing sugar and starch need to be demonstrated to the pupils so that they can test for the results.

- Ask the pupils to think about water absorption in the large intestine. What would happen if water was not absorbed? What happens if too much water is absorbed?

Plenary Suggestions

Digestion mnemonics or 'Te-To-Tum'
Pupils should make up a mnemonic to help them remember the sequence of parts of the digestive system. (5–10 mins)

Digestion song
Pupils should write a song or poem summarising some of the features of the learning objectives of the lesson. Share confident examples with the rest of the class. Mark by how many key words they have managed to include. (10–15 mins)

Practical Support

Main lesson demonstrations

Equipment and materials required
Chocolate bar and knife to illustrate the action of teeth, hard-boiled egg/tennis ball and sock or leg of pair of tights to demonstrate peristalsis, pieces of rolled up carpet to illustrate structure of small intestine, rubber glove and felt tip pens for a model villus.

Details
The liquidised food should be made using a blender. It would be a good idea to have some lumps still in it, but there does need to be a fair amount of liquid so that it is readily pushed through.

Safety
Be aware of nut allergies.
Food should not be consumed by the pupils in the laboratory.

A model intestine

Equipment and materials required
Per group: Visking or dialysis tubing, dropping pipettes, elastic bands, starch and enzyme solutions (the strength of the solutions should be adjusted to give results in a lesson session), water baths, beakers, Bunsen burner, 2 test tubes and a stand, 1 test tube of warm water, iodine solution, Benedict's solution, eye protection.

Details
Each group of pupils will need two 15 cm lengths of dialysis (Visking) tubing, which has been soaked in water. Each piece should be knotted securely at one end. Using a dropping pipette, fill one length of the tubing with 3% starch solution and place it in a test tube. Fold the top of the tubing over the rim of the test tube and secure with an elastic band. Remove all traces of the starch solution from the outside of the tubing by filling the test tube with water and emptying it several times. Finally, fill the test tube with water and place it in a rack.

Repeat the procedure with the second length of tubing but add 5 cm³ saliva or amylase solution to the starch solution, and shake before filling the dialysis tubing.

The test tubes should be labelled A and B and placed in a water bath at 35°C for 30 minutes. The water in the test tubes should then be tested for starch, using iodine solution, and sugars, using Benedict's solution.

Safety
Iodine: CLEAPSS Hazcard 54B.
Benedict's solution is harmful: CLEAPSS Hazcards 27C and 95A.
Eye protection.

Differentiation

SEN
Use a cloth intestines tabard to illustrate the parts of the digestive system.

Extension
Using the chocolate bar illustration from the starter, suggest to the pupils that they calculate how the surface area of an 8 cm cube sweet bar increases each time it is divided, i.e. untouched, cut into 2,4,8,16,32. Pupils could graph these out and try to come up with an equation linking the two.

Homework Suggestion

Give the pupils a list of the key words and ask them to write a paragraph about the digestive system in their notebooks.

Ask them to finish their mnemonic or song if time is short at the end of the lesson.

B1.3 Digesting Food

NC links for the lesson
- Organisms, behaviour and health.
- Life processes are supported by the organisation of cells into tissues, organs and body systems.

Learning Objectives

Pupils should learn:
- How digestion occurs.
- That starch, protein and fat have to be digested before they can be absorbed.
- How these large molecules are broken down by enzymes.

Learning Outcomes
- All pupils should be able to recognise that large molecules cannot be absorbed but smaller ones can.
- Most pupils should be able to match the food types to their component parts.
- Some pupils should also be able to give a detailed description of the digestion of the major food types including enzyme names.

How Science Works
- Describe how the use of a model or analogy supports an explanation (1.1a1).

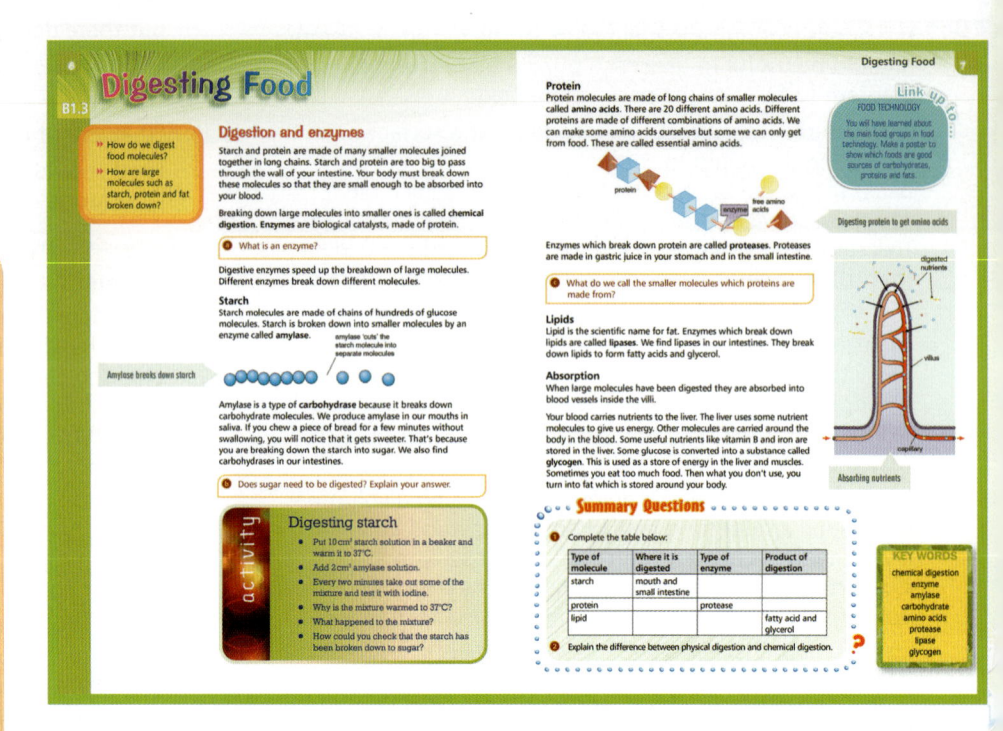

Learning Styles

Visual: Observing the results of the experiment.
Auditory: Listening to the exposition on enzymes.
Kinaesthetic: Carrying out the Lego bricks exercise.
Interpersonal: Taking part in 'Squeezy fists' or 'Breakdown duel'.
Intrapersonal: Completing summary table on breakdown of foods.

Answers to in-text questions

a) A substance made of protein, which speeds up reactions in living things/breaks down large molecules.

b) No, the molecules are small enough to fit through the holes in the intestine wall.

c) Amino acids.

Answers to Summary questions

1.

Type of molecule	Where it is digested	Type of enzyme	Product of digestion
starch	mouth and small intestine	carbohydrase/amylase	sugar/monosaccharide
protein	stomach and small intestine	protease	amino acids
lipid	small intestine	lipase	fatty acid and glycerol

2. Physical digestion is the breakdown of large lumps of food to smaller ones; chemical digestion is the breakdown of large molecules to smaller ones.

Digesting Food

The Lesson

Starter Suggestions

Squeezy fists
Get the pupils to put their hands into the air and squeeze their fists. Ask them how they are doing that and keep questioning about where the energy comes from to enable them to keep doing it. How many times can they carry on doing it before they get tired? Why do their fists get tired? This should link them to the previous lesson and the idea of substances from food getting into the blood and being used by the muscles. (5–10 mins)

Dissolving race
Get two volunteers to come to the front of the class. Give each a large clear beaker of water and a plastic or wooden spoon. Say that you are going to have a dissolving race. Give one pupil a sugar cube and the other a potato cube. Have two more volunteers as judges. Start the race and stop it when the sugar has dissolved. Discuss this with the class. If you cannot dissolve potatoes, how do they act as a food? (10–15 mins)

Main Lesson

- Explain that enzymes are proteins, biological catalysts, which speed up reactions in living organisms but are not themselves used up. It could be useful to ask if pupils know what a catalyst is and to link with knowledge they may have gained from Chemistry. Explain that enzymes are specific, i.e. that one enzyme will only speed up the rate of one reaction and another reaction will require a different enzyme.
- Show the pupils a PowerPoint or animation of the breakdown of starch by amylase, protein by a protease and fats by lipase.
- Give each group of pupils a set of six identical Lego bricks (or laminated cards with Velcro patches) with the letters 'S', 'T', 'A', 'R', 'C' and 'H' written on the front of them. On the back of each brick write the word 'sugar' (or 'glucose' if you prefer). Ask the pupils to assemble the bricks into a block and then to separate them using a plastic knife labelled 'amylase'.
- Use the experiment 'Digesting starch' described in the pupil book either as a class demonstration or in groups. The pupils should remember the tests for starch and sugar from the activity 'A model intestine' in the last lesson.
- The process of digestion of a meal can be demonstrated by placing some food into a blender and liquidising it. Pour the liquidised food into the leg of a pair of tights and squeeze. The liquid part will come through the gaps. Emphasise that this is going into the blood and not the body cavity and that for most food, digestive enzymes are needed to make the food small enough to go through the gaps. This is best done as a class demonstration.

Plenary Suggestions

Digestion rags to riches
Carry out a 'Who wants to be a millionaire?' style rags to riches game constructed using a set of Java tools such as Quia (www.quia.com). (5–10 mins)

Breakdown duel
In pairs, get pupils to play a game where one writes down the name of a food type (either protein, fat or starch) on a 'Show me' board and the other writes down the name of an enzyme (protease, lipase or amylase). On the count of three, they show each other the boards. If the enzyme cannot digest the food stuff, the foodstuff player gains a point. If the enzyme can digest the foodstuff, that player gains a point. The first to reach 'five' wins, then the pupils swap roles. (10–15 mins)

Practical Support

Starter: Dissolving race

Equipment and materials required
Sugar cubes, potato cubes, wooden/plastic spoon, two 500 cm^3 beakers, eye protection.

Digesting starch

Equipment and materials required
Starch solution, glass beaker, water bath at 37°C, amylase solution (or saliva), iodine solution (less than 1 mol/dm^3). Liquidised food and a pair of tights to demonstrate the function of digestion.

Details
See pupil book.

Safety
Amylase solution is an irritant: CLEAPSS Hazcard 33, Recipe card 23.
Iodine solution: CLEAPSS Hazcard 54B.
Eye protection.

Differentiation

SEN
Pupils could look at simple digestion animations on the intranet.

Extension
Ask pupils to research the consequences of cystic fibrosis (which blocks the pancreatic duct) in terms of enzymes and digestion, then report their findings.

Homework Suggestion

Having explained that enzyme names end in '-ase', ask pupils to find as many different names for enzymes as they can.

B1.4 Food and a Balanced Diet

NC links for the lesson
- Organisms, behaviour and health.
- Life processes are supported by the organisation of cells into tissues, organs and body systems.

Learning Objectives
Pupils should learn:
- The food types needed in a balanced diet.
- How the body uses the different nutrients contained in foods.
- To use chemical tests to identify carbohydrate, protein and fat.

Learning Outcomes
- All pupils should be able to name the six major food types with aid.
- Most pupils should be able to list the major food types, giving examples, and describe the tests for them.
- Some pupils should also be able to give detailed descriptions of the types of foodstuffs and how they are used by the body.

How Science Works
- Explain how the observation and recordings methods are appropriate to the task (1.2d).

Learning Styles
Visual: Matching tri-ominoes in the plenary.
Auditory: Listening to discussion of food requirements for different occupations.
Kinaesthetic: Carrying out the food tests.
Interpersonal: Working together on food tests.
Intrapersonal: Making a personal 'food types' booklet in the plenary.

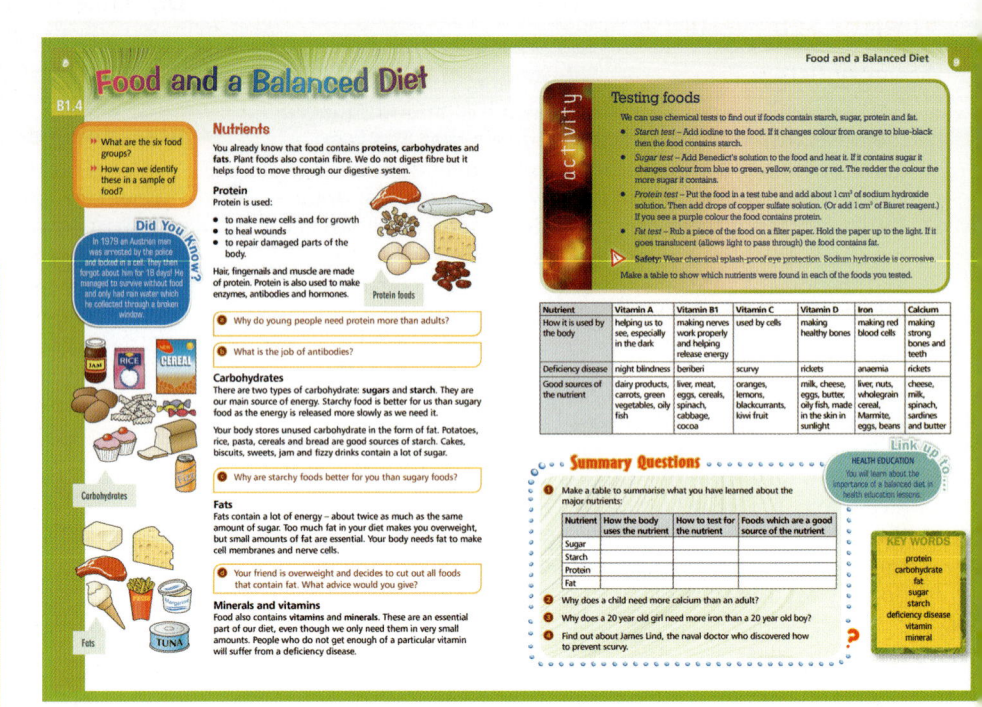

Answers to in-text questions

a. Because young people are growing.

b. To kill microbes/protect against certain diseases.

c. They release energy more slowly.

d. We need some fat in our diet for things like making cell membranes.

Answers to Summary questions

1

Nutrient	How the body uses the nutrient	How to test for the nutrient	Foods which are a good source of the nutrient
Sugar	As a source of energy	Add Benedict's solution and heat. If sugar is present it changes colour from blue to green, yellow, orange or red.	Cakes, biscuits, sweets, jam, fizzy drinks
Starch	As a source of energy	Add iodine solution. If starch is present it changes colour from orange to blue-black.	Potatoes, pasta, rice, bread
Protein	For growth and repair, and making enzymes	Add Biuret reagent (sodium hydroxide solution and copper sulfate solution). If protein is present a purple colour appears.	Meat, fish, eggs, cheese, pulses
Fat	As a source of energy	Rub a piece of the food on a filter paper. Hold the paper up to the light. If it has gone translucent the food contains fat.	Meat, cheese, fried foods, butter

2 To help make strong teeth and bones as they grow.

3 To replace iron lost in menstrual bleeding.

4 Pupil research. [Mark by overall impression.]

The Lesson

Starter Suggestions

Food for thought

It is said that humans can survive on a diet of beans on toast. Show either a real plateful or a large colourful PowerPoint photograph of beans on toast. Discuss this and draw out from the pupils any funny family or friends' anecdotes about people's strange eating habits. Enlarge this into a discussion of what we actually need. In small groups, pupils should write down their thoughts on this and then share them with the class. (5–10 mins)

Shopping sort out

Show the pupils a large bag with shopping items in, or display large posters with pictures of the items. Ask the pupils to sort them into groups according to the food type. Do not introduce the scientific notion of food types at this stage, just see what emerges. Discuss the types of food and see if a consensus is present. (10–15 mins)

Main Lesson

- Using PowerPoint, go over the main food types according to scientific understanding. Give the pupils a worksheet with a table of food types, examples and uses and ask them to fill in the appropriate bits. They could use the materials from the 'Shopping sort out' starter and take the opportunity to correct any misconceptions.

- Demonstrate the main standard food tests: iodine solution for starch, Benedict's reagent for sugars (don't bother with the distinction between reducing and non-reducing at this level – if necessary alter the instructions so that both will show positive, see 'Practical support'), Biuret for protein (sodium hydroxide solution and copper sulfate solution) and either the emulsion test (shaking with alcohol) or the grease mark test on translucent paper for fats.

- Give the pupils a variety of simple foods, such as pieces of apple, potato, bread, egg albumen to test. Give them a sheet with the foods tabulated and spaces to fill in the results of the tests they do on each one.

- Show pictures of several different occupations e.g. a clerical assistant, a bricklayer, a sumo wrestler, an athlete or any other relevant types, being careful not to stereotype them. You could also include a toddler and an elderly person. Carry out a matching exercise with the occupations and a range of different diet types. Put a time limit on this and then discuss the results.

- Using computers, carry out a 'drag and drop' exercise where pupils have to put food examples into the correct food type bin or on to the correct shelf.

Plenary Suggestions

Food type booklet

Provide each pupil with a piece of plain A4 paper and show them how to fold and cut it to make an eight page booklet. Using one page as a cover and one as a back sheet for sticking the booklet into notes if so desired, allow one sheet for each of the major food groups. Ask the pupils to illustrate colourfully and complete notes on each type. This can be finished for homework. (5–10 mins)

Food tri-ominoes

Pupils play a game like dominoes but with triangular playing pieces. Each piece has one food type, one example and one use on it. The different categories are colour-coded. The object is to match one face of the tri-omino with a matching face of one already lying on the table, e.g. 'fats' as the food type could go with 'energy storage and insulation' as the use or 'lard' as the example. (10–15 mins)

Practical Support

Testing foods

Equipment and materials required

Per group: small pieces of foods such as apple, potato, bread, egg albumen, test tubes, test tube rack, water bath, dropping pipettes, watch glasses or white tiles, iodine solution (starch), Benedict's reagent (sugars), Biuret reagent (proteins) and translucent paper (fats).

Details

Starch test: Add a drop of iodine solution to the food to be tested.

Benedict's test: A small piece of food should be placed in a test tube and about 3 cm^3 of Benedict's solution added. Heat in a water bath.

Biuret test: Add a small quantity of Biuret reagent to the food in a test tube and observe the colour change (alternatively add 1 cm^3 0.1 mol/dm^3 sodium hydroxide solution to some food in a test tube and add a few drops of copper sulfate solution).

Fat test: Rub the food to be tested on to a piece of paper.

Safety

Eye protection.

Care with water baths.

Care with chemicals: wash off with water if there is contact with the skin. Iodine solution: CLEAPSS Hazcard 54B; Benedict's solution: CLEAPSS Hazcard 27C and 95A; Biuret reagent: CLEAPSS Recipe card 13; 0.1 mol/dm^3 sodium hydroxide solution: CLEAPSS Hazcard 91 and 27C (Copper Sulphate).

Also useful: CLEAPSS Student Safety Sheet 4 Food Testing (1).

Differentiation

SEN

Pupils could use a 'cut and stick' exercise to sort food items on to appropriate shelves drawn on a pantry sheet. Check, then pupils glue cut-out food into their exercise books.

Extension

Continue the exercise on occupation and appropriate diet to include more detailed information on the changes in the food requirements of an individual at different stages of their life. Do they change? Why might they need to change?

Homework Suggestion

Complete the 'food types' booklet.

Ask the pupils to take a photograph using their mobile phones (or find an appropriate picture from a magazine) of an example of a food which is representative of each one of the food types. This can be peer-assessed as part of an assessment of learning session.

B1.5 Breathing

NC links for the lesson
- Organisms, behaviour and health.
- Life processes are supported by the organisation of cells into tissues, organs and body systems.

Learning Objectives
Pupils should learn:
- The basic structure of the lungs.
- How our lungs work.
- How we breathe in and out.

Learning Outcomes
- All pupils should be able to describe the basic structure of the lungs.
- Most pupils should be able to describe how the breathing process occurs.
- Some pupils should also be able to explain the effects of breathing in and breathing out on the different parts of the thorax.

Functional Skills Link-up
ICT skills
- Enter, develop and organise numerical information that is fit for purpose (level 2).

Learning Styles
Visual: Observing nostrils.
Auditory: Listening to the PowerPoint exposition.
Kinaesthetic: Making their own lung model.
Interpersonal: Discussing the results of the observations on chest movements.
Intrapersonal: Completing a word search in the plenary.

Answers to in-text questions
a. Breathing in.
b. Breathing out.

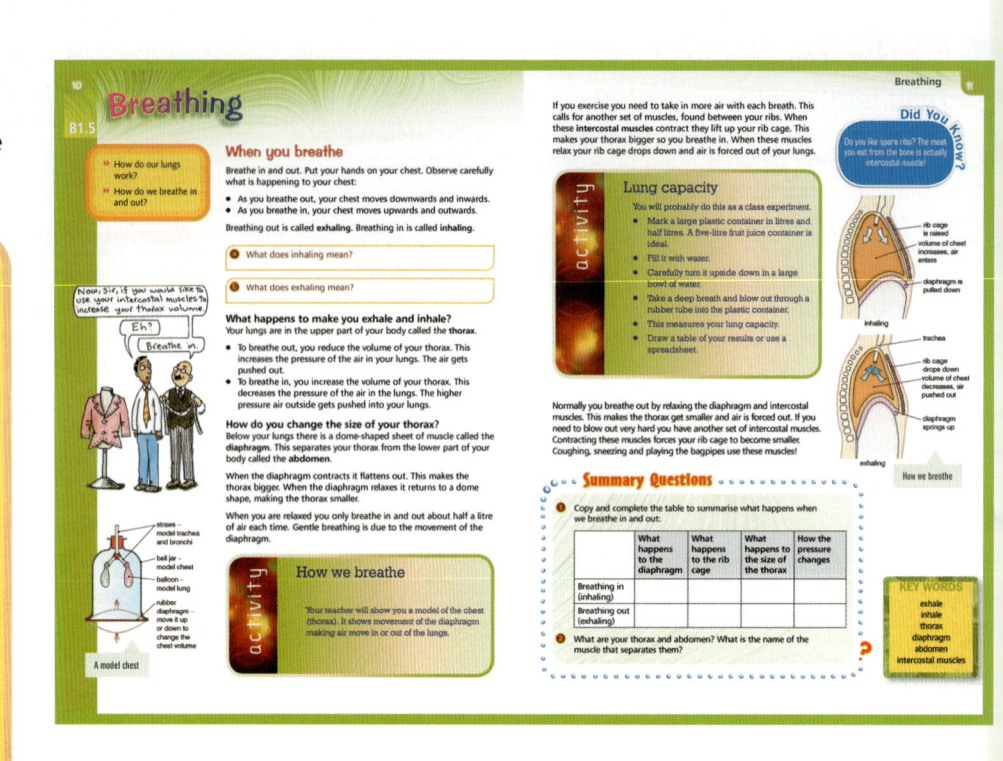

The Lesson

Starter Suggestions

Breathing line up
As the pupils come through the door, say to each one in turn 'You are a mouth, you are an epiglottis, you are a larynx, you are a trachea, you are a bronchus, you are bronchioles, you are air sacs, you are alveoli.' Give the pupils slips of paper with these on if they may not remember them. Go straight into an anatomical diagram of the respiratory system and get the pupils to line up in sets in the correct order that inhaled air would meet them. Ask them to call out their part names in order. (5–10 mins)

In and out, or up and down
Working in pairs of the same gender, ask pupils to observe each other from the side as they breathe in and out and to record the movements made by the chest when they are sitting on a chair and when they are lying flat. Ask: 'Does any other part of the body move during these movements?' (During quiet breathing, the abdomen may be observed to rise and fall – discuss how this could be involved with the alteration in volume.) If the hands are placed on the ribs during breathing, what movements can be felt? Use a tape measure to find out how much the chest size alters when breathing lightly (normally) and when breathing

Answers to Summary questions

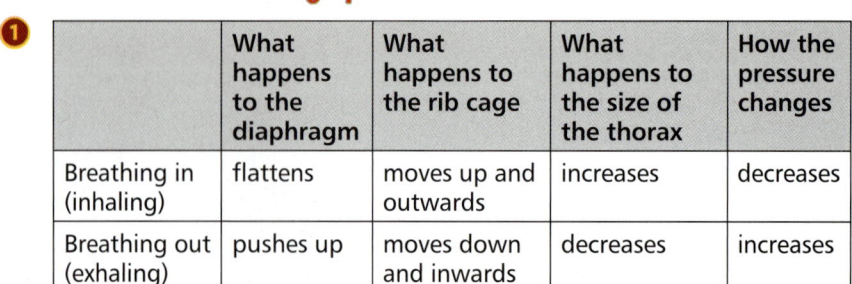

1.

	What happens to the diaphragm	What happens to the rib cage	What happens to the size of the thorax	How the pressure changes
Breathing in (inhaling)	flattens	moves up and outwards	increases	decreases
Breathing out (exhaling)	pushes up	moves down and inwards	decreases	increases

2. The thorax is the chest cavity; the abdomen is the space below; they are separated by the diaphragm.

Breathing

deeply. Ask the pupils to run carefully on the spot for a minute and then repeat the observations. Get each pair to write down their observations and discuss what is happening to the volume of the chest cavity. (10–15 mins)

Main Lesson

- Ask if anyone has ever choked on a food item. Some may remember George Bush nearly dying by inhaling a pretzel. Set up a demonstration model of how an epiglottis works by having a Y-junction section from a domestic waste pipe cut in two, lengthways. Arrange a hinged sprung flap of plastic, so that as a ball rolls down one tube it shuts the other one off so that it can't go down it. Go through some basic first aid on how to save someone if they are choking. If the person can speak and is breathing, do not interfere. If they can't breathe, carry out the Heimlich manoeuvre, details of which can be found on the intranet.

- How we breathe activity: use the classic bell jar with a pair of balloons in it as a breathing model. Ask the pupils to say what the parts of the model represent in a mammal, e.g. the balloons are the lungs. Demonstrate how the model works by pulling down the 'diaphragm' and then letting go. Get the pupils to describe and explain what is happening. Ask: 'How does the model differ from a human chest?'

- Loosen the plug at the top of the bell jar and ask a pupil to try to get the balloons to inflate. They may a little, but very poorly. State that this is why chest wounds are very dangerous – they do not have to pierce the lungs to stop you from being able to breathe properly, as by raising your rib cage and lowering your diaphragm you will draw air in through the wound and into the cavity around the lungs, expelling it when you try to breathe out. You might add that sometimes if a wound is bleeding into an un-punctured chest cavity it needs to be let out so that the pressure difference can be established allowing the victim to breathe.

- Carry out the activity 'Lung capacity' as described in the pupil book. Alternatively, using a peak flow meter and either disposable cardboard mouthpieces or disinfection between users, take peak flow readings of all the class members. The data can be used to see if there are any interesting correlations. Is there a gender difference? What difference does sport make? How might the readings from smokers differ from those of non-smokers? [Make sure pupils are fit and happy to do this.]

Plenary Suggestions

Passengers will kindly remember to breathe

In pairs, write and rehearse a spoof version of the familiar airline safety announcements given at the start of flights. Their version should, in a humorous yet accurate way, tell the passengers how to breathe. Get some of the more enthusiastic pairs to enact theirs. Particularly good ones can be videoed for other classes. (5–10 mins)

Chest injury guide card

Give the pupils a blank business card. State that they have to make a guide card to tell people what to do in case they encounter anyone who has an open chest wound which appears to be frothing as they breathe. Include reasons related to how the breathing system works. Laminate the best ones and place on display. If assistance is needed with this, an army guide is available at this website: http://www.armystudyguide.com.

Practical Support

Starter: In and out, or up and down
Equipment and materials required

Tape measures to measure chest sizes.

Main lesson: Demonstration of epiglottis
Equipment and materials required

Plumbers' Y-piece and valve, ball to fit, hinged sprung flap of plastic.

How we breathe
Equipment and materials required

For the class demonstration breathing model: bell jar with a cork in the top, sheet of rubber, two balloons, Y-shaped glass tube inserted through the cork at the top of the bell jar.

For the pupils' models: plastic soft drinks bottles, balloons, plastic bags, elastic bands, scissors, Sellotape, tape.

Details

For the pupils' models: put a balloon onto the neck of a soft drinks bottle, cut off the bottom and secure a circle cut from a plastic bag over the open end using an elastic band. They can then stick a loop of tape onto the bag as a handle and pull and push it in and out to inflate and deflate the balloon lung.

For the demonstration model: the balloons are attached to the ends of the Y-shaped tube and the piece of rubber should be firmly fixed over the bottom of the bell jar. The cork in the top of the bell jar should fit firmly.

Lung capacity
Equipment and materials required

Large plastic container (five-litre fruit juice container) marked with litres and half litres, large bowl, rubber tubing.

Main lesson: Taking peak flow readings
Equipment and materials required

Peak flow meter and disposable mouthpieces.

Safety

If mouth pieces are not disposable, use disinfection. See CLEAPSS handbook/CDROM section 15.12.3.

Differentiation

SEN

Give the pupils the key words for the topic, but with either all the vowels or all the consonants missing and ask them to fill in the missing letters.

Extension

Pupils could produce a poster to show how the Heimlich manoeuvre is carried out and explain how it works.

Homework Suggestion

Pupils should write up the results of the 'Lung capacity' activity or peak flow meter activities, making a table of results and commenting on any difficulties with the experiment, differences in results from different groups (age, gender, etc.) and conclusions that can be drawn from the results.

B1.6 Lungs

NC links for the lesson
- Organisms, behaviour and health.
- Life processes are supported by the organisation of cells into tissues, organs and body systems.

Learning Objectives
Pupils should learn:
- How the lungs are adapted for gaseous exchange.
- The structure of the lungs and associated organs.
- How our lungs are kept clean.

Learning Outcomes
- All pupils should be able to label windpipe, voice box, bronchi and air sacs.
- Most pupils should be able to label larynx, trachea, bronchi, bronchioles, alveoli, ribs and diaphragm, and be able to describe how the lungs are adapted for gaseous exchange.
- Some pupils should also be able to link structure and function for all the above parts and give explanations of how the lungs are kept clean.

Learning Styles
Visual: Observing PowerPoint or video presentations.
Auditory: Listening to the ideas of others in the starter activities.
Kinaesthetic: Sequencing the stages in breathing.
Interpersonal: Working in pairs to carry out the starter and/or plenary activities.
Intrapersonal: Making own notes on the sequence of breathing.

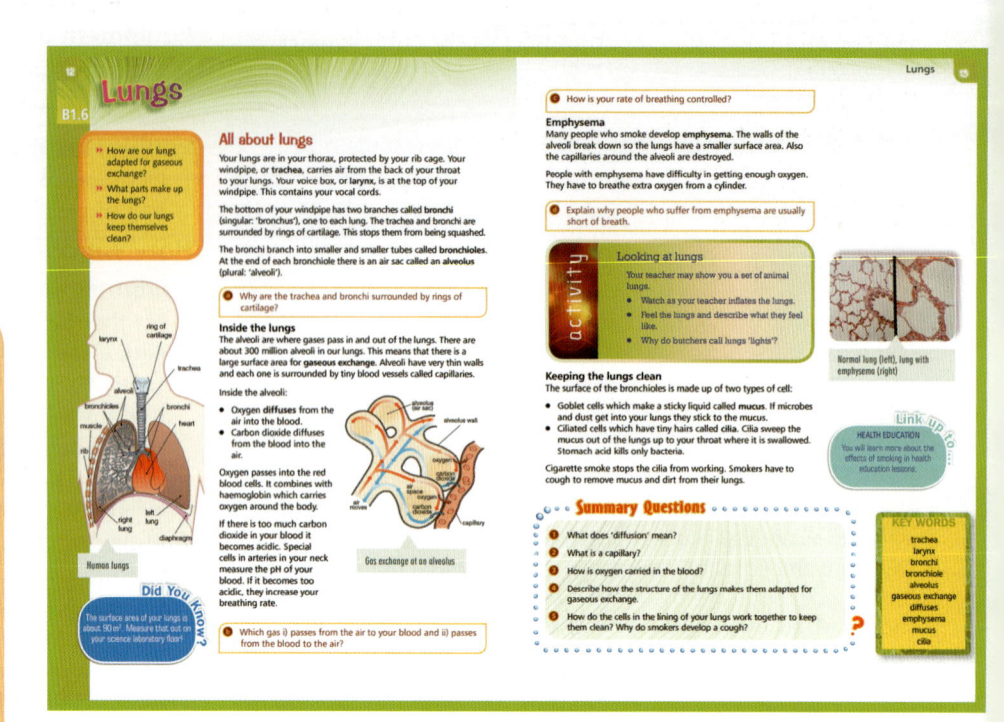

The Lesson

Starter Suggestions

Chest parts word search
Ask the pupils to complete a word search with the key words in it. Gear the difficulty of this to the ability of the pupils. (5–10 mins)

Syringes don't suck!
Draw a gravestone on the board. On it write R.I.P. 'sucks'. Explain that you are not allowed to use the word 'sucks' in this lesson. No suckers allowed. Give each pair of pupils a syringe (without a needle!) and get them to interact with it, putting their fingers over the end and pushing and pulling. Do not allow access to water. After a couple of minutes, ask them to explain how the air is drawn into the syringe when the plunger is pulled back. Get volunteers to explain their ideas to the rest of the class. (10–15 mins)

Answers to Summary questions

1. Movement of molecules from an area of high concentration to an area of low concentration.
2. The smallest type of blood vessel, with a very thin wall, allowing substances to move in and out of the blood.
3. It is combined with haemoglobin to form oxyhaemoglobin in red blood cells.
4. They have a large surface area, a thin wall, and lots of capillaries.
5. Bacteria and dirt stick to the mucus produced by goblet cells, movement of cilia sweeps mucus out of the lungs. In smokers the cilia stop moving.

Lungs

Main Lesson

- Show video footage of an endoscope camera going down the trachea and into the bronchi and bronchioles. This can be found on a number of recently broadcast science TV programmes.
- Show the pupils a head of broccoli and draw analogies. For a bit of goriness, inform the pupils that a favourite Viking execution method was to open the chest of a victim up and spread the lungs out as far as they would go – they called this the 'Blood Eagle'. Show the pupils a tennis court and relate to the area of the gas exchange surface of the lungs (the alveoli).
- There are some excellent simulations available to show what goes on in terms of gas exchange in the alveoli. They can be found on Multimedia Science School and Sunflower.
- Show the pupils a PowerPoint, or a video, on the process of breathing and how it takes place.
- Carry out a dissection of a set of pigs' lungs. [Check pupil sensitivities and/or religious objections.] If you ask at a good butcher for a pigs pluck, you should get a set. Ask if you can have ones which have not been cut up too much (the meat inspectors have to look internally for signs of disease). Get them as fresh as you can and keep them refrigerated. Either use them straight away or freeze them straight away. Do not re-freeze once thawed out. The lungs can be inflated by introducing a piece of Bunsen hose, attached to a foot pump or cycle pump for inflating, into an airway leading into an intact lobe. If your school policy allows it, the pupils will enjoy touching the inflated lung (wash hands well straight afterwards and beware of wiping).
- Show photographs of the structure of the different parts of the lungs, particularly of the alveoli. A microscope slide of alveoli, emphasising the nature of the thin walls and the close proximity to the blood vessels should link the gross structure to the gas exchange surface. Refer the pupils back to the dissection and the pink colour of the lungs. Ask: 'Why were they so pink?'
- Get the pupils to carry out a sequencing exercise on the stages in breathing. The 'In and out, or up and down' starter from the previous lesson could be a good starting point for this. Once the sequence has been established, the pupils should make notes in their exercise books summarising the process.
- To reinforce the idea of changes in volume of the chest cavity, use a male volunteer and measure chest size inflated and deflated. Tie this in with pressure changes. Link with observations made in the starter to the previous lesson and to the homework exercise below, if done.

Plenary Suggestions

Key word pairs

On the board, place laminated cards with all the names of the key words on the anatomy of the lungs, well spaced out. Demonstrate how to make a key word pair by joining two words with an arrow and writing above the arrow to create a sentence. Ask volunteers to do this until all key words have at least one connector. (10–15 mins)

Structure to function mind map

Ask the pupils to complete a mind map showing the parts of the respiratory system, relating them to their functions. (5–10 mins)

Practical Support

Looking at lungs

Equipment and materials required

Pig's lungs (pluck), dissecting tools, a piece of rubber hose, a foot pump or cycle pump.

Safety

Place pig's lungs in a large, clear plastic bag when inflating: CLEAPSS handbook/CD-Rom section 14.7.2.

Pupils to wash hands thoroughly after touching the pig's lungs.

Differentiation

SEN

Provide cards with the stages of breathing on them and ask the pupils to put them in the correct order.

Using a large poster of the lungs and associated structures, ask pupils to label the key structures or provide labels for them to put in the correct places.

Extension

Ask the pupils to find out how you can breathe for someone who is unconscious and not breathing. Link to PSHE and remind them of what happens on programmes such as *Casualty*. If possible, let them investigate the models used to teach CPR. Emphasise that this should never be done on a conscious person or if a conscious person is breathing unaided.

Homework Suggestion

Pupils should finish writing up their notes on the sequence of breathing.

Get pupils to count and record how many breaths per minute they take when carrying out different activities. Ask: 'Are there changes in chest volume associated with the number of breaths?'

Answers to in-text questions

a It stops them from collapsing, especially when the pressure is low.

b i) Oxygen.   ii) Carbon dioxide.

c By special cells which measure the amount of carbon dioxide in your blood. If there is too much carbon dioxide the breathing rate speeds up.

d They cannot absorb enough oxygen because the surface area of their lungs is reduced.

B1.7 Inhaled and Exhaled Air

NC links for the lesson
- Organisms, behaviour and health.
- Life processes are supported by the organisation of cells into tissues, organs and body systems.

Learning Objectives
Pupils should learn:
- That respiration releases energy from food.
- The differences between inhaled and exhaled air.
- That the differences between inhaled and exhaled air are related to the release of energy.

Learning Outcomes
- All pupils should be able to state that inhaled air has more oxygen and less carbon dioxide than exhaled air.
- Most pupils should be able to state that inhaled air has more oxygen and less carbon dioxide than exhaled air and give the percentages.
- Some pupils should also be able to give a balanced equation for respiration.

Functional Skills Link-up
ICT skills
- Enter, develop and organise numerical information that is fit for purpose (level 2).

Learning Styles
Visual: Watching film and video footage; observing the Joseph Wright picture.
Auditory: Listening to discussions and the views of others.
Kinaesthetic: Carrying out the practical experiment.
Interpersonal: Working in a group in the 'Respiration modelling' plenary.
Intrapersonal: Reflecting on their own views about the Joseph Wright picture.

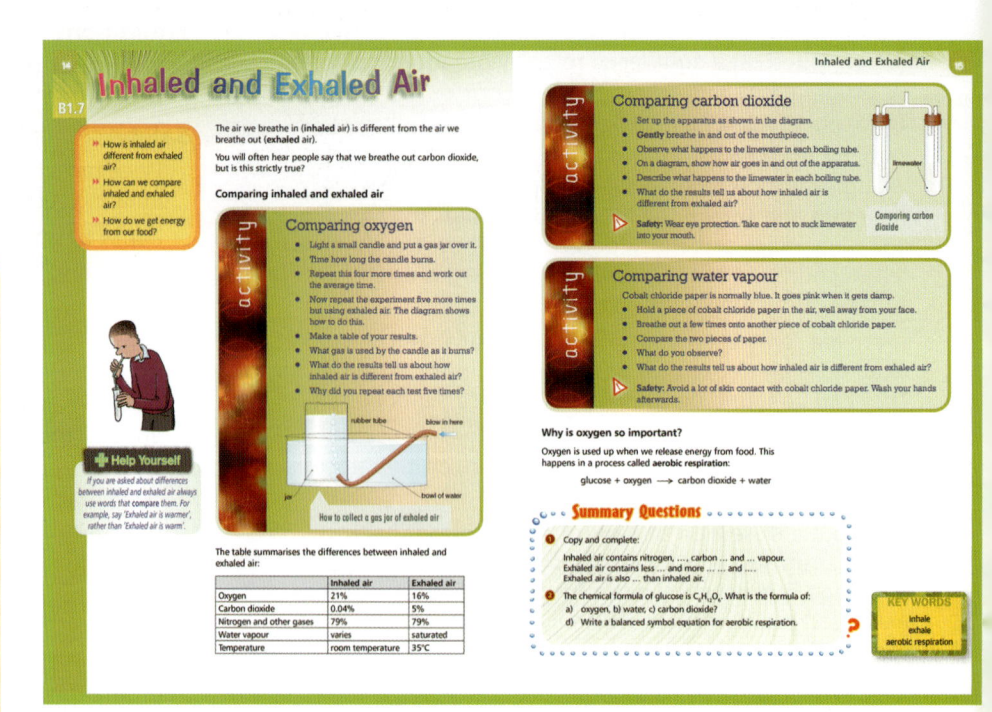

The Lesson

Starter Suggestions

Pupil breath samples

Get a popular volunteer to blow up a balloon. State that this is a sample of (*name*)'s breath. Ask the rest of the class to discuss in pairs what will be different about it, compared to the air in the rest of the room. Say that you are going to pick on someone to give their responses and give a short time limit. Collect several responses from around the room and use this to launch the lesson. Ask the pupils to think about the amount of water vapour and the temperature of the air in the balloon, if they do not come up with these differences themselves. (5–10 mins)

Watch the birdy

Show the pupils the painting 'Experiment on a bird in the air pump' by Joseph Wright (go to National Gallery website). Allow them to respond in any way to the painting. Draw out, through discussion, what is going on and what will happen to the bird if it is left inside the pump and why. Expand this to explore what is currently known by the class about the differences between inhaled and exhaled air. (10–15 mins)

Main Lesson
- Remind the pupils of the structure and function of the respiratory system as covered in the previous two lessons. This could be done as a question and answer session, a sequencing exercise or by means of a simple one word answer test.

Answers to Summary questions

1. Inhaled air contains nitrogen, **oxygen**, carbon **dioxide** and **water** vapour. Exhaled air contains less **oxygen** and more **carbon dioxide** and **water**. Exhaled air is also **hotter/warmer** than inhaled air.

2. a) O_2 b) H_2O c) CO_2 d) $C_6H_{12}O_6 + 6O_2 \longrightarrow 6CO_2 + 6H_2O$

Inhaled and Exhaled Air

- Show film footage of a person being given mouth to mouth resuscitation. Ask pupils what is happening and how breath which you exhale will be OK for someone else to inhale. If the extension work from the previous lesson was carried out, ask the pupils who did it to begin the explanation or give a commentary on the film or video footage.
- Show a picture of an oxygen mask being used. Ask: 'How would this be different from the mouth-to-mouth situation?'
- Ask if anyone remembers the film *Castaway* starring Tom Hanks, and see if they can remember how he started his fire. Get someone to act it out. Alternatively, ask if anyone has been to scout or guide camp and lit a fire? Ask how blowing on the embers makes the fire go better?
- For each group of three or four pupils, set up two gas jars filled with water, inverted over water. Give each pair within the four a stubby candle on a float and a stop-watch. One pair is to allow the jar to fill with ordinary air by letting the water out. The other pair breathe out through a rubber hose to expel the water. Keep the mouth of this jar beneath the water surface to keep the exhaled air trapped. Seal each jar by sliding a lid covered with Vaseline over the mouth. Light the candles, take the lids off the jars and invert the jars over the candles. Start the stop-watches. Record when each candle goes out. Repeat the procedure. Get the pupils to compare their results and discuss. Ask: 'Why is there a difference between the lengths of time the candles will burn? Can it be linked to the composition of the exhaled air?'
- As a comparison, you could demonstrate what happens when you use a jar of pure oxygen and what happens when you use a jar of pure carbon dioxide. Emphasise that carbon dioxide is heavier than air and will sink, so don't let it fall out of the jar. Brewery workers have to wear breathing apparatus when they get into the fermenting vats to clean them or carry out repairs, otherwise they would pass out and die (some have in the past).
- Use the experiment 'Comparing carbon dioxide' described in the pupil book as a demonstration.
- Carry out the 'Comparing water vapour' activity as described in the pupil book. Link with the starter 'Pupil breath samples'. Ask the pupils to think of other ways of showing that there is more water vapour in exhaled air (breathing on to a cold surface or a mirror, etc.) and ask them to suggest why this should be so. Ask: 'Why is the air we breathe out warmer?'
- Show a video animation clip of Priestley's experiment where he put a mouse in an air tight glass bottle with and without the plant. Draw out from discussion of this that animals respire. Compare this experiment with the candle one. What is the link?
- This should then lead to the formulation of a generalised equation for respiration, involving the uptake of oxygen and the release of carbon dioxide. Use PowerPoint to reinforce the respiration equation.

Plenary Suggestions

Respiration modelling: O_2 in, CO_2 out
Give some pupils cards to hold with the names of the parts of the respiratory system written on them. Give one pupil a card with 'O_2' written on it. Ask them to pass down the system in the correct sequence, eventually into the blood and to the cells, where they join with a pupil who has a card labelled 'C'. They both come back out as 'CO_2'. Get the pupils involved so that they describe what is happening at each stage. Give some pupils cards with 'H_2O' and 'energy' on them, and ask whereabouts in the system they should be. (5–10 mins)

Slimming through your lungs
Show the pupils a picture of an obese person eating a chocolate bar alongside a very slim person. Ask the pupils if the obese person goes to the gym and takes lots of exercise and cuts down their calorific intake, what will happen? [They will lose weight.] Then ask the pupils, how will this weight actually get out from their bodies? Where does the mass come out? This should lead to an interesting discussion on the composition of urine, faeces and sweat, and should eventually lead to the fact that it comes out through their breath. This challenges understanding and will provide cognitive conflict for some – link it with the summary equation for respiration. (10–15 mins)

Practical Support

Starter: Pupil breath samples
Equipment and materials required
Balloons.

Comparing inhaled and exhaled air
Equipment and materials required
Drinking straws, test tubes, limewater, candles, gas jars, Vaseline, cover slips, floats, stop-watches, rubber hose, cobalt chloride paper, thermometer (0–110°C), matches.

Apparatus as shown in the pupil book for the 'Comparing carbon dioxide' experiment.

Safety
Eye protection should be worn.

Limewater is an irritant: CLEAPSS Hazcard 18.

Cobalt chloride paper should be handled as little as possible, wash hands afterwards and avoid skin contact: CLEAPSS Hazcard 25.

Warn about the use of matches.

Differentiation

SEN
The 'Respiration modelling' plenary could be extended for these pupils.

Extension
Pupils could produce a balanced equation for respiration. To extend further, ask: 'if a person inhales and exhales 3 litres of air, assuming the inhaled air has 0.04% carbon dioxide and exhaled has 4%, how much more would the exhaled breath weigh than the inhaled one?'

Homework Suggestion

Pupils could imagine they are one of the people in the picture by Joseph Wright and write a short account of what they saw, giving a scientific explanation of what was happening.

B1.8 The Heart and Circulation

NC links for the lesson
- Organisms, behaviour and health.
- Life processes are supported by the organisation of cells into tissues, organs and body systems.

Learning Objectives
Pupils should learn:
- That the heart pumps blood around the body.
- That the blood is carried to and from body organs in blood vessels.
- The structure and functions of the different types of blood vessel.

Learning Outcomes
- All pupils should be able to state that the heart pumps blood around the body and the names of the different types of blood vessel.
- Most pupils should be able to describe how the heart works and the differences between arteries, veins and capillaries.
- Some pupils should also be able to give detailed descriptions of the tissues and anatomical features involved linked to their functions.

Learning Styles
Visual: Observing the heart dissection.
Auditory: Describing the double circulation.
Kinaesthetic: Taking pulse rates.
Interpersonal: Taking part in the 'double circulation' chanting.
Intrapersonal: Making their own diagrams of the circulatory system.

Answers to in-text questions
a The left side has to pump blood to all parts of the body. The right side only has to pump blood to the lungs.
b They ensure that blood flows in the right direction.

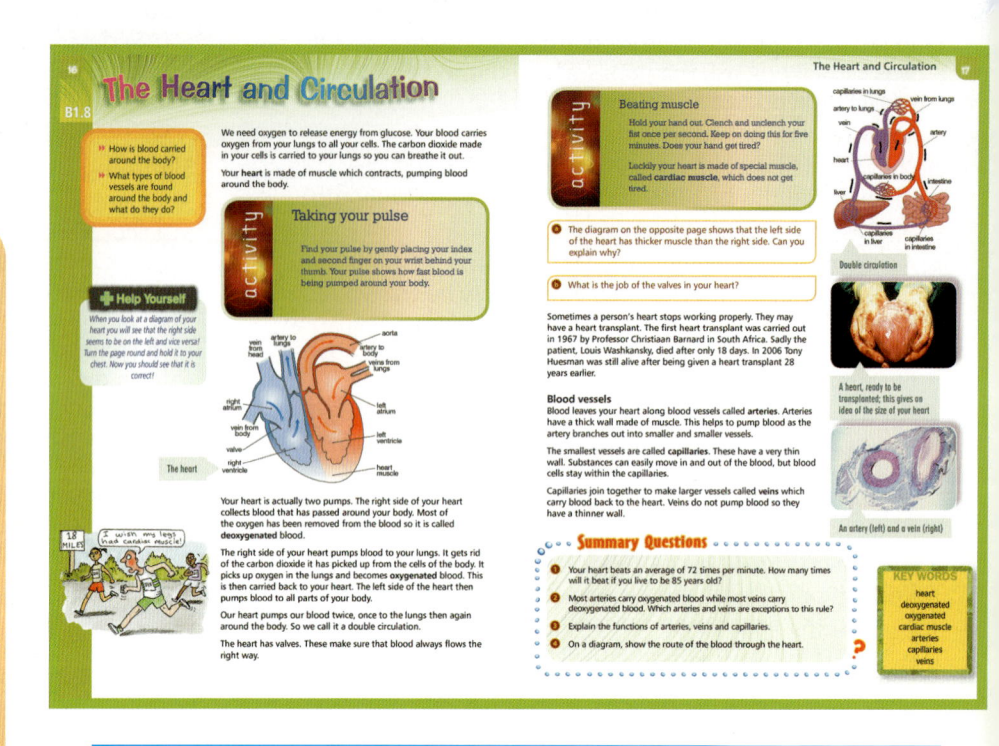

Answers to Summary questions
1. $72 \times 60 \times 24 \times 365 \times 85 = 3,216,672,000$ (approx!)
2. The pulmonary artery carries deoxygenated blood, the pulmonary vein carries oxygenated blood.
3. Arteries carry blood from the heart under high pressure. They have a thick wall to resist the pressure and to help in pumping. Capillaries allow substances to move in and out of the blood so they are very small with a very thin wall. Veins carry blood to the heart at low pressure. Their walls are thin and they have valves to prevent backflow of blood.
4. Pupil diagram should show flow from heart to lungs then back to the heart, then around the body and back to the heart.

The Lesson

Starter Suggestions
All change
Give the pupils a cloze passage to complete, or ten quick questions to answer, on the basic knowledge gained last lesson on the gas exchanges which happen in the lungs. This can then be peer marked. (5–10 mins)

Heart expectations
Tell the pupils that later on this lesson we will be dissecting a heart. Ask them to write down or draw diagrams of what they will be expecting to see in the way of structures when the heart is cut open. Remind them that the heart receives blood from two places and pushes blood out to two different places. Read out some examples. (10–15 mins)

Main Lesson
- Reinforce the idea of double circulation. Get the pupils to describe the flow of blood in a rhythmical manner, chanting with you that it goes 'from the body to the heart, to the lungs to the heart, to the body to the heart, to the lungs to the heart' reinforcing this by actions, moving your fist in appropriate semicircles coming to rest over the heart each time.

The Heart and Circulation

- Use an interactive animation of the heart if available.
- Ask the pupils to label a blank diagram of the heart and use coloured pencils to colour in the left side red and the right side purple. Draw a stick man with the flag in one hand to remind pupils of the opponent L–R inversion of diagrams.
- Carry out the activity 'Taking your pulse' as described in the pupil book. Ask: 'Are there other places where a pulse can be determined and measured?' Working in pairs, pupils should practise taking someone else's pulse. Gather up the results for the class and determine a mean rate. Ask: 'What are the extremes?' If time permits, a distribution curve could be plotted of the class results and this could show how variable pulse rates can be.
- Carry out the activity 'Beating muscle' as described in the pupil book. Each pupil should count how many times they can clench and unclench their hand in five minutes. Again, the class results could be recorded and any differences (age, gender, fitness, etc.) discussed. The rate at which the clenching and unclenching can be done will vary. Ask the pupils to account for this.
- Carry out a dissection of a pig's heart. [Check pupil sensitivities and religious objections.] Using a flexicam will help engagement. Start at the right atrium mentioning that it means 'porch'. Cut down through the curved ventricle. Show the valves and the cords or tendons, which stop the valves from blowing inside out. Stick your finger out through the pulmonary artery and then cut alongside it to open out and expose the semilunar valves. Explain that the blood now goes to the lungs and comes back in through the left atrium. Dissect this and follow down through, opening up the left ventricle, asking the pupils to comment on the thickness and why it is much thicker than the right ventricle. Ask them to suggest reasons why this might be. Again stick your finger through the aorta. If a long section of aorta has been left, you can cut off some sections of it for pupils to put their fingers into to feel how elastic it is (they should wear gloves or wash hands immediately afterwards). Show them the semi-lunar valves again, lifting up each flap with a seeker, so they can see their half-moon shape. Just above the semi-lunar valves a narrow opening goes into the heart muscle. Explain that this is the coronary artery, which gives the heart the oxygenated blood it needs and which gets blocked during heart attacks.
- Show the pupils a video clip of open heart surgery. [Be aware of sensitive pupils or those whose relatives may have had such an operation.] The oxygenated and deoxygenated blood in the transparent tubes should be identifiable by their colours. This is probably best done after the heart dissection as the pupils will be able to recognise the different parts more easily.
- Listen to a heart using a stethoscope, if available.
- Imitate the way the heart makes sounds using a film canister with small holes pieced in the lid and the base. Stick a flap of plastic on the base, so that it can cover the hole but is hinged at one side. Breathe through the cap and the plastic will act like a valve and make a sound each time it closes.

Plenary Suggestions

Cute cuticles
Draw cells on a cardboard tube from a roll of kitchen paper and pass around to show what capillary structure is like. Put some moving eyes on it and suggest that it looks like a caterpillar. Choose a volunteer, cover the nail cuticle in clove oil and focus carefully down a binocular microscope. Capillary loops with curved heads towards the nail should be visible under high magnification. (5–10 mins)

Arteries away and veins in
Use PowerPoint to show a diagram of the complete circulatory system, including details of arteries and veins. Ask the pupils to name the organs which the arteries are supplying. Pupils can compose their own diagrams, with the heart in the middle and arrows 'away' (representing the arteries) to the organs and arrows back to the heart ('in') representing the veins. As an aid to memory, ask them to write down at the top of their diagram 'Arteries away' and circle the two letter 'A's , explaining that they go away from the heart. Also ask them to write down the word 'Veins' and circle the letters 'in' within the word, emphasising that veins go in towards the heart. This can be finished for homework. (10–15 mins)

Practical Support

Taking your pulse and Beating muscle
Equipment and materials required
Stop-watches or stop-clocks.

Main lesson: Heart dissection
Equipment and materials required
Pig's heart and dissecting instruments.

Details See 'Main lesson'.

Safety
Wear eye protection when carrying out the dissection: CLEAPSS handbook/CD-Rom section 14.7.2.

If pupils touch the pig's heart, then gloves should be worn or hands washed immediately after touching any of the tissue.

Main lesson: Heart imitation
Equipment and materials required
Film canister with flap and holes.

Plenary: Cute cuticles
Equipment and materials required
Kitchen roll tube, felt-tipped pens, moving eyes, clove oil, binocular microscope.

Differentiation

SEN
Give the pupils name cards to place in the correct positions on a large heart diagram. Also provide some arrows so that the passage of blood through the heart can be indicated.

Extension
Get the pupils to do some more research on Galen or William Harvey and to make a poster for the classroom, summarising their ideas and contrasting them with the knowledge we have today.

Homework Suggestion

Ask the pupils to imagine that they are red blood cells and get them to describe how they circulate around the body, picking up oxygen and delivering it to the cells. To make it more exciting, they could be told to think of it as a motor rally circuit or a Grand Prix race track, where there are different hazards and they may travel at different speeds.

B1.9 Supplying the Cells

NC links for the lesson
- Organisms, behaviour and health.
- Life processes are supported by the organisation of cells into tissues, organs and body systems.

Learning Objectives
Pupils should learn:
- How ideas about the circulation of the blood have developed over time.
- That oxygen, carbon dioxide, dissolved food and waste are carried in the blood.
- How different substances are carried to the tissues and organs.

Learning Outcomes
- All pupils should be able to state that the red cells carry oxygen.
- Most pupils should be able to state that the red cells carry oxygen and that the plasma carries carbon dioxide, dissolved food and waste.
- Some pupils should also be able to do the above in detail and describe how the different substances reach the tissues and organs.

How Science Works
- Describe how scientific evidence from different sources carries different weight in supporting or disproving theories (1.1a3).

Learning Styles
Visual: Observing each other's arterioles and venules.
Auditory: Listening to the job descriptions for blood.
Kinaesthetic: Making a timeline.
Interpersonal: Taking part in the floor dominoes plenary.
Intrapersonal: Working out the number of molecules of oxygen carried by the bag of sweets.

Answers to in-text questions
a. In red blood cells.

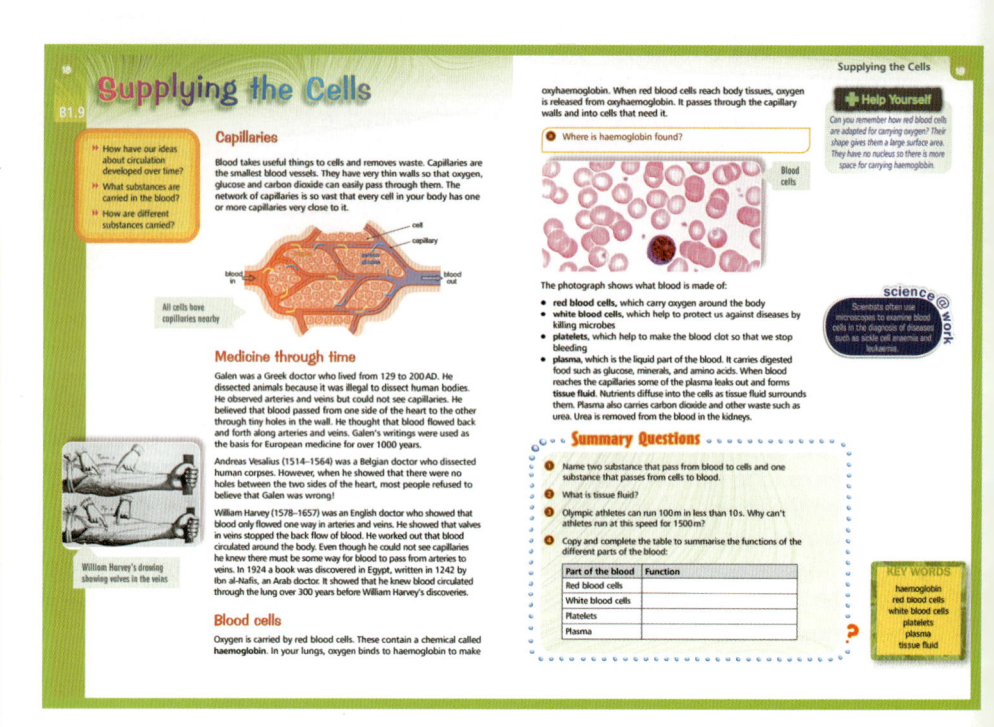

The Lesson

Starter Suggestions

True or false?
Give the pupils a list of questions based on the previous lesson. They have to write down whether they are 'true' or 'false' in the back of their books. They self-mark this exercise. (5–10 mins)

Just the bloody job
What jobs does the blood have? Ask the pupils to write out a job description for blood. Tell them to make it as imaginative and vivid as possible. At first, get the pupils to exchange and read them to each other, and then read out loud from the front some of the best offerings. Get a volunteer to write down the key points on the board. (10–15 mins)

Main Lesson
- Using video, if available, and/or PowerPoint, go over the history of thought on the human circulation, from Galen's ideas through Ibn al-Nafis's work on pulmonary circulation to that of William Harvey. There is a cross-curricular tie-in with the popular GCSE History topic 'The History of Medicine'.

Answers to Summary questions

1. Blood to cells: oxygen + glucose; cells to blood: carbon dioxide.
2. Liquid that leaks out of capillaries and flows between cells.
3. They cannot get enough oxygen to the muscles, so respiration is anaerobic which produces lactic acid.
4.

Part of the blood	Function
Red blood cells	Carry oxygen
White blood cells	Fight diseases/kill microbes
Platelets	Clot blood
Plasma	Carries nutrients, carbon dioxide, urea, antibodies, hormones, etc.

Supplying the Cells

- Bare your arm and have a trusty pupil place a tourniquet made from rubber tube around your upper arm. Slap the inside of your elbow until the veins stand out. The valves should stand our proud of your skin. Rub your hand downwards over them, deflating the valves and ask the pupils to comment on what happens. Rub your hand upwards over them causing the valves to distend and get them again to comment on why this might happen. Draw this out into a discussion on evidence for a one way flow of blood around the body. Relate to the work of William Harvey, as shown in the pupil book. [Make sure this is a teacher demonstration only.]
- Ask the pupils to make a timeline using a till roll. Using a scale of 20 cm per 100 years, start at CE Year 0. The relevant dates are in the pupil book. Ask: 'Why did it take so long for the details to be worked out? How were the workings of the human body discovered?'
- If possible get a supply of fresh blood from an abattoir. Put a little sodium citrate solution into the bottom of the collecting flask as an anti-coagulating agent. Using an oxygen cylinder or generator (manganese dioxide and hydrogen peroxide will do this), bubble some oxygen through the blood to observe the colour change.
- Working in pairs, get the pupils to look at the inside of each other's lower lip or under the tongue to see both oxygenated and deoxygenated blood within the arterioles and venules. Relate this to why blood is always bright red when you cut yourself, but is purple/blue when you have a blood sample taken from a vein.
- Show the pupils a PowerPoint slide show of red blood cells carrying oxygen molecules. Have a packet of sweets which are shaped like a biconcave disc (Refreshers will do). Hand these around in a sealed transparent bag and give them as prizes to be eaten after the class (no eating during the lesson). Each red cell contains about 250 million haemoglobin molecules, and each of these can carry four oxygen molecules, so each red cell carries about a billion oxygen molecules on its journey around the body. Ask the pupils to estimate how many sweets there are in the bag and then to work out how many oxygen molecules can be carried by the sweets (representing red cells). The correct answer can be rewarded at the end of the lesson with the bag of sweets.
- There are about five million red cells per micro-litre (millimetre cubed) so a tiny drop that would fit on a full stop would carry five million billion oxygen molecules (5,000,000,000,000,000,000). To get a view on this show the pupils a sheet with a million dots on it arranged into blocks of 100 and 1000.
- Show an animation of the body tissues with capillaries running through them. Observe how the molecules of oxygen and dissolved food diffuse from the capillaries into the tissues and how the carbon dioxide and waste molecules diffuse from the tissues into the capillaries. Get the pupils to summarise these exchanges in their exercise books. Framework will be necessary for lower attaining pupils.
- The following class activity could be useful in reinforcing the idea of exchange of materials between the tissues and the blood. Prepare sets of cards with the names of substances carried by the blood on them (oxygen, carbon dioxide, glucose, amino acids, fatty acids, glycerol, water, hormones, urea, heat). Prepare sets of carrier cards (red blood cells, plasma) in appropriate numbers for the class. Arrange posters or labels, showing names or pictures of the body organs on the wall. Include a label for body cells. Give out cards randomly; about 50:50 materials cards to carrier cards to begin with. Pupils are to move around the room until they meet an appropriate partner, when they need to decide where to deliver their material. For example, oxygen meets red blood cell and delivers it to a body cell. The red blood cell is then free to pick up another oxygen card: the other pupil could then return to the pool of cards for another go. Look at all the cards deposited by the labels and discuss the findings. It could be worth pointing out here that the cells of the lungs, kidneys and so on do need oxygen and glucose in order to function.

Plenary Suggestions

Blood dominoes
Carry out a floor dominoes game relating the parts of the blood and their functions. (5–10 mins)

Artificial blood
Tell the pupils that there has been research going on for a long time into the possibility of 'artificial' blood or blood substitutes. Discuss with the pupils the advantages of artificial blood or blood substitutes; refer back to the Starter 'Just the bloody job.' Ask: 'Does it seem like a good idea? When could it be used?' (10–15 mins.)

Practical Support

Main lesson: Making a timeline
Equipment and materials required
Till roll or long strips of paper.

Main lesson: Colour of oxygenated blood
Equipment and materials required
Fresh blood from abattoir, sodium citrate and a source of oxygen.

Safety
Care with the handling of the fresh blood and risk assess hydrogen peroxide if generating oxygen.

Main lesson: Looking at arterioles and venules
Safety
Make sure pupils hands are clean when examining each other's mouths and tongues.

Main lesson: Number of oxygen molecules
Equipment and materials required
Packets of sweets to represent red blood cells, e.g. Refreshers.

Safety
Do not eat sweets!

Differentiation

SEN
Pupils could make Plasticine models of red blood cells to fit the capillary tubes made in the previous lesson. They could use red Plasticine for oxygenated and purple for deoxygenated.

Extension
Ask: 'Are all vertebrate red blood cells the same?' Get pupils to find out how the blood of other animals differs from human blood. This leads to a discussion of the importance of forensic science in the investigation of blood stains at the scene of a crime.

Homework Suggestion
Ask pupils to write a short passage or a poem about the duties of a red blood cell.

B1.10 Exercise

NC links for the lesson
- Organisms, behaviour and health.
- Life processes are supported by the organisation of cells into tissues, organs and body systems.

Learning Objectives
Pupils should learn:
- That heart rate increases when we exercise.
- What happens to our breathing rate when we exercise.
- What happens when we cannot get enough oxygen to our muscles.

Learning Outcomes
- All pupils should be able to relate heart rate to exercise.
- Most pupils should be able to explain why heart rate increases with exercise.
- Some pupils should also be able to predict accurately the effects of increased exercise on the rate of return to the resting heart rate.
- Describe and suggest, with reasons, how planning and implementation could be improved (1.2e).

Learning Styles
Visual: Recording pulse rates.
Auditory: Listening to explanations.
Kinaesthetic: Carrying out practical activities.
Interpersonal: Working in pairs on pulse rate activity.
Intrapersonal: Displaying personal results on graphs.

Answers to in-text questions
a) Hot, sweating, short of breath, heart rate high, breathing faster and deeper, red in face.
b) Jogging, cycling, walking, swimming, football, rugby, tennis, badminton, etc.

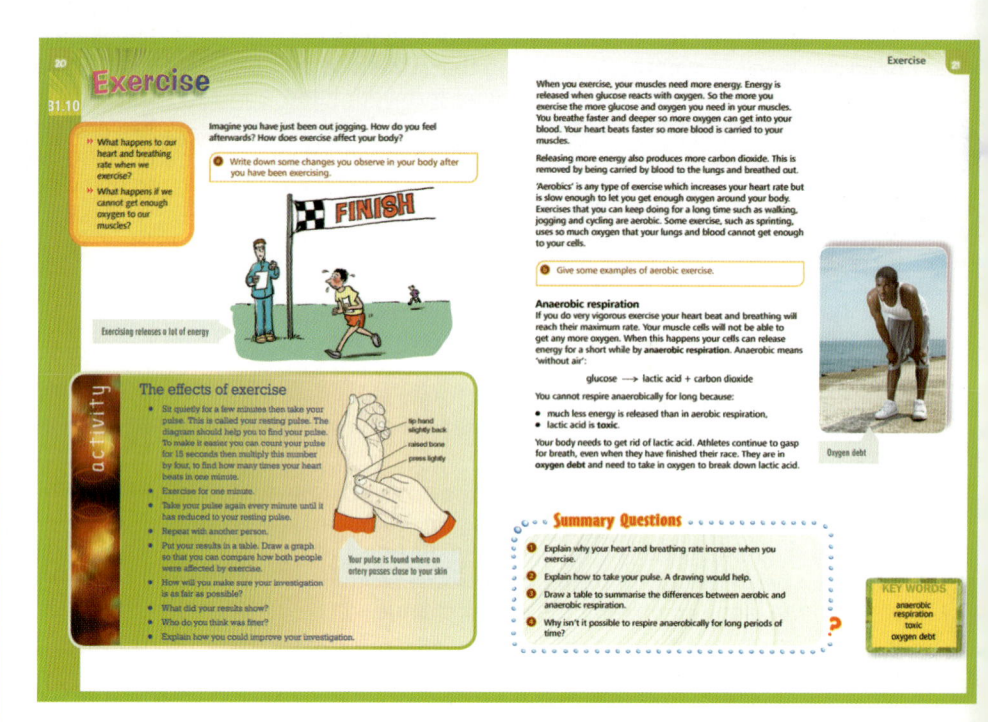

The Lesson

Starter Suggestions

Why does that happen?
Show the pupils a video clip from a cartoon chase, such as *Road Runner*, where a character is shown with a pounding heart following vigorous exercise. Working in small groups, ask the pupils to say why this happens in as much detail as possible. Discuss the responses with the class, getting them to draw out as much existing knowledge as possible. (10–15 mins)

Blood flow arrows
This is a review of previous learning. Using an interactive computer projection for concept mapping, where one can attach flexible arrows from one box to another which stay connected when the boxes are moved (such as Smart Ideas), get the pupils to link up text boxes containing names of parts of the

Answers to Summary questions

1. More oxygen is needed in the muslces so the breathing rate increases. This gets more oxygen into the blood and the heart rate increases to carry this oxygen to the muscles. Meanwhile more carbon dioxide is produced in the muscles which is carried to the lungs in the blood then breathed out. The muscles also need more glucose which is carried by the increased blood flow.

2. Show position on wrist below thumb, taken with fingers not thumb (or neck method.)

3.

Aerobic	Anaerobic
Uses oxygen	Does not use oxygen
Produces carbon dioxide	Produces lactic acid
Produces lots of energy	Produces a small amount of energy

4. Lactic acid, which builds up in the lungs, is toxic.

circulatory system. Use red arrows for oxygenated blood and purple arrows for deoxygenated blood. Ask volunteers to join up a pair of boxes, correctly showing the blood flow direction, and then let them pick others to continue the process, asking for help from their peers if they need it. (5–10 mins)

Main Lesson

- Through imagination and scene setting, provide another link from the energy in food to the oxygen needed to get the energy out. Pick two pupils and put them each into an imaginary midget submarine. Both have water supplies. In one there is plenty of oxygen in the tanks, but no food. In the other there is plenty of food, but no oxygen. Ask: 'Who is going to die first, and why and from what?' Draw out through questioning details of why the air-less one would die first, linking it with the energy in the food.

- Using PowerPoint and demonstration, show the pupils how to take their own pulse and that of a partner. Use both the wrist and the neck method. Get the pupils to count the beats in 15 seconds and then, by multiplying by four with a calculator, get the heart rate or pulse rate in beats per minute (BPM). Introduce these terms carefully and ensure by questioning that the pupils understand them. Collect some rates and draw out that there appears to be a big range (the pupils are generally poor at carrying out this task accurately). Discuss what the range may be due to, leading to identification of human error as a factor. Ask if they can think of a way of avoiding human error.

- Show the pupils how to use data-loggers with heart rate monitors connected. If possible, have a range of these, including the commonly used chest belt and wrist-watch style recorders used by athletes to assess their training performance. Some monitors are better than others. Generally, they can function intermittently which can be irritating. The TTS group's pulse meter is simple and easy to use.

- Use the practical 'The effects of exercise' as described in the pupil book. Either get the pupils to draw up their own results tables or pre-print blank ones. Demonstrate the method first (see third bullet point above).Let the pupils work in pairs, one as exerciser and one as timer and recorder. Take an initial reading when the pupil is seated and resting. Record this result. Have them carry out safe, sensible but vigorous exercise (discuss and agree on this in advance) for two minutes. This is best done en masse to avoid prolonged disruption. Get the pupils to take a pulse reading immediately after exercise and record it, starting a stop-watch at the same time. After one minute, take the next reading, keeping the stop-watch running (many will turn them off) measure and record again. Continue this for another two or three minutes. Repeat the whole exercise, reversing roles.

- Pupils can plot their results on a graph, either by hand or using a suitable computer programme, such as Simple Data Handling. They can compare their individual results with their partner and the class results can be collated. Discuss the results and draw out by questioning the reasons behind the increase in rate. Aim to get them to recall the links to the energy in food and to the necessity of oxygen, and of getting both of these to the muscles for respiration to occur.

- Show footage of athletes at the end of very exhausting exercise, such as a boxing match or a rowing competition (Olympics or Boat Race). Get a volunteer to hold a chair out at arm's length until they can no longer do so. Ask them to talk through what they are feeling as they do this. Ask the rest of the class to look for signs that they are becoming fatigued. Ask: 'How can you tell what is happening?'

- Ask pupils to flex the forefinger of their right hand up and down for as long as they can. You could make this a competition, if they time how long they can do it. Ask: 'Why do you slow down and eventually stop?'

- Supply pupils with a Lego model of glucose, made using six identical bricks in a stack and the word 'glucose' written across the front. Let them break the model into two halves, each labelled 'lactic acid'. Relate this to the pained look on the faces of the volunteers' faces as lactic acid builds up in their muscles. Explain that the lactic acid can be broken down to carbon dioxide as soon as there is sufficient oxygen available and that this is known as the 'oxygen debt'.

Plenary Suggestions

Why did that happen again?

Repeat the *Road Runner* clip used at the start. Put up on the board, either as cards or digitally, the key words for the unit so far. Ask pupils to repeat their explanations for the increase in heart rate during exercise, gaining a point for each in-context key word they use. (5–10 mins)

The long-distance runner

Show a video of Kenyan long-distance runners or other athletes training at altitude. Ask pupils to think of reasons why training at altitude is beneficial for long-distance or endurance events. Discuss the reasons and then compare long-distance training with training for sprint events. (10–15 mins.)

Practical Support

The effects of exercise

Equipment and materials required

Stop-watches or a clock with a second hand to time pulse rates.

If available, examples of data-loggers with heart rate monitors/pulse monitors such as used in athletic training.

Safety

Check exercises suggested for suitability and safety.

Main lesson: Model of glucose

Sugar, spoon, Bunsen burner, mat. Six identical bricks in a stack with the word 'glucose' written across the front. Two labels of 'lactic acid'.

Differentiation

SEN

Pupils should be able to participate in the practical activities with assistance.

Using pictures cut out from newspapers and magazines, pupils could make a poster showing examples of aerobic exercise.

Extension

Pupils could devise a training programme for an athlete who wishes to compete in a marathon. The programme should include reasons for the training and suitable diets, both during training and on the day before the marathon.

B1.11 Excretion and Homeostasis

NC links for the lesson
- Organisms, behaviour and health.
- Life processes are supported by the organisation of cells into tissues, organs and body systems.

Learning Objectives
Pupils should learn:
- How the temperature and water content of the body is controlled.
- The functions of the kidney in the removal of toxins and the control of the water content of our bodies.

Learning Outcomes
- All pupils should be able to state that the temperature and water content of the body are controlled and that the kidneys clean the blood.
- Most pupils should be able to describe how temperature and water content are controlled and how toxins are removed from the body by the kidneys.
- Some pupils should also be able to explain in greater detail how these homeostatic mechanisms work.

Learning Styles
Visual: Watching videos clips and demonstrations.
Auditory: Listening to the responses to discussions.
Kinaesthetic: Carrying out practical activities.
Interpersonal: Working in a group to design an investigation.
Intrapersonal: Writing an e-mail to a person in the arctic or the tropics.

Answers to in-text questions
a. In the brain.
b. In the winter.
c. Summer urine.

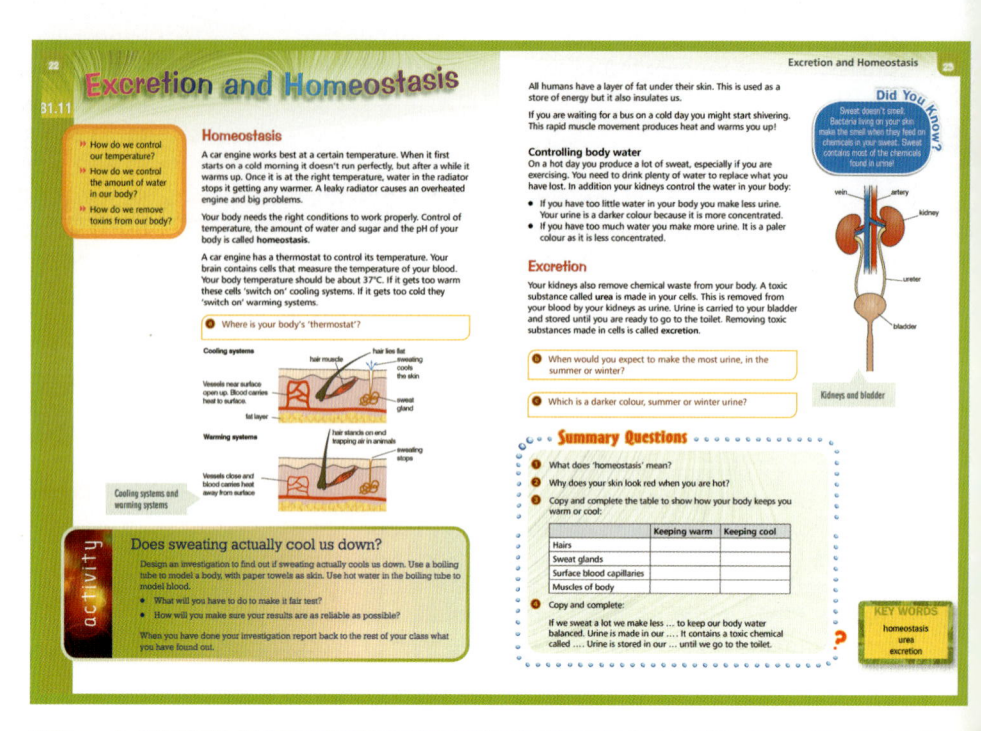

The Lesson

Starter Suggestions

Running hot and cold
Divide the class into two groups. Ask the pupils in one group to write e-mails to a person living in arctic conditions suggesting how they can keep warm. Ask the pupils in the other group to write e-mails to a person living in the tropics suggesting how they can keep cool. Give them a time limit and then draw up a list of suggestions on the board – one column for the arctic and one for the tropics. Discuss the responses and match contrasting advice (e.g. wear thicker clothing/wear thinner clothing). From this, establish the current state of the pupils' knowledge of the importance of establishing and maintaining a steady body temperature. (10–15 mins)

What is a thermostat?
Pose this question to the pupils and gauge responses. If possible, display a thermostat in action – a mini-fridge used for camping may be an appropriate prop. As an alternative example to discuss in class, you could

Answers to Summary questions

1. Maintaining a constant internal environment.
2. Blood flows closer to the surface of the skin so it can be cooled down.
3.

	Keeping warm	Keeping cool
Hairs	Stand on end	Lie flat
Sweat glands	Do not make sweat	Make sweat
Surface blood capillaries	Close (constrict)	Open up (dilate)
Muscles of body	Nothing special	Shiver

4. If we sweat a lot we make less **urine** to keep our body water balanced. Urine is made in our **kidneys**. It contains a toxic chemical called **urea**. Urine is stored in our **bladder** until we go to the toilet.

Excretion and Homeostasis

use thermostatically controlled radiators and domestic hot water systems. Discuss and ask pupils to make notes on how these systems work. (5–10 mins)

Main Lesson

- Show a video clip of a boxing match or other sporting event with plenty of sweat flowing (any of the 'Rocky' films would do or any current 'frothy' sporting clip). Discuss situations where we get sweaty, concentrating on drawing out the reason why we get sweaty and getting past the responsive answer (because we are exercising hard) to establish the rational answer as to what is the function of sweating.
- Using volunteers, swab down the skin of the right forearm with water. Ask pupils to describe how it feels and to explain why. Then swab down the skin on the left forearm with ethanol (reminding the pupils of previous injections they might have had). Ask pupils again to describe how it feels and to explain why. Then ask for any differences between using water and ethanol.
- The above activity can be followed up by dipping thermometers into ethanol and waving them around gently until the ethanol has evaporated. Record the starting temperature and then the lowest temperature reached when all the ethanol has evaporated. Then repeat the process, using water instead of the ethanol. Collect the results together, analyse them and ask the pupils to state the relationships between how easily the substance evaporates and the extent to which cooling takes place. Bear in mind the heating effect of human breath and ask pupils how the investigation could be made more reliable.
- Use the activity suggested in the pupil book, 'Does sweating actually cool us down?'. Each group of pupils could be given the same set of apparatus (boiling tubes, paper towels, thermometers, hot water), and asked to consider how they can make it a fair test and how to ensure that the results are as reliable as possible. The design of the investigation could be a homework task and then the ideas could be put into practice during another lesson.
- Show a video clip of the effect of cold on the human body. A suitable video clip could be from *The Mighty Boosh*, in the episode where they visit the North Pole in search of a precious stone and meet an ice monster. Comment on the processes involved in trying to keep itself at the correct temperature. Get the pupils to summarise these processes in a table. Ask for a volunteer to act out being very cold and discuss with the class the importance of shivering. Ask why the face would be pale. Draw the discussion to a close by getting the pupils to summarise the effects of excessive heat and cold on the human body.
- Show the pupils a bottle of concentrated orange squash. Discuss what the best concentration to drink is and whether or not grown-ups make it too weak. Ask a pupil to pour out a glass of the concentrated squash and then ask another to make a 50:50 dilution with water. Another pupil could make up a very dilute mixture. Discuss the appearance of these dilutions. Relate to the text in the pupil book on urine colour and its implications. **Safety:** Do not drink.
- Ask if anyone has ever seen a bird urinate. No – because the urea is the white part of a bird dropping: the dark part being the faeces. What is the advantage to birds of not having a bladder? [It reduces the mass of the bird; the bird does not need lots of water to get rid of excretory material.]

Plenary Suggestions

Homeostasis of the wallet
Ask the pupils to draw out a flow chart of decision making regarding the amount of money that they have and how much they spend. Include directions on feedback links, e.g. the more money you have, the more you can spend, but the less you have the less you can spend. Be aware of, and sensitive to, social ramifications in the class. (5–10 mins)

Steady as she goes
Ask pupils to devise homoeostatic mechanisms for 'Bender' the robot from *Futurama* – a suitable clip would be useful here. Ask: 'What sort of sensors would he need and how would they respond to the environment?' Use a background track for this activity 'Steady as she goes' by The Raconteurs. (10–15 mins)

Practical Support

Does sweating actually cool us down?
Equipment and materials required
Boiling tubes, stand, thermometers, paper towels, hot water.

Safety
Care needed with hot water and the handling of thermometers.

Main lesson: Evaporation
Equipment and materials required
Cotton wool balls, thermometers, ethanol.

Safety
Ethanol is highly flammable, no naked flames: CLEAPSS Hazcard 40A.
Care needed with the handling of thermometers.

Main lesson: Concentrations
Equipment and materials required
Orange squash, beakers, measuring cylinders (100 cm^3).

Differentiation

SEN
Supply pupils with two outlines of the human body, one labelled 'Too hot' and the other 'Too cold'. Pupils can label and illustrate how each is feeling or what is happening. For example, the hot person could have a red face and drops of sweat and the cold person could look pale and be shivering.

Extension
These pupils could be given pigs' kidneys to dissect. Supply an instruction sheet and a set of flag labels so that they can label the parts for the rest of the class as a demonstration. [Be aware of pupils' sensitivities and/or religious objections.] **Safety:** Wear eye protection and wash hands after experiment. Care with scalpels.

Homework Suggestion

Pupils could design the investigation suggested in the pupil book, showing how the apparatus could be set up, how to make it a fair test and how to ensure the results are reliable. This could then be used during a practical session.

The plenary 'Homeostasis of the wallet' could be used as a homework exercise.

B1.12 The Nervous System

NC links for the lesson
- Organisms, behaviour and health.
- Life processes are supported by the organisation of cells into tissues, organs and body systems.

Learning Objectives

Pupils should learn:
- That reflex actions protect us because they are fast and automatic.
- How a reflex action works.
- The ways in which the skin is sensitive to different types of stimuli.

Learning Outcomes
- All pupils should be able to name a reflex action.
- Most pupils should be able to name a reflex action and describe how it works.
- Some pupils should also be able to describe the details of a named reflex action.

How Science Works
- Describe ways in which the presentation of experimental results through the routine use of tables, chart and line graphs makes it easier to see patterns and trends (1.2d).

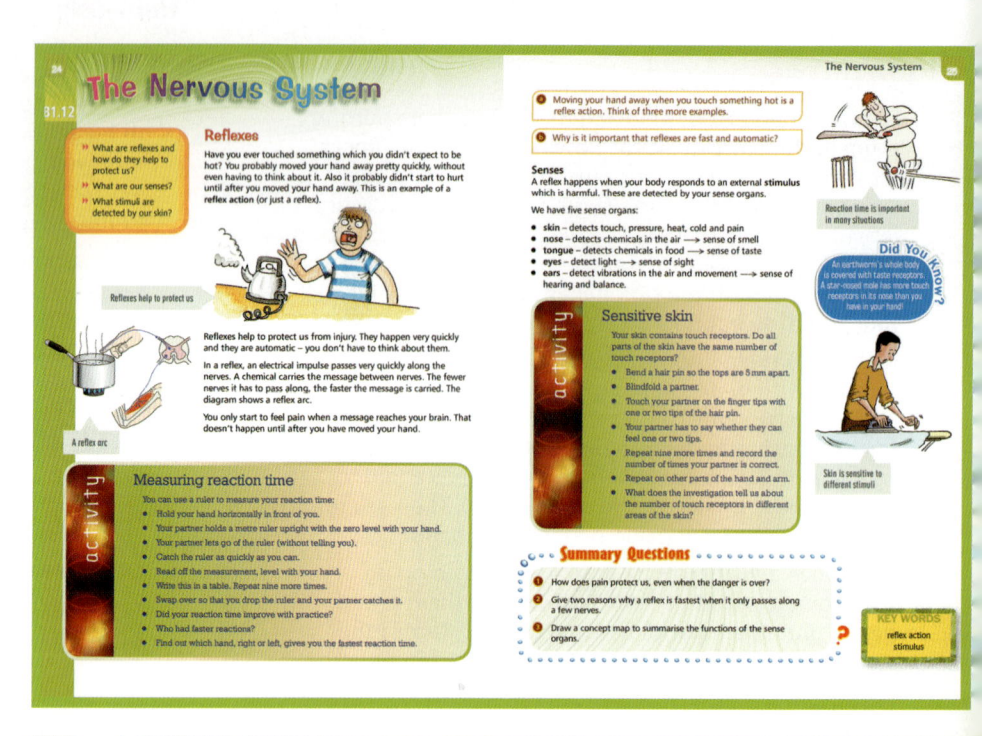

Answers to Summary questions

1. 'Reminds' us not to use injured limb, etc.
2. Less distance to travel; avoids having to pass from nerve to nerve as often.
3. Pupil concept map. [Mark by impression.]

The Lesson

Starter Suggestions

Senses for safety
Ask the pupils to list the five sense organs in their notebooks, or write up a list on the board. Give them five minutes to write down what each does and, for each one, an example of how the sense organ makes life safer. It might be necessary to give them an example to get them going – standing on a pin or touching a hot saucepan. Gather together the ideas and discuss how important the sense organs are. (5–10 mins)

Nervous 'Rex'
Get the class settled into a very quiet mode if possible and then unexpectedly make a very loud noise, for example, by exploding a hydrogen/oxygen balloon (CLEAPSS check beforehand) or banging a slab of wood hard down against a desk. Get the pupils to gauge their responses (increased heart rate, rapid breathing, dilated eyes, paler skin, blinking and other involuntary movements) and to attempt to describe which sense organs are involved, what has happened and why. (10–15 mins)

Learning Styles
Visual: Observing PowerPoint presentation on reflex action.
Auditory: Listening to explanations.
Kinaesthetic: Carrying out practical activities.
Interpersonal: Working in groups at the practical activities.
Intrapersonal: Responding to 'Nervous Rex' starter.

The Nervous System

Main Lesson

- Ask the pupils to identify their sense organs (if not already done as a starter), and discuss why we need sense organs. Let them imagine that they lost each one. Get them to arrange a set of cards in the order in which they would prefer to have their senses. Discuss this and draw group conclusions. Link this to empathy with people who have these problems, e.g. think about the problems of people who are hearing-impaired or sight-impaired. Discuss why some people enter sensory deprivation chambers voluntarily.
- Show a PowerPoint presentation on the reflex pathway. Provide the pupils with a worksheet that they fill in as the pathway is explained. This sheet can then be fixed in their notebooks. It would be a good idea to choose something different from the example in the pupil book, e.g. a knee jerk reflex. Introduce the relevant terms, if appropriate, and ensure that the flow of nerve impulses from receptor to effector in the pathway is clearly shown.
- The activity 'Measuring reaction time' can be carried out as described in the pupil book. Alternatively, there are Internet-based reaction timers that can be used.
- The activity 'Sensitive skin' can be carried out as described in the pupil book. Variations could include testing other parts of the body, such as the leg or the back. Map out the results from various parts of the body.
- The skin also has temperature receptors, but how do they work? Provide a bowl of hot water, a bowl of iced water and a bowl of warm water. Get a volunteer to place one hand in the hot water and the other in the iced water. Leave the hands in the water for one minute, after which time both hands are placed in the warm water. Ask the volunteer what they are feeling. Draw out an explanation of what information the hot and cold sensory receptors are sending to the brain.
- Draw up a list of different sporting activities. Ask the pupils which of the senses are important in order to be successful in each one. Link this in with the measurement of reaction times. If there are pupils who have done extension work on the stick-drop test, find out how much difference practising makes.

Plenary Suggestions

Sixth sense
Ask the pupils to imagine another sense that they would like to have. Ask: 'How would it work? What would it enable you to do?' Share this with other members of your group or neighbours and with the rest of the class. (5–10 mins)

Super-sensory animals
Give the pupils a set of sheets, or information cards, on animals which have senses over and above those which we have, such as dogs' noses, sharks' electromagnetic detectors, spiders' vibration detectors, a bee's ability to see colours that we never can. Ask the pupils to relate these to the animal's way of life. Discuss which one they would like to have and why. (10–15 mins)

Practical Support

Starter: Hydrogen/air balloon CLEAPSS Hazard 48.

Measuring reaction time

Equipment and materials required
Metre ruler, pre-printed sheets to fill in.

Sensitive skin

Equipment and materials required
Small pieces of blunt wire (hair pins, unbent paper clip, blunt tapestry needles) mounted in pieces of cork. If two wires are used, they should be about 1 cm apart.

Safety
Avoid the use of sharp needles or pieces of wire.

Main lesson: Temperature receptors

Equipment and materials required
Three washing-up bowls; hot, warm and iced water.

Safety
Make sure hot water is safe to put hands in.

Differentiation

SEN
Pupils should be able to take part in the practical activities with assistance.

Provide the pupils with a set of cards with the components of a reflex pathway on them. Pupils can then put them into the correct order.

Extension
Pupils could complete a worksheet summarising the flow of nerve impulse from receptor to effector.

Pupils could find out if practising the stick-drop test improves reaction times. They could try the test out on younger pupils and older people. Ask: 'Do the times vary significantly? Is there a difference between the times for boys and those for girls?'

Homework Suggestion

If using the 'Senses for safety' starter, pupils could build up a table of functions and examples in their notebooks, using the information from the lesson.

As a follow-up to the activity on losing senses, ask pupils to write a short paragraph in their notebooks explaining which sense they think is the most important for human survival.

There are several opportunities here to follow up the practical activities: writing up the method, making a table of results, comparison of results etc.

Answers to in-text questions

a E.g. touching something sharp; blinking if insect flies near eye; ducking on hearing loud noise.

b Fast so we react quickly; automatic so we don't waste time thinking about it.

Answers to Body Systems – End of Topic Questions

Answers to know your stuff questions

1. a) i) D. [1]
      ii) E. [1]
      iii) B. [1]
      iv) Any *one* from: [1]
          in blood [accept 'plasma']
          in blood vessels [accept a named blood vessel, accept 'arteries'].
   b) For energy. [1]
   c) i) Sitel [accept 'cola drink and biscuit']. [1]
      ii) Faye [accept '(double) cheeseburger and chips' *or* 'burger and chips']. [1]
      iii) Any *one* from: [1]
           It causes heart disease.
           It could give you a heart attack *or* stroke.
           It clogs your arteries *or* blood vessels.
           It makes you fat.

2. a) It will increase it [accept 'make it go up' *or* 'make it faster']. [1]
   b) Carbon dioxide, urea. [2]

3. a) i) Answers may be in either order:
         Vitamins [accept 'vitamin C'], [1]
         water. [1]
      ii) Answers may be in either order:
          Fats, [1]
          proteins. [1]
   b) Answers may be in either order:
      Minerals, [1]
      fibre [accept 'roughage']. [1]
   c) Any *two* from: [2]
      It increases the surface area of the food *or* orange.
      It breaks it into smaller pieces.
      It breaks open cells [accept 'so you can get the nutrients out'].
      It mixes it with saliva for easy swallowing [accept 'for ease of swallowing' or 'to stop you choking'].
      It mixes with saliva to start digestion occurring.

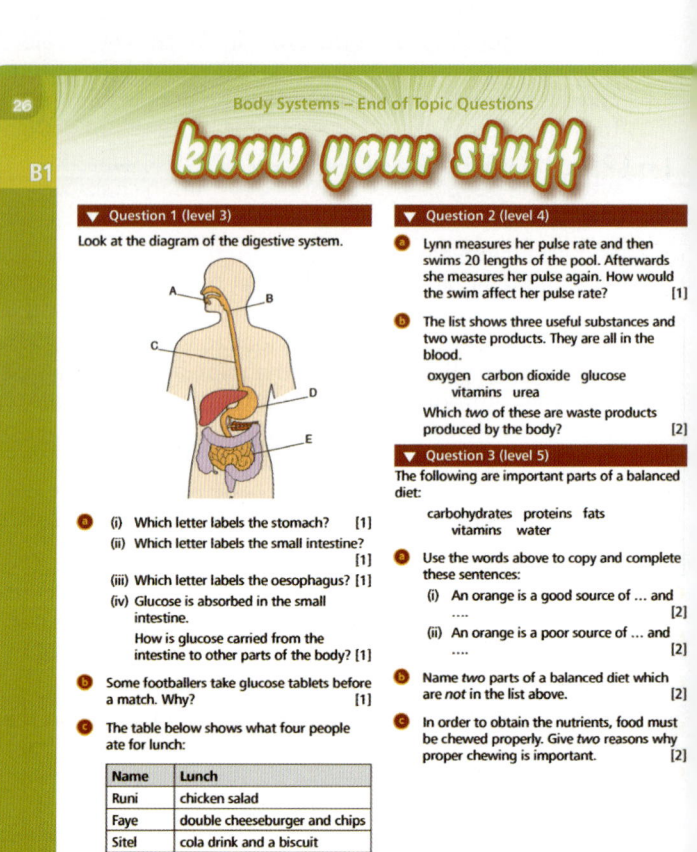

Body Systems – End of Topic Questions

How Science Works

Question 1 (level 6)

The table shows the amount of six different nutrients in three types of mashed potato.

Kidzmash is an instant mash, specially made for children.

Nutrient	100 g Mashed potatoes	100 g Instant mash made up ready to eat	100 g 'Kidzmash' made up ready to eat
Carbohydrate (g)	12.0	12.6	12.5
Protein (g)	1.4	1.4	1.4
Fat (g)	0.1	0.1	0.1
Vitamin C (mg)	20	10	60
Fibre (g)	1.3	1.2	1.2
Sodium chloride (mg)	75	80	78

a A scientist compared the three types of mash. Why was it a fair comparison? [1]

b All types of mash include some sugar. Why isn't it listed in the table? [1]

c What ingredient helps the movement of food through the intestines? [1]

d What evidence is there that vitamin C is added when making Kidzmash? [1]

e A boy said, "There is more sodium chloride than protein in mashed potato". How can you tell from the table that the pupil is wrong? [1]

Question 2 (level 7)

Jasdeep and Mandeep carried out an investigation into the digestion of starch by the enzyme called amylase.

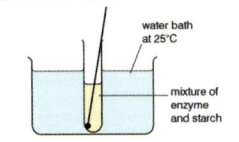

a Why was the mixture kept in a water bath? [1]

Jasdeep and Mandeep put drops of iodine solution on a white tile.

Every 30 seconds they added a drop of the mixture of enzyme and starch to a drop of iodine solution. At first the drops turned blue, but after four minutes they stayed brown.

b Why did the mixture stop turning the drops of iodine solution blue after four minutes? [1]

c They then carried out the experiment with the water bath at 35°C. This time, the drops stopped turning blue after two minutes. Explain why. [1]

d Sadie and Tom want to compare the experiment at 35°C with the results from the experiment at 25°C. Describe what they need to do to make this a fair test. [1]

Answers to How Science Works questions

1
  a They analysed 100 g / the same amount of each potato.
  b Sugar is in the carbohydrate.
  c Fibre.
  d There is more vitamin C in Kidzmash than in potato.
  e Sodium chloride is measured in mg / milligrams and protein is in g / grams.

2
  a Any *one* from: [1]
  To keep the temperature constant.
  So that the experiment was not affected by a change in temperature in the room.
  To control the temperature *or* a variable.

  b Any *one* from: [1]
  The starch had been digested *or* broken down *or* used up.
  There was no starch left.

  c Any *one* from: [1]
  It doubled the speed [accept 'it made it quicker' *or* 'it increased the speed'].
  It halved the time taken [accept 'it takes less time'].

  d Any *one* from: [1]
  Use the same amount of mixture *or* the same amount of enzyme and starch.
  Stir the mixture *or* stir the enzyme and starch.
  Use the same type of mixture.

B2.1 Ecology

NC links for the topic
- Organisms, behaviour and health.
- Life processes are supported by the organisation of cells into tissues, organs and body systems.
- All living things show variation, can be classified and are interdependent, interacting with each other and their environment.

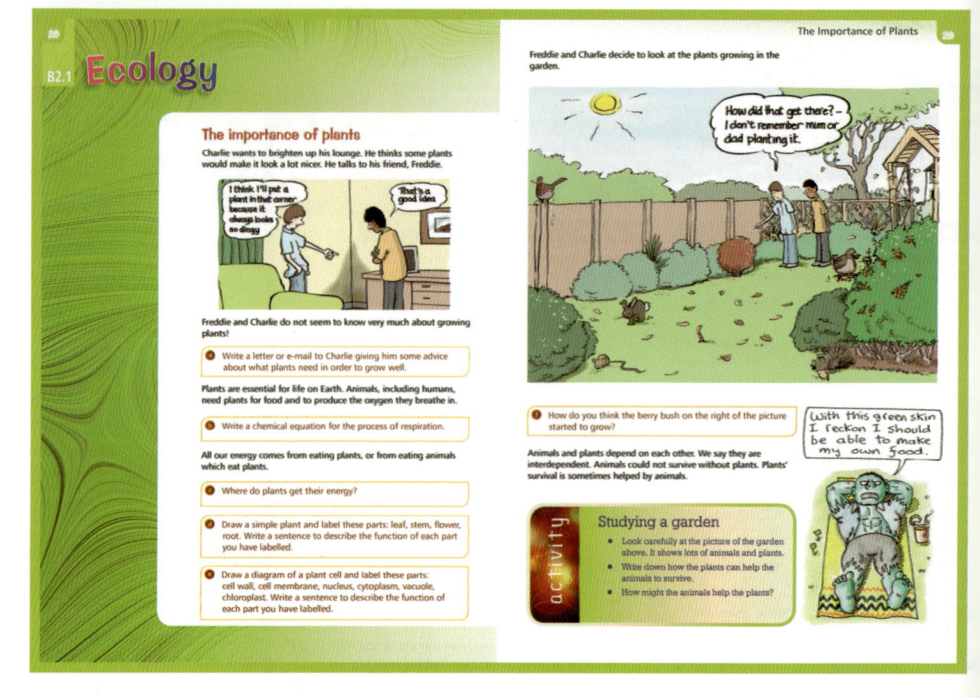

Learning Objectives
Pupils should learn:
- That plants are essential for the existence of life on Earth.
- How animals and plants depend on each other.
- How plants obtain their energy for growth.

Learning Outcomes
- All pupils should be able to state that animals and plants are interdependent.
- Most pupils should be able to describe the structure of a plant and the functions of its parts.
- Some pupils should also be able to describe examples of the inter-relationships between plants and animals.

Learning Styles
Visual: Watching the PowerPoint presentation.
Auditory: Listening to other pupils' views about whether or not plants should be taken into space.
Kinaesthetic: Taking part in the understanding energy activity.
Interpersonal: Taking part in discussions.
Intrapersonal: Reflecting on own ideas for the 'Society for the preservation of plants'.

The Lesson

Starter Suggestions

Society for the preservation of plants
Suggest to the pupils that they are going to set up a society for the preservation of plants. Working in groups, get them to write a short list of rules for membership: for example, how to help plants grow well or how to help reproduction in plants. For each rule, they will need to give a scientific explanation. After a time limit, invite groups to suggest rules and discuss how successful they could be, linking to the necessities of life for plants. Have small rewards available for the best list. (10–15 mins)

Plants in space
Working in groups, get the pupils to discuss why humans may one day take plants into space with them if they have to go on very long missions. Discuss their answers, drawing out the interactions between plants, animals and the environment. This could be extended by getting them to suggest which plants would be good to take and the logistics of the project. (5–10 mins)

Main Lesson

- As a revision exercise, let teams of pupils compete in a race to label the plant parts and plant cell parts on a pair of diagrams. It would be useful to have several versions of these diagrams available according to the ability of the class members, some with more structured support than others.

- Use a PowerPoint summary of the need for energy in living organisms, revising the process of respiration and including a 'drag and drop' section for pupils' involvement. Emphasise that all living organisms need energy and the differences in the ways that plants and animals obtain their energy.

- Burn some food, such as sugar, over a bench mat and ask where the energy comes from. Show the pupils a carbon dioxide fire extinguisher and ask why a squirt from it would put out the flames. Establish, through questioning, that the energy originally came from the Sun and that oxygen is necessary for the conversion of the stored chemical energy into other forms.

- Ask the pupils what 'going green' means. Following a discussion, which should be kept brief, show a slide of the Jolly Green Giant or a video clip of the sweet corn advert, if available. Ask the pupils to imagine what it would be like if they could lie down in the sunshine any time they felt hungry and their skin would make them some food. If the 'Plants in space' starter has been used, you could ask whether or not it would be a good idea to have a genetically engineered green-skinned crew member, and what additional benefits and requirements this would bring.

- Using the activity 'Studying a garden' in the pupil book, and using a writing frame if necessary, fill in all the ways that are shown (plus any additional ones you can envisage) in which plants and animals are of benefit to each other. Summarise the relationships in a PowerPoint series of slides to include plants providing food and oxygen for animals and animals providing nutrients for plants through their excreta and remains, plus providing them with carbon dioxide as a raw material for photosynthesis.

- Run an activity to help understand energy. Place four stations around the room labelled glucose, oxygen, water and carbon dioxide, each with cards labelled as such. Give pupils an indentity sticker either animal or plant. Plants get a green sticker with the word (chlorophyll) in brackets. Pupils who are plants have to get a water and a CO_2 card and then go to you. You stand by a light or a board drawing of the sun. Give them glucose and an O_2 card in exchange for their H_2O and CO_2 cards. Also place a removeable 'energy' sticker on the glucose card. Pupils who are animals must get the glucose cards from the plants and remove the energy stickers. They need an oxygen card to do this and must put a CO_2 and water card back on the piles after exchanging. After a suitable interval discuss how the cards are exchanged.

- Ask the pupils to list other ways in which plants can assist animals and vice versa, including seed distribution, pollination, use of toxins, human use of plants, and so on.

Plenary Suggestions

Key word spotter
Using PowerPoint flash up definitions of some of the key words in this section and ask the pupils to write down on 'Show me' boards which word is being defined. (5–10 mins)

Plant adaptation
As a follow-up to the 'Society for the preservation of plants' starter, give the pupils a set time to write down as many ways in which plants are adapted to survive being eaten or damaged by animals: for example, possession of thorns, prickles, poisonous substances. When the time is up, discuss the ideas, getting the pupils to say how the animals are deterred. (10–15 mins)

Practical Support

Main lesson: Burning food (sugar)

Equipment and materials required
A suitable food is needed, dish, Bunsen burner, safety mat and eye protection.

Safety
Eye protection.
Burning sugar is very hot.

Differentiation

SEN
Have a simplified version of the card game.
Provide a list of words to choose from in the 'Key word spotter' plenary.
Provide ready-prepared labels for the naming of the parts of a plant and a plant cell.

Extension
Ask pupils to draw up a food web of the scene depicted in 'Studying a garden'.
Pupils could search the Internet for references to the way in which vegetables and fruit are grown in water culture at Achiltibuie, Scotland, and assess whether it would be possible to set up such a system on the Moon.

Homework Suggestion
Pupils could gather together all the information from the lesson about the ways in which plants help animals and vice versa and either write a paragraph about each or summarise in the form of a table.

Answers to in-text questions

a [Mention should be made of water and light, with higher level answers also referring to nutrients/minerals and possibly warmth.]

b glucose (or sugar) + oxygen $\longrightarrow$ carbon dioxide + water

c From the Sun.

d Leaf – absorbs light and site of photosynthesis; water exits via leaf.
Stem – supports plant; contains vascular system.
Flower – makes pollen and ovules; responsible for spread of pollen (by insects or wind).
Root – anchors plant; absorbs water and minerals.

e Cell wall – helps maintain shape and strength of cell.
Cell membrane – allows substances in and out of cell; holds contents together.
Nucleus – contains genetic information; controls cell.
Cytoplasm – where chemical reactions take place.
Vacuole – used for storage/removal of unwanted materials.
Chloroplast – site of photosynthesis/absorbs light energy.

f From a seed from a fruit, eaten by a bird and passed through its digestive system.

B2.2 Making Food

NC links for the lesson
- Organisms, behaviour and health.
- Life processes are supported by the organisation of cells into tissues, organs and body systems.
- All living things show variation, can be classified and are interdependent, interacting with each other and the environment.

Learning Objectives
Pupils should learn:
- That plants can make their own food by photosynthesis.
- That plants need light to make glucose and other carbon containing compounds.
- How we can show the presence of starch in the leaves of plants and the need for light.

Learning Outcomes
- All pupils should be able to state that photosynthesis is the way in which plants make their food.
- Most pupils should be able to describe the tests for the presence of starch in leaves and the necessity for light.
- Some pupils should also be able to explain why glucose is built up into starch for storage.

How Science Works
- Adapt the stylistic conventions of a range of genres for different audiences and purposes in scientific writing (1.1c) (see Van Helmont plenary).

Learning Styles
Visual: Observing the colour changes in the experiments.
Auditory: Listening to the interviews with van Helmont in the plenary.
Kinaesthetic: Carrying out the practical investigations.
Interpersonal: Working in groups to write a script for the interview in the plenary.
Intrapersonal: Imagining the effect of the comet impact in the plenary.

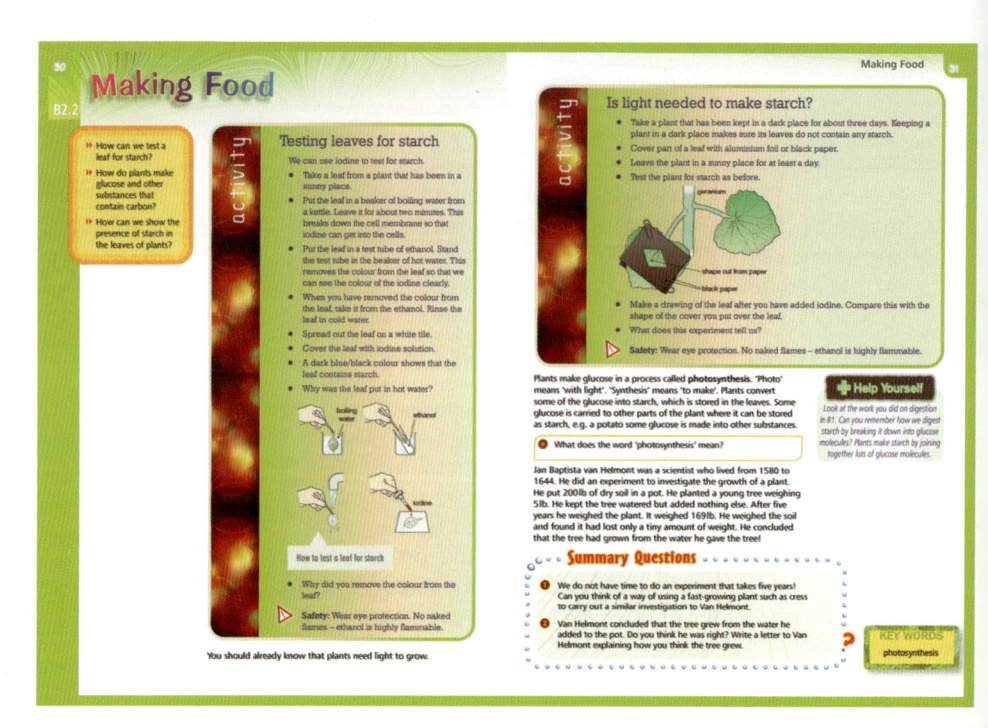

The Lesson

Starter Suggestions

Starch strip
Show the pupils a glucose sweet, such as a barley sugar. Say you've just eaten one and ask the pupils where the sugar (glucose) in the sweet will be in a few minutes. With some persistence, you may establish that the sugar could be all over your body, being carried in the blood (blood is sticky because it is full of sugar). Draw out that plants can make their own sugar, but may want to keep it in one place. Show the pupils six Duplo or large Lego-style bricks, each with the word 'Glucose' on them. Stick them together and turn them around to show the pupils that you have written the word 'Starch' on the back and state that starch is lots of glucose molecules stuck together. Give each pupil a strip of paper with six hexagons printed end-to-end on it. Get them to write the word 'Glucose' in each hexagon and then turn the strip over and draw the letters spelling 'Starch' on the reverse. Let them stick their strip into their books as a foldout using a tab. (10–15 mins)

Autumn leaves
Show the pupils some beautiful photographs of autumn leaves (or real leaves if the time of the year is right) and then some bare winter branches. Compare this with some pictures of palms and bananas from the tropics. Ask the pupils why the trees shed their leaves here but not in the tropics. Link this to the conditions needed for photosynthesis. (5–10 mins)

Main Lesson

- Testing leaves for starch: You could use PowerPoint and a demonstration to illustrate the classic starch test on leaves. Use the instructions set out in the pupil book. The best leaves to use are from geraniums or zonal pelargoniums, which have been well-illuminated either in natural sunlight or by a suitable light source for several days. The plants need to have been kept in an ambient temperature of 15° C and well-watered. If available, use a video camera connected to a projector to display the stages on a screen for better viewing. Give out laminated summaries of the stages for constant reference (or have them projected, but beware of screen-saver kick-in). Discuss the potential hazards associated with this practical work. Make sure there are no naked flames in the room before issuing the bottles of ethanol. Care needs to be taken when moving around the room distributing boiling water from a kettle.

Making Food

The pupils should be standing and wearing eye protection. Remind pupils that they do not need to heat the water when the tube with the ethanol is resting in it, as the boiling point of ethanol is less than that of water (link this to the distillation of spirits for real-life interest). Ensure that the pupils do not confuse the instructions and pour the ethanol with the leaf into the hot water. Use a glass rod to stir the ethanol while the leaf is in it and to remove the leaf when blanched. Pupils should avoid getting iodine on their skin or clothes. Check that the dropper bottles are filled to a suitable level or use pipettes. The colour change for a positive result can be demonstrated in advance by getting a pupil to squirt some iodine on to a slice of white bread.

- For the experiment 'Is light needed to make starch?', have the de-starched plants ready. Allowing pupils to cut out black paper or aluminium foil shapes can add stimulus to this investigation, as can attaching photocopied transparency sheets with the emblems of football clubs (some have clearer graphics than others – Notts Forest is particularly good for this). You may like to set one up yourself and get the pupils to guess which team the plant supports. Use miniature clothes pegs (available from craft stores) or paperclips to hold the paper or foil templates on to the leaves.

- As an alternative, you may like to make a negative of a high contrast digital photograph (Microsoft Photo Editor can perform this) and project it for an hour on to a leaf. This should be sandwiched in glass (a CD crystal case will do) with a backdrop of black paper soaked in weak sodium hydrogencarbonate solution as a carbon source. When developed using iodine, a positive image will be formed on the leaf which can be most striking. When the templates are used, the plants need to be left illuminated and in a warm temperature, so that the leaves can be tested for starch in a later lesson.

Plenary Suggestions

Interview with Van Helmont

Organise the pupils, in small groups, to write a script for an interview with Van Helmont where he describes how he carried out his experiment. Groups could either stage the interview as a news item and use 'our science correspondent' or a Newsnight-type interview. Using a digital recorder, collect versions from around the groups and share some good ones with the whole class. (10–15 mins)

Winter all year?

Discuss the effect of a large impact on the Earth by a comet or an asteroid, including the dust thrown up into the atmosphere obscuring the Sun. Ask: 'What effects would it have on all life and why?' Discuss the probability that this did actually happen and ask pupils to suggest the likely timing from their knowledge of the history of our planet. What living forms were best adapted to survival in such conditions? (10–15 mins)

Practical Support

Starter: Starch strip

Equipment and materials required

Barley sugar, 6 Duplo or Lego-style bricks and paper strips of hexagons (one per pupil).

Safety

Do not eat sweet!

Starter: Autumn leaves

Photographs of leaves or real leaves and bare branches.

Testing leaves for starch

Equipment and materials required

Geraniums or zonal pelargoniums illuminated, water baths, test tubes, ethanol, white tiles, dilute iodine solution, glass rods, forceps.

Safety

Need eye protection.

Pupils should be told to keep iodine solution off their clothes and hands. Iodine solution: CLEAPSS Hazcard 54B.

Careful with hot water and ethanol (no naked flames). Ethanol is highly flammable: CLEAPSS Hazcard 40A.

Is light needed to make starch?

Equipment and materials required

Plants should be de-starched (keep in dark for at least 48 hours).

Black paper or aluminium foil, miniature clothes pegs or paperclips, materials for the starch test as above.

If used, photocopied transparency sheets with the emblems of football clubs or negative of a high contrast digital photograph, CD crystal case, black paper soaked in weak sodium hydrogencarbonate solution.

Safety

Need eye protection.

Pupils should be told to keep iodine solution off their clothes and hands. Iodine solution: CLEAPSS Hazcard 54B.

Careful with hot water and ethanol (no naked flames). Ethanol is highly flammable: CLEAPSS Hazcard 40A.

Differentiation

SEN

Use a sequencing sheet to show flow through the stages of the practical.

Extension

Pupils to plan out a mini version of Van Helmont's experiment using cress seeds.

Homework Suggestion

Pupils could write up accounts of the practical work done in the lesson.

Answers to Summary questions

1. Using light to make something.

2. Description of experiment, e.g. weigh damp cotton wool and seeds then weigh again after they have grown adding in any extra water they have been given. Keep under cover, reducing water loss due to evaporation/transpiration.

3. Yes, partly but it also used carbon dioxide.

B2.3 Photosynthesis

NC links for the lesson
- Organisms, behaviour and health.
- Life processes are supported by the organisation of cells into tissues, organs and body systems.
- All living things show variation, can be classified and are interdependent, interacting with each other and with their environment.

Learning Objectives
Pupils should learn:
- That chlorophyll is needed for photosynthesis.
- That carbon dioxide and water are needed as raw materials for the process of photosynthesis.
- That glucose and oxygen are produced.

Learning Outcomes
- All pupils should be able to name the raw materials and the products of photosynthesis.
- Most pupils should be able to describe the experiments to show that the raw materials are needed and that the products are glucose and oxygen.
- Some pupils should also be able to explain the results of the experiments in detail.

How Science Works
- Describe an approach to answer a scientific question using sources of evidence, and where appopriate, making relevant observations or measurements using appropriate apparatus (1.2a).

Learning Styles
Visual: Observing the PowerPoint presentations and the results of the experiments.
Auditory: Listening to instructions about the practical.
Kinaesthetic: Carrying out the practical work.
Interpersonal: Working in groups to do the 'Photosynthesis card match' plenary.
Intrapersonal: Writing out the 'Green cloze' passage.

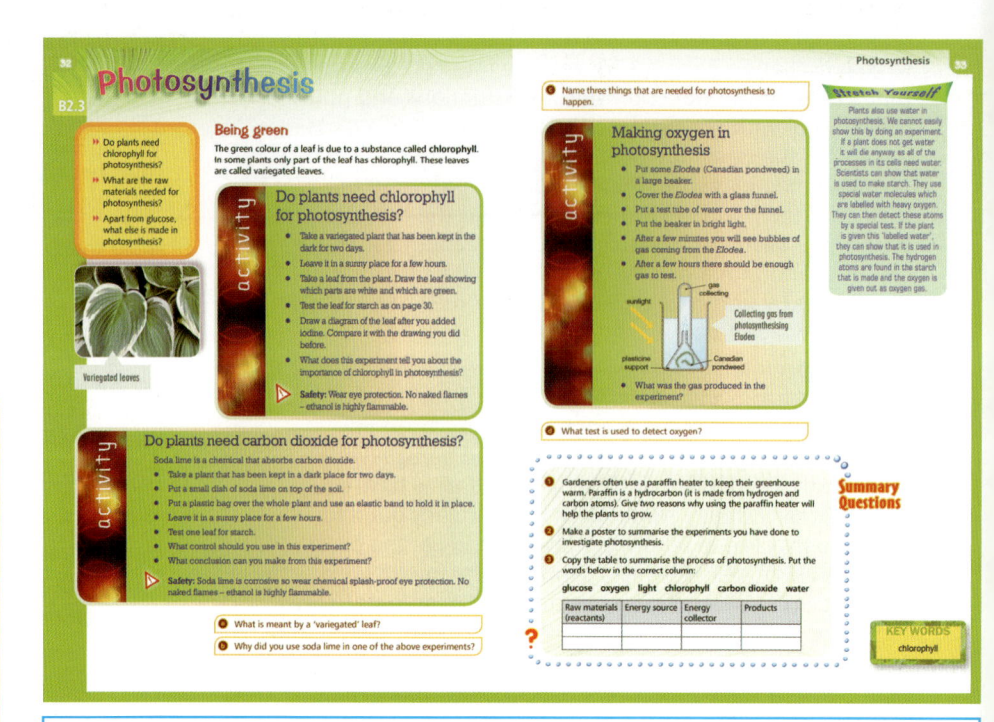

Answers to Summary questions

1. It gives warmth and carbon dioxide.
2. Pupil poster. [Mark by overall impression.]
3.

Raw materials (reactants)	Energy source	Energy collector	Products
carbon dioxide	light	chlorophyll	glucose
water			oxygen

The Lesson

Starter Suggestions

What's in a word?
Write up or project the word 'Photosynthesis' onto the board. Split it into two parts, using different colours to emphasise the 'photo' bit and the 'synthesis' bit. Ask the pupils if any one can think of any words connected to either of the sub-units. If necessary give clues, such as showing a photograph or the sound of a synthesiser. It should be possible to draw out words such as 'photograph' (defined as pictures using light), 'photography' and possibly 'photon'; also 'synthesiser' and 'synthetic'. Illustrate each of these words and draw out the meaning of 'photosynthesis' as making new things using light. (5–10 mins)

Why are colours coloured?
Show the pupils a number of different coloured objects. Ask why they appear to be the colours they are, acknowledging but then dispelling simplistic notions (e.g. 'because of the dye or paint'). Show the pupils a simple PowerPoint presentation of arrows in spectral colours hitting various coloured objects, with the arrows of un-reflected colours staying pointed at the object but those of the reflected colour bouncing off and into an eye. Repeat with several colours. It might be relevant here to introduce a black object and a white object. Ask the pupils to predict what will happen with a green object. Show them a slide of this. Establish that green plants absorb a lot of light owing to their green pigment absorbing all colours except green. (10–15 mins)

Photosynthesis

Main Lesson

- Show the pupils a piece of clothing, such as a white T-shirt or a pair of cricket trousers, with grass stains on it. Establish that there is a green colouring in grass and other plants. Some fresh grass or really green vegetable, such as spinach or watercress, could be used to make a stain on white paper or a piece of white cloth. Name this as chlorophyll, writing it in large green letters on the board and get the pupils to repeat the name out loud a couple of times. Make a point of the unusual spelling, getting them to pronounce it emphasising the syllables. Make it clear that the job of chlorophyll is to absorb the light energy from the Sun to be trapped in the manufacture of glucose by the leaf if this was not not done in the starter.
- Demonstration of the extraction of chlorophyll. Cut up some grass or green vegetable (spinach or watercress) and place in the bottom of a mortar with a little sharp sand. Add a few millilitres of ethanol (**care**: no naked flames) and grind to a pulp. Filter the mixture into a test tube and show it in a bright light. It should be an intense green colour. Allow the pupils to use it as a pigment, writing the word 'chlorophyll' using paint brushes, or filling an empty fountain pen ink cartridge with the liquid.
- Show the pupils a microscope slide or photomicrograph of chloroplasts in the cells of a leaf. It is not difficult to show chloroplasts in living leaves by mounting moss leaves in water on microscope slides. The moss leaves are thin and the chloroplasts show up well. Carry out a written exercise to record this information about chlorophyll, either as a worksheet or a self-composed text.
- Show the pupils a number of variegated plants, such as spider plant and variegated ivy. Establish that the white parts of the leaves do not contain chlorophyll. Carry out the practical 'Do plants need chlorophyll for photosynthesis? as described in the pupil book. This practical can either be done as a demonstration, with worksheets for the pupils, or it can be done in groups using one plant per group. Pupils should make a drawing of their leaf before the starch test and then again afterwards (or keep the dried leaf).
- The activity 'Do plants need carbon dioxide for photosynthesis?' is best set up beforehand as a demonstration for the class. Using PowerPoint, take the pupils through the procedure, emphasising the need for the plant to be de-starched beforehand, the purpose of the soda lime and the need for a control.
- 'Making oxygen in photosynthesis' can be set up beforehand as a demonstration as described in the pupil book – it benefits from being left for a long time.

Plenary Suggestions

Photosynthesis card match

Make up sets of laminated cards with the pre-requisites (light, chlorophyll), the raw materials (water, carbon dioxide) and the products (glucose, oxygen) written on them. Hand these out around the class randomly and ask the pupils to carry out a matching game and organise themselves into groups to make a word equation for photosynthesis. Get the pupils to take photos on their mobile phones of the finished card sets to use as reminders. (5–10 mins)

Green cloze

Working in pairs, ask the pupils to write out a cloze passage for their peer. They may need to be told this is a 'fill in the gaps' exercise. Give them a limit of ten missing words and a few key words which they must include. Peer mark and read out some of the best ones. (10–15 mins)

Practical Support

Demonstration: Extraction of chlorophyll

Equipment and materials required

Grass/spinach/watercress, ethanol, mortar and pestle, sharp sand, filter funnel, filter paper, test tubes and stand, paint brushes or empty fountain pen ink cartridges.

Do plants need chlorophyll for photosynthesis?

Equipment and materials required

De-starched spider plant (or other variegated plant), materials for starch test.

Do plants need carbon dioxide for photosynthesis?

Equipment and materials required

De-starched potted plants, plastic bags, soda lime, materials for starch test.

Making oxygen in photosynthesis

Equipment and materials required

Elodea, large beaker, funnel, test tube, source of bright light, splint, matches.

Safety

Iodine solution: CLEAPSS Hazcard 54B.

Ethanol is highly flammable, no naked flames: CLEAPSS Hazcard 40A.

Eye protection needed.

CLEAPSS handbook section 15.5.1.

Soda lime is corrosive: CLEAPSS Hazcard 91.

Differentiation

SEN

Using large diagrams of the apparatus used and pre-formed labels, ask pupils to label the apparatus used in the experiments.

Extension

If the 'Why are colours coloured?' starter was used, ask the pupils to think of what colour a plant would be if it developed a perfectly efficient photosynthetic method [black] and to write creatively about an invasion of black plants.

Homework Suggestion

Using the word equation devised in the plenary, summarise the experiments used to show the reactants, pre-requisites and products of photosynthesis. This could either be a poster, as suggested in the pupil book, or a spider diagram.

Complete worksheets given out in the lesson.

Answers to in-text questions

a Green and white, only has chlorophyll in parts.

b To absorb carbon dioxide.

c Light, carbon dioxide and water.

d It relights a glowing splint.

B2.4 Leaves and Photosynthesis

NC links for the lesson
- Organisms, behaviour and health.
- Life processes are supported by the organisation of cells into tissues, organs and body systems.

Learning Objectives

Pupils should learn:
- That the leaves of plants are where photosynthesis occurs.
- The ways in which leaves are adapted for photosynthesis.
- To plan an investigation into the factors that can affect the rate at which photosynthesis occurs.

Learning Outcomes

- All pupils should be able to state that the leaves are where photosynthesis occurs and to describe their main adaptations.
- Most pupils should be able to identify the internal tissues of a leaf and state their functions.
- Some pupils should also be able to design an investigation and explain how environmental factors may affect the rate of photosynthesis.

How Science Works

- Describe and identify key variables in an investigation and assign appropriate values to these (1.2b).

Answers to in-text questions

a) Carbon dioxide.
b) Oxygen.

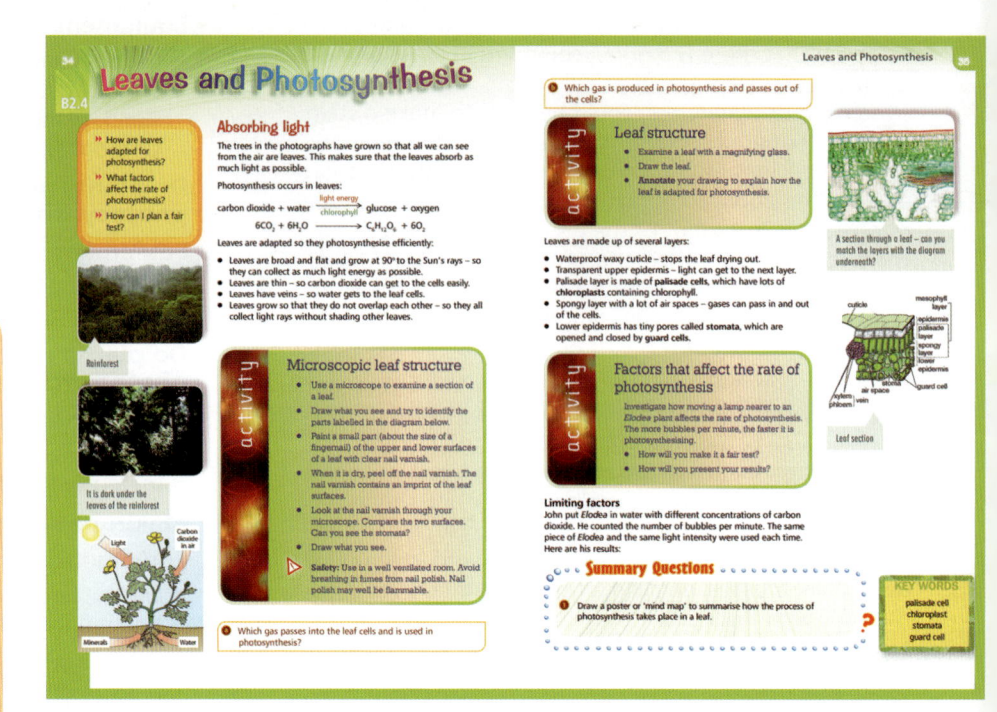

Learning Styles

Visual: Observing stomata and leaf structure using microscopes.

Auditory: Listening to discussions and explanations of the different parts of the leaf.

Kinaesthetic: Using microscopes to look at leaf sections.

Interpersonal: Working together on the 'Dining hall leaf model' plenary.

Intrapersonal: Thinking up some more rules for the 'Captain Blackfinger's cruelty to plants club' for homework.

The Lesson

Starter Suggestions

Captain Blackfinger's cruelty to plants club

Tell the pupils that you are Captain Blackfinger and that you have started a 'Cruelty to Plants' club. As your first activity, you are going to pull all the leaves off a plant, one by one, without anaesthetic. Do so (make sure the plant is not toxic) and get grizzly minded volunteers to help you. When the leaves are all off, ask the pupils to write down what will happen to this plant now and why. Discuss the answers and draw out the obvious implications. (5–10 mins)

Agent Orange

Show the pupils a photograph of a forest with a soldier in camouflage. Explain that in the 1960s, America was at war in Vietnam and the soldiers of their enemy were hiding in the trees so that the Americans couldn't find them to kill them. The Americans decided to spray the forests with a special chemical that would make all the leaves drop off. Show some stills from the Internet of the defoliant Agent Orange (herbicide 2,4-D) in use during the Vietnam war and a defoliated area. Ask the pupils to write down why the trees die when their leaves are removed. Discuss their responses. (10–15 mins)

Main Lesson

- Leaf Structure: Ask the pupils how the water gets into the leaves. Some pupils will probably answer 'through the leaves', but dispel this suggestion by demonstrating that leaves can be waterproof. Ask a volunteer to hold

Leaves and Photosynthesis

a leaf under a running tap and let pupils see the water running off. Show how a scoop can be made from most leaves that will hold water. Link to survival in the wild – what to do if you do not have a cup! Hand out blank un-labelled leaf diagrams or use a projected blank diagram and label the waxy cuticle, linking the name to the root of the nail.

- Using a stick of celery, show the veins in a plant. Tell the pupils that these make up the transport system of plants. Some pupils will learn that the xylem [link to xylophones for pronunciation] consists of the water tubes and phloem transports food. Link the xylem to the way in which water gets to the leaves, show the pupils real leaves and let them see (hold leaves up to light if thin) and feel the veins. Label veins on the blank leaf diagrams.

- Elicit that leaves are spongy and that spongy things have air in them. Imagine shrinking a pupil and sending them inside the leaf. You might like to link this to SpongeBob Squarepants. Show that there is air in leaves by plunging geranium leaves into near boiling water and observing the bubbles which emerge from the underside. Draw attention to the fact that the air bubbles are coming from the underside of the leaf. Ask: 'why?' Label the spongy mesophyll.

- Ask the pupils how the air can get into the leaves (they might get a clue from the previous demonstration). Show them micrographs of stomata, introducing the name (tell them not to mix it up with tomatoes), and the singular form 'stoma'. Draw eyes above a stoma or get the pupils to do so on a diagram, so that the stoma looks like a mouth. Explain that 'stoma' is Greek for mouth and that's where we get the word 'stomach' from. Ask pupils to remind each other of what goes in and what comes out of the stomata in the leaf.

- Microscopic leaf structure: Well before the lesson, paint transparent nail varnish on to the underside of *Tradescantia* leaves, enough for one between two pupils. Get the pupils to peel a section of the varnish off and examine it under a microscope on low magnification at first, and then on higher magnification. Give the pupils a half A4 sheet of plain paper and tell them to draw what they see, complete with magnification (show some good previous examples). Demonstrate the role of the guard cells by partially inflating a pair of long balloons, holding them side by side, sticking a strip of Sellotape down the inside of each. Inflate them a little more and hold them together again to show the stoma formed. Label the stomata, guard cells and lower epidermis.

- Show the pupils a box of pens, pencils or glue sticks. Ask one pupil to tip them out into a tray. Ask another to come and arrange them so that they take up as little space as possible. Tie this in with structure of the palisade layer, pointing out the regular arrangement of the cells on a projected diagram. Label the palisade layer and the transparent upper epidermis, drawing out why it is transparent. Tie in with chlorophyll in the equation.

Plenary Suggestions

Dining hall leaf model
Take the pupils to the hall and arrange tables and chairs to represent the various tissues in the leaf, e.g. line of chairs for upper epidermis, closely stacked tables for palisade cells, spaced-out chairs for spongy mesophyll, chairs again for lower epidermis with gaps between them for the stomata. If your school has PVC cloths for the tables, these could be placed along the first row of chairs to represent the waxy cuticle. This model could be activated by allowing pupils to move in through the stomata and circulate through the spongy mesophyll to reach the palisade cells and out again, thus demonstrating the passage of gases into and out of the leaf tissues. (5–10 mins)

Pupils could draw up some more rules for 'Captain Blackfinger's cruelty to plants club'. Suggest that such rules could apply to anything concerned with preventing the plant from carrying out photosynthesis (for example, blocking up the stomata, depriving the plant of water, keeping a plant out in the cold, etc.). For each new rule, they should say why it is cruel.

Practical Support

Captain Blackfinger's cruelty to plants club
Equipment and materials required
Plant

Main lesson: Seeing veins and microscopic leaf structure
Equipment and materials required
Stick of celery or leaves from a chestnut tree, geranium leaves, micrographs of stomata, nail varnish, *Tradescantia* leaves, microscopes, collection of dry leaves, eggs.

Safety
Nail varnish might be flammable.

Differentiation

SEN
Give the pupils printed labels to place on large diagrams of leaf structure. This can be done for both the external adaptations and the internal structure of the leaf.

Extension
Ask the pupils to investigate limiting factors, by making a list and then working out what would be the best combination of factors to set up in a glasshouse in order to produce crops all the year round.

Homework Suggestion

Pupils could finish labelling diagrams and organise them to be stuck into notebooks.

Answers to Summary questions

1. A poster or 'mind map' to summarise how the process of photosynthesis takes place in a leaf.

B2.5 Food Chains

NC links for the lesson
- Organisms, behaviour and health.
- Life processes are supported by the organisation of cells into tissues, organs and body systems.
- All living things show variation, can be classified and are interdependent, interacting with each other and with their environment.

Learning Objectives
Pupils should learn:
- What is meant by a food chain.
- How organisms are classified in food chains.
- Which groups of organisms act as decomposers.

Learning Outcomes
- All pupils should be able to describe and construct simple food chains, using the correct terminology.
- Most pupils should be able to describe the energy flow through a food chain and classify the organisms in the food chain.
- Some pupils should also be able to explain the importance of the decomposers.

Learning Styles
Visual: Looking at the slides of organisms and identifying the different categories.
Auditory: Listening to the advice in the 'Hat badge food chain' starter.
Kinaesthetic: Changing the fish into another animal or joining up the food chains.
Interpersonal: Working in groups in the activities.
Intrapersonal: Unscrambling the key words.

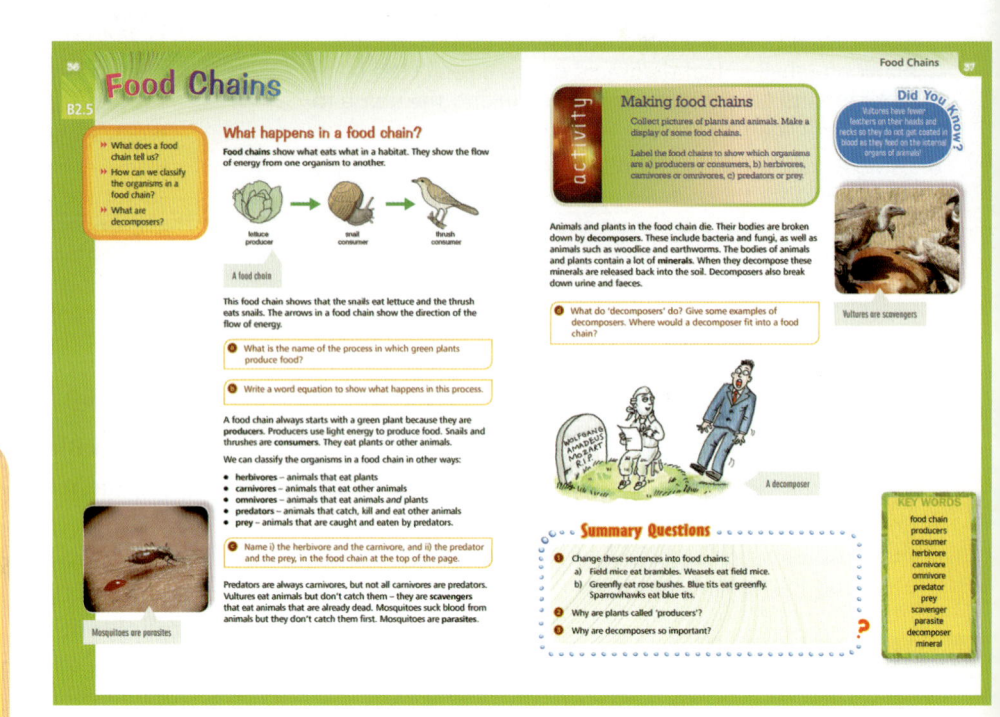

The Lesson

Starter Suggestions

Hat badge food chains

Get four volunteers to stand at the front of the class. Give each volunteer a hat with a badge on the front: one with a picture of the Sun, one with a picture of some grass, one with a picture of a rabbit and one with a picture of a fox. Place the hats on the pupils from behind, so that they can see other people's badges but not their own. They are not allowed to tell each other what is on their hat badges. Ask them to advise each other in which order they should line up. On completing their order, get them to give reasons to the class for the order and let them guess what is on their own hat. Finally, let them take off the hats and look at their own badges. Iron out any unorthodox reasoning for their chosen order in discussion following the exercise. Elicit any previously learned vocabulary and record it. (10–15 mins)

Food chains 'drag and drop'

Use a digital projected 'drag and drop' exercise with the parts of a simple food chain. Ask a volunteer, or small team of volunteers, to assemble the chain and explain their reasoning. As above, sort out any unorthodox responses (a common one is getting the arrows the wrong way round) and draw out and record currently known vocabulary associated with the topic. (5–10 mins)

Main Lesson

- Through exposition, go over the concept of a food chain as being a way of showing energy flow from its source through a succession of organisms. Explain that matter is also passed from the producers to the rest of the consumers. Re-emphasise the convention that the arrow shows the direction of energy flow. To help them to remember this, get the pupils to recite 'The arrow shows where the food goes'. Illustrate this with suitable pairs of organisms, using questioning to reinforce this, e.g. 'Does the grass go into the rabbit or does the rabbit go into the grass?'.

- A PowerPoint presentation of a food chain would be a useful reinforcement at this stage, as would a section of video. Many widely known science video series have sections on food chains.

Food Chains

- Show a slide of a range of organisms. Ask which ones make (produce) their own food. Highlight these and introduce the word 'producers'. Highlight all the other organisms and introduce the word 'consumers'. Show a slide of a cow eating grass and introduce the word 'herbivores', passing around some mixed herbs to smell as a sense engager. Point out that 'herb' is another word for plants and that the 'vore' bit means 'eating' (remind them of 'voracious'). Show a slide of a dog eating dog food. Draw out the word 'carnivore'. Link it with the word 'carnival' (a short video clip or a still photograph could be used) and tie this to the fact that people used to give up eating meat during Lent, or link it with 'chilli con carne'. Show a slide of a BLT (bacon, lettuce and tomato) sandwich and draw out that we are 'omnivores', and what this means in terms of eating both meat and plants. Many pupils will have seen the feature film *Predator*. Remind them of this film, or view an appropriate clip, and link with the word 'prey'. Show a slide of vultures and introduce the word 'scavengers' as being eaters of dead things. Show a slide of a head louse and introduce the word 'parasites' as feeding off living things without killing them. Show your original slide of the range of organisms again and ask the pupils to identify the different types of consumer, classifying them with the words you have introduced.
- Show the pupils a simple flat model of a fish made out of Lego bricks. Ask a volunteer to disassemble it and build a model of another animal with the bricks (rather like 'Transformers'). During this activity, show some slides or footage of decomposition and introduce the word 'decomposer', linking it with 'compost' and 'composition'.
- Carry out a bookwork exercise, copying the correct key words, with the correct definitions, for producer, consumer, food chain, carnivore, herbivore, omnivore, predators, prey, scavengers, parasites and decomposers.
- Organise the pupils into pairs and give each pair an A3 sheet with the names of many organisms on it and a set of coloured highlighter pens. Explain that they have to make food chains by joining the organisms together using arrows, and that they should then make a key showing which colour represents each one of the key words used in the previous exercise. They should highlight the words accordingly, going around them with more than one colour. When finished, they can check out other groups' sheets. As an extension, ask them to add more examples of their own. Also see the activity 'Making food chains' in the pupil book.

Plenary Suggestions

Unscramble key words
Give the pupils sheet with the key words scrambled up and get them to unscramble them. Alternatively, write out the key words with either the vowels or the consonants missing. As an extension, get them to make up some of their own and try them out on other pupils. (5–10 mins.)

Spot the blots
Give the pupils a sheet with a number of food chains incorrectly assembled (e.g. no producer at the start, arrows in the wrong direction, consumers labelled as producers). Ask the pupils to identify the errors and produce corrected versions. A small prize for the first correct solution aids motivation. As an extension, get the pupils to make up their own incorrect versions and test them out on their peers. (10–15 mins)

Practical Support

Main lesson: 'fish to another animal' activity
Equipment and materials required
Lego bricks.

Differentiation

SEN
Play hangman with the key words. If necessary put in initial letters, or all the vowels.

Extension
Introduce the phrase 'trophic levels'. Pupils should find out what the word 'trophic' means and see how many words they can find which incorporate it.

Using the Internet, ask the pupils to draw out as long a food chain as they can find, writing down the URLs (uniform resource locator) of each site as evidence.

Homework Suggestion

Pupils could write out a set of definitions of the key words which can be used to test their peers' knowledge at the beginning of the next lesson.

Ask pupils to work out food chains for the meals they have eaten in one day. It is interesting for them to see how high up the food chain their food is.

Answers to in-text questions

a Photosynthesis.

b carbon dioxide + water $\longrightarrow$ glucose + oxygen

c i) The snail is the herbivore and the thrush is the carnivore.
ii) The thrush is the predator and the snail is the prey.

d Decomposers make dead animals and plants decay, releasing minerals, etc. Bacteria and fungi are examples. They fit in a food chain at each stage.

Answers to Summary questions

1 a) bramble $\longrightarrow$ field mouse $\longrightarrow$ weasel
b) rose bush $\longrightarrow$ greenfly $\longrightarrow$ blue tit $\longrightarrow$ sparrowhawk

2 They produce food from simple chemicals.

3 They ensure that nutrients are recycled.

B2.6 Food Webs

NC links for the lesson
- Organisms, behaviour and health.
- All living things show variation, can be classified and are interdependent, interacting with each other and their environment.

Learning Objectives
Pupils should learn:
- That food chains link together to make food webs.
- That populations can be affected by changes in feeding relationships.
- That food webs can be upset by introducing organisms into a different habitat.

Learning Outcomes
- All pupils should be able to understand that food chains link together to make food webs.
- Most pupils should be able to understand that a change in the size of a population of one species in a food web can affect other species.
- Some pupils should also be able to predict the effects of such changes on the other organisms in a food web.

Answers to Summary questions

1.
   a) Pupils draw a food web.
   b) Seaweed.
   c) Winkle and limpet.
   d) Crab, octopus, starfish, seal, seagull, killer whale.
   e) Winkles and limpets may increase because fewer are eaten; seals and seagulls may decline due to reduced food availability; octopuses and starfish may decline as more are eaten by seals and seagulls.
2. [Mark by overall impression.]

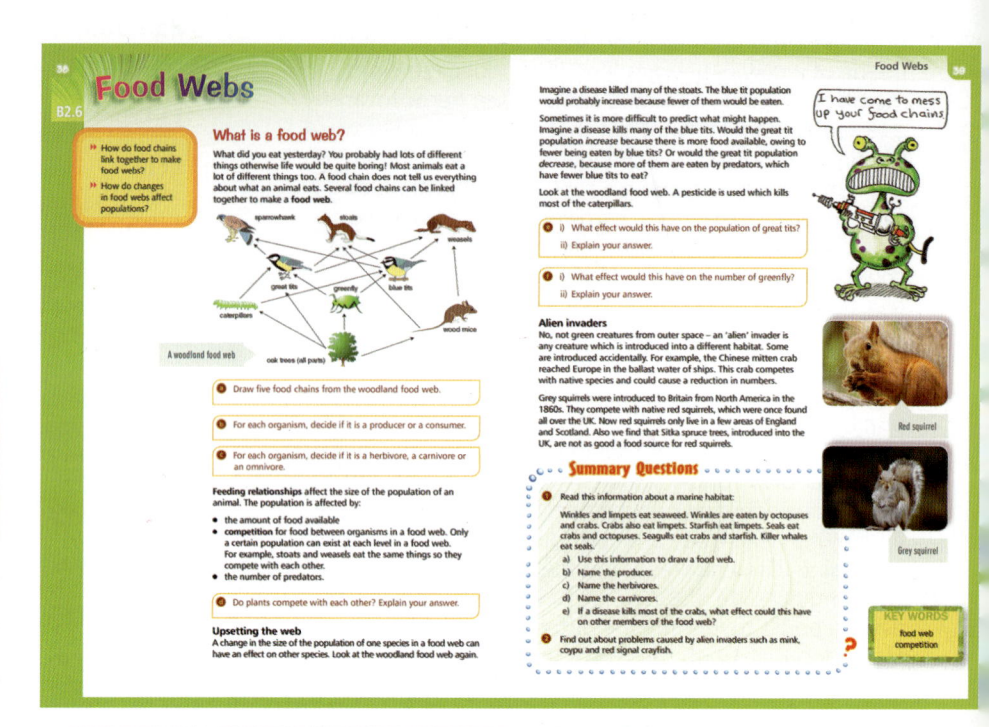

Learning Styles
Visual: Observing the food webs and miming activity.
Auditory: Listening to discussions about changes in population numbers.
Kinaesthetic: Taking part in the Floor food web activity.
Interpersonal: Working in groups and pairs in the activities.
Intrapersonal: Completing the crossword puzzle; completing the food web diagram.

The Lesson

Starter Suggestions

Key word revision charades
Ask a volunteer to pick one of the key words from the last lesson and carry out a mime to help the class to guess which one it is. The rest of the pupils can put their hands up when they think they know the key word. The pupil who is miming can pick one of them to answer. If they get it right, they are now 'on' and have to pick and mime the next key word. Lower attaining pupils could look up the words beforehand or have them on a projected list. If the homework exercise from the last lesson was carried out, pupils should have definitions of the key words which can be read out and answered in a similar way as an alternative exercise. (5–10 mins)

Crossword race
Give the pupils a crossword puzzle of all the key words from the previous lesson. Using a projected, large display count-down timer, such as the Cool timer (available as a free download from Harmony Hollow), give them a fixed time limit in which to complete the puzzle. Get them to complete the puzzle, recording how much time there was left on the timer. As an extension, let them create new clues for the existing words or add more appropriate words (and clues) of their own. (10–15 mins)

Main Lesson
- Ask pupils in the front row if they know the name of a producer. Select a pupil to answer and write down the name of the producer they gave onto a sheet of A4 paper in thick pen in large bold letters. Get the pupil to stand up and hold the paper. Ask if anyone in the second row knows an organism which would

Food Webs

eat the producer. Again, take the suggestion, write it onto A4 and ask the pupil to stand up and hold it. Using a ball of string, make a connection between the two pupils, getting them to hold the string and cutting it to length. Blu-tack an arrow head onto the string, getting the pupils to recite 'the arrow shows where the food goes'. Ask if anyone else in the second row knows of something different which could eat the producer, and repeat the procedure. The next row behind should think of secondary consumers, and so on. Continue until you have built up a web of string arrows throughout the class. Introduce the idea of trophic levels by relating to the distance from the front of the class. Set up a picture, model or projection of the Sun at the very front and remind the pupils that the webs describe energy flow and that the Sun is the source of it all.

- Show the pupils a video clip of a food web if available.
- Floor food web activity: Arrange the pupils into groups of four or five. Give them each a pack, containing the laminated words 'grass', 'corn', 'rabbit', 'sheep', 'cow', 'fox', 'hawk' and 'human'. Also include in each pack some much smaller labels, saying 'producer' (2 of these), 'consumer' (6), 'herbivore' (3), 'carnivore' (1) and 'omnivore' (2). [Pupils may not realise that a fox is an omnivore and eats lots of berries and other plant food.] The packs should also contain strips of paper, about 2 cm wide, and paper arrow heads with Blu-tack on the back. The objective is to use a pack to construct a floor diagram of a food web, using the paper arrows to show feeding relationships. Tell the pupils to put the producers at the bottom, then the primary consumers in the next layer above, then the secondary consumers. Don't let them forget that secondary consumers can eat producers, too (e.g. humans eating corn). Space the groups around the room, using adjacent spaces, such as corridors, if appropriate. When each group has completed the exercise, take a digital photograph of the completed diagram (the pupils may be able to do this themselves on their mobile phones) to print out later as a record. Let the groups examine and assess each other's work.
- Exposition: show a slide of a food web. Pick out an organism and ask the pupils to discuss how other organisms would be affected if the numbers of this organism (population) increased. Repeat this with the numbers going down (population decreasing).
- Give the pupils a written exercise to define a food web and give them a pre-printed food web diagram to complete by filling in the arrows and missing words.
- Use PowerPoint to illustrate the effect that introducing an alien species, such as those mentioned in the pupil text, will have on the food web. There are a number of good videos available about this. Try searching the BBC for their news report video 'The case for culling grey squirrels'.

Plenary Suggestions

Net spotting
Give the pupils, in pairs, an A3 sheet with the names of lots of organisms on it, but no links. Each pair should spend five minutes drawing in as many links as they can and five minutes circulating the class to look at others, adding in any extra links they have found in a different colour. If time permits, compare sheets and keep as a record. (5–10 mins)

All are members, one of another
Using the same individuals and string links, re-establish the net set up at the start of the lesson. Ask a pupil to select an organism and say whether its numbers will go up or down. Use the string links to identify where connections can be made and get the pupils to describe what will happen. Repeat for several organisms. Eventually, ask all the producers to die and see what happens. Relate this to the mass extinction events of the past, and fears of future asteroid or comet impacts, or super volcano eruptions, such as that predicted for Yellowstone Park, USA. (10–15 mins)

Differentiation

SEN
Use a simpler food web floor chart or give a printed model of what their floor chart should look like.

Extension
Give the pupils a list of websites and ask them to produce a synopsis of the alien species problems which are currently in high profile internationally.
Let the pupils choose one alien species, use the Internet for research and produce a poster about it for display. For example, the impact of the different ladybird species from the continent could be relevant.

Homework Suggestion

Draw out another food web of your own.

Answers to in-text questions

a) Five of:
Oak tree ⟶ caterpillar ⟶ great tit ⟶ sparrowhawk
Oak tree ⟶ caterpillar ⟶ blue tit ⟶ weasel
Oak tree ⟶ caterpillar ⟶ great tit ⟶ stoat
Oak tree ⟶ caterpillar ⟶ great tit ⟶ weasel
Oak tree ⟶ greenfly ⟶ great tit ⟶ stoat
Oak tree ⟶ wood mouse ⟶ weasel
Oak tree ⟶ wood mouse ⟶ stoat

b) Tree is a producer, all others are consumers.

c) Great tit is omnivore; wood mouse, greenfly and caterpillar are herbivores; the others are carnivores.

d) Yes, as they compete for water and minerals from the soil and for light.

e) i) The population will probably fall.
ii) The great tits will have less food.

f) i) and ii) The greenfly population may increase as there are fewer tits eating them or the greenfly population may fall as tits eat more of them due to the lack of caterpillars.

B2.7 Food Pyramids and Energy Flow

NC links for the lesson
- Organisms, behaviour and health.
- All living things show variation, can be classified and are interdependent, interacting with each other and with their environment.

Learning Objectives
Pupils should learn:
- What pyramids of numbers are.
- How pyramids of numbers can show energy flow through ecosystems.
- How bioaccumulation occurs in ecosystems.

Learning Outcomes
- All pupils should be able to construct a pyramid of numbers from given data and link it to energy flow.
- Most pupils should be able to interpret pyramids of numbers and describe how persistent chemicals accumulate in ecosystems.
- Some pupils should also be able to explain why bioaccumulation occurs.

Learning Styles
Visual: Identifying organisms by means of keys.
Auditory: Discussing problems with pyramids.
Kinaesthetic: Carrying out the practical activities.
Interpersonal: Working in groups in the 'Tightest on the tigers' plenary.
Intrapersonal: Drawing the answer to 'When is a pyramid not a pyramid?' plenary.

Answers to Summary questions
1. a) = i), b) = ii).
2. Pupils to show DDT passing up the food chain and concentration increasing.
3. Corn → human provides most energy as there is no waste caused by animals moving, keeping warm, etc.

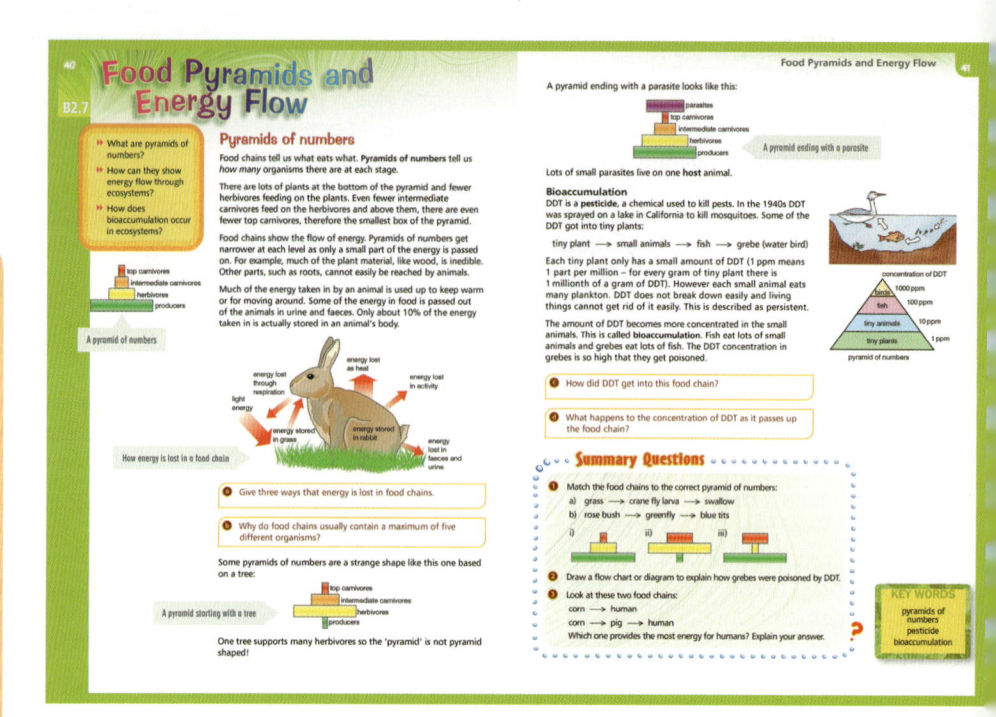

The Lesson

Starter Suggestions

What makes a pyramid a pyramid?
Show a slide of the great pyramids in Egypt, playing some suitable Middle Eastern background music. If available, show them, or talk to them about the Simpson's episode 'Sweets and Sour Marge' (series 13 1308 DABF03), where the inhabitants of Springfield try to get into the Duff book of records for the largest human pyramid and finish up getting in as the fattest town in America. Ask the pupils to write down what makes a pyramid a pyramid. Share responses, perhaps quoting a dictionary definition, and draw out that it is a 3-D shape in which each higher layer occupies less area than the one below it. (10–15 mins)

Big fleas have little fleas
Tell the pupils about *Ichneumon* flies, which are wasp-like insects that lay their eggs in the bodies of butterfly and moth larvae (caterpillars). The caterpillar is the host and the *Ichneumon* fly larvae feed parasitically inside the caterpillar. The fly larvae are parasitised by the larvae of another group of wasp-like insects. This second lot of parasites are called 'hyperparasites'. Assuming that each parasite has only one hyperparasite, ask the pupils to suggest what shape the pyramid of numbers would be. Choose a pupil to draw it on the board. (5–10 mins)

Main Lesson
- Pyramids of numbers in a freshwater habitat: This is a fieldwork and laboratory-based activity. This will take more time than one lesson and is suitable for a field day or as a special project. Alternatively, sampling could be carried out beforehand and the pupils can use keys and so on in the laboratory to identify and count the organisms. Keys such as the Aidgap series (Aids to Identification of Difficult Groups of Animals) produced by the Field Studies Council will help in the identification. The aim is to provide some hands-on experience of how pyramids are built, using information collected from a habitat. The collected animals should be kept in a bucket (with some pondweed) in a cool place and then they can be identified and put into groups according to their feeding habits. Count the numbers of carnivores, herbivores and detritivores (those that eat dead and decaying material). Draw a pyramid of numbers. There should be fewer carnivores than herbivores, but this does not always happen and pupils could discuss why (could be

Food Pyramids and Energy Flow

sampling technique, time of day collected, time of year, whether sample was from a pond or flowing water etc.). All animals should be returned to the habitat from which they came. Care should be taken to avoid water-borne diseases, therefore emphasise the importance of washing hands.

- **Pyramids of numbers in a terrestrial habitat**: This is similar to the activity above, but may be easier to carry out in the laboratory and within one lesson period. Collect leaf litter from a 50 × 50 cm area of woodland (or other suitable habitat) and place in a bag for transport to the laboratory. Tip the litter out into a large tray or on to a large sheet of paper. Get the pupils to catch any animals they can spot, using pooters, pipettes, paintbrushes (emphasising that they need to be careful to separate out the animals and keep them in specimen tubes). Identify the animals, using references, into carnivores, herbivores and detritivores, and build a pyramid for the leaf litter. All animals should be returned safely to their original habitat.

- **Exposition**: Show the pupils a PowerPoint presentation of the concept of pyramids of numbers, building up each layer in turn, using all the terminology (consumers, etc.). Use some actual figures for this, either from the exercises above or from data. The pyramid should relate to a specific habitat or situation. Give them a worksheet to complete as the presentation proceeds, with a table of numbers to fill in and then plot a pyramid to scale on graph paper. Ensure that they have clearly grasped the definition of a pyramid of numbers (a representation of the number of organisms at each level in a food chain).

- In discussion, draw out any problems which have occurred in understanding pyramids, such as the classic tree at the base of a pyramid of numbers being represented by a very small rectangle and therefore the analogy breaking down. Illustrate the solutions to this through PowerPoint, including a version for parasites, where the top layer is larger than the lower ones. Make this gory with stories of rats being struck and dying followed by a mass exodus of fleas from the cooling corpse, hunting for other hosts. Dogs catching rats can often pick up thousands of fleas if they carry the prey in their mouths for any distance after the kill. Link with the 'Big fleas have little fleas' starter.

- **Bioaccumulation**: Explain the concept using Minamata Bay and mercury poisoning, and DDT on birds of prey as examples. As reinforcement, use a drag and drop exercise where a series of boxes containing plant symbols are sprayed with pesticide. The pupils have to move the contaminated plants into boxes containing caterpillars where the plants disappear but the poisons do not. The next group of pupils drag the caterpillars into small birds, and the next group drag the small birds into a bird of prey, the toxins accumulating each time. The eggs of the bird of prey crack due to thin shells and cannot breed successfully. Pupils can then complete a differentiated worksheet to summarise the process.

Plenary Suggestions

When is a pyramid not a pyramid?
Ask the pupils to write this question on one half of a folded piece of A4 and on the other side to draw out, in words and pictures, the answer to this riddle. [In a pyramid of numbers where the bottom layer can be of smaller volume than the ones above.] The best one can be scanned and put on the school Intranet or used as a science week poster question. (5–10 mins)

Tightest on the tigers
Tell the pupils they are all going to be eaten by tigers at the end of the day. In groups of three or four, ask them to work out how they can be tight on the tigers and give them as little food as possible (i.e. how they can lose as much weight as possible before the end of the day). Ask them to write their responses down ready to reply to the class through a leader. Draw out the ways in which energy is lost from one trophic level to the next (respiration, excretion, movement, heat, reproduction etc.) and summarise in a 'How to be tight on the tigers' paragraph which can be completed for homework. (10–15 mins)

Practical Support

Main lesson: Freshwater habitat pyramid

Equipment and materials required
Pond net, bucket plus lid, pondweed, Pasteur pipettes, Petri dishes, forceps, identification keys.

Safety
Follow local guidelines and risk assessments for outside activities.
Wash hands and cover cuts with waterproof plasters.

Main lesson: Terrestrial pyramid

Equipment and materials required
Leaf litter, bag, large tray or sheet of paper, specimen tubes, forceps, pooters, pipettes, paint brush, identification keys.

Safety
Follow local guidelines and risk assessments for outside activities.
CLEAPSS laboratory handbook/CDROM section 17.1.

Differentiation

SEN
If available, have a magnetic balls model and get a pupil to build a pyramid from it. Stick stickers on the balls to state which layer represents which type of organism. Alternatively, use building bricks and stick-on labels.

Extension
Research the use of dung as fuel and present as a PowerPoint.

Homework Suggestion

Suggested paragraph on 'Tightest on the tigers' plenary. Pupils could complete pyramids of numbers activities.

Answers to in-text questions

a Three of: used in moving around, keeping warm, in breathing, in faeces and urine and in inedible parts of the animals such as bones.

b So much energy is lost at each stage that there would not be enough energy to reach a sixth level.

c Absorbed by tiny plants which are eaten by small animals.

d It increases due to bioaccumulation.

B2.8 Predators and Prey

NC links for the lesson
- Organisms, behaviour and health.
- All living things show variation, can be classified and are interdependent, interacting with each other and with their environment.

Learning Objectives
Pupils should learn:
- How predators are adapted to catch prey.
- How plants and prey are adapted to avoid being eaten.
- How populations of predators and prey affect each other.

Learning Outcomes
- All pupils should be able to describe how predators are adapted to catch prey and how plants and prey avoid being eaten.
- Most pupils should be able to describe how predators and prey affect each other.
- Some pupils should also be able to explain the fluctuations in predator and prey populations.

Learning Styles
Visual: Observing PowerPoint presentations and viewing pictures of animals.
Auditory: Discuss adaptations of predators and prey.
Kinaesthetic: Carrying out practical activity on density of prey.
Interpersonal: Working in pairs on predator–prey graphs in the 'jigsaw graph' plenary.
Intrapersonal: Writing a 'harey story' for the plenary.

Answers to Summary questions
1. [Mark by overall impression.]
2. [Mark by overall impression.]
3. Graph should reflect that predator numbers are smaller than prey and that they increase and decline slightly after prey numbers. Annotations should show the link between them.

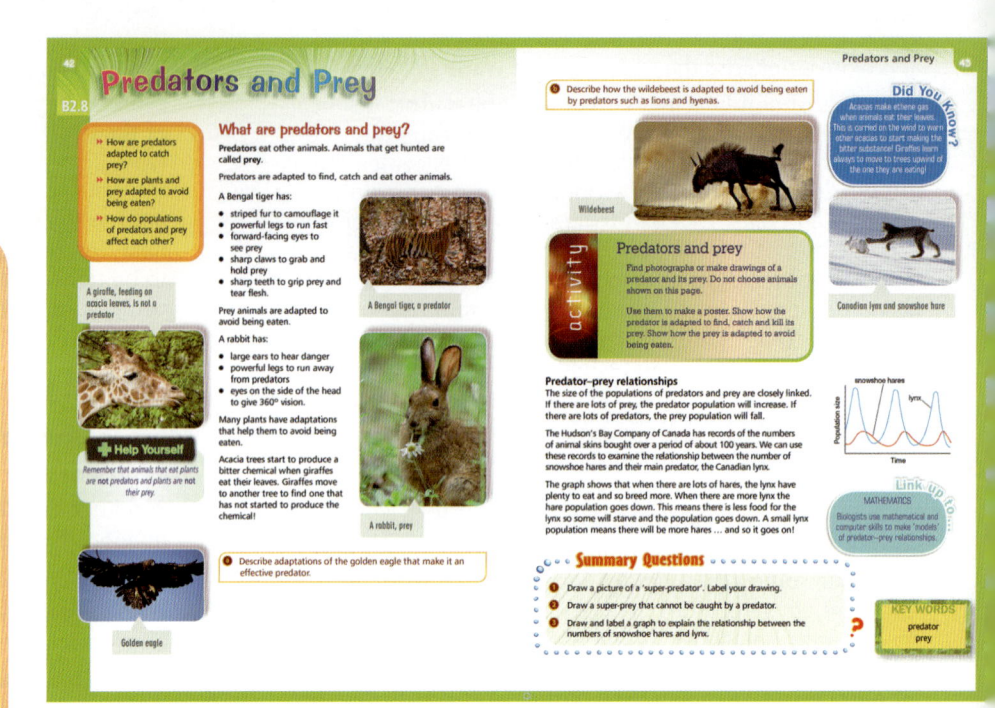

Answers to in-text questions
a. Good eye sight, strong claws to grip prey, sharp beak to rip meat, big wings for soaring to spot prey.
b. Long legs for running fast, horns for protection.

Functional Skills Link-up
ICT Skills
- Use of computer modelling software such as that in Multimedia science school if available.

The Lesson

Starter Suggestions

Predator, prey, both or neither?
Remind the pupils what the words 'predator' and 'prey' mean. Place the words 'predator', 'prey', 'both' and 'neither' on to the board and assign them each a letter: 'a', 'b', 'c', or 'd'. Show the pupils a series of photographs of various animals, including some which are obviously predators, such as lions, hawks; some which are obviously prey species, such as rabbits and deer; some which could be both, such as small birds; and some which are neither, such as plants. Using small individual white boards, get the pupils to write the letter they think best sums up each organism in turn and, on a signal, hold them up. Discuss the class views. (5–10 mins)

Animal part jobs
Give each pupil a sheet of paper with some photographs of functional parts of animals, which are adaptations to help them as predators to catch prey or as prey to escape from predators. Examples might include owl eyes, tiger stripes, ibex prongs (horns), and rabbit's tails. Get the pupils to write, underneath the photos, which animal it comes from, whether it is to help the hunters or the hunted and how it helps. Alternatively, have large, numbered pictures of these parts around the room and let pupils identify as many as they can, writing down the information. After a time limit (5–8 minutes) go through the answers allowing pupils to share their reasons for identification with the rest of the class. (10–15 mins)

Predators and Prey

Main Lesson

- If possible, collect a large box full of various common children's plastic toy animals. An appeal to parents usually brings in plenty. Hand groups of these around to groups of four or five, and ask the pupils to describe to the class what the adaptations are and how they help. As an alternative, request a box of books which contain animal photographs from the library and carry out the same exercise. Ask the pupils to draw up a table showing some of the adaptations and how they help the organism to survive. A pre-printed template may help those who take a lot of time drawing tables.

- Demonstrate some plant adaptations, using specimens either from the school glasshouse or brought in. Examples could include thorny plants, stinging plants, smelly plants (latex laden). Using computers connected to the Internet, give the pupils a finite time limit to investigate plant adaptations which help them to avoid being eaten.

- Choose a pair of organisms in a feeding relationship and ask the class what will happen to the number of the prey species if the number of predators increases, and what will happen to the number of prey if the number of the predator species decreases. Show a section of video, if available, of the inter-relationship of the populations of the arctic fox and the snowshoe hare. As an extension activity, show a computer model of this relationship in graphical form (try an Internet search for Sound toys Periodic Rhythm by Philip Gaedke – scroll down to see the graphs draw themselves out as the simulation progresses). In addition, if available, use modelling or simulation software, such as the relevant tool in Multimedia science school, and allow the pupils to interact with the system, changing variables and seeing the effect on the numbers of predators and prey.

- To demonstrate the effect of the density of prey on the relationship, mark out a 1 m square area on the bench and place dried peas (or similar) randomly within the marked-out area. The dried peas represent the prey. Blindfold one member of the group (the predator) and ask them to tap their finger inside the area at a constant rate for exactly one minute. Any pea that is touched is picked up and placed in a beaker. This represents the time taken by the predator to eat the prey and should be kept as constant as possible. Repeat with different prey densities. Keep a record of the 'prey' caught and eaten at each density and plot class results as the mean number of prey captured per minute against prey density. It is also possible to plot the percentage of prey captured against prey density. Discuss the results and relate to graphs of predator–prey relationships.

- Project a PowerPoint slide of a section of a typical predator–prey pair of graph lines onto a white board, which is suitable for writing on, or a transparent pull down overlay on an interactive board. Get a pupil to draw out, with a dry wipe pen, a predicted line or a specific point where they think the line will go when the graph continues. Give a small reward if they get it correct, repeat if they do not. Get the pupils, in pairs, to come up with a predator and a prey species which could show this type of relationship. Ask them to write the species pairs onto Post-it notes and put them on the board at the front. Ask a volunteer to read them out and, as a class, write down some examples. Fill in a cloze passage worksheet summarising the relationships and get the pupils to stick this into their exercise books.

- Carry out the exercise 'Predators and prey' from the pupil book. This activity focuses on one predator and prey, whereas the activity suggested earlier looks at the different habitats and their predator–prey relationships. The poster activity could be set as homework.

Plenary Suggestions

Jigsaw graph
Give the pupils a slip of paper, wide enough to stick into their books, with the predator–prey graph on it. Using letters, mark several points on the graph at different phases of the cycle. Mark the graphs with faint vertical lines every 2 cm or so. Each pupil has to cut their graph into strips along the faint lines and give these to their partner, who has to reassemble it, glue it into their book and write down what is happening at each of the lettered points. Check each other's work when completed. Lower-attaining pupils can be helped by higher attaining ones. (5–10 mins)

A harey story
Ask the pupils to compose a piece of prose (or poetry if they prefer!) from a hare's point of view, to encapsulate the family history of a snowshoe hare. Allow the pupils to anthropomorphise and tell dramatic tales of the fluctuating fortunes of the family history, to include suitable references e.g. to lynx numbers, predation, competition, food supply, disease. Read out some examples, or encourage the pupils to do so themselves. This activity could be started as a plenary and continued for homework. (10–15 mins)

Practical Support

Starter: Predator, prey, both or neither
Equipment and materials required
Photographs of various animals.

Starter: Animal part jobs
Equipment and materials required
Photographs of animal and plant parts.

Main lesson: Introduction
Equipment and materials required
Box of toy animals or library books, plants with adaptations.

Main lesson: The effect of the density of prey
Equipment and materials required
Dried peas or similar, blindfold, sticky tape to mark out areas, beakers for peas, graph paper, stop watch.

Plenary: Jigsaw graph
Equipment and materials required
Scissors, glue and graph.

Differentiation

SEN
Provide differentiated worksheets to summarise the information and use templates and clue sheets for recording the adaptations.

Extension
Some predators hunt at night and some during the day. Ask the pupils to research and discuss any differences between the adaptations of those that hunt at night and those that hunt during the daytime.

Homework Suggestion

Pupils could continue with the plenary 'A harey story'.

Ask the pupils to make the poster as described in the 'Predators and prey' activity.

B2.9 Habitats and Adaptation

NC links for the lesson
- Organisms, behaviour and health.
- All living things show variation, can be classified and are interdependent, interacting with each other and their environment.

Learning Objectives

Pupils should learn:
- That a habitat is the place where organisms live.
- That animals and plants are adapted to live in a particular habitat.

Learning Outcomes

- All pupils should be able to explain that different animals and plants live in different habitats.
- Most pupils should be able to describe some adaptations of animals and plants to their habitats.
- Some pupils should also be able to explain how specific adaptations enable organisms to survive.

Functional Skills Link-up

ICT Skills
- Obtain, insert, size, crop, and position images that are fit for purpose (level 2).

Learning Styles

Visual: Identifying and linking organisms to habitats.
Auditory: Listening to the discussions and reports from other pupils and groups.
Kinaesthetic: Taking part in the fieldwork or compiling the master sheets.
Interpersonal: Working in groups on the activities.
Intrapersonal: Making a personal contribution to the group activity.

Answers to Summary questions

1.
   i) Polar bear – arctic; fish and seals; white fur for camouflage, thick fur to keep it warm, sharp claws to grip prey, sharp teeth to rip meat.
   ii) Camel – desert; plants; sandy colour acts as camouflage, large feet stop it sinking in sand, hump made of fat which acts as store of energy and acting as insulation (if fat was evenly distributed).
   iii) Orca – arctic and other seas; seals and fish; blubber acts as insulation, streamlined shape enables it to swim fast, powerful fluke helps it to swim, sharp teeth to chew meat.
   iv) Cheetah – savannah; small mammals; powerful legs to outrun prey, sharp claws to grip prey, sharp teeth to rip meat, camouflage helps it to stalk prey.
   v) Howler monkey – rainforest; fruit and other plant material; hands, feet and tail help it to grasp branches.

The Lesson

Starter Suggestions

Creature features
On the board, draw out a grid with five columns. Title the columns as follows: 'Name of organism', 'Food', 'Water', 'Shelter', 'Oxygen'. Ask the pupils to suggest the names of different organisms, ensuring that there is a variety of both plants and animals. Taking each suggested organism in turn, discuss where they get these necessities from and what feature they have that enables them to do so. Get the pupils to fill in the table accordingly. Alternatively, or additionally, the table could be printed on an A4 sheet and a copy given to each pupil, so that they can stick them into their notebooks when completed. Use a list of possible answers as a cue sheet for differentiation. (10–15 mins)

Habitat matching
Arrange a set of A3 pictures of various named habitats around the room. As each pupil enters the room, give them a slip of paper with the name of an organism (or its picture) large enough to be seen from the whole room. The picture or label should have a tiny blob of Blu-tack on the back (beware of pupils throwing this at each other). Let the pupils circulate around the room and stick their organisms on to the appropriate habitat sheet. When complete,

Habitats and Adaptation

hold each sheet up in turn and, choosing organisms from those stuck on, ask the pupils who put them there, what particular feature the organism has that would enable it to survive in that habitat. (5–10 mins)

Main Lesson

- Divide the class into groups of five or six pupils. Give each group a large sheet of coloured or sugar paper, a set of pens, scissors, glue and sheets of plain and lined A4 paper. For each group, provide a range of texts and library books, which relate to a particular habitat (such as deserts, forests, ponds, arctic, seas), in order to identify habitats and the organisms within them. If possible, arrange in advance for the pupils to have supervised access to a photocopier. Before starting the task, discuss with the class the nature of the information to be obtained. This should include the name of the habitat, its physical features such as temperature, rainfall/ moisture, sunlight, soil, as well as identifying organisms which live there and how they get food, oxygen, water and a space to live. Also include a section on plant life in the habitat and where the plants get the carbon dioxide, light and nutrients they need. Make visible a large master list of these expectations on the board at the front of the class as well as having an individual prompt sheet for each group to refer to as it goes along.

- Each pupil has to choose one of the aspects discussed and produce an individual contribution to the overall sheet. Assign them, if volunteers are not forthcoming. The individual pupils' written contributions will be cut out, if necessary, and stuck on to the master sheet on completion. Circulate among the class to ensure that all pupils are actively involved. Set a fixed time limit (about 30 minutes should suffice) and on completion get each group in turn to come to the front of the class and report their findings, allowing time for questioning.

- As an alternative carry out the activity 'Adaptations for a habitat' as described in the pupil book. The finished results could be displayed around the room.

- If the weather is clement and the facilities are available, an alternative activity would be to look at a habitat by carrying out fieldwork. The class teaching environment must be stable and positive to allow this type of work. For further details see B2.11 and B2.12 later.

- Another alternative is to use the Internet, providing a series of questions relating to individual websites relating to a variety of habitats. The URLs for these can be hyperlinked from a page of text in a Word document on the school's intranet. Pupils could place their finished documents into a shared area for their peers to review.

Plenary Suggestions

Habitat display sheets

If the book research option is taken in the main lesson, the pupils' reports back to the group will form a large part of the plenary. Draw together generalised findings into a few sentences, display these using board work or PowerPoint and share them with the class on conclusion of the exercise. Put up the large display sheets around the room and, if time allows, get the pupils to circulate and look at their peers work. As an AfL activity, they could attach Post-it notes giving praise and suggesting improvements. (5–10 mins)

What we found

If the habitat investigation fieldwork option has been taken in the main lesson, groups can choose leaders to report back to the class on which organisms they found, what their adaptations for survival are and the physical features of the environment which make these a necessity. If the Internet trawl option is taken, pupils can view each other's work and collectively appraise it. (10–15 mins)

Practical Support

Starter: Habitat matching

Equipment and materials required

A3 pictures of habitats, names or pictures of organisms, Blu-tack.

Main lesson: Paper work

Equipment and materials required

Sugar paper, pens, scissors, glue, plain and lined A4 paper, reference books.

Main lesson: Fieldwork

Equipment and materials required

It depends on the habitat, e.g. pond nets, dishes and specimen tubes for ponds.

Safety

Follow local guidelines and risk assessments for outside activities.

CLEAPSS laboratory handbook/CDROM section 17.1.

Differentiation

SEN

You could use differentiated worksheets and have simplified practical expectations during the fieldwork.

Extension

As an extension, some individuals may wish to investigate how the environmental conditions in a habitat have dictated the features of the organisms which live there. This could lead to a consideration of evolution and natural selection. An information file (either electronic or paper) and a list of pertinent open-ended questions will be of assistance here.

Answers to in-text questions

a Desert – hot, little water, nights may be very cold, lots of light.

Arctic – very cold, not much available fresh water in winter, very dark in winter and light in summer.

Rainforest – dark, wet, humid, hot.

Sea shore – little fresh water, waves pulling at organisms, under water then exposed twice each day.

b Desert – lack of water.

Arctic – cold.

Rainforest – number of predators.

Sea shore – damage caused by waves.

c Desert – camels, snakes, lizards, gerbils, etc.

Arctic – polar bear, killer whale, musk ox, arctic fox, reindeer, etc.

Rainforest – monkeys, sloth, parrots, toucans, frogs, snakes, jaguar, etc.

Sea shore – limpet, crab, sea gull, winkles, anemones, etc.

B2.10 Habitats Changing

NC links for the lesson
- Organisms, behaviour and health.
- All living things show variation, can be classified and are interdependent, interacting with each other and with their environment.

Learning Objectives
Pupils should learn:
- How habitats change daily.
- How habitats change with the seasons.
- The ways in which animals and plants cope with these changes.

Learning Outcomes
- All pupils should be able to describe how habitats can change daily and with the seasons.
- Most pupils should be able to describe ways in which animals and plants cope with daily and seasonal changes.
- Some pupils should also be able to explain the adaptations of organisms to seasonal changes.

Learning Styles
Visual: Watching video clips and viewing slides.
Auditory: Listening to exposition on the reasons for the seasons and the tides.
Kinaesthetic: Constructing a mind map of the key words in the plenary.
Interpersonal: Discussing in groups the reasons for migration in the plenary.
Intrapersonal: Completing their worksheets on key words and definitions.

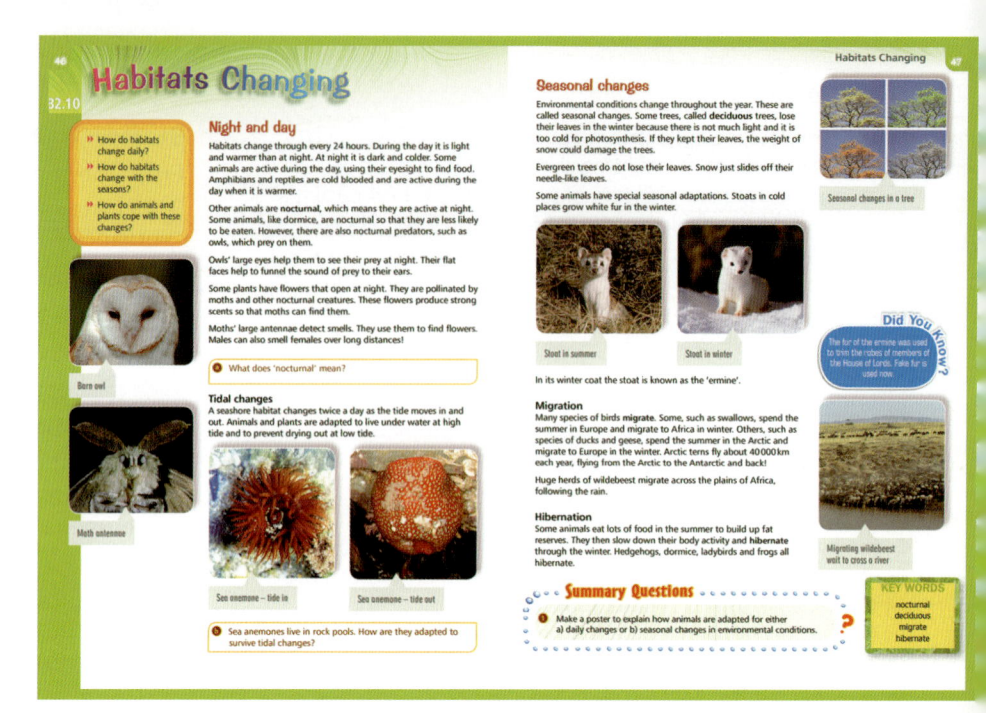

The Lesson

Starter Suggestions

Guess the graphs
Show the pupils three graphs, one showing a cyclical fluctuation in light level every 24 hours (this could be set up at the end of a previous lesson by attaching a light probe to a data-logger and showing the resulting graph), one showing a cyclical fluctuation in temperature over 12 months and one showing a cyclical fluctuation in sea water level over 12 hours. Do not put titles on these graphs, but label the axes. The pupils have to guess what the patterns are representing (day and night, seasons and tides) and describe them. As an extension, ask them to give reasons for each of these phenomena. (5–10 mins)

Clothes for thought
Give the pupils pictures of a large range of different types of clothing, to include pyjamas and slippers, school uniform, casual wear such as jeans, beachwear and sunhats, high visibility jackets, woolly hats and scarves. You may choose to bring in examples. Ask the pupils to state which time of day or year the clothes are for and draw out what the daily and seasonal changes are. (10–15 mins)

Main Lesson
- Recap through exposition, board work and the use of a lamp and a globe, the reasons for day and night and for the seasons, emphasising that the tilted angle of the Earth's spin is what is responsible for these. Relate it to the relative lengths of day and night time, the number of hours above the horizon, the elevation of the Sun in the sky and changes in the relative concentration of the rays. Take care to kill the idea that summer is when we are closer to the Sun – this is a very persistent misconception! Ask the pupils, in pairs or small groups, to discuss and list the changes which take place every day and every year. Collect the ideas on a board, following a class discussion and get the pupils to add any changes they had not already listed, as well as writing down or filling in a summary sheet on the rhythmical changes, the reasons for them and the consequences.
- Introduce the word 'nocturnal'. A short video clip or some stills of nocturnal creatures would be helpful. Ask the pupils to write a brief definition, with some examples, in their exercise books.

Habitats Changing

- Show a slide with the frame cut into quarters, each containing a picture of the same tree in each of the seasons (not in order). Label each shot with a letter and ask the pupils to put the pictures in to the correct seasonal order, starting with winter. They should write down the corresponding letters on to an individual white board, keeping it face down until the command 'Show me' is given. Ask the pupils to discuss with each other why some of the trees lose their leaves in the winter and some do not. Introduce the words 'deciduous' (getting the pupils to pronounce this out loud) and 'evergreen'. Project a slide showing four reasons why this loss of leaves might happen, prefixed by letters. Only two of the answers should be correct. Ask the pupils to write down the ones they think are right on their 'Show me' boards. Write out a brief summary. A suggested backing track is 'Four Seasons in One Day' by Crowded House.

- Ask the pupils to recall the story of King Cnut unsuccessfully trying to command the tide to stay still. Show some stop motion footage of the tide rising and falling, for example in a harbour. Ask if anyone knows why this should happen. For added grisliness, describe how in past times prisoners were sometimes shackled to posts at low tide and left to die as the water slowly rose (partly through cruelty, partly to maintain purported innocence of their bloodless deaths). Draw out the role of the Moon through discussion and show an animation (several good ones are available on the Internet) or a series of PowerPoint slides to illustrate this. Pupils may recall a point in the Jim Carey film *Bruce Almighty* where Bruce is being God for a while and during a romantic dinner draws the Moon closer to the Earth to impress his girlfriend. They could discuss what effect this would have upon the tides and the knock-on effect on the animals and plants living on the seashore, and then write this up. A suggested backing track is 'Bad Moon rising' by Creedence Clearwater Revival or 'Blue Moon' by Showaddywaddy.

- Show a video clip from the film *Ice Age* if available, where the animals are discussing, then setting off on the great migration. Discuss the reasons for migration and get the pupils, in small groups, to list as many animals as they can which migrate. Check their lists and provide a small motivational prize for the group which gets the most.

- Show some video footage of animals hibernating, defining the word. Draw out through questioning (some pupils may have pets which hibernate) what 'hibernation' means, why some animals do it and some examples. If dormice are used as an example, link to 'dormant' and 'dormitory'. Pupils can then complete a concise worksheet summarising migration and hibernation.

Plenary Suggestions

Mind map key words
Ask the pupils to make a mind map joining together the key words used in the lesson. Ask them to annotate the arrows so that they make complete sentences. (5–10 mins)

Summer visitors or winter visitors
Show slides, or provide still pictures, of a variety of birds that migrate to the British Isles. Choose some that are winter migrants (some geese, ducks, swans) and some that are summer migrants (the swallow family). Also include some like puffins, razorbills and guillemots that arrive in spring to breed and then depart far out to sea. A good bird book, or the RSPB website, will give details and pictures. Ask the pupils to sort out which come in the winter and which are summer visitors (their knowledge will depend on the locality and their familiarity with garden birds). Discuss where the birds are likely to spend the rest of the year and why (food, breeding grounds), and ask for suggestions as to what triggers their migration. If there is time, the large distances travelled could be shown on a map or globe. (10–15 mins)

Practical Support

Starter:
Equipment and materials required
Graphs, various clothing.

Main lesson:
Equipment and materials required
Lamp and globe.

Differentiation

SEN
Give the pupils a mind map of the key words, but give them all the key words in a box at the bottom of the map. Put in all the arrow link phrases for them and, if necessary, put in initial letters and correct numbers of spaces for the number of letters into the text boxes where the key words are to go. The colours of the empty boxes and their correct key words can also be correlated.

Extension
As an extension to the day and night and seasons recap at the start of the lesson, higher-attaining pupils could envisage what dramatically changing the rate of, and angle of, the Earth's spin would have. Get the pupils to come up with some extreme scenarios and describe the consequences of them in terms of the effects of the changes and of how life would be constrained on such a planet.

Pupils could follow up the 'Summer visitors or winter visitors' plenary with some research on how birds navigate during migration.

Homework Suggestion

Ask pupils to choose one bird from a suggested list that migrates to the British Isles and to write a short account of its activities, entitled 'A year in the life of …'. For reference see RSPB or BTO websites and good bird identification guides.

Answers to in-text questions

a) Animals that are active at night.

b) They close up when tide is out so they can conserve water and/or prevent dehydration.

Answers to Summary questions

1) [Mark by overall impression.]

B2.11 Investigating a Habitat (1)

NC links for the lesson
- Organisms, behaviour and health.
- All living things show variation, can be classified and are interdependent, interacting with each other and with their environment.

Learning Objectives
Pupils should learn:
- How to use keys to help identify living organisms.
- How to collect animals and plants in a habitat.

Learning Outcomes
- All pupils should be able to identify a living organism using a simple key and to describe some ways in which organisms can be collected in a habitat.
- Most pupils should be able to use equipment to collect and identify the organisms in a habitat.
- Some pupils should also be able to use more complex keys to identify organisms and to select appropriate equipment for sampling specific habitats.

How Science Works
- Describe an appropriate approach to answer a scientific question using sources of evidence, and where appropriate, making relevant observations or measurements using appropriate apparatus (1.2a).

Learning Styles
Visual: Identifying organisms using keys.
Auditory: Discussing the different techniques used.
Kinaesthetic: Carrying out the sampling methods.
Interpersonal: Collaborating in groups during the investigation.
Intrapersonal: Telling others what was the best bit for them.

The Lesson

Starter Suggestions

What's it for?
Put out around the lab examples of the equipment the pupils will be using during the practical, e.g. sweep nets, pooters, sheets for tree beating, Petri dishes, identification books and keys, and so on. Allow the pupils to circulate and interact with the materials for a short specified time (five minutes should be fine for most groups). Call the class together and go through the names and functions of each piece of equipment, taking as much lead as possible from the members of the class. Conclude by giving instructions about what the outcomes of the habitat investigation should be. (5–10 mins)

Balls key
Show the pupils a slide with eight types of ball with different characteristics (e.g. snooker, table tennis, golf, rugby, cricket, bowling, tennis, football). Give one pupil a question-based key on a sheet of A4 and ask them to step outside the room, while the rest of the class choose a ball for them to identify. When the pupil returns, they must ask the series of questions, to which the class answers either 'Yes' or 'No'. The pupil should soon arrive at the type of ball chosen by the class. Repeat several times with different pupils, then introduce and demonstrate keys for the organisms which will be looked for during the habitat investigation. (10–15 mins)

Main Lesson

- Studying a habitat: Remind the pupils of the definition of a habitat and get them to give some examples. In advance of the lesson, it is a very valuable use of time to seek out a suitable nearby habitat and carry out some initial research by yourself, in order to become familiar with the species to be found and their locations. At the same time, a risk assessment can be carried out.
- Give a briefing regarding behavioural expectations and safety. Allocate sampling methods to different groups: for example, one group to set up pitfall traps, another to use sweep nets, according to the habitat sampled. The information can be collected together in a plenary session.
- Choose sampling techniques to suit the environment. If using pooters, ensure that the correct method of use has been demonstrated and that one person only uses each mouthpiece (bring out beakers of disinfectant

Investigating a Habitat (1)

and washing water). Ensure that the pupils are not trying to suck up into the pooter animals which will not comfortably fit up the tube. If using pitfall traps, ensure that they have a loose cover to protect the captured organisms from birds, and that they are examined and the organisms are released within a suitable time period (no more than 24 hours).

- If tree beating, ensure that this is done sensibly and in a safe manner, and that the trees or bushes are not damaged. If pond dipping, ensure that an adequate depth of water is in all containers and that these are not left in very sunny conditions for too long. (It is tempting for the pupils to see if they can observe some feeding relationships by putting a predator in with a prey species – this is to be discouraged.)
- Take identification keys into the field for use there and prepare frameworks for recording the findings. Pre-printed record sheets on clipboards, with a pencil or ball-point pen attached, are ideal. Laminated key cards are really useful in these situations. A good range of these (Aidgap: Aids to Identification of Difficult Groups of Animals) are available from the Field Studies Council, who also provide much support material. A laptop with a suitable identification key programme, such as those produced by Gatekeeper Education Limited, is also of much benefit, as are field guide books. Encourage the pupils to observe the behaviour of the animals and to look at their structure and relate it to their function.
- Time in the habitat could be limited, so it might be necessary to take organisms back to the classroom for identification. Specimen tubes should be used for the organisms, which should be returned to their habitat as soon as possible.
- Use graphs, tables, pie charts, and so on to present the findings. Get the pupils to explain how each organism is adapted to the place in which it is found. Further research on the organisms (what they eat, who eats them) could result in building up a food web for the habitat studied.

Plenary Suggestions

Who's eating who?
Collect on the board, the names of all the species which have been found. Split the board with horizontal lines, one for each trophic level, and label them 'producers', 'decomposers' (more accurately 'detritivores'), 'primary consumers', 'secondary consumers', and so on. As the pupils add the names to the board, get them to think of which trophic level their organism should go in. When a suitable number of organisms have been put up on the board, arrows to show feeding relationships can be added to form a food web. (5–10 mins)
(This could be extended and linked with food pyramids, if the numbers of the different organisms have been counted. See B2.7 'Food Pyramids and Energy Flow'.)

The best bit for me
Discuss, in open forum, the findings of the investigation. Ask pupils if the sampling methods worked, whether they caught the organisms they expected and what were the advantages and disadvantages of the methods used. This session would be particularly useful if different groups had used different sampling methods. Encourage the pupils to share with each other what they found out and what they were enthused by or found stimulating. (10–15mins)

Practical Support

Studying a habitat

Equipment and materials required
To investigate organisms within a habitat: pitfall traps, pooters, beakers of disinfectant and washing water, card or sheets for tree beating, sweep nets, plastic trays, hand lenses, beakers, Petri dishes, digital camera, identification guide books and laminated key cards appropriate to the area studied. Clipboards with writing frames for recording findings.

Details
Discuss with the class the methods of collection to be used and demonstrate them. Break the class into groups of about three and allow them to explore the environment, providing them in advance with a worksheet framework of what they are expected to find. Record specimens using a digital camera. Ensure that the welfare of the organisms is of highest priority.

Safety
Risk assess any outdoor work. See CLEAPSS laboratory handbook/CDROM section 17.1.
Caution regarding falling in or pushing in around ponds.
Be aware of allergies to plants and of any toxic stinging species in the habitat.
Wash hands after handling organisms and before eating.
Make sure any cuts are covered by waterproof plasters.
If using microscopes, beware of breaking slides.

Differentiation

SEN
Picture keys could be used for identification and pupils could be asked to look for specific organisms.

Extension
Pupils could be asked how such an investigation could be made quantitative and could be introduced to the idea of random sampling techniques.
Give the pupils a selection of the plants in the habitat and ask them to devise a key to identify or separate them.

Homework Suggestion

Ask pupils to write a full description of one technique they used in the investigation of the habitat.

Answers to Summary questions

1. Pupil key. [Check that the key actually works for each item.]
2. Pupil poster. [Mark by overall impression.]

Answers to in-text questions

1. i) ladybird ii) ground beetle iii) spider iv) centipede v) snail

B2.12 Investigating a Habitat (2)

NC links for the lesson
- Organisms, behaviour and health.
- All living things show variation, can be classified and are interdependent, interacting with each other and with their environment.

Learning Objectives

Pupils should learn:
- That there are physical factors affecting the organisms in a habitat.
- How to measure some of the physical factors in a habitat.
- How to estimate the number of plants in a habitat.

Learning Outcomes

- All pupils should be able to list the physical factors in a habitat and describe a random sampling technique.
- Most pupils should be able to describe how some physical factors are measured.
- Some pupils should also be able to explain how physical factors may affect the distribution of organisms.

How Science Works

- Describe an appropriate approach to answer a scientific question using sources of evidence, and where appropriate, make relevant observations or measurements using appropriate apparatus (1.2a).

Answers to in-text questions

a Samples which are taken at random so that there is no bias in where they are chosen.

b So that results are not affected by choosing samples which are not representative of the whole area.

c In any area the first 2 or 3 digits are usually the same.

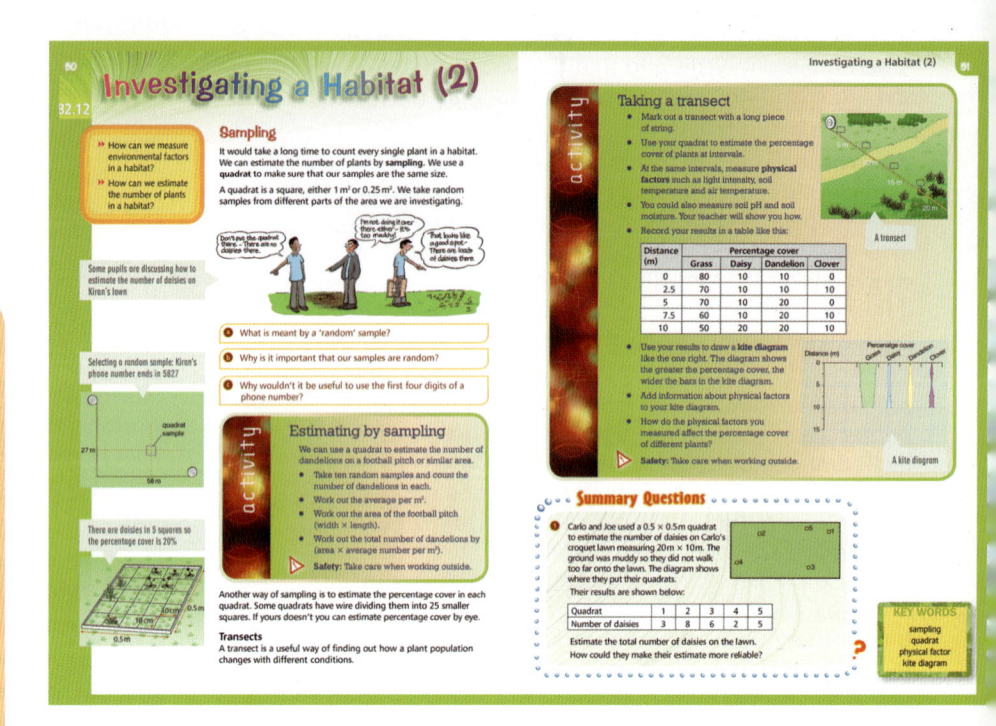

Learning Styles

Visual: Estimating the percentage cover of the plants in the quadrat.
Auditory: Listening to discussions in starters and plenaries.
Kinaesthetic: Carrying out the practical investigation.
Interpersonal: Working in a group to do the sampling.
Intrapersonal: Writing description of random sampling for homework.

The Lesson

Starter Suggestions

That's really random!

Ask a pupil to pick the name of another pupil. Ask the class why they think that person was chosen. Possible reasons may include friendship (most likely), proximity (first person they looked at), popularity (being chosen adds kudos, adding kudos to a popular person may make you more noticed by them), bullying (picking a person who you know will not like being picked, either to get at them or to gain favour with another who would like to get at them) and so on. Discuss these reasons and then give the pupils, working in pairs, one minute only to come up with methods of choosing a truly random person (an opportunity for some humour here). Review the discussion which ensues and relate this to the choice of sample in an ecological investigation. (5–10 mins)

It could be you!

Ask the pupils to think about the National Lottery, projecting an image of the Smiling Hand logo with the 'It could be you!' tag. Imagine that the numbers, instead of being on balls, were written in large 1 × 1m squares on the ground and that the person in charge of the lottery had to throw a series of bean bags to choose the numbers. Ask: 'Would this be fair? How could they cheat? How could you stop them cheating?' Relate this to the distribution of quadrats in a plant survey, and then continue with the practical plan. (10–15 mins)

Main Lesson

- **Estimating by sampling:** Put some quadrat frames, if available, around the room or one to each bench. Discuss the need for random samples of plants in a habitat. Discuss methods of random sampling, if not already covered during the

Investigating a Habitat (2)

starter, and introduce the class to the quadrats. This is a good time to kill the idea that throwing a quadrat in any form, either in front of you, behind you or blindfold, is any way of ensuring a non-biased distribution of samples. Introduce random number tables, showing the pupils examples from the Internet. You could also use random number generating software which runs from the Internet. Try searching for 'random integer generator'. In advance, measure out the area you are going to investigate and either mark it out in some way or identify landmarks which define it. Measure the area and decide which will be your x-axis and which your y-axis, for the purpose of working out co-ordinates. You will need to define the range of these when using a digital random number generator or a table of random numbers, so as to get co-ordinates which fit the available space.

- When quadrats are introduced in the classroom, make clear other linguistic references, such as 'quad bikes', 'quadrilaterals', 'quads' as being four babies born at the same time (as a bit of obscure interest, you may like to point out here that armadillos always give birth to identical quads), and the military term 'squad', for a group of troops, comes from the Latin *exquadra*, referring to a square formation of soldiers, RAF squadrons, etc.

- Often quadrats in schools are home-made from coat hanger wire or similar. This is not ideal, as sub-divisions are difficult to make. However, if this is the only option then string dividers to break the frame into 25 sub-units are fairly easy to make. It is better to use purpose-built frames, with 100 sub-units, but these can be expensive. Try using plastic trellis netting, sold in garden centres for training climbing plants. This is relatively cheap and can be cut into appropriate squares without sharp edges.

- To estimate the distribution of a species in an area, first work out and record the total area by measurement and multiplication. Decide how many quadrats can be taken and analysed in the time available (probably not more that two per group). Show the pupils the species to be recorded (one only).

- Show them in advance, through PowerPoint or diagrams, how to estimate percentage cover, as this is easier to assess than other ecological measures. To do this, assess the squares within the grid, accounting the appropriate percentage to each. If the species occupies more than 50% of a square, then that percentage is counted, if less than 50 %, it is not counted. Calculate the sum for each quadrat. As an alternative, if local conditions are appropriate, you could count the number of individuals per quadrat by tracing each down to the tap root.

- Assign co-ordinates for each group of pupils from the random number tables or generator. Collect the data. Ask those who finish early to help those who are taking more time. As a class, carry out the investigation and collect individual results. Calculators may help with the maths of recording and for all, except higher attaining pupils, a pre-printed sheet to help with recording will be of great benefit.

- The physical factors can be measured by assigning one factor to each group of pupils, so that one group record air temperature, another group soil temperature, another light intensity and so on, depending on the equipment available to you. Simple thermometers can be used for temperature, a light meter for the light intensity and some soil brought back to the classroom to test for soil pH and moisture content.

- On return to the classroom, collect all the class data and calculate an average (an Excel spreadsheet will do this automatically). From the average percentage cover per quadrat and the total area, calculate the total cover area (or if an individual count has been carried out, the estimated total number of plants of the chosen species in the area).

Plenary Suggestions

Results summary
Collectively pool results: ask each group of pupils to write a summary sentence and randomly (using table or a generator) choose a group to read out their summary. (5–10 mins)

Improvements gambling
Discuss the practical and, in groups, ask the pupils to come up with ways in which the assessment could be improved. As an imaginary incentive, get them to envisage a situation where, if they got their estimate correct to within say 10%, they would get triple pocket money all year, but if they got it wrong they would lose all their pocket money all year. Ask: how would they make sure they had got it right?

Practical Support

Estimating by sampling and Taking a transect
Equipment and materials required
Quadrat frames, string to mark out area, pre-printed recording sheets, digital thermometers, light meter, plastic bag and trowel to collect soil samples, pH meters or universal indicator papers.

Safety
Usual risk assessments and precautions for outside work. See CLEAPSS laboratory handbook/CDROM section 17.1.

Differentiation

SEN
Give pupils a picture of the plant being investigated, so that they can help locate them in the quadrats.

Extension
Introduce the pupils to the point frame for sampling vegetation and get them to work out what information it could provide about the nature of the vegetation in a habitat.

Homework Suggestion
Each pupil could write a description of how to carry out random sampling, including an explanation of its importance.

Answers to Summary questions

1. Average per quadrat = $\frac{24}{5}$ = 4.8 per 0.25 m²

   Total area = 200 m²

   Total number of daisies = $4.8 \times \frac{200}{0.25}$ = 3840

   The results could be made more reliable by increasing the number of quadrats sampled.

   Also the quadrats do not appear to be random – most are near the edge of the lawn.

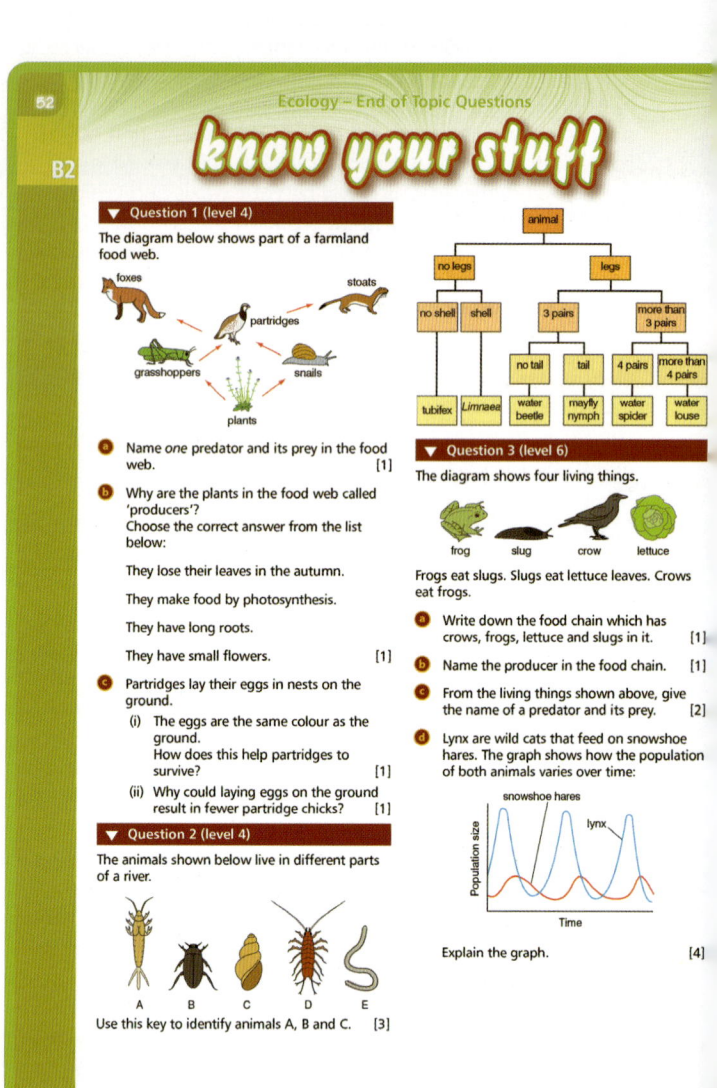

Answers to Ecology – End of Topic Questions

Answers to know your stuff questions

1 **a** Any *one* from: [1]
Predator*:* partridge; prey*:* grasshopper *or* snail.
Predator*:* fox; prey*:* partridge.
Predator*:* stoat; prey*:* partridge.
[*Both* the predator and its prey are required.]

b They make food by photosynthesis. [1]

c i) Any *one* from: [1]
Fewer will be found by predators.
Fewer will be eaten.

ii) Any *one* from: [1]
They may be trodden on *or* damaged.
Predators can get to them easily.

2 A = mayfly nymph [1]
B = water beetle [1]
C = *Limnaea* [1]

3 **a** lettuce → slugs → frogs → crows
[Order must be correct.] [1]

b Lettuce. [1]

c [One mark is for the name of a predator and one mark is for its prey.] [2]
Either:
Predator: crow.
Prey: frog.
or
Predator: frog.
Prey: slug.

d When there are lots of hares, the lynx population goes up as they have plenty of food and breed more. [1]
When there are more lynx the hare population goes down. [1]
This results in less food for the lynx so some will starve and their population goes down. [1]
This in turn results in more hares etc. [1]

Ecology – End of Topic Questions

How Science Works

▼ Question 1 (level 6)

Manpreet did an investigation to find out how temperature affects the number of bubbles produced by waterweed in one minute. Her apparatus is shown below.

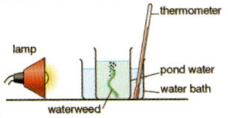

When the temperature of the water was 10°C the waterweed did *not* produce bubbles.

a The waterweed started to produce bubbles when Manpreet increased the temperature of the water in the water bath to 20°C. She waited two minutes before counting the bubbles. Why did she wait two minutes before she started to count the bubbles? [1]

b Manpreet counted the number of bubbles made at six different temperatures. Here is a table of her results:

Temperature of water bath (°C)	10	20	30	40	50	60
Number of bubbles produced per minute	0	8	12	12	8	2

(i) Draw a graph of Manpreet's results. [4]
(ii) Draw a smooth curve on the graph. [1]
(iii) At what temperature were the most bubbles produced per minute? [1]

c Manpreet made a prediction that the higher the temperature the more bubbles would be produced. Which parts of the graph support Manpreet's prediction? [1]

d Manpreet's results do *not* show the exact temperature at which most bubbles were produced. How could she improve the results she collects so she can find this temperature? [1]

▼ Question 2 (level 7)

In the 17th century a Belgian scientist, Van Helmont, planted a small tree in a tub of dry soil. For the next five years he watered the plant with rain water when it got dry. He did not add anything else to the tub.

After five years he took the tree from the tub and weighed it. He also dried and weighed the soil. Here is a table of his results:

	Mass of willow tree (kg)	Mass of dried soil (kg)
At the start	2.3	90.6
Five years later	76.7	90.5

a Van Helmont reached the conclusion that the increase in mass of the willow tree was due to a gain in water.
(i) What *two* pieces of evidence led Van Helmont to this conclusion? [2]
(ii) We now know that Van Helmont's conclusion is *not* correct. Explain why the mass of the willow tree increased. [2]

b Van Helmont thought that a plant would always grow faster if it was given more water. We now know that this is *not* true. Give *two* environmental conditions which can slow down the growth of a plant, even when it has plenty of water. [2]

c The **fresh mass** of a plant includes water. To measure plant growth accurately, scientists work out the increase in **dry mass** rather than the increase in fresh mass of a plant. Why is finding the increase in dry mass a more reliable way to measure plant growth? [1]

Answers to How Science Works questions

1
a Any *one* from: [1]
To make sure the water in the beaker had reached the required temperature.
To make sure the rate stabilised or adjusted to the new temperature.

b i) Correct x- and y-axes labelled. [1]
Sensible scale. [1]
All points plotted to within half a square. [2]
[If only five points plotted to within half a square, give 1 mark instead.]
ii) A smooth curve through all six points. [1]
iii) A temperature from 32 to 38°C. [1]
[Accept any reading consistent with the maximum point on the drawn curve.]

c Any one from: [1]
Between 10°C and 30°C.
Between 10°C and 40°C.
10°C, 20°C and 30°C.

d Any one from: [1]
Use smaller intervals of measuring the temperature.
Use temperatures between 30°C and 40°C.

2
a i) Only water was added. [1]
The mass of the soil did not go down much. [1]
ii) Any two from: [2]
Photosynthesis took place. [Accept 'the plant uses light to make food'.]
Biomass / carbohydrate / wood was produced.
The tree took in carbon dioxide.

b Any two from: [2]
Not enough light.
Not enough carbon dioxide.
Not enough minerals.
Too cold or temperature too low.

c Any one from: [1]
The fresh mass of a plant depends on the availability of water.
Water can be lost by evaporation.
The water content varies from day to day.
Dry mass is due to the manufacture of compounds or named carbon compound or biomass.
Water is not part of the biomass.

C1.1 Elements and Compounds

NC links for the topic
- The particle model provides explanations for the different physical properties and behaviour of matter.
- Elements consist of atoms that combine together in chemical reactions to form compounds.
- Use ideas and models to explain phenomena and develop them to generate and test theories.
- Analyse and evaluate evidence critically from observations and experiments.
- Critically analysing and evaluating evidence from observations and experiments.
- Use a range of scientific methods and techniques to develop and test ideas and explanations.
- Assess risk and work safely in the laboratory, field and workplace.
- Carry out practical and investigative activities, both individually and in groups.
- Obtain, record and analyse data from a wide range of primary and secondary sources, including ICT sources, and use their findings to provide evidence for scientific explanations.
- Evaluate scientific evidence and working methods.
- Use appropriate methods, including ICT, to communicate scientific information and contribute to presentations and discussions about scientific issues.

Level descriptors for the topic
- **AT3 level 4:** Pupils recall simple scientific knowledge and terminology of the properties and classification of materials such as solids, liquids and gases or elements and compounds. They describe some phenomena and processes, such as chemical reactions, drawing on scientific knowledge and understanding. They recognise that evidence can support or refute scientific ideas, for example the classification of reactions as reversible and irreversible. They recognise some applications and implications of science, such as the safe use of acids and alkalis.
- **AT3 level 5:** Pupils recall straightforward scientific knowledge and terminology of materials and their properties. They describe phenomena and processes, drawing on abstract ideas. They explain processes and phenomena such as the formation of compounds. They apply and use knowledge and understanding in familiar contexts, such as identifying changes of state. They recognise that both evidence and creative thinking contribute to the development of scientific ideas, such as elements and their compounds displaying different properties. They describe applications and implications of science, such as the uses of metals based on their specific properties.
- **AT3 level 6:** Pupils recall detailed scientific knowledge and terminology of properties of materials. They describe phenomena and processes using abstract ideas, such as the particle model applied to solids, liquids and gases and to elements and compounds. They take account of a number of factors or use abstract ideas or models, such as word equations, in their explanations of phenomena and processes. They apply and use knowledge and understanding, such as predicting compound names, in unfamiliar contexts. They describe some evidence for some accepted scientific ideas, such as the properties of a compound being independent of how it is formed. They explain the importance of some applications and implications of science, such as the production of new materials with specific desirable properties.
- **AT3 level 7:** Pupils recall detailed scientific knowledge and terminology of properties of materials and make links between different areas. They describe a wide range of phenomena and processes using abstract ideas and sequencing a number of points, such as compound formation. They make links between different areas of science in their explanations, such as between the nature and behaviour of materials and their particles. They apply and use more abstract knowledge and understanding, such as the particle model of matter, and symbols and formulas for elements and compounds, in a range of contexts. They explain how evidence supports some accepted scientific ideas, such as the location of elements in the Periodic Table. They explain, using abstract ideas where appropriate, the importance of some applications and implications of science, such as the need to consider the availability of resources, and environmental effects, in the production of materials.

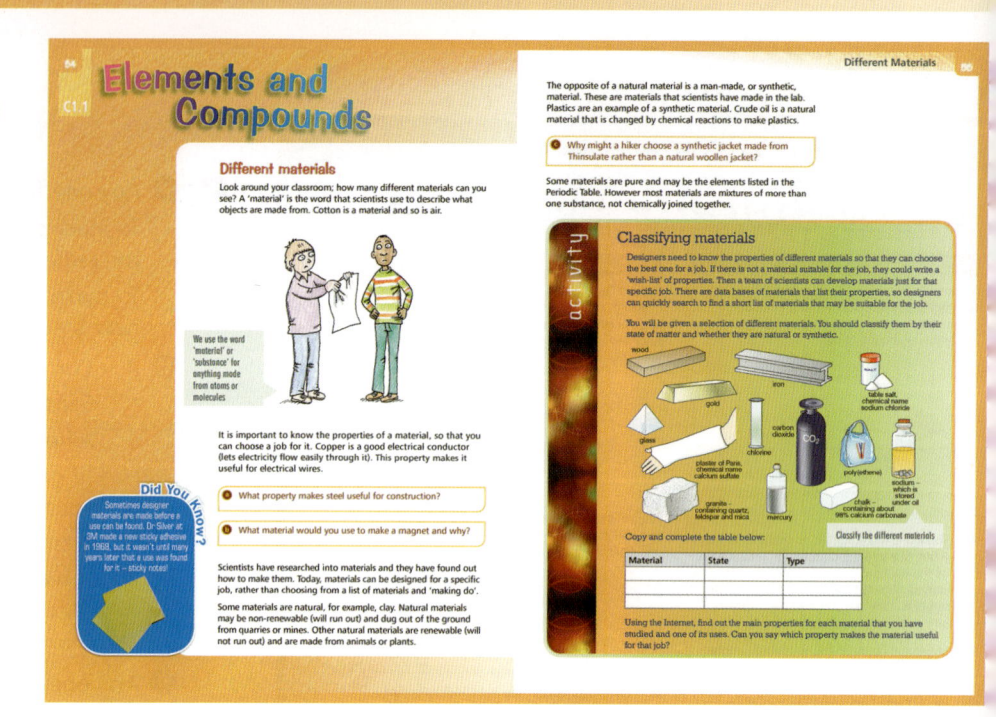

Learning Styles
Visual: Making observations of materials.
Auditory: Describing their observations.
Kinaesthetic: Carrying out practical work and using a computer.
Interpersonal: Sharing ideas with other pupils.
Intrapersonal: Understanding why a material is chosen for a particular purpose.

The Lesson

Starter Suggestions

Material gain
Show pupils photos of buildings or other large objects. Ask them to state the main material used in the construction of each. Choose photos which clearly show the material used, such as a building made of stone or glass, a bridge made from steel or wood. (5 mins)

Safety first
If this is the first Chemistry lesson of the year, it may be a good time to remind pupils of their responsibilities while in a laboratory. Show a picture, or set up a demonstration, of an unsafe laboratory. Ask pupils to identify as many hazards as they can. If you choose to set up a situation, ensure that no-one can actually be harmed. Link any pupil responses back to your school's laboratory rules. (10 mins)

Main Lesson

- Ask pupils to describe what a solid, a liquid and a gas are like. You may wish to extend this to discussing particle arrangements which pupils learned about in Fusion 1.
- Ask pupils to carry out the 'Classifying Materials' activity described in the pupil book. Any materials are suitable but some suggestions are given in the 'Practical Support' section.

Learning Objectives

Pupils should learn:
- How materials can be grouped.
- To suggest the right material for a job.

Learning Outcomes

- All pupils should be able to sort materials into groups.
- Most pupils should be able to name specific groups, such as solids, liquids and gases.
- Some pupils should also be able to explain why a material belongs to a particular group.

How Science Works

- Pupils should recognise that science is a communal activity (1.1a2).

Functional Skills Link-up

ICT
- Select and use appropriate ICT-based and other forms of information which match requirements (level 2).

Answers to in-text questions

a It is strong.

b Cobalt, iron or nickel (or alloys of) as these are the only magnetic metals.

c Thinsulate is designed for sports people by regulating the body's temperature, it is non-allergenic; wool is heavier and absorbs water if it rains.

- Once the pupils have completed their investigation, review their findings. Then, using books or an ICT resource, they should find a use of each of the materials seen. It is important for them to try to suggest a reason why that material is used for that purpose.

Plenary Suggestions

Designer materials
Ask pupils what properties the material used to make the body of a spacecraft should have. [For example: low density so the rocket can take off more easily, high melting point so it won't melt as it enters a planet's atmosphere, easy to shape and join so the rocket can be manufactured, strong so the craft will keep its shape when subjected to large forces.] (5 mins)

Material fact
Show pupils a picture of an object made of several materials, such as a car. Ask them to identify the different materials and to say why each is used. [For example: glass for windows as it's transparent and hard; steel for bodywork as it is strong, relatively cheap and easily shaped; rubber for tyres so they can be inflated and are soft enough to grip the road, ABS plastic for bumpers so they can flex to absorb bumps without breaking.] (10 mins)

Practical Support

Classifying Materials

Equipment and materials required
Labelled samples of different materials, such as copper, steel, aluminium, a magnet, diamond (which could be represented by a picture or by a substitute colourless crystal, such as cubic zirconium – often used in jewellery), wood, cotton cloth, nylon cloth, wool, polyester, polycarbonate (Perspex), poly(ethene) (polythene), liquid glue.

Details
Ask pupils to observe the materials and to complete the table. It may be best to place the materials around the room in small groups so that pupils can visit each 'station' as a circus.

Safety
Do not use large pieces of metal which could injure feet if dropped.

Differentiation

SEN
A sorting activity worksheet would help pupils link different materials with their properties and suggested uses.

Extension
Encourage pupils to differentiate between different metals and not just describe a material as 'metal'. They should also try to do the same for polymeric materials (plastics). Ask pupils to research different types of plastic.

Homework Suggestion

Find out what material is used to make the windows of space rockets. [Diamond, so it's hard enough to withstand the massive pressure differences between the inside and outside of the craft but is still transparent.]

C1.2 Building Blocks

NC links for the lesson
- Elements consist of atoms that combine together in chemical reactions to form compounds.
- Use scientific ideas and models to explain phenomena.

Learning Objectives
Pupils should learn:
- What matter is made from.
- What an element is.
- Why we use models in science.

Learning Outcomes
- All pupils should be able to list examples of elements.
- Most pupils should be able to recall a definition of 'element'.
- Some pupils should also be able to explain why a given model is an example of an element and explain advantages and disadvantages of using a particular model.

How Science Works
- Describe more than one model to explain the same phenomenon and discuss the strengths and weaknesses of each model.
- Describe how the use of a particular model or analogy supports an explanation (1.1a1).

Functional Skills Link-up
English
- Present information on complex subjects concisely and clearly (level 2)

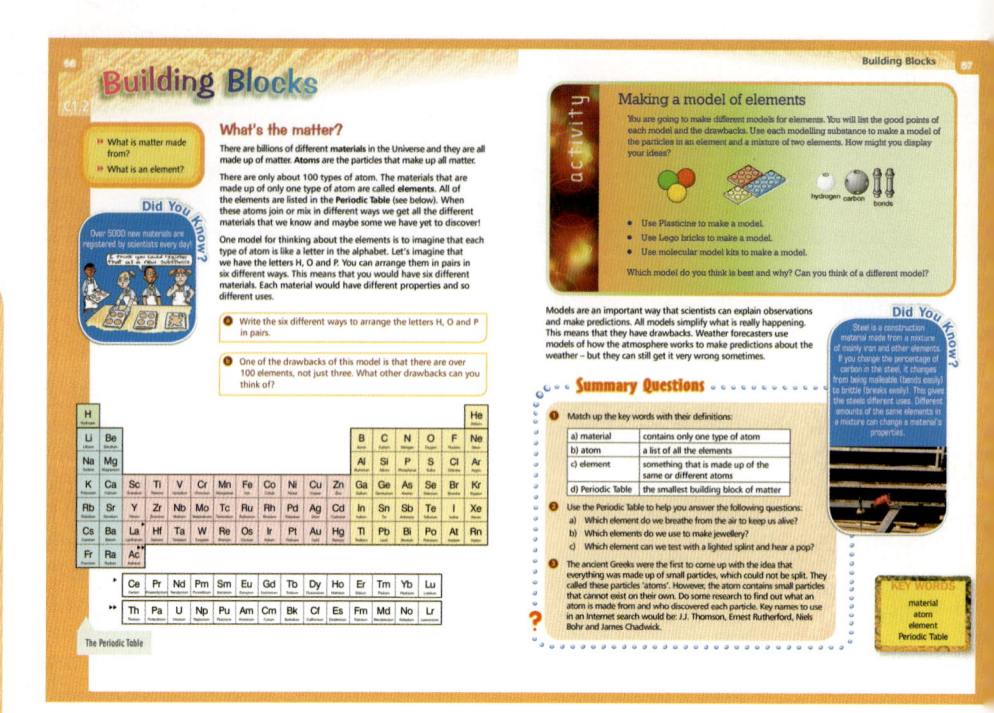

Answers to in-text questions

a) HOP; HPO; POH; PHO; OPH; OHP.

b) Sometimes the elements are joined, other times they are mixed. In this model the elements are always mixed.

Learning Styles
Visual: Making models of elements.
Auditory: Describing their observations.
Kinaesthetic: Making models of elements.
Intrapersonal: Understanding the concept that matter is made of atoms which are too small to see.

Answers to Summary questions

1. a) Material – something that is made up of the same or different atoms.
   b) Atom – the smallest building block of matter.
   c) Element – contains only one type of atom.
   d) Periodic Table – a list of all the elements.

2. a) Oxygen.
   b) Any suitable metal e.g. gold, silver, platinum, copper. Consider answers about precious stones, e.g. carbon for diamond.
   c) Hydrogen.

3. Research.

Building Blocks

The Lesson

Starter Suggestions

Building blocks
Pupils must guess how many different substances there are in the universe [billions] and how many different types of atom there are [about 100]. (5 mins)

Material world
Ask pupils to list all the different materials they can see in the room. This will help identify any pupils who are having difficulty distinguishing materials from objects. Longest list wins. (10 mins)

Main Lesson

- Remind pupils of the work they did last lesson on materials and discuss the number and range of different materials on Earth. Scientists are registering around 5000 new materials every day. Ask pupils why we cannot be sure how many different substances there are in the universe. [There are too many to catalogue reliably and people have not visited the whole universe.]

- Show pupils a copy of the Periodic Table of the elements [This is the full title.] There is one in the pupil book on page 56. Explain to them that scientists believe that all the substances in the universe are made from just the elements in the Periodic Table. Establish that there are about 100 elements listed in the Periodic Table. Only elements are listed in the Periodic Table.

- Establish that each of the elements is made up of a different type of atom and that the definition of an elemental substance is that it contains only one type of atom. All the other substances in the universe are made from combinations of the elements.

- Get pupils to carry out the activity, 'Making a model of elements'. The purpose of this activity is to test different ways of modelling elements and to consider their limitations. They could record their opinions about the suitability of each model in a table. [Plasticine is the weakest model as it does not show that atoms of an element have a uniform size nor that they can be taken apart easily and re-assembled. Lego provides a very good model if bricks of the same colour are used. However, the bricks should also be the same size. The molecular model kits provide, unsurprisingly, the best model as they show uniform atoms which can only be joined in particular ways. They also allow groups of atoms to be broken apart and reassembled easily. With all the models pupils will not have successfully represented an element unless they choose pieces of one colour.]

- Give pupils the opportunity to discuss their ideas with each other and to debate the merits of each model.

Plenary Suggestions

Elementary
Show pupils pictures of models of elements made from Lego, Plasticine and molecular models. Ask them to identify which ones are elements and to explain why. [The models only represent an element if they show only one colour or atom (particle).] (5 mins)

What's it like?
Ask pupils to produce a poster to define an element, which could be put on the classroom wall. (10 mins)

Practical Support

Making a model of elements

Equipment and materials required
Per group: selection of Lego bricks, of different sizes and colours; 2–3 golf-ball-sized lumps of Plasticine, each lump a different colour; molecular model kit (Moly-Mod or similar).

Details
Refer to pupil book and to lesson outline. If you do not have sufficient equipment for each group, stations could be placed around the room for the pupils to move between.

Safety
Normal laboratory rules apply.

Differentiation

SEN
Some pupils may cope better with a more basic definition of an element: 'a substance is only an element if it is listed on the Periodic Table or if it can't be broken down into a simpler substance'.

Extension
Ask pupils to research the most recently discovered element. [It will have an atomic number greater than 110 and will, almost certainly, have been discovered in a nuclear reaction such as those carried out at CERN, Switzerland.]

Homework Suggestion

Pupils could find out as much as they can about a particular element. You could choose one yourself or allow pupils free choice.

C1.3 Elements and their Properties

NC links for the lesson
- Elements consist of atoms that combine together in chemical reactions to form compounds.
- Use a range of scientific methods and techniques to develop and test ideas and explanations.
- Explore the ethical and moral implications of using and applying science.
- Carry out practical and investigative activities, both individually and in groups.
- Contribute to presentations and discussions about scientific issues.

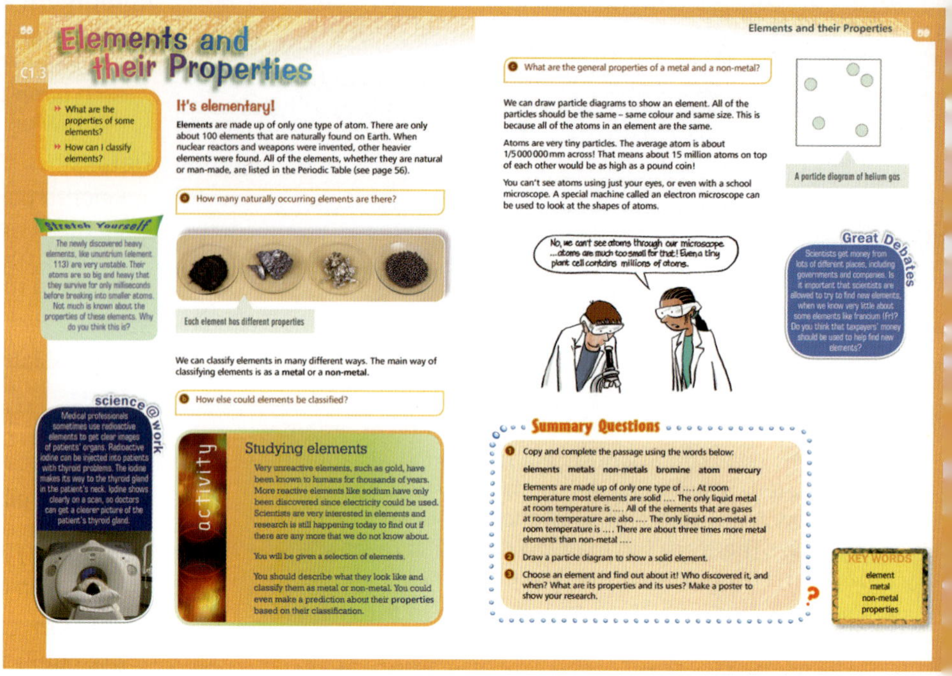

Functional Skills Link-up
English
- Make significant contributions in discussions, helping to move discussion forward to reach decisions (level 2).

Learning Styles
Visual: Making observations of elements.

Auditory: Describing their observations.

Kinaesthetic: Carrying out practical work.

Interpersonal: Taking part in the class debate.

Intrapersonal: Understanding the idea that there may be more elements left to discover.

Learning Objectives
Pupils should learn:
- How to test and record the properties of elements.
- How to classify elements.

Learning Outcomes
- All pupils should be able to determine some properties of elements.
- Most pupils should be able to group elements into metals and non-metals.
- Some pupils should also be able to predict an element's properties based on its position in the Periodic Table.

How Science Works
- Recognise that decisions about the use and application of science and technology are influenced by society and individuals and how these could impact on people and the environment (Great Debates) (1.1b).

Answers to in-text questions
a About 100 (92 in fact), the rest occur as a result of nuclear reactions.

b State of matter at room temperature, hazard, alphabetically, etc.

c Metal: conductor, shiny, high melting and boiling point, ductile, malleable, sonorous.

Non-metal: insulator, dull, low melting and boiling point, brittle.

Answers to summary questions
1 Elements are made up of only one type of **atom**. At room temperature most elements are solid **metals**. The only liquid metal at room temperature is **mercury**. All of the elements that are gases at room temperature are also **non-metals**. The only liquid non-metal at room temperature is **bromine**. There are about three times more metal elements than non-metal **elements**.

2

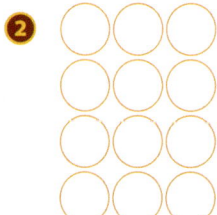

3 Research.

Elements and their Properties

The Lesson

Starter Suggestions

Elements song
Play pupils the *Elements Song,* by Tom Lehrer. Search for it on Google. You should be able to find it easily by typing in 'Elements Song Tom Lehrer' into any search engine. Ask them to try to count how many elements he mentions and if they can think of any he doesn't. (5 mins)

What the use?
Show pupils a selection of materials and a list of possible uses. Ask them to match the material to the use. (10 mins)

Main Lesson

- Remind pupils of the work they did about elements last lesson. Ask them to describe what an element is [a substance made from only one type of atom (and listed on the Periodic Table)].
- Discuss the fact that some elements are radioactive, in conjunction with the 'science @ work' section in the pupil book. [Radioactive elements are used in medicine, even though they may harm the patient. They may be given to a patient because they are the only way to see if a body organ is functioning or because the alternative is complex surgery which carries a greater risk of complications than a dose of radiation.]
- Explain to pupils that they are going to investigate some of the properties of elements by carrying out the 'Studying elements' activity described in the pupil book. See details in the 'Practical Support' section
- Ask pupils to decide which elements they think are metals and which are not, suggesting why. Establish that metals are usually shiny in appearance, solid and conduct electricity, though there are exceptions. For example, mercury metal is liquid at room temperature and the non-metal carbon in the form of graphite can conduct electricity.
- Refer to the Periodic Table on page 56 of the pupil book and locate the elements pupils have met today on it. Establish that the Periodic Table is arranged to place elements with similar properties together and that all the metals are on the left-hand side while the non-metals are on the right. In fact about 75% of the elements are metals, only a triangle of elements on the upper right-hand side of the table are non-metals.
- If you have time, ask pupils to debate the issue raised in the pupil book in the 'Great Debates' section. Pupils may need you to explain to them what tax is. Draw out that without scientific research new discoveries are harder to come by and we would not be able to develop new medicines, materials or energy sources so easily. They may also consider that scientific research is slow, expensive and, as private companies make money from new products, they should pay for all the research themselves. They could follow this up with some homework to extend the scope of their understanding.

Plenary Suggestions

What's a metal?
Ask pupils to sort a list of properties into those they think apply to metals and those which apply to non-metals. [Metals: conduct heat and electricity, sonorous, ductile, malleable, high melting point and boiling point, shiny appearance. Non-metals: opposites of metal properties, brittle rather than malleable, etc.] (5 mins)

Metal mad
Give pupils a paper Periodic Table and ask them to colour in the squares for any element they are sure is a metal. Check their answers and show them which ones are metals on a large Periodic Table. (10 mins)

Practical Support

Studying elements

Equipment and materials required
Per group: circuit to test electrical conductivity: 6V power supply/cells, lamp and three wires, piece of charcoal/graphite, labelled 'Carbon' [non-metal], piece of 'Sulfur' [non-metal], sealed jar labelled 'Oxygen' [non-metal], small phial of 'Iodine' crystals (sealed) [non-metal], mercury thermometer, labelled 'Mercury' [metal], piece of 'Copper' foil [metal], piece of 'Magnesium' ribbon, [metal], 'Iron' nail, [metal], piece of 'Zinc' foil [metal].

Details
Refer to pupil book and lesson outline. Get pupils to complete a table noting their observations of an element's appearance, electrical conductivity, state at room temperature, if it bends, and so on.

Pupils should only attempt to test the electrical conductivity of solid elements, noting 'Unable to test' in the table where they cannot. Charcoal (carbon) may conduct electricity but it is still a non-metal and shows an exception.

Safety
Sulfur: CLEAPSS Hazcard 96A.

Magnesium: CLEAPSS Hazcard 59A.

Do not warm the iodine as it may vaporise. Do not touch iodine: CLEAPSS Hazcard 54A.

Differentiation

SEN
Instead of having a whole class debate, ask pupils to consider specific statements in small groups. They could consider ideas like: 'Without scientific research there would be no new cures for diseases' or 'The money wasted in scientific research would be better spent on new schools and hospitals'. Pupils may then feel able to join in with the whole class debate.

Extension
Give pupils some cards giving brief details about elements, including physical and chemical information. Ask them to sort the cards into groups of their choosing. Then ask them to compare their groups to the locations of elements on the Periodic Table. The aim of this activity is for pupils to realise that the Periodic Table was originally worked out in this way and that elements which are close together in the Periodic Table have similar properties.

Homework Suggestion

Find out which non-metals conduct electricity. [Silicon and carbon are the main ones.] To extend the 'Great debates', you could ask pupils to find out what scientific research two commercial companies carry out. [For example, a television manufacturer is always looking for ways to improve picture quality, and pharmaceutical companies search for new drugs.] Ask pupils to say whether they think the work is important, who makes the decisions and what are the impacts on people of the new developments.

C1.4 Symbols

NC links for the lesson
- Elements consist of atoms that combine together in chemical reactions to form compounds.
- Use a range of scientific methods and techniques to develop and test ideas and explanations.

Learning Objectives
Pupils should learn:
- Why elements have symbols.
- How to find out the symbol for an element.

Learning Outcomes
- All pupils should be able to recall that elements can be represented by a symbol as well as a name.
- Most pupils should be able to use the Periodic Table to find the name or symbol of an element.
- Some pupils should also be able to explain why the element symbols are useful for scientists.

How Science Works
- Use a range of scientific vocabulary and terminology consistently in discussions and written work (1.1c).

Functional Skills Link-up
ICT
- Select and use appropriate sources of ICT-based and other forms of information which match requirements (level 2).

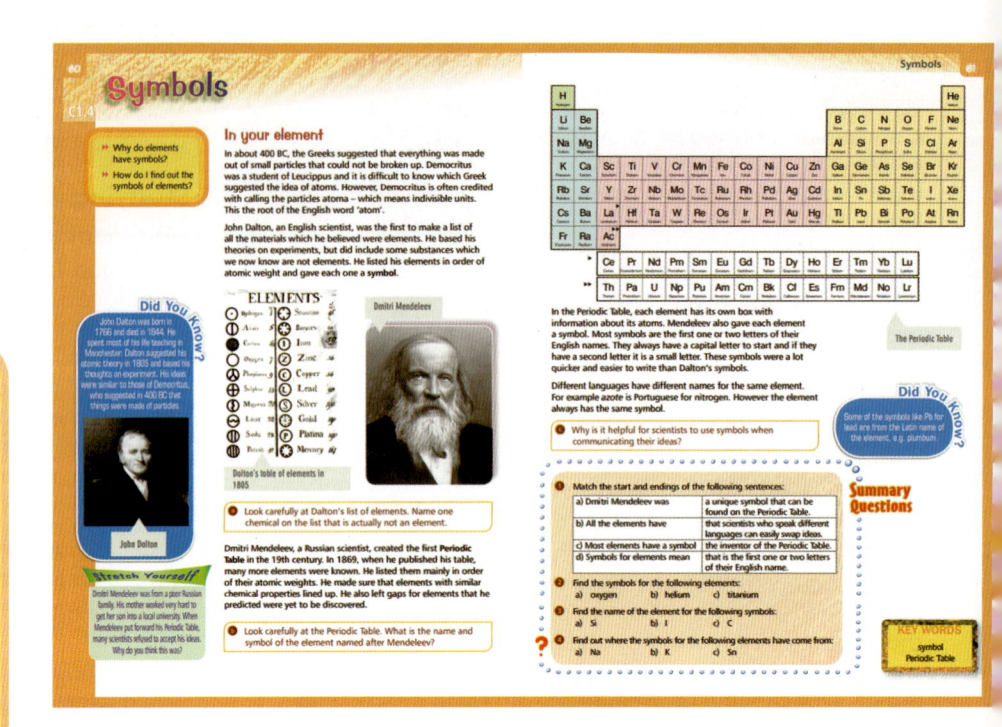

Answers to Summary questions

1
a) Dmitri Mendeleev was the inventor of the Periodic Table.
b) All the elements have a unique symbol that can be found on the Periodic Table.
c) Most elements have a symbol that is the first one or two letters of their English name.
d) Symbols for elements mean that scientists who speak different languages can easily swap ideas.

2
a) O
b) He
c) Ti

3
a) Silicon.
b) Iodine.
c) Carbon.

4
a) Natrium.
b) Kalium.
c) Stannum.

Learning Styles
Visual: Looking at the Periodic Table.
Auditory: Reading element names and symbols.
Kinaesthetic: Manipulating card sorts.

Symbols

The Lesson

Starter Suggestions

Metal or non-metal?
Give pupils the names of some elements and ask them to sort them into metals or non-metals. (5 mins)

Shorty
Give pupils some commonly used abbreviations and ask them to say what the full word/term is. They could be from written English, (such as e.g. – for example, etc. – etcetera), from scientific language (such as cm – centimetres, kg – kilograms) or text-speak (such as B4 – before, CUL8R – see you later, btw – by the way, lol – laugh out loud). (10 mins)

Main Lesson

- Remind pupils of the work they have done on elements over the past few lessons and of the Periodic Table.
- Use the pupil book to find out how the Periodic Table was developed. Pupils could extend this phase of the lesson by using other sources of information, such as the Internet.
- Ask pupils why we use abbreviations and establish that they are a quick way of writing a long word or phrase. Introduce the idea that elements have a symbol which works like an abbreviation of their name.
- Give the pupils a copy of the Periodic Table and start to look at the symbols for the elements. Emphasise that where there is more than one letter in a symbol, only the first is capitalised and any others written in lower case. This is very important as, for example, Co is cobalt but CO is a compound called carbon monoxide.
- Make a set of cards with different symbols from the Periodic Tables. The pupils can use these to play snap.
- Pupils may ask about some of the symbols which don't appear to be related to the name, such as Pb for lead and Fe for iron. Explain that not all element symbols were decided by English speaking scientists and that many are based on other languages. Sometimes the obvious symbol is not chosen to avoid a clash. For example, sulfur and sodium can't both be 'S'.

Plenary Suggestions

Fastest finder
Call out the names of some elements and ask pupils to find the symbol. Fastest correct response wins. You could reverse it and call out the symbol. Make this more difficult by asking about some less common elements that pupils will have to look up on the Periodic Table rather than remember. (5 mins)

Code name
Ask pupils to try to write their name in code using element names. [For example, Nick could be Nickel carbon potassium. If there isn't a symbol they could take one symbol away from another, e.g. one way to get an 'm' is to say manganese — nitrogen.] (10 mins)

Differentiation

SEN
Focus on the more obvious symbols first, such as S for sulfur and O for oxygen before moving on to the two-letter symbols and, perhaps, to symbols which don't seem to match the name.

Extension
Ask pupils to research why elements don't have symbols which match their names, such as Ag, Pb and Fe. [Fe comes from the word 'ferrous'. Materials containing iron are often described as ferrous. Pb is from the latin word for lead which is *plumbum*. Water pipes used to be made of lead and the people who fitted them became known as 'plumbers' so the word does appear in English. Ag is from the Latin word for silver. Today the French word for money, which used to be made from silver, is *argent*.]

Homework Suggestion

The pupils could find out who John Newlands was and what influence he had on the development of the Periodic Table.

Answers to in-text questions

a. Magnesia, lime, soda, potash, barytes [platina and azote are elements but have modern names: platinum and nitrogen, respectively].

b. Md, Mendelevium.

c. It is a shorthand way (saves time) and also every scientist understands – no matter which language they speak.

C1.5 Compounds and their Elements

NC links for the lesson
- Elements consist of atoms that combine together in chemical reactions to form compounds.
- Use a range of scientific methods and techniques to develop and test ideas and explanations.
- Assess risk and work safely in the laboratory, field and workplace.
- Carry out practical and investigative activities, both individually and in groups.

Learning Objectives
Pupils should learn:
- What a compound is.
- How compounds are different from elements.

Learning Outcomes
- All pupils should be able to give examples of compounds.
- Most pupils should be able to recall a definition of a compound and recognise a model of a compound.
- Some pupils should also be able to explain why a model of a compound represents a compound.

How Science Works
- Explain how to take action to control the risks to themselves and others, and demonstrate competence in their practical techniques (1.2c).

Answers to in-text questions

a Electricity. Electricity has enabled different experiments to be carried out and analysis machines to be developed. It has also made communication tools, e.g. the telephone and computers possible, letting scientists share ideas with each other.

b It is made up of two types of atom (hydrogen joined (or bonded) to oxygen).

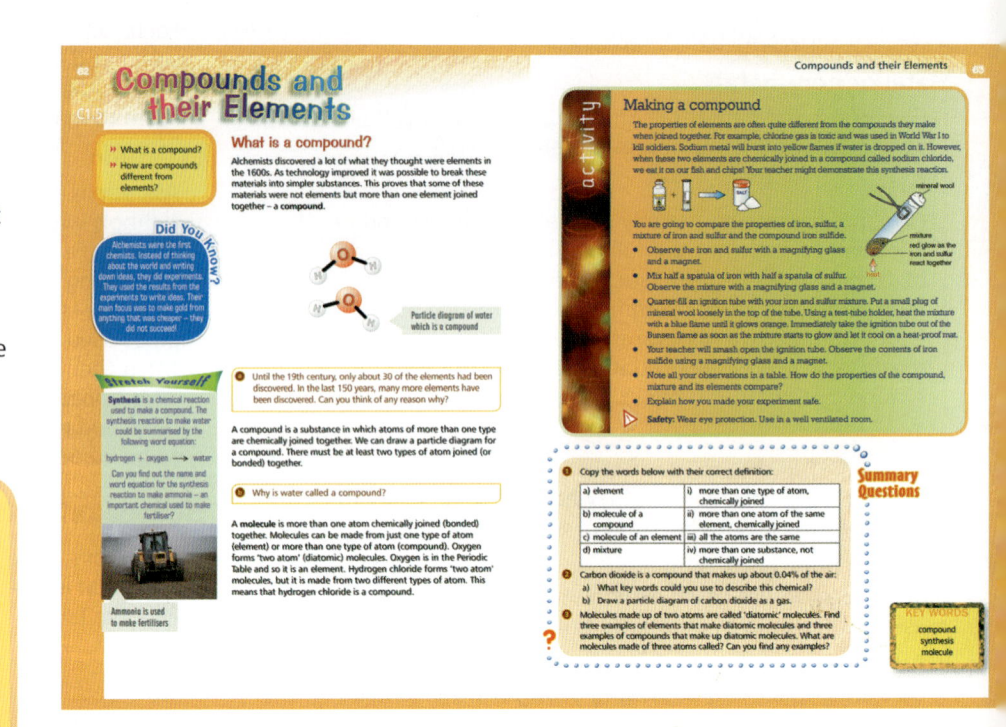

The Lesson

Starter Suggestions

Odd one out
Show pupils four pictures (or just give them the names) of: sulfur, iron, gold and water. Ask them to decide which one is the odd one out and why. [Water is not an element and does not appear on the Periodic Table.] (5 mins)

Element symbols
Give pupils a recall test involving element names and symbols. Either give them the element name and ask them to recall the symbol, or the other way around. If they have to write the symbol, give two marks for a correct answer; one for the correct letters and one for using upper case for the first letter and lower case for any others. (10 mins)

Main Lesson

- Remind pupils of the work they have done on elements and symbols. Refer to work earlier in the unit about the existence of millions of different substances in the universe which are made from only a few (about 100) elements.
- Demonstrate the reaction between sodium and chlorine gas, which produces sodium chloride. The method for this is described in the 'Practical Support' section. Guidance and extra information for pupils is contained in the pupil book.
- Establish that the product does not seem to be like either of the elements it was made from.
- Get pupils to make iron sulfide, as described in the activity 'Making a compound' in the pupil book.

Learning Styles
Visual: Making observations.
Auditory: Describing their observations.
Kinaesthetic: Carrying out practical work to make a compound.
Intrapersonal: Understanding the concept that atoms can join together to form molecules of elements or compounds.

Compounds and their Elements

- Review the practical with the pupils looking for evidence of differences between the properties of the elements and the compound formed. [The sulfur powder is yellow and the iron filings are slightly shiny and magnetic. The iron sulfide compound is dull in appearance and non-magnetic. Un-reacted iron may mean that the compound appears to be magnetic still.]

Plenary Suggestions

Txt spk
Ask the pupils to write what they have learned in this lesson as a text message. They can use text abbreviations if it helps but they must not use more than 100 characters, including spaces. (5 mins)

Spot the compound
Show pupils some particle diagrams, representing elements and compounds. Pupils must correctly identify the compounds. (10 mins)

Practical Support

Demonstration: Reaction between chlorine gas and sodium metal

Equipment and materials required
For demonstration: 2 gas jars filled with chlorine gas and a lid placed on top, 2 small pieces of sodium, cubes approx 2–3 mm each side, deflagrating spoon (unless using alternative method, see under 'Safety'), matches, Bunsen burner, fume cabinet, eye protection (goggles).

Details
Place a piece of sodium onto the deflagrating spoon and ignite using the Bunsen burner. Immediately slide the lid off the gas jar and place the spoon and sodium into the chlorine. White fumes of sodium chloride will be seen. The fumes may be grey if the sodium is contaminated with oil. Repeat with the other piece of sodium and jar of chlorine if the first fails.

Safety
Chlorine: CLEAPSS Hazcard 22A.
Sodium: CLEAPSS Hazcard 88.
To avoid using a deflagrating spoon, see CLEAPSS L195 for an alternative method.
Must be carried out in a fume cabinet.
Wear eye protection or a full-face visor.
Asthmatics must take care not to breathe in any gases.

Making a compound (iron sulfide)

Equipment and materials required
Per group: half a spatula of sulfur powder, half a spatula of fine iron filings, magnifying glass, magnet, ignition tube (use old tubes as they will be broken during the experiment), small piece of mineral wool to plug ignition tube, Bunsen burner and flame-proof mat, spatula, test-tube holder, matches, eye protection.
For class teacher: small hammer, old rag (to prevent broken ignition tube pieces from escaping), eye protection.

Details
Refer to pupil book. Once the contents of the tube begin to glow red, the reaction should continue on its own and should be taken from the flame. Pupils will need help to break the ignition tube, which should be wrapped in a rag before breaking with a hammer. An alternative is to demonstrate the breaking of a single tube and the testing of the product inside it. When asking pupils to check the magnetic properties of the iron filings, make sure that the iron is inside the test tube and the magnet outside. Filings are very difficult to remove from the surface of a magnet.

Safety
Sulfur: CLEAPSS Hazcard 96A. See L195.
Only fill ignition tube one-quarter full.
Ensure the room is well ventilated, especially if there are asthma sufferers in the room. Plug tube with mineral wool.
If the sulfur ignites, sulfur dioxide will be produced, which is an irritant.
Ensure no sulfur is on the outside of the ignition tubes before it is put into the flame.
Beware of fragments of glass from broken ignition tubes.

Differentiation

SEN
Concentrate on the concrete idea that compounds do not have the same properties as the elements they are made from, rather then the much more conceptual issue of molecule formation.

Extension
Challenge pupils to explain why water doesn't burn. [Burning is generally thought of as an oxidation reaction. Since, in forming water (H_2O), hydrogen must have already reacted with oxygen in some sort of 'burning' reaction and cannot, therefore, burn again. Oxygen, contrary to popular belief, does not burn as it cannot react with oxygen.]

Homework Suggestion

The pupils could find out who Alchemists were. [Alchemists were early chemists, usually considered to have been working around the 1600s to 1700s. Many were attempting to turn metals into gold.]

Answers to Summary questions

1. a) Element: all the atoms are the same: (iii).
   b) Molecule of a compound: more than one type of atom, chemically joined: (i).
   c) Molecule of an element: more than one atom of the same element, chemically joined: (ii).
   d) Mixture: more than one substance, not chemically joined: (iv).

2. a) Compound / molecule.
   b)

3. Examples of diatomic elements include [three of]: oxygen, chlorine, fluorine, nitrogen, hydrogen, bromine.
   Examples of diatomic compounds include: HCl, HF and HBr [as gases and not dissolved in water, which causes them to ionise].

C1.6 Compound Names

NC links for the lesson
- Elements consist of atoms that combine together in chemical reactions to form compounds.

Learning Objectives
Pupils should learn:
- How to name a compound.
- To state the elements in a compound from the compound name.

Learning Outcomes
- All pupils should be able to recognise the metal and non-metal in an -ide compound.
- Most pupils should be able to name simple compounds.
- Some pupils should also be able to name the elements in more complex compounds, such as -ates

How Science Works
- Use a range of scientific vocabulary and terminology consistently in discussions and written work (1.1c).

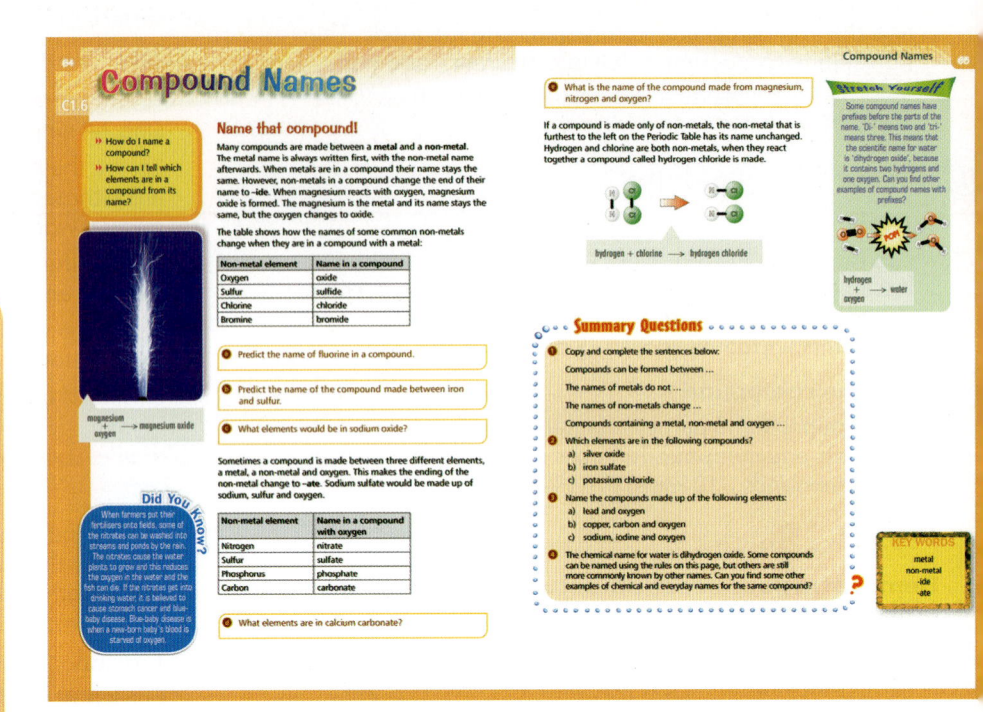

Learning Styles
Auditory: Describing and discussing the rules for naming compounds.
Kinaesthetic: Card sort.
Interpersonal: Discussing with others.
Intrapersonal: Understanding that names have an origin.

Answers to Summary questions

1. E.g. Compounds can be formed between elements, a metal and non-metal or more than one non-metal.
   The names of metals do not change in a compound.
   The names of non-metals change when they are in a compound.
   Compounds containing a metal, non-metal and oxygen have the ending -ate.

2. a) Silver, oxygen.
   b) Iron, sulfur and oxygen.
   c) Potassium, chlorine.

3. a) Lead oxide.
   b) Copper carbonate.
   c) Sodium iodate.

4. For example, poly(ethene) is usually called polythene. Teflon, the non-stick pan coating, has the chemical name poly(tetrafluoroethene).

Compound Names

The Lesson

Starter Suggestions

What's in a name?
Ask pupils why they think a 'bicycle' is so called and where the name 'television' comes from. [A 'bi-cycle' has two wheels. 'Tele-vision' refers to the sending of pictures over a distance.] (5 mins)

Word up!
Make as many words as you can using the letters contained in the words 'magnesium oxide'. (10 mins)

Main Lesson

- Remind pupils of the work they have done on elements and compounds and explain that the name of a compound can tell you what is in it. This lesson is essentially about learning the 'rules' for naming compounds and much of it can be achieved by following the pupil book.
- Demonstrate the reaction between magnesium and oxygen (air). Explain that the white powder formed is magnesium oxide and is so called because it contains only magnesium and oxygen. This would be a very good opportunity to reinforce the idea that compounds are different to the elements they are formed from, which the pupils learned in the last lesson.
- Ask the pupils to refer to the 'rules' for naming compounds described in the pupil book and to discuss why the rules are necessary. [They are important so that scientists developing new compounds can describe what they have made to others without confusion.]

Plenary Suggestions

What's in a name (part 2)?
Ask pupils which elements they think are found in 8-hydroxy-7-iodo-5-quinolinesulfonic acid ($C_9H_6NSO_4I$). They are unlikely to guess all the elements involved but should at least get H, O, I and S. (5 mins)

Sort it out!
Give pupils cards with element names and compound names on them and ask them to match them up. (10 mins)

Practical Support

Demonstration: Reaction between magnesium and oxygen

Equipment and materials required
For teacher: magnesium ribbon (2 cm strip, heatproof mat, tongs, Bunsen burner, eye protection.

Details
Hold the ribbon in tongs and ignite in a Bunsen flame. Remove ribbon from the Bunsen flame as soon as it lights.

Safety
Magnesium ribbon: CLEAPSS Hazcard 59A.
Warn pupils not to look directly at flame.
Pupils should observe the reaction through blue glass.

Differentiation

SEN
Avoid moving onto compounds of three elements, such as 'ates'. Ensure pupils can understand the elemental origins of basic compounds like magnesium oxide and iron sulfide. It may be better to use the plenary card sort as the main activity.

Extension
Find out the difference between carbon dioxide and carbon monoxide. [Carbon dioxide (CO_2) contains two oxygen atoms, while carbon monoxide (CO) only contains one.]

Homework Suggestion

Pupils could find out what elements are contained in the compound ethane. [Carbon and hydrogen.]

Answers to in-text questions

a Fluoride.

b Iron sulfide.

c Sodium and oxygen.

d Calcium, carbon and oxygen.

e Magnesium nitrate.

C1.7 Compound Formulas

NC links for the lesson
- Elements consist of atoms that combine together in chemical reactions to form compounds.
- Use a range of scientific methods and techniques to develop and test ideas and explanations.

Learning Objectives
Pupils should learn:
- How to write the formula for a compound.
- How to recognise the atoms in a compound from its formula.

Learning Outcomes
- All pupils should be able to name the elements in a compound from its formula.
- Most pupils should be able to state the number and type of particle from a compound formula.
- Some pupils should also be able to generate the formula of a compound from its name.

How Science Works
- Use a range of scientific vocabulary and terminology consistently in discussions and written work (1.1c).

Functional Skills Link-up
Mathematics
- Solve simple problems involving ratio, where one number is a multiple of the other (level 1).

Learning Styles
Visual: Making observations.
Auditory: Describing the rules for reading formulas.
Kinaesthetic: Forming molecules using themselves as atoms.
Interpersonal: Working with others to form molecules.
Intrapersonal: Understanding the concept that atoms can only bond in a certain way.

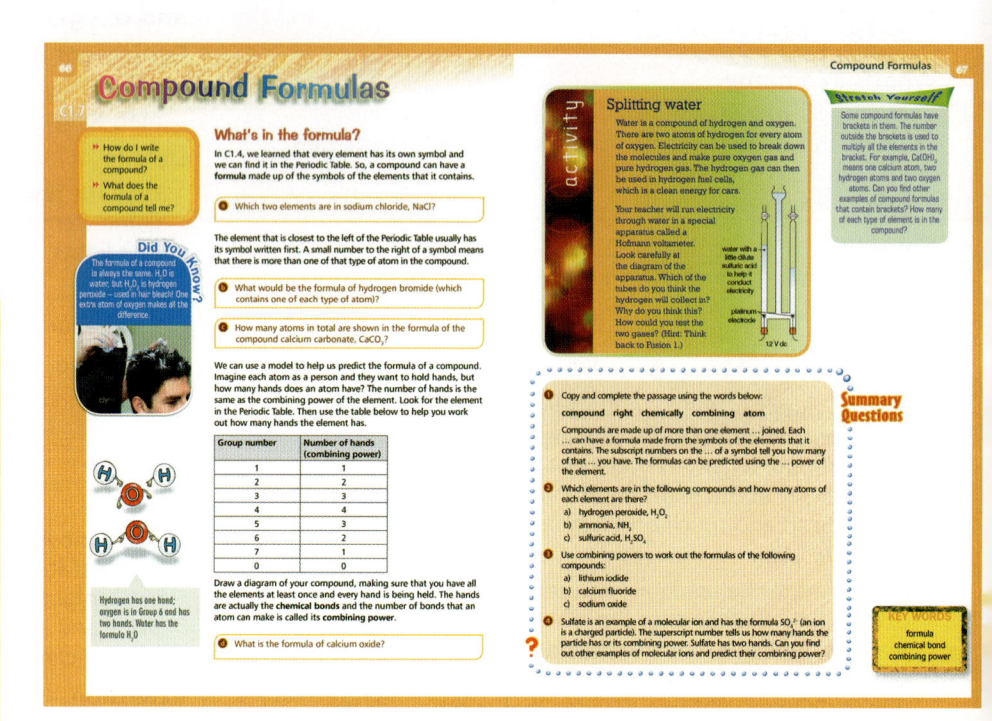

The Lesson

Starter Suggestions

Tessellation mania
Ask pupils to tessellate hexagons on a page and then to try to do the same thing with octagons. [They will find that octagons leave small squares between them.] This starter will link to the idea that atoms can only be joined together in certain ways. (5 mins)

Some of the pieces are missing!
Give pupils a sheet with parts of a house on it: roofs, buildings, doors and windows. The pupils must cut out the pieces and make as many complete houses as they can. A complete house has walls, a roof, a door and four windows. Make sure that pupils have some spare pieces that they cannot use. If pupils ask, allow them to swap pieces with each other or give them away. The purpose of this activity is to help pupils realise that a house, like a molecule, is not complete unless it has the right pieces. (10 mins)

Answers to Summary questions

1. Compounds are made up of more than one element **chemically** joined. Each **compound** can have a formula made from the symbols of the elements that it contains. The sub-script numbers on the **right** of a symbol tell you how many of that **atom** you have. The formulas can be predicted using the **combining** power of the element.

2. a) 2× hydrogen, 2× oxygen = 4
   b) 1× nitrogen, 3× hydrogen = 4
   c) 2× hydrogen, 1× sulfur, 4× oxygen = 7

3. a) LiI
   b) CaF_2
   c) Na_2O

4. Research.

Compound Formulas

Main Lesson

- Remind pupils of the work they have done regarding forming compounds. Explain that compounds are made of molecules which are groups of atoms that are joined together.
- Demonstrate the electrolysis of water using a Hofmann voltameter. You will obtain twice the volume of hydrogen as oxygen. This is an excellent opportunity to review the tests for hydrogen and oxygen which the pupils should have met in Year 7. [Hydrogen burns with a squeaky pop and oxygen relights a glowing splint.]
- Pupils may well know that the formula for water is H_2O. Explain that this means that each molecule of water has two atoms of hydrogen and one atom of oxygen. This is shown by the results of the electrolysis experiment.
- Ask pupils to work in groups of six and use themselves as atoms to make up some molecules using the 'hands' suggestion in the pupil book. They could start by making two water molecules and then move on to making other simple molecules like hydrogen bromide (HBr) and carbon dioxide (CO_2). You will need to tell pupils what atoms are involved and how many of each. Suggested molecules to start with include: NaCl, MgO, $MgBr_2$, HF, $CaCl_2$, Na_2O. Higher attaining pupils could then move on to trying to find a way to model these: NH_3, $AlCl_3$, CO_2, N_2, O_2, C_2H_4. This would provide another good opportunity to consider the drawbacks of this way of modelling formulas.
- Lower attaining pupils may find the activity suggested above more accessible if Moly-Mod kits are used. The kits could be used to make models of a series of compounds (as above), and then they could make their own designs of compounds and use them to write the formulas.
- Explain to pupils that molecules can only have one formula as the atoms can only be joined together in a certain way. Run through the 'rules' for reading formulas. [If there is no number after an element symbol, then there is one atom of that element. In other cases, the number after an element indicates the number of atoms of that element in the molecule.]
- Give pupils some examples of formulas and ask them to describe what atoms and how many of each type are present. For example MgO contains one magnesium atom and one oxygen atom, C_2H_6 contains 2 carbon atoms and 6 hydrogen atoms.

Plenary Suggestions

True or false?
Show pupils a formula and then a suggestion of which atoms and how many are present. Ask them whether it is true or false. If it is false, ask them to correct the information. (5 mins)

Rules is rules
Ask pupils to summarise the rules for writing and reading a chemical formula, in five bullet points. (10 mins)

Practical Support

Demonstration: Splitting water

Equipment and materials required
For teacher: Hofmann voltameter and power supply, $100\,cm^3$ $0.5\,mol/dm^3$ sulfuric acid (tell the pupils it's water), two test tubes, matches, splints, eye protection.

Details
Pure water will not electrolyse so very dilute acid, which is almost entirely water, is used instead. Set up the apparatus and, with the taps on the voltmeter closed, allow it to operate for a few minutes. Once some gas has collected, show the pupils that about twice the volume of hydrogen collects as the volume of oxygen. The hydrogen will form over the cathode (negative electrode) and the oxygen over the anode (positive electrode). Test the gases.

Safety
Do not leave equipment operating unattended, as a build-up of explosive hydrogen will occur. Equipment is fragile. See CLEAPSS handbook/CD-Rom 11.4.2.

Sulfuric acid. CLEAPSS hazcard 98A.

No naked flames.

Use eye protection when filling.

Differentiation

SEN

Bond formation between atoms is a highly conceptual idea. A simpler model, though one with some flaws, can be found through the use of building blocks, such as Lego.

As a simple starting point, ask pupils to assemble a 'wall' two bricks high by 10 dots (Lego bricks have dots on top) long. There are only certain ways they can do this. Tell them that this is one compound and that another compound might be two bricks high and 15 dots long. Get them to make this too.

Whilst this model is a good way to teach that only certain combinations of blocks (atoms) will work the flaw lies in the fact that, unlike a compound, there is more than one way to make a given sized wall.

Extension

Use the 'Stretch yourself' section described in the pupil book.

You may also like to get pupils to consider for themselves the flaws in the suggested SEN model.

Homework Suggestion

Pupils could research who August Wilhelm von Hoffman was. Ask pupils to find out about what his contribution to chemistry was. [He was the first director of the Royal College of Chemistry, London and did much work on dyes and organic chemistry.]

Answers to in-text questions

a Sodium and chlorine.

b HBr

c 5

d CaO

C1.8 Properties of Compounds

NC links for the lesson
- Elements consist of atoms that combine together in chemical reactions to form compounds.
- Assess risk and work safely in the laboratory, field and workplace.
- Carry out practical and investigative activities, both individually and in groups.
- Use a range of scientific methods and techniques to develop and test ideas and explanations.

Learning Objectives
Pupils should learn:
- How to make a compound from elements.
- Whether the properties of a compound depend upon how it is made.

Learning Outcomes
- All pupils should be able to produce carbon dioxide by two different methods.
- Most pupils should be able to recognise that carbon dioxide has the same properties however it is produced.
- Some pupils should also be able to explain why compounds have the same properties however they are made.

How Science Works
- Explain how to take action to control the risks to themselves and others, and demonstrate competence in their practical techniques (1.2c).

Learning Styles
Visual: Making observations.
Auditory: Describing their observations.
Kinaesthetic: Carrying out practical work.
Interpersonal: Working with others during the practical and discussing ideas with other pupils.
Intrapersonal: Understanding that as the molecules are always the same, a compound has constant properties.

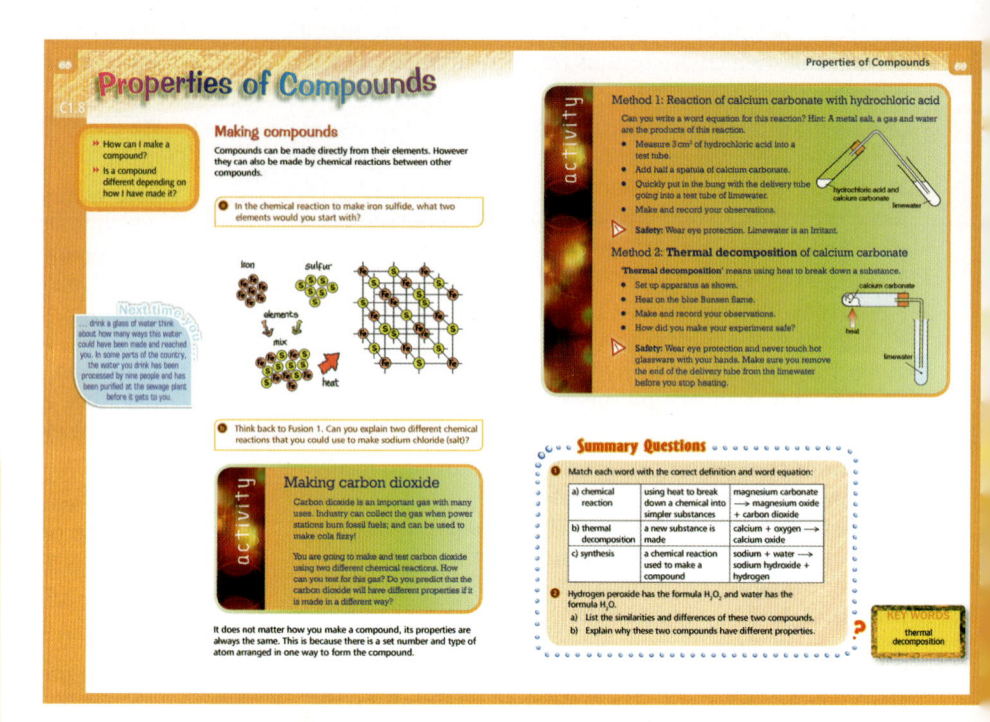

The Lesson

Starter Suggestions

Word up!
Ask pupils to make as many words as they can using the letters from 'compound' and 'element'. Longest list wins. (5 mins)

Making water
Show pupils a beaker of water and test it with blue cobalt chloride paper, showing that the paper turns pink. Hold an ice-cold watch glass over a candle or spirit burner flame for a few seconds. Show that the liquid which condenses on the glass is also water by testing it with the cobalt chloride paper. See 'Practical Support' section for details. (10 mins)

Main Lesson
- Remind pupils of their study of compounds and how forming a compound involves joining the atoms of more than one element together to form molecules.
- Pose the question: 'Are the properties of a compound different if it's made different ways?'

Answers to Summary questions

1.
   a) Chemical reaction: a new substance is made: sodium + water ⟶ sodium hydroxide + hydrogen
   b) Thermal decomposition: using heat to break down a chemical into simpler substances: magnesium carbonate ⟶ magnesium oxide + carbon dioxide
   c) Synthesis: a chemical reaction used to make a compound: calcium + oxygen ⟶ calcium oxide

2.
   a) Similarities: they are both compounds; they both contain the same elements, H and O; they both contain 2 hydrogen atoms.
      Differences: hydrogen peroxide contains an extra oxygen atom.
   b) Hydrogen peroxide has one extra oxygen atom in it. This means that the compound will have a different structure and will react differently.

Properties of Compounds

- Invite pupils to discuss the matter in pairs or small groups for a few moments and then gather the class' opinion and their reasons for their ideas. You could even get them to vote on it. This is an excellent opportunity to introduce the idea of making a prediction. After pupils are asked to make their prediction, they should explain it and suggest ways of testing it.
- Get pupils to carry out the 'Making carbon dioxide' activity described in the pupil book. They will make carbon dioxide by two different methods and show that, however it is made, it behaves the same.
- Remind pupils that the formula of carbon dioxide is CO_2. Ask them if they can now, having seen the evidence, explain why carbon dioxide always reacts with limewater in the same way. [The experiment is evidence that all molecules of carbon dioxide are the same.]

Plenary Suggestions

Mix and match
Give pupils the names of the gases oxygen, hydrogen and carbon dioxide, along with the tests for the gases and the outcomes of those tests mixed up. The challenge is to sort them out. (5 mins)

Share – pair, square
In pairs to start with, then with the table in front of/behind them, ask pupils to identify the key things they have learnt in this lesson. You could get them to share in larger and larger groups until the whole class can agree. (10 mins)

Practical Support

Demonstration: Making water
Equipment and materials required

For teacher: small beaker filled with tap water, 2–3 pieces of blue cobalt chloride paper, candle or ethanol-filled spirit burner, watch glass with ice in, tongs, matches, eye protection.

Details

Show the beaker of water and prove that it is water by dipping in a piece of blue cobalt chloride paper. The paper will turn pink. Light the candle or burner and then hold the watch glass over the flame for a few seconds. The ice on the top of the glass will cause water vapour from the flame to condense on the underside. Do not hold the glass over the flame for more than a few seconds or any vapour which condenses will re-vaporise. Test the condensation with the cobalt chloride paper to show that it too is water.

Safety

Avoid skin contact with cobalt chloride paper: CLEAPSS Hazcard 25.

Ethanol is highly flammable and harmful: CLEAPSS Hazcard 40A.

Ensure glass is heat resistant and so less likely to crack on exposure to the flame, wear eye protection.

Making carbon dioxide
Equipment and materials required

Method 1: Reaction of calcium carbonate with hydrochloric acid

Per group: 3 cm³ of 0.5 mol/dm³ hydrochloric acid, half a spatula of calcium carbonate powder (precipitated), spatula, 2 test tubes, bung to fit test tube with delivery tube attached, limewater, test tube rack, eye protection.

Method 2: Thermal decomposition of calcium carbonate

Per group: 3–4 spatulas full of calcium carbonate powder (precipitated), spatula, Bunsen burner, matches, retort stand, boss and clamp, boiling tube, bung to fit boiling tube with delivery tube attached, test tube, limewater, test tube rack, eye protection.

Details

Refer to pupil book. Emphasise that carbon dioxide is being produced and that the same result is seen each time. [Limewater turns cloudy/milky.]

Safety

Eye protection must be worn.

Limewater is an irritant: CLEAPSS Hazcard 18.

Hydrochloric acid: CLEAPSS Hazcard 47A.

Care must be exercised when heating the calcium carbonate powder to avoid fluidisation. Do not heat strongly initially.

The boiling tube containing the limewater must be taken away from the delivery tube before the heat source is removed from the carbonate or 'suck-back' will occur. Cold limewater could be sucked into the hot boiling tube and may cause it to shatter.

Differentiation

SEN
The idea of molecules is highly conceptual but pupils may find it much easier to handle the concrete evidence that carbon dioxide gas behaves the same however it is formed.

Extension
Ask pupils to use molecular model kits to demonstrate why the carbon dioxide formed is the same in each part of the practical or you could explain to them that calcium carbonate has the formula $CaCO_3$. When they heated it, one of the products was carbon dioxide, CO_2. Ask them to work out the formula, and then the name, of the other product. They should then write word and symbol equations to show the reaction.

Homework Suggestion

Pupils to find out why sherbet is fizzy. [When it gets wet, carbon dioxide is produced. Sherbet contains sodium bicarbonate and tartaric acid, as well as sugar for sweetness. As a dry powder the acid and bicarbonate do not react, when the acid does get wet, such as in the mouth, it will dissolve. This allows it to react with the sodium bicarbonate. One of the products of this acid–carbonate reaction is carbon dioxide whose presence we sense as fizzing.]

Answers to in-text questions

a Iron and sulfur.

b E.g. sodium hydroxide or sodium carbonate and hydrochloric acid.

C1.9 Word Equations

NC links for the lesson
- Elements consist of atoms that combine together in chemical reactions to form compounds.
- Use a range of scientific methods and techniques to develop and test ideas and explanations.
- Assess risk and work safely in the laboratory, field and workplace.
- Carry out practical and investigative activities, both individually and in groups.

Learning Objectives
Pupils should learn:
- How to use a word equation to describe a chemical reaction.
- What a word equation is.
- How to write a risk assessment.

Learning Outcomes
- All pupils should be able to make and record observations, recording simple hazards.
- Most pupils should be able to write simple word equations and a simple risk assessment.
- Some pupils should be able to list reactants and products from a given word equation, and write a detailed risk assessment.

How Science Works
- Explain how to take action to control the risks to themselves and others, and demonstrate competence in their practical techniques (1.2c).
- Explain how the observation and recording methods are appropriate to the tasks (1.2d).

Learning Styles
Visual: Making observations.
Auditory: Describing their observations and writing word equations.
Kinaesthetic: Carrying out practical work and creating word equations in the plenary.
Interpersonal: Working with others during practical.
Intrapersonal: Understanding how to work safely.

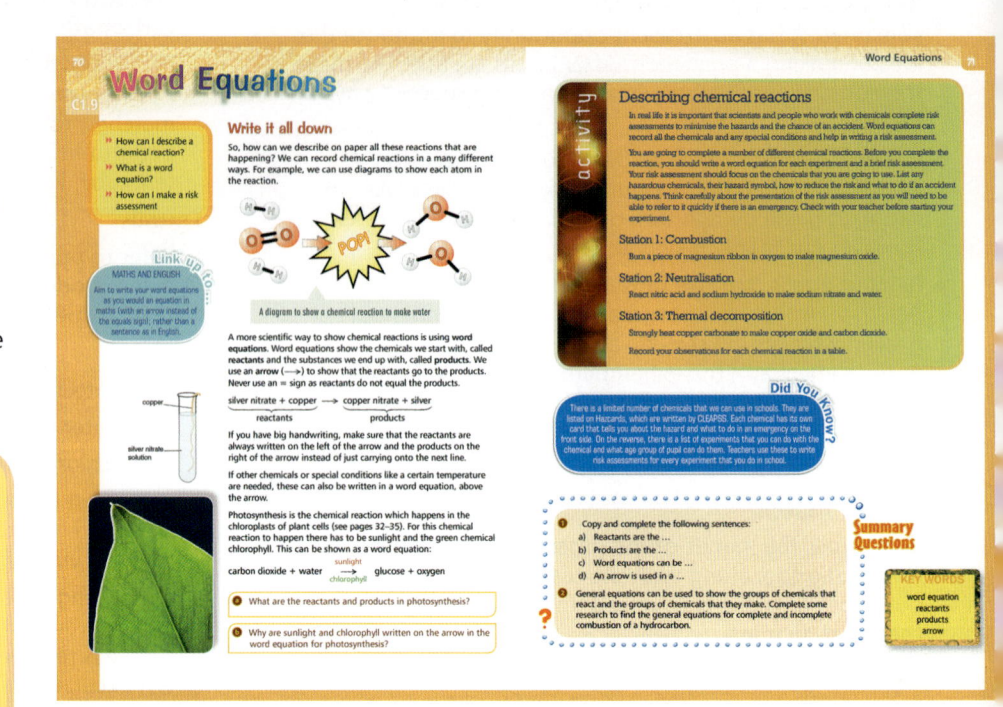

The Lesson

Starter Suggestions

Sum it up
Write *one sentence* to describe how to boil an egg and what happens to the egg when you do. (5 mins)

Chemical story
Show pupils the reaction between magnesium and hydrochloric acid. Ask them to write just one sentence to describe what they saw. For example, 'when the magnesium was placed in the acid, bubbles of gas were given off and the magnesium dissolved.' (10 mins)

Main Lesson
- Remind pupils of the reactions they have seen so far in this unit, such as that between iron and sulfur, forming iron sulfide. Establish that it would be very useful to have a simple and quick way to describe a chemical reaction. You could liken the process to writing a mathematical equation, where only the

Answers to Summary questions

1
a) Reactants are the starting chemicals in a chemical reaction.
b) Products are the ending chemicals in a chemical reaction.
c) Word equations can be used to summarise a chemical reaction.
d) An arrow is used in a word equation to show the reactants go to the products.

2 Complete combustion: hydrocarbon + oxygen $\longrightarrow$ water + carbon dioxide
Incomplete combustion: hydrocarbon + oxygen $\longrightarrow$ water + carbon dioxide + carbon monoxide + carbon

Word Equations

important information is given. Explain that, once the pupils have safely carried out some reactions, they are going to describe them using word equations.

- Ask pupils to plan and then carry out the 'Describing chemical reactions' activity from the pupil book. The emphasis here is on them planning a safe procedure and taking note of the chemicals used so they can construct word equations later. Hazard information is available from CLEAPSS and this could be shared with pupils to help them plan. Make sure pupils' risk assessments are safe before they proceed.
- Once the pupils have carried out the experiments, remind them that they need to explain what happened in each one in a shorthand format. As an example you could explain that a simple way of describing how to make chocolate might be: cocoa + milk + sugar makes chocolate. This doesn't explain exactly how to make chocolate but it does tell you what materials you start with and what you end up with.
- Establish that, in general, a word equation is written: Starting materials or reactants ⟶ Finishing materials or products
Explain to pupils that they must try to write these on one line, just as they would a mathematical equation. Chemical equations are not sentences and don't make sense if they are wrapped over more than one line. You could encourage them to write them correctly by starting with the arrow in the middle of the line on the page. If pupils have large writing, ask them to write long chemical names, like carbon dioxide, with the word carbon above dioxide.
- Ask pupils to identify the reactants from the reactions they have just carried out. Then get them to start to write the word equations. They may need help to name the products so they can complete the word equations.

Plenary Suggestions

What do you know?
Ask pupils to write an answer to the learning objective questions in the pupil book. (5 mins)

What happened?
Divide pupils up into groups of about six. Give each team a set of cards with the reactants and products they have seen in this lesson marked on them. They will also need an arrow card. Teams should take a card each and form the word equations for the reactions seen in the lesson. Fastest team wins. (10 mins)

Practical Support

Demonstration: Describing chemical reactions
Equipment and materials required for Station 1
2 cm long piece of magnesium ribbon, Bunsen burner and heat mat, matches, tongs, pieces of blue glass, eye protection.

Details
Suggested method: light burner and hold magnesium in tongs. While looking through blue glass, ignite magnesium in flame. Continue to observe through blue glass until magnesium burns out.

Safety
Flame should be observed through blue glass as it is so bright.
Magnesium ribbon: CLEAPSS Hazcard 59A. Highly flammable.

Equipment and materials required for Station 2
50 cm^3 of 0.1 mol/dm^3 nitric acid, 50 cm^3 of 0.1 mol/dm^3 sodium hydroxide, few drops of universal indicator, boiling tube, rack for boiling tube, 2 pipettes, 10 cm^3 measuring cylinder, eye protection.

Details
Suggested method: measure out 3 cm^3 of acid in the measuring cylinder and add to the boiling tube. Add 1–2 drops of universal indicator. Using a pipette, add sodium hydroxide to neutralise the acid, making the indicator turn green. If the indicator shows the solution to be alkaline, use another pipette to add a small quantity of acid.

Safety
Eye protection must be worn.
Ensure pupils behave with pipettes.
Nitric acid is an irritant: CLEAPSS Hazcard 67.
Sodium hydroxide is an irritant: CLEAPSS Hazcard 91.
Universal indicator may be flammable.

Equipment and materials required for Station 3
3–4 spatulas full of copper carbonate powder, spatula, Bunsen burner, matches, retort stand, boss, clamp, boiling tube, bung to fit boiling tube with delivery tube attached, test tube, limewater, test tube rack, eye protection.

Details
Refer to pupil book, topic C1.8, Method 2: Thermal decomposition of calcium carbonate.

Safety
Eye protection must be worn.
Care must be exercised when heating the copper carbonate powder to avoid fluidisation. Do not heat strongly initially. Use a loose mineral wool plug.
Limewater is an irritant: CLEAPSS Hazcard 18.

Differentiation

SEN
Pupils could use the cards for the 'What happened?' plenary on their own to sort out the equations.

Extension
Pupils could find out how scientists and engineers try to ensure nuclear power stations are safe. Ask pupils to write a risk assessment for Homer Simpson's job. You could show them the opening credits to *The Simpsons* as inspiration.

Homework Suggestion

Pupils could write word equations for household tasks such as baking a cake and making toast. Pupils should not aim to describe what is happening chemically but to explain the overall process. For example, flour + egg + margarine + baking powder ⟶ sponge cake.

Answers to in-text questions

a Carbon dioxide and water and glucose and oxygen.

b They are neither reactants nor products but are vital for the chemical reaction to happen.

C1.10 Symbol Equations

NC links for the lesson
- Elements consist of atoms that combine together in chemical reactions to form compounds.
- Use a range of scientific methods and techniques to develop and test ideas and explanations.
- Assess risk and work safely in the laboratory, field and workplace.
- Carry out practical and investigative activities, both individually and in groups.

Learning Objectives
Pupils should learn:
- What a symbol equation is.
- How to balance a symbol equation.

Learning Outcomes
- All pupils should be able to understand that atoms are not created or destroyed in a reaction, just rearranged.
- Most pupils should be able to recognise when a simple symbol equation is balanced.
- Some pupils should also be able to balance a symbol equation by themselves.

How Science Works
- Use a range of scientific vocabulary and terminology consistently in discussions and written work (1.1c).

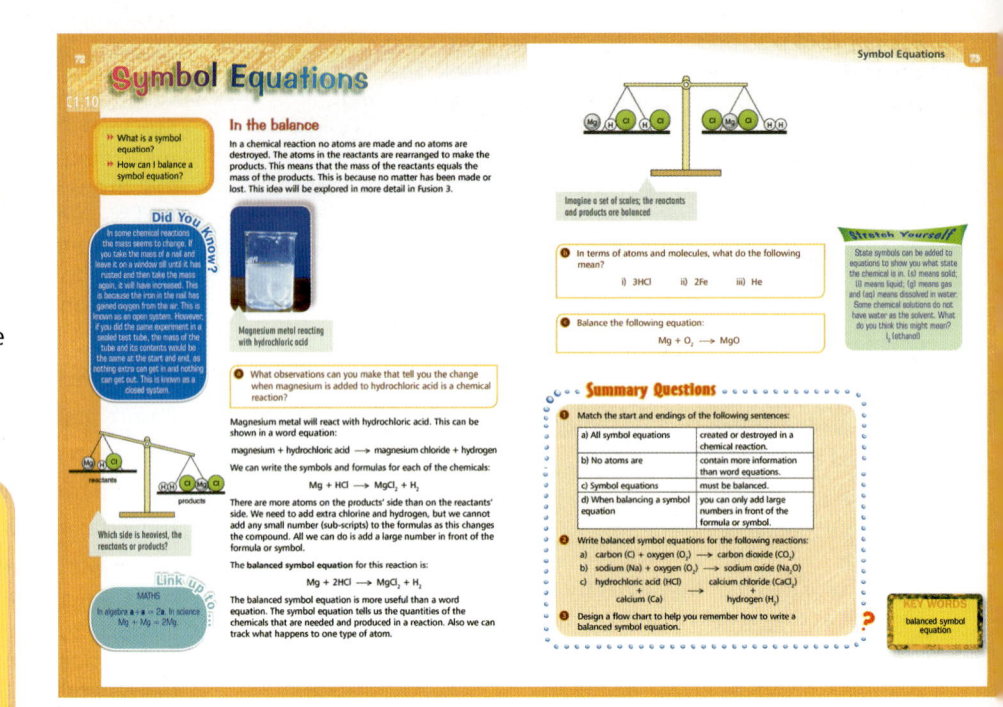

Answers to Summary questions

1.
   a) All symbol equations must be balanced.
   b) No atoms are created or destroyed in a chemical reaction.
   c) Symbol equations contain more information than word equations.
   d) When balancing a symbol equation you can only add large numbers in front of the formula and symbol.

2.
   a) $C + O_2 \longrightarrow CO_2$
   b) $4Na + O_2 \longrightarrow 2Na_2O$
   c) $2HCl + Ca \longrightarrow CaCl_2 + H_2$

3. Pupil's own flow chart.

Learning Styles
Auditory: Describing their observations.
Kinaesthetic: Completing a cut and stick equation balancing exercise.
Intrapersonal: Understanding that atoms are not created or destroyed during a reaction.

Symbol Equations

The Lesson

Starter Suggestions

Elementary
Give pupils a quick-fire element name and symbol quiz. If you give them the name, they must respond with the symbol. (5 mins)

Recyling
Give pupils a few Lego bricks or a lump of Plasticine. Tell them they must make one model and then another. The aim here is for pupils to realise that they only have a fixed amount of Lego/Plasticine and one model must be dismantled before a new one can be made. (10 mins)

Main Lesson
- Discuss with pupils the purpose of a word equation and then some of the drawbacks. The principle problem is that a word equation doesn't tell you how much of a chemical is needed and so doesn't make a good 'recipe'. It's a bit like a cake recipe which reads just: eggs, flour and butter.
- Introduce the idea that we need an equation that shows us what happens to the atoms during a chemical reaction. Explain that, during a chemical reaction, no atoms are made or destroyed. Whatever is present at the start must be there at the end. You could refer to the 'Recycling' starter if pupils undertook this.
- Show pupils how to balance an equation. Establish that the same number of each type of atom must appear on each side of the equation.
- Ask pupils to complete a cut and stick equation balancing exercise. Stress to them that only whole molecules are acceptable and they must add a whole extra molecule if they need just a part of it.
- Ask pupils to complete further equation balancing exercises on a worksheet. Encourage them to make use of a tally chart to account for the atoms of each type.

Plenary Suggestions

Balancing act
Show pupils some symbol equations and ask them to say whether they are balanced or not. If they are not, ask pupils to suggest what is wrong. (5 mins)

In the balance
Ask pupils to write a set of rules/instructions for balancing equations. (10 mins)

Differentiation

SEN
This lesson is highly conceptual and may be missed by lower attaining pupils. Focus on the more concrete aspects of the lesson.

Extension
Ask pupils to add state symbols to their symbol equations, after each substance. [(s) for solids, (l) for liquids, (g) for gases and (aq) for solutions in water (aqueous).]

Homework Suggestion
Pupils could write a story imagining what might happen to an oxygen atom when breathed in. [During respiration the atom would become part of, either a carbon dioxide molecule which could take part in photosynthesis, or a water molecule which could be breathed out and form part of the water cycle.]

Answers to in-text questions

a Hear fizzing/see bubbles implies a gas is being made, this is a new chemical and therefore a chemical reaction has happened.

b
i) 3 molecules of HCl
ii) 2 atoms of Fe
iii) 1 atom of He

c $2Mg + O_2 \longrightarrow 2MgO$

C1.11 Mixtures

NC links for the lesson
- Elements consist of atoms that combine together in chemical reactions to form compounds.
- Use a range of scientific methods and techniques to develop and test ideas and explanations.
- Assess risk and work safely in the laboratory, field and workplace.
- Carry out practical and investigative activities, both individually and in groups.

Learning Objectives
Pupils should learn:
- The difference between elements and mixtures.
- The difference between compounds and mixtures.

Learning Outcomes
- All pupils should be able to list examples of mixtures and compounds.
- Most pupils should be able to recall definitions of elements, compounds and mixtures in words and diagrams.
- Some pupils should also be able to explain the properties of compounds and mixtures when considering the elements that make them.

How Science Works
- Describe an appropriate approach to answer a scientific question using sources of evidence and, where appropriate, making relevant observations or measurements using appropriate apparatus (1.2a).

Functional Skills Link-up
English
- Present information concisely and logically (level 2).

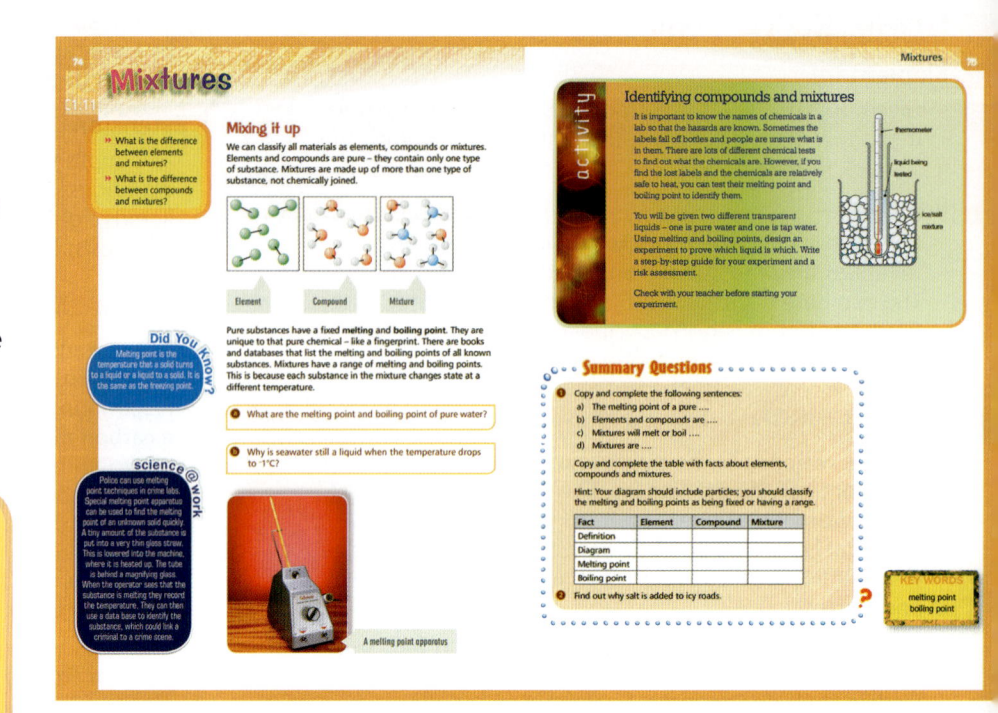

Learning Styles
Visual: Making observations.
Auditory: Describing their observations.
Kinaesthetic: Carrying out practical work.
Interpersonal: Working with others during practical work.

Answers to Summary questions

1.
   a) E.g. The melting point of a pure substance is fixed.
   b) E.g. Elements and compounds are pure substances.
   c) E.g. Mixtures will melt or boil over a range of temperatures.
   d) E.g. Mixtures are impure substances.

Fact	Element	Compound	Mixture
Definition	Only one type of atom, can be found on the Periodic Table	More than one type of atom, chemically joined	More than one type of substance, not chemically joined
Diagram	○	○●	○ ●
Melting point	Fixed	Fixed	Range
Boiling point	Fixed	Fixed	Range

2. Salt mixes with the water to make a solution. This is a mixture and lowers the melting point and therefore the ice melts.

Mixtures

The Lesson

Starter Suggestions

Mix it up
Pupils to plan a procedure to separate sand from water and salt from water. (5 mins)

Tea time
Ask pupils to imagine that the four ingredients [water, tea, milk and sugar] in a cup of tea are 'elements'. They should describe how each of these elements affects the mixture. Ask them to suggest how this shows that a cup of tea is not a compound. [The properties of the individual elements are still apparent, e.g. adding more sugar makes it sweeter.] (10 mins)

Main Lesson

- Ask pupils to recall different ways to separate mixtures which they met in Year 7, such as filtering, evaporation and distillation. Ask them to suggest differences in the properties of mixtures, compounds and elements, referring to earlier lessons in this unit.
- Ask pupils what the melting point and boiling point of water are. Establish that they are 0°C and 100°C, respectively. Ask pupils why we put salt onto roads and establish that it makes it less likely that the roads will freeze in the winter. [Salt lowers the melting point of water and so it freezes at a temperature lower than 0°C.]
- Explain that impure substances (mixtures) have different melting points and boiling points from their pure substances and melt over a range of temperature rather than at one sharp point.
- Ask pupils to plan and carry out activity 'Identifying compounds and mixtures' as described in the pupil book. Pupils could look at one or both of the following situations: comparing freezing point and comparing boiling point. Pupils may need reminding that melting and freezing points are the same thing, but the name used is usually chosen to indicate the direction of the change of state. Rather than use a freezer to compare freezing points, it is probably simpler to use an ice–salt mixture to cool containers of the two test substances.

Plenary Suggestions

True or false
Ask pupils if some statements about elements, mixtures and compounds are true or false. (5 mins)

Defining moment
Ask pupils to write a definition for an element [substance made of only one type of atom], a compound [substance made of more than one type of atom chemically joined], and a mixture [more than one element or substance that can be easily separated]. (10 mins)

Practical Support

Identifying compounds and mixtures

Equipment and materials required
Per group: 200 cm³ distilled water, 200 cm³ of brine solution labelled 'tap water' (doctored to ensure pupils see a difference), two 250 cm³ beakers, two 100 cm³ beakers, two thermometers (–10°C to 110°C), Bunsen burner, tripod, gauze and heat mat, plastic bowl, filled with ice, 50 g of sodium chloride, eye protection.

Details
Refer to pupil book. Suggested method for testing boiling point: pour 100 cm³ of test water into a 250 cm³ beaker and heat over a Bunsen burner. Record the temperature at which the water boils. Repeat for the other test water. The pure water should boil at 100°C.

Suggested method for testing freezing point: mix sodium chloride into the ice and check the temperature. Stop adding salt when the temperature ceases to fall. Pour 50 cm³ of test water into a 100 cm³ beaker and place the beaker in a well in the ice. Repeat for the other test water. Observe the temperature of each beaker until they begin to freeze. The pure water should freeze at 0°C.

Safety
Pupils must not drink the water.
Take care with boiling water.
Wear eye protection.

Extension: Melting point apparatus

Equipment and materials required
Per group: organic compound with a low melting point, such as salol or stearic acid, eye protection.

Details
Refer to manual supplied with your melting point apparatus.

Safety
Wear eye protection.
Salol is an irritant: CLEAPSS Hazcard 52.

Differentiation

SEN
Use a jumbled-up suggested method for the investigation that the pupils need to sort.

Extension
Write an instruction manual for the use of a melting point apparatus.

Homework Suggestion

Pupils could find out how scientists use melting points to identify compounds.

Answers to in-text questions

a 0°C and 100°C, respectively.

b The freezing point of water is lowered because of dissolved substances in the water.

C1.12 Discovering Oxygen

NC links for the topic
- Elements consist of atoms that combine together in chemical reactions to form compounds.
- Use a range of scientific methods and techniques to develop and test ideas and explanations.
- Applying scientific ideas brings about technological developments and consequent changes in the way people think and behave.

Learning Objectives
Pupils should learn:
- How we know about oxygen.
- How ideas about burning have changed over time.

Learning Outcomes
- All pupils should be able to recognise burning and recall what is needed.
- Most pupils should be able to understand that ideas about elements have changed over time.
- Some pupils should also be able to explain why scientific ideas change over time.

How Science Works
- Identify a range of scientific data and other evidence to back an argument and the counterclaim in more complex and/or less familiar contexts (1.1a3).
- Describe how scientific evidence from different sources carries different weight in supporting or disproving theories (1.1a3).

Functional Skills Link-up
English
- Use a range of different styles of writing for different purposes (level 2).

ICT
- Produce information that is fit for purpose and audience, using accepted layouts and conventions as appropriate (level 1).

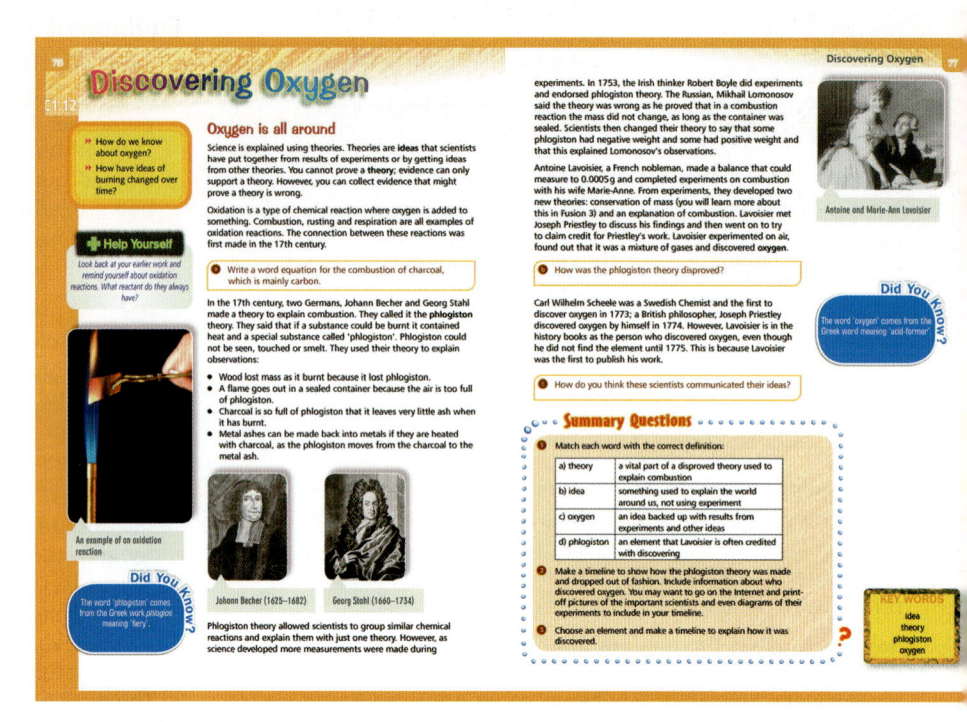

Learning Styles
Visual: Preparing the timeline.
Auditory: Writing text for the timeline.
Intrapersonal: Understanding that the scientific development is slow and ideas often change over time.

Answers to Summary questions

1.
   a) Theory: an idea backed up with results from experiments and other ideas.
   b) Idea: something used to explain the world around us, not using experiment.
   c) Oxygen: an element that Lavoisier is often credited with discovering.
   d) Phlogiston: a vital part of a disproved theory used to explain combustion.

2. 17th century Becher and Stahl generate phlogiston theory.
   17th century Boyle did experiments and endorsed phlogiston theory.
   Lomonosov tried to copy Boyle's experiment and disproved phlogiston theory.
   Phlogiston theory was changed to incorporate positive and negative mass phlogiston.
   1773, Scheele discovered oxygen.
   1774, Priestly discovered oxygen.
   1775, Lavoisier discovered oxygen, and got the credit!

3. Pupils own time line.

Discovering Oxygen

The Lesson

Starter Suggestions

Magic teabag
Show pupils how a teabag can be made to float up on its own convection current when it is burned. See 'Practical Support' section for details. (5 mins)

Burning problem
Show pupils a candle burning in the open, and one burning inside an upturned jar. Ask them to explain why the one in the jar goes out. [The oxygen is used up by conversion to carbon dioxide and water.] (10 mins)

Main Lesson

- Find out what pupils know about burning. They should say that a fuel and oxygen are needed.
- Ask pupils how they know that oxygen is needed and lead on to a discussion about how people found out about oxygen.
- Using the pupil book as a starting point, ask pupils to assemble a strip cartoon or timeline about the history of peoples' understanding of burning. They will need access to other sources of information, such as the Internet. They could produce their work as a PowerPoint presentation rather than hand-written.

Plenary Suggestions

Tricky problem
Ask pupils to debate why people used to think that the Sun went around the Earth and what changed our minds. They could do this in pairs, groups or as a whole class. [People used to think that the Sun went around the Earth because that is what appears to happen. It was only once we were able to study other planets and stars that we had enough information to change that view.] (5 mins)

Famous last words
Ask pupils to write an epitaph for Joseph Priestley, who, along with Antoine Lavoisier, discovered oxygen. (10 mins)

Practical Support

Starter: Magic teabag

Equipment and materials required
For demonstration: teabag (of the type which is folded up and has a tag), heat mat, matches.

Details
Undo the teabag carefully and remove the tea. You should be left with a cylinder of paper which can be opened out and stood on its end. Light the top of the cylinder. The heat generated by the flame will cause a convection current which will lift the very light bag off the desk.

Safety
Pupils should be kept well back in case any burning embers drop onto them.

Starter: Burning problem

Equipment and materials required
For demonstration: two candles or nightlights, one jar big enough to fit over one of the candles, matches.

Details
Light both the candles and then place an upturned jar over one of them. Observe the candle inside the jar going out once all the oxygen inside has been used.

Safety
Make sure hair and loose clothing are tied back.

Differentiation

SEN
Give pupils some of the key facts about the people involved so they don't have to do so much research, which is a high level skill.

Extension
Pupils should find out how scientists developed our understanding of what atoms are like, from Dalton through Rutherford, Bohr and Chadwick. Encourage them to find out about work that is still being done in places like Harwell, Oxfordshire and in CERN, Switzerland.

Answers to in-text questions

a carbon + oxygen ⟶ carbon dioxide

b Conservation of mass theory developed and the discovery of oxygen.

c They would have had to have written letters by hand or travelled to visit each other, slowly over land and sea.

Answers to Elements and Compounds – End of Topic Questions

Answers to know your stuff questions

1 **a** Oxygen. [1]

  b Carbon dioxide. [1]

  c i) Atom: smallest particle of a substance that can exist on its own.
  ii) Element: only one type of atom and listed on the Periodic Table.
  iii) Compound: more than one type of atom chemically joined. [3]

2 **a**

Material	Metal	Non-metal
Steel	✓	
Sulfur		✓
Wood		✓
Cobalt	✓	

[3]

  b Cobalt (Co). [1]

  c It is strong. [1]

3 **a** Substance containing only one type of atom [1]
  listed on the Periodic Table. [1]

  b A and B. [2]

  c D. [1]

  d D. [1]

4 **a** Chemical. [1]

  b 5 [1]

  c 4Fe + 3O$_2$ $\longrightarrow$ 2Fe$_2$O$_3$

  [For correct symbols for the reactants, [1]

  for the correct symbols for the products, [1]

  for the correct balancing.] [1]

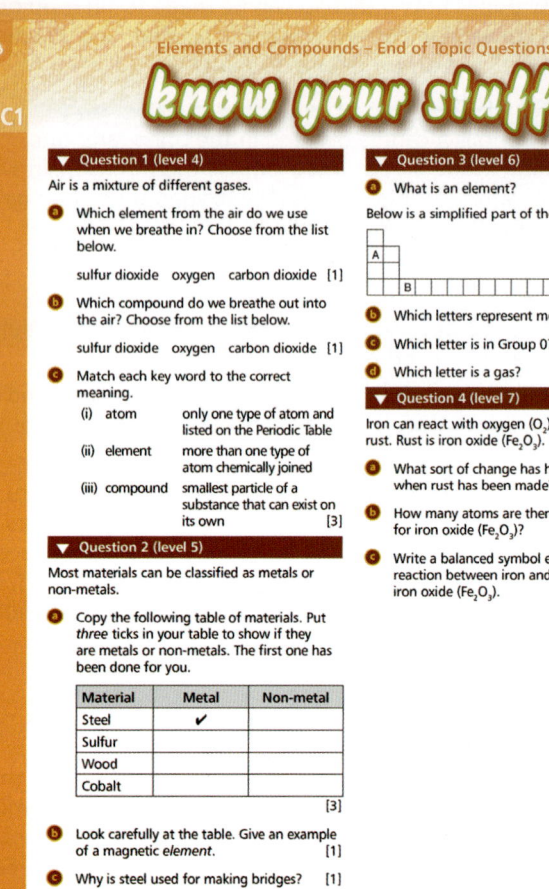

Elements and Compounds – End of Topic Questions

How Science Works

Question 1 (level 4)

Dave and Bill are going to classify three different elements as metals or non-metals.

a) Draw a table for Dave and Bill to record their results. [2]

Dave knows that metals often have a high density. To calculate the density of a substance you need to record the mass and volume.

b) What is the unit of mass? [1]

c) Explain how you could work out the volume of a sample of a material using water and a measuring cylinder. [3]

d) Why might it be dangerous to measure the volume of some elements using the method in part (c)? [1]

Question 2 (level 5)

Maria decided to investigate how the percentage of oxygen affected how quickly magnesium burned. She decided to time how long the reaction took from start to finish.

a) What is the symbol for the metal in this reaction? [1]

b) What is the name of the compound made in this reaction? [1]

c) On the packet of magnesium there was the following hazard symbol:

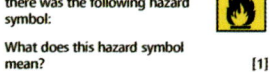

What does this hazard symbol mean? [1]

d) On the oxygen cylinder there was the following hazard symbol:

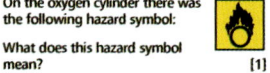

What does this hazard symbol mean? [1]

e) What is the independent variable in Maria's experiment? (The independent variable is the one Maria chose to vary.) [1]

f) How could Maria record her results? Select two options from the following list.

table   pie chart   line graph   [2]

Question 3 (level 6)

Hydrogen peroxide (H_2O_2) decomposes into oxygen (O_2) and water (H_2O). Special chemicals called catalysts can speed up this chemical reaction.

Merendeep wanted to investigate how different amounts of manganese dioxide affected how quickly oxygen was made. She used the following equipment:

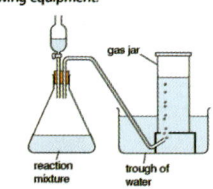

a) Write a word equation for this reaction. [2]

b) What piece of equipment could Merendeep have used to measure the volume of oxygen? [1]

Merendeep recorded her results in the following table:

Mass of manganese dioxide (g)	Volume of oxygen in 5 minutes (cm³)
0	1
1	100
1.5	99
2	100
2.5	98
3	97

c) What conclusions can you draw from Merendeep's experiment? [2]

d) Why did Merendeep complete the experiment without any manganese dioxide? [1]

e) Are Merendeep's results reliable? Choose from the list below.

Yes   No   Don't know

Explain your answer. [2]

Answers to How Science Works questions

1
a) [For correct column headings, [1]
for three rows to put the materials.] [1]
b) kg or g. [1]
c) Record the volume of water in a measuring cylinder. [1]
Put in the sample and record the new volume of water. [1]
Calculate the difference in volumes of water and this is the volume of the sample. [1]
Or Fill a container to the brim with water. [1]
Put in the sample and catch all the water that spills out. [1]
Measure the volume of the spilled water and this is the volume of the sample. [1]
d) Some elements react dangerously with water. [1]

2
a) Mg [1]
b) Magnesium oxide or MgO. [1]
c) Flammable. [1]
d) Oxidising. [1]
e) Percentage oxygen. [1]
f) Table and line graph. [2]

3
a) Hydrogen peroxide ⟶ water + oxygen
(Correct reactant)   (Correct products) [2]
b) Any one of the following: measuring cylinder, gas syringe, graduated test tube, burette. [1]
c) Manganese dioxide increases the amount of oxygen produced in 5 minutes / a given time. [1]
The actual mass of manganese dioxide does not affect the amount of oxygen produced, as long as there is some there. [1]
d) To act as a control. [1]
e) Don't know.
To be reliable the results must be similar when the experiment is repeated. [1]
Merendeep did not repeat her experiment, therefore we cannot say if the results are reliable or not. [1]
Or
No.
She should repeat her experiment. [1]
Then similar results would indicate better reliability. [1]

C2.1 Our Planet

NC links for the topic
- Geological events are a combination of chemical and physical processes.
- Human activity and natural processes can lead to changes in the environment.
- Using ideas and models to explain phenomena and developing them to generate and test theories.
- Critically analysing and evaluating evidence from observations and experiments.
- Use a range of scientific methods and techniques to develop and test ideas and explanations.
- Assess risk and work safely in the laboratory, field and workplace.
- Carry out practical and investigative activities, both individually and in groups.
- Obtain, record and analyse data from a wide range of primary and secondary sources, including ICT sources, and use their findings to provide evidence for scientific explanations.
- Evaluate scientific evidence and working methods.
- Use appropriate methods, including ICT, to communicate scientific information and contribute to presentations and discussions about scientific issues.

Level descriptors for the topic
- **AT3 level 4:** Pupils recall simple scientific knowledge and terminology of the properties and classification of materials such as rocks. They describe some phenomena and processes, such as separation methods and rock weathering, drawing on scientific knowledge and understanding. They recognise that evidence can support or refute scientific ideas, for example the classification of reactions as reversible and irreversible. They recognise some applications and implications of science, such as the safe use of acids and alkalis.
- **AT3 level 5:** Pupils recall straightforward scientific knowledge and terminology of materials and their properties. They describe phenomena and processes, drawing on abstract ideas. They explain processes and phenomena such as the formation of sedimentary rocks in more than one step or using a model. They apply and use knowledge and understanding in familiar contexts, such as identifying changes of state. They recognise that both evidence and creative thinking contribute to the development of scientific ideas, such as basing separation methods for mixtures on physical and chemical properties. They describe applications and implications of science, such as the uses of metals based on their specific properties.
- **AT3 level 6:** Pupils recall detailed scientific knowledge and terminology of properties of materials. They describe phenomena and processes using abstract ideas, such as the particle model applied to solids, liquids and gases. They take account of a number of factors or use abstract ideas or models, such as word equations, in their explanations of phenomena and processes. They apply and use knowledge and understanding, such as relating changes of state to energy transfers, in unfamiliar contexts. They describe some evidence for some accepted scientific ideas, such as the patterns in the reactions of acids with metals and the reactions of a variety of substances with oxygen. They explain the importance of some applications and implications of science, such as the production of new materials with specific desirable properties.
- **AT3 level 7:** Pupils recall detailed scientific knowledge and terminology of properties of materials and make links between different areas. They describe a wide range of phenomena and processes using abstract ideas and sequencing a number of points, for example in the rock cycle. They make links between different areas of science in their explanations, such as between the nature and behaviour of materials and their particles. They apply and use more abstract knowledge and understanding, such as the particle model of matter, and symbols and formulas for elements and compounds, in a range of contexts. They explain how evidence supports some accepted scientific ideas, such as the reactivity series of metals. They explain, using abstract ideas where appropriate, the importance of some applications and implications of science, such as the need to consider the availability of resources, and environmental effects, in the production of materials.

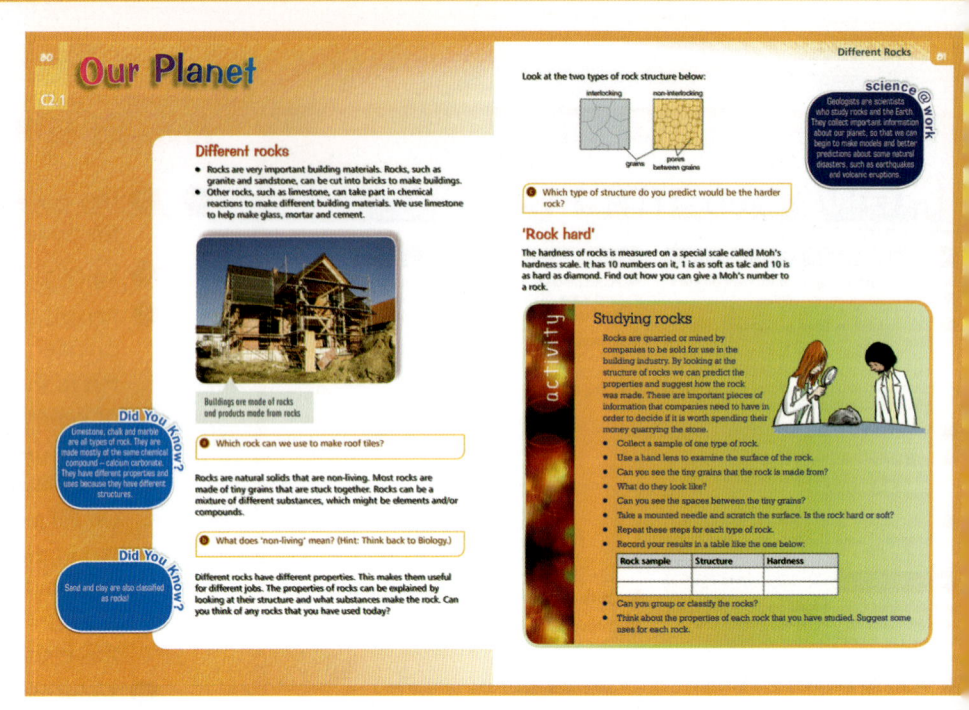

Different Rocks

The Lesson

Starter Suggestions

Rock on!
Ask pupils to list as many items made from rock that they can see in the room. Longest list wins. [Allow items made from metal if pupils know that metals are extracted from rock ores.] (5 mins)

Spot the difference
Give pupils a 'spot the difference' photo from a newspaper or magazine if you have one available. They will be using similar skills in the main lesson. (10 mins)

Main Lesson

- Open the lesson by talking about mountains and volcanoes and asking pupils whether they think the Earth has always looked like it does now. Perhaps allow a short, open discussion on this area.
- Ask pupils what mountains are made from – establish that they are made from rock.
- Suggest to pupils that there are many different sorts of rock and that they are going to observe some rocks to see if they can identify any differences. Ask pupils what sort of things might make different rocks appear different from each other.
- Ask pupils to carry out 'Studying rocks' as described in the pupil book.
- After pupils have carried out the activity, draw together any common themes they observed, e.g. the presence of crystals in some of the rocks or whether any rocks were particularly hard or soft.

Plenary Suggestions

Think you're hard?
Ask pupils to sort rock samples into order of hardness. You could relate this to Moh's scale. (5 mins)

Sort it out!
Ask pupils to put the rocks they have seen in this lesson into different groups, by properties of their choosing. For example, they could choose to sort by whether the rocks have crystals or not. (10 mins)

Practical Support

Studying rocks

Equipment and materials required
Per group: 5–6 rock samples (such as granite, slate, limestone, basalt, sandstone), mounted needle or short nail, hand lens.

Details
Refer to pupil book. Pupils may need help to identify some of the features of rocks, such as what crystals actually are.

Safety
Large rock samples may present a hazard if dropped. Mounted needles are sharp.
If breaking rocks, wear eye protection.

Differentiation

SEN
Emphasise the obvious features of rock and stick to examples which are easy to observe, such as granite and sandstone.

Extension
Ask pupils to find out about Moh's scale and how it was developed.

Homework Suggestion

Pupils could find out what sort of stone a local historic building is made from, where the stone was quarried and how long ago.

Learning Objectives

Pupils should learn:
- What a rock is.
- What rock is made from.
- How rock is useful to us.

Learning Outcomes

- All pupils should be able to recognise a rock.
- Most pupils should be able to recall what a rock is made from.
- Some pupils should also be able to relate the structure of a rock to its uses.

How Science Works

- Describe an appropriate approach to answer a scientific question, making relevant observations (1.2a).

Learning Styles

Visual: Making observations of rocks.
Auditory: Describing their observations of rocks.
Kinaesthetic: Carrying out practical work.
Interpersonal: Sharing ideas with other pupils.

Answers to in-text questions

a Slate.
b A substance that never has and never will do the seven life processes.
c Non-interlocking.

C2.2 Igneous Rocks

NC links for the lesson
- Geological events are a combination of chemical and physical processes.
- Human activity and natural processes can lead to changes in the environment.
- Use a range of scientific methods and techniques to develop and test ideas and explanations.
- Assess risk and work safely in the laboratory, field and workplace.
- Carry out practical and investigative activities, both individually and in groups.

Learning Objectives
Pupils should learn:
- What igneous rock is.
- How igneous rock is formed.
- How to get reliable results.

Learning Outcomes
- All pupils should be able to recognise igneous rock and to give an example of it.
- Most pupils should be able to recall the general properties of igneous rock and explain the concept of reliability.
- Some pupils should also be able to relate the properties of igneous rock to how it was formed and explain the concept of reliability and accuracy.

How Science Works
- Explain how the observation and recording methods are appropriate to the task (1.2d).

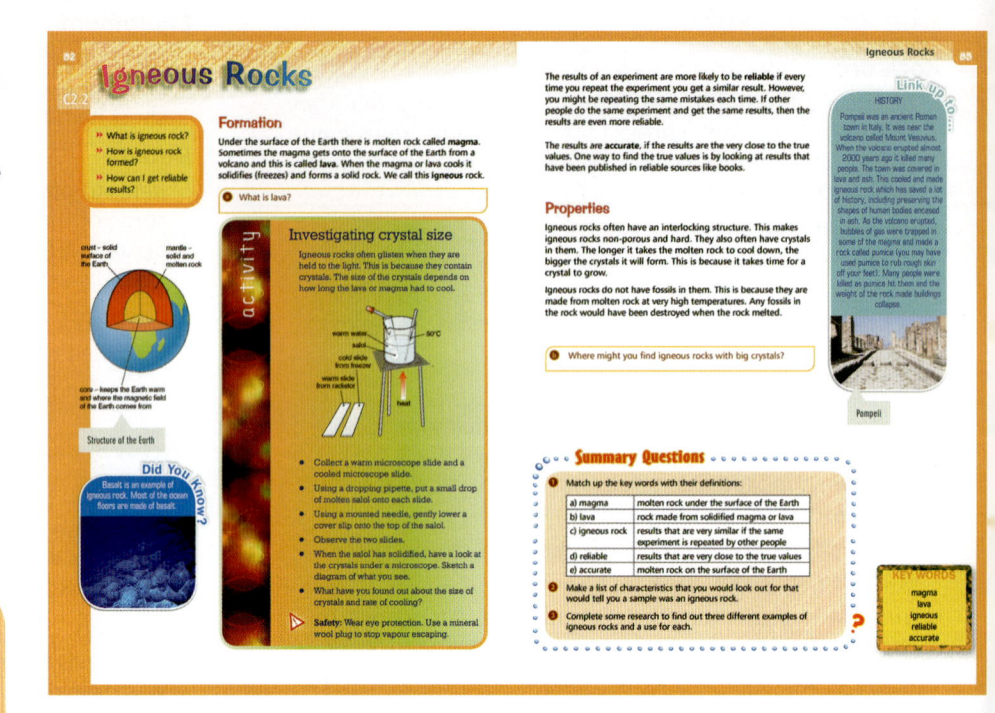

Learning Styles
Visual: Making observations of igneous rock.
Auditory: Describing their observations.
Kinaesthetic: Carrying out practical work on crystal sizes in igneous rock.
Interpersonal: Working with others during practical.
Intrapersonal: Linking crystal size to cooling rate.

Answers to Summary questions

1.
   a) Magma: molten rock under the surface of the Earth.
   b) Lava: molten rock on the surface of the Earth.
   c) Igneous rock: rock made from solidified magma or lava.
   d) Reliable: results that are very similar if the same experiment is repeated by other people.
   e) Accurate: results that are very close to the true values.

2. Crystals, interlocking structure, non-porous, no fossils.

3. For example: pumice – removing hard skin; granite – tomb stones, kitchen surfaces; basalt – garden stone.

Igneous Rocks

The Lesson

Starter Suggestions

Crunchie!
Cut through a Cadbury's Crunchie bar and observe the bubbles. [The bubbles are largest in the centre where the cinder toffee cooled slowly, but you may choose not to reveal the reason at this stage of the lesson.] (5 mins)

Volcano
Show pupils a video clip of a volcano erupting (if you have access to one on the Internet). Ask them to describe what they see happening and to try to explain what is going on. (10 mins)

Main Lesson

- Remind pupils of the observations they made of rocks in the last lesson and of the fact that some rocks have crystals. Explain that 'geologists' are people who study rocks and they divide rocks up into three categories: igneous, sedimentary and metamorphic.
- Give pupils some pieces of igneous rock to observe with a hand lens, such as basalt, granite, gabbro, rhyolite or pumice.
- After they have looked at them, establish that igneous rocks have crystals but that those crystals can vary in size. Explain to pupils how igneous rock forms. [It forms from magma from the Earth's mantle (the layer under the crust) which has cooled and solidified. Magma which escapes from a volcano becomes known as lava.]
- Ask pupils to carry out the 'Investigating crystal size' activity described in the pupil book.
- Establish that large crystals are formed when magma cools slowly. This typically happens when magma cools inside the Earth's crust where it is insulated. The crystals are much smaller when the magma cools quickly as it usually does when it cools on the surface.

Plenary Suggestions

Odd one out
Show pupils pictures or real rock samples, but preferably ones they haven't seen so far this lesson. Make three of them igneous and one non-igneous. (5 mins)

Sort it out
Give pupils some sentences describing how igneous rocks form but do not give them the statements in the right order. The challenge is to sort them out correctly. (10 mins)

Answers to in-text questions

a Lava is magma that gets to the surface of the Earth from a volcano.

b Where the rock has had a long time to cool, e.g. rocks formed under the ground.

Practical Support

Main lesson: Observing igneous rocks

Equipment and materials required
per group: hand lens, samples of igneous rocks, such as basalt, granite, gabbro, rhyolite or pumice.

Details
Ask pupils to observe each of the rocks and to describe their appearance.

Safety
Large rock samples may cause damage if dropped.

Investigating crystal size

Equipment and materials required
Per group: microscope, 5–6 drops of liquid salol (melting point 42°C; warm inside a boiling tube in a water bath at about 60°C to melt it), a microscope slide at room temperature, a microscope slide which has been kept in the freezer until just before use, a mounted needle, 2 microscope slide cover slips, dropping pipette.

Details
Refer to pupil book. It is probably simplest to provide central access to one container of liquid salol than to provide each group with their own source. The cold microscope slides could be kept on ice to keep them cold. Place them in a plastic bag to keep them dry. The slide at room temperature can be placed on a radiator to make sure it is warm.

Safety
Normal laboratory rules, making sure pupils do not abuse the dropping pipette.
Salol is an irritant: CLEAPSS Hazcard 52.

Differentiation

SEN
Concentrate on getting lower attaining pupils to recognise the crystalline nature of igneous rock rather than crystal size. These pupils could also drop a droplet of liquid salol into a beaker of cold water during the 'Investigating crystal size' practical, to model igneous rocks forming under the sea in 'pillow' shapes.

Extension
Ask pupils to find out about pumice and why it has such a low density. [It is effectively a solid foam. Hot gas created bubbles in the lava and the lava then set quickly.] This can be followed up by research into the formation of obsidian.

Homework Suggestion

Pupils could find out about some buildings which are made from granite.

C2.3 Sedimentary Rocks

NC links for the lesson
- Geological events are a combination of chemical and physical processes.
- Human activity and natural processes can lead to changes in the environment.
- Use a range of scientific methods and techniques to develop and test ideas and explanations.
- Assess risk and work safely in the laboratory, field and workplace.
- Carry out practical and investigative activities, both individually and in groups.

Learning Objectives

Pupils should learn:
- What a sedimentary rock is.
- How sedimentary rock is formed.
- How to evaluate an investigation.

Learning Outcomes
- All pupils should be able to recognise sedimentary rock and to give an example of it, as well as giving some examples of errors.
- Most pupils should be able to recall the general properties of sedimentary rock, as well as classifying errors in their investigation.
- Some pupils should also be able to explain how the properties of sedimentary rock relate to how it was formed, as well as giving a detailed evaluation of their investigation.

How Science Works
- Describe and suggest, with reasons, how planning and implementation could be improved (1.2e).

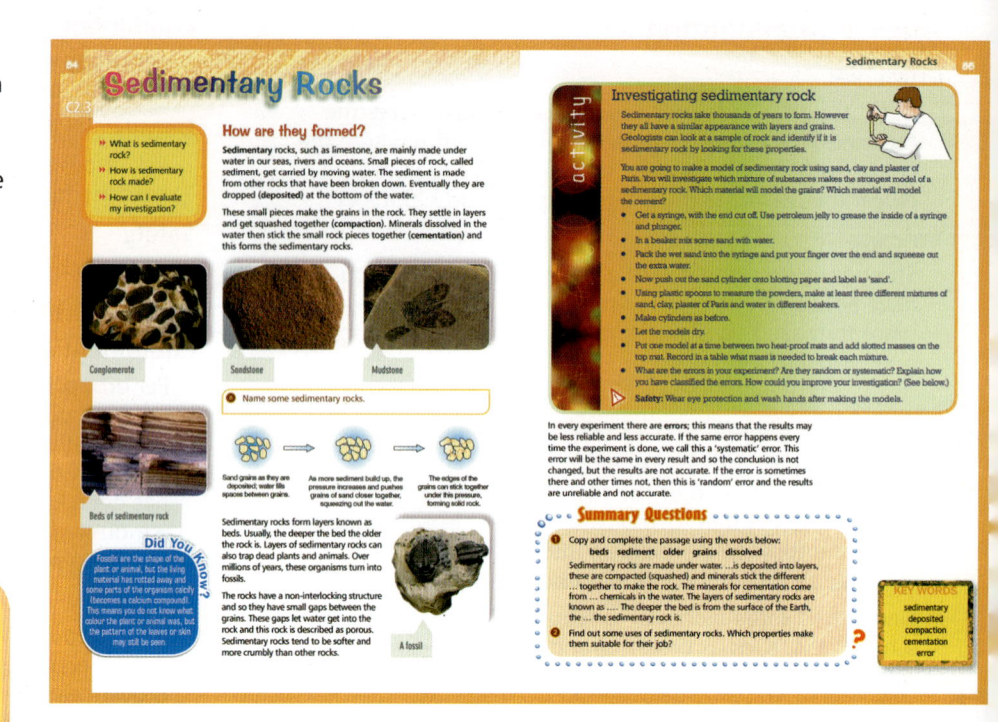

Learning Styles

Visual: Observing the structure of sedimentary rock.
Auditory: Taking part in the class evaluation of the experiment.
Kinaesthetic: Making and testing the rock samples.
Interpersonal: Working with others to make and test the rock samples.
Intrapersonal: Reflecting on the idea that sedimentary rocks take millions of years to form.

Answers to Summary questions

1. Sedimentary rocks are made under water. **Sediment** is deposited into layers, these are compacted (squashed) and minerals stick the different **grains** together to make the rock. The minerals for cementation come from **dissolved** chemicals in the water. The layers of sedimentary rocks are known as **beds**. The deeper the bed is from the surface of the Earth, the **older** the sedimentary rock is.

2. E.g. Chalk – for writing on black boards; it is soft and non-toxic.

   E.g. Sandstone/limestone – used to make sculptures; they are aesthetically pleasing and easy to work.

Sedimentary Rocks

The Lesson

Starter Suggestions

Fossilised
Ask pupils to describe what a fossil is. [Fossils are the mineralised remains or impressions in rock of plants and animals. Allow answers which refer to the remains of dinosaurs.] (5 mins)

Stripes
Show pupils a picture of sedimentary rock strata, which clearly shows the layers. Ask them to describe what they see and to guess as to how the rock formed. (10 mins)

Main Lesson

- Remind pupils of the work they did on igneous rocks last lesson. Explain that other rocks are not formed in the same way and that sedimentary rocks are formed from the remains of other rocks.
- Show pupils some samples of sedimentary rocks, such as sandstone, limestone and chalk. Explain that they are made of grains of other rocks which have been compressed and cemented together. Show pupils that some sedimentary rocks are quite soft, by scratching the rock with a nail.
- Ask pupils to carry out 'Investigating sedimentary rock' as described in the pupil book. The emphasis here should be on getting pupils to consider the validity of the tests and to evaluate the experiment.
- After they have completed the practical, hold a class discussion to evaluate the experiment. [There are several key areas of error; little consistency in the way the 'rock' is made; it is difficult to apply force onto the pillars]. Invite pupils to suggest how they could make the experiment more reliable.

Plenary Suggestions

Sort it out
Give pupils statements which describe how sedimentary rock forms, but in the wrong order. Ask them to place the statements into the correct order. (5 mins)

Show me
Give groups of pupils a piece of car cleaning sponge and some text books. Ask them to use the props to explain how sedimentary rock forms. (10 mins)

Practical Support

Demonstration: Investigating sedimentary rocks

Equipment and materials required
Samples of sedimentary rock (such as limestone, chalk and sandstone), hand lens, nail, small amount of water and a watch glass.

Optional: visualiser or camera connected to a large display to allow class to see more easily.

Details
Show pupils the rock samples and their grainy structure. Use the nail to scratch the rock revealing it to be soft. Place the sample in a watch glass and show that it absorbs some water indicating that it is porous.

If you wish to carry out the investigation with your group, this demonstration could easily be converted into a class activity.

Safety
Normal laboratory rules.

Investigating sedimentary rock

Equipment and materials required
Per group: syringe with nozzle end cut off, petroleum jelly to grease syringe, 100 g of sand, 100 g of clay, 50 g of plaster of Paris, 3–4 beakers (you may wish to use disposable cups), 3 spatulas (or plastic spoons), small sheet of blotting or filter paper, 2 heat-proof mats, set of slotted masses, eye protection.

Details
Refer to pupil book. Pupils need to make different mixtures of sand, clay and plaster, and press cylinders in the syringe to make a column of 'sedimentary rock'. As the rocks take a while to dry the waiting time could be used by pupils to record what they have done. Once dried the column should be tested to breaking point with the masses. This experiment can be messy. It may be a good idea to cover the desks with newspaper before starting.

Safety
Care should be taken when testing the rock in case masses fall or the rock shatters.
Eye protection should be worn.

Differentiation

SEN
Concentrate on getting pupils to recall the names of some sedimentary rocks and on identifying their key features. Pupils may need prompts in order to be able to take part in evaluating the investigation. Ask them why it would be better if three samples of the same rock column were made at the same time. [It would allow the test to be repeated.]

Extension
Allow pupils to repeat the investigation, putting into place all their suggested improvements, to see if the outcome is improved.

Invite pupils to work out how the age of a rock can be determined by the fossils found in it. [If we know when the fossilised animal was alive, we know when the rock must have begun to form.]

Homework Suggestion

Pupils could produce a poster about a particular geological period and the fossils we find from that time, e.g. Cretaceous.

Answers to in-text questions

a. Limestone, chalk, conglomerate, sandstone, clay, shale, mudstone.

C2.4 Metamorphic Rocks

NC links for the lesson
- Geological events are a combination of chemical and physical processes.
- Human activity and natural processes can lead to changes in the environment.
- Use a range of scientific methods and techniques to develop and test ideas and explanations.

Learning Styles
Visual: Observing metamorphic rocks and developing the formation model.

Kinaesthetic: Developing the model showing how metamorphic rocks form.

Interpersonal: Working with others to develop the model.

Intrapersonal: Understanding the concept that the process of forming metamorphic rock is too slow to see.

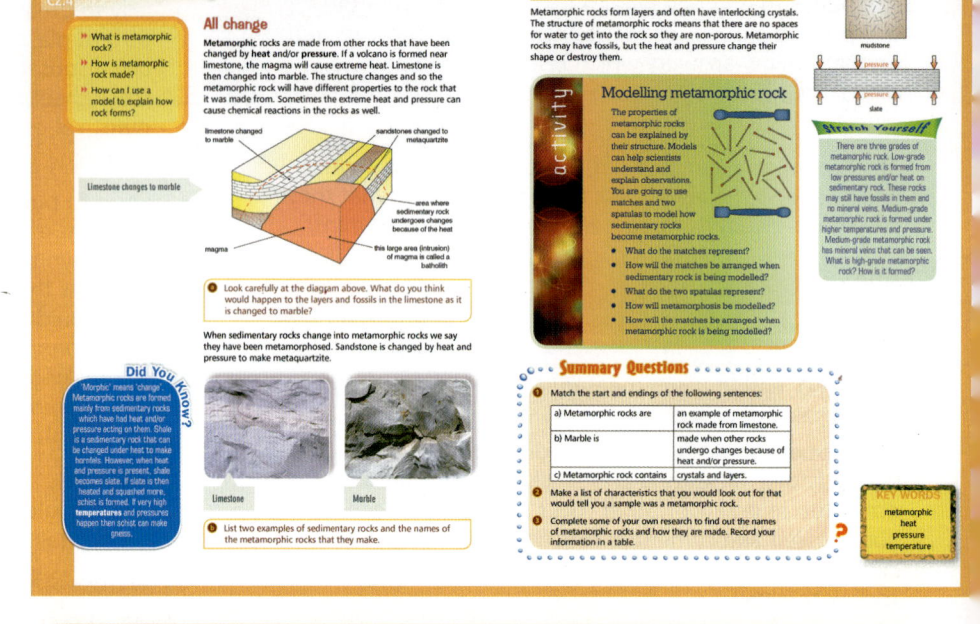

Learning Objectives
Pupils should learn:
- What a metamorphic rock is.
- How a metamorphic rock forms.
- How we can model rock formation.

Learning Outcomes
- All pupils should be able to recognise metamorphic rock and to give an example of it, as well as modelling how the rock was formed.
- Most pupils should be able to recall the general properties of metamorphic rock and explain the model of rock formation.
- Some pupils should also be able to relate the properties of metamorphic rock to how it was formed and evaluate the model of rock formation.

How Science Works
- Describe how the use of a particular model or analogy supports an explanation (1.1a1).

Answers to Summary questions

1. a) Metamorphic rocks are made when other rocks undergo changes because of heat and/or pressure.
   b) Marble is an example of metamorphic rock made from limestone.
   c) Metamorphic rock contains crystals and layers.
2. Layers, crystals, interlocking structure, fossils, non-porous.
3. Research.

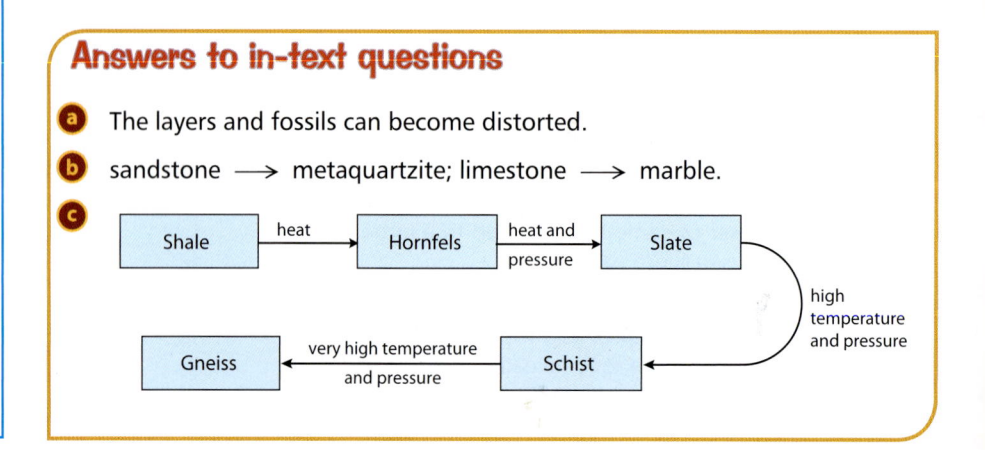

Answers to in-text questions

a) The layers and fossils can become distorted.

b) sandstone → metaquartzite; limestone → marble.

c) Shale —heat→ Hornfels —heat and pressure→ Slate —high temperature and pressure→ Schist —very high temperature and pressure→ Gneiss

Metamorphic Rocks

The Lesson

Starter Suggestions

Spot the difference
Give pupils a sample of limestone and of marble. Ask them to describe all the differences they can see and feel. [Limestone is softer, with obvious grains. Marble is much harder and often has lines of recrystallised minerals in it.] (5 mins)

'Morph'
Show pupils a video clip of the 'Morph' animation. Searching for 'Morph' on video clip websites such as YouTube.com should yield a suitable one. Ask them to explain what is special about Morph's character. [Morph can change his shape at will. Use this as a lever to explain that 'metamorphic' refers to the fact that the rock has been changed in some way.] (10 mins)

Main Lesson

- Remind pupils of the work they have done so far on igneous and sedimentary rocks. Ask pupils to explain briefly how each is formed.
- Explain that inside the Earth it is very hot and that very slowly, the continents are moving around. You may wish to use terms such as 'tectonic plates' and to discuss earthquakes and volcanoes here, but it is not necessary and may divert attention from the aims of the lesson.
- Explain that the high temperatures and the forces involved in the slow movement of the crust can change the rocks by softening and putting them under immense pressure. Use the information in the pupil book to help describe how rocks are metamorphosised. [It is a common misconception that the rock fully melts during the process. It just softens as, despite the very high temperatures involved, the high pressure prevents full melting. Metamorphic rocks can be formed from either igneous or sedimentary rocks. The processes involved often mean that any fossils present in the latter become distorted.]
- Show pupils some samples of metamorphic rocks, such as marble, slate, gneiss and schist. You may wish to give them time to examine the samples.
- Ask pupils to carry out the activity 'Modelling metamorphic rock' which is described in the pupil book.
- After they have done this, ask the class, in groups or together, to consider how they could improve the model.

Plenary Suggestions

Sort it out
Give pupils statements which describe how metamorphic rock forms, but in the wrong order. Ask them to place the statements into the correct order. (5 mins)

Are you hard enough?
Ask pupils to consider where the rocks they have seen today should fit into Moh's Scale and if they should all go in the same place. [Moh's scale is included in C2.1. Most metamorphic rocks are quite hard. Gneiss is the hardest, while slate is relatively soft.] (10 mins)

Practical Support

Starter: Spot the difference

Equipment and materials required
Per group: sample of limestone, sample of marble, hand lens.

Details
Refer to starter information.

Main lesson (optional): Studying metamorphic rocks

Equipment and materials required
Per group: samples of metaquartzite, marble, slate, gneiss, schist; hand lens.

Details
Ask pupils to study the samples. They should look to see if they can see the remains of layers from the original sedimentary rock.

Safety
Normal laboratory rules.

Modelling metamorphic rock

Equipment and materials required
Per group: 50–100 matchsticks, 2 laboratory spatulas.

Details
Refer to pupil book. The matches are the grains within the rock. In sedimentary rock the grains are randomly arranged (such as by dropping the matches on the desk). In metamorphic rocks the grains are aligned. The spatulas can be placed above and below the matches and used to apply even pressure to all the matches; they mimic the layers of rock above and below.

Safety
Normal laboratory rules. Use spent matches.

Differentiation

SEN
Give pupils a set of instructions to help them form the model when undertaking 'Modelling metamorphic rock' rather than them having to develop the model by themselves.

Extension
Invite pupils to undertake the 'Stretch yourself' section described in the pupil book. [High-grade metamorphic rock, such as gneiss, is formed by high temperature and pressure.]

Homework Suggestion

Pupils could find out about the use of slate as a building material. [Slate is mainly found in North Wales and the Lake District in the UK. It can be split along the layers in the rock, allowing thin sheets to be obtained. These were often used as roof tiles until they were replaced by moulded tiles.]

C2.5 Which Rock?

NC links for the lesson
- Geological events are a combination of chemical and physical processes.
- Human activity and natural processes can lead to changes in the environment.

Learning Objectives
Pupils should learn:
- How to tell which type of rock they have.
- How to identify rocks.

Learning Outcomes
- All pupils should be able to use a key to identify rocks.
- Most pupils should be able to develop a simple key to identify rocks.
- Some pupils should also be able to make a flow chart or couplet key to identify rocks.

How Science Works
- Describe an appropriate approach to answer a scientific question, making relevant observations [devising a key] (1.2a).

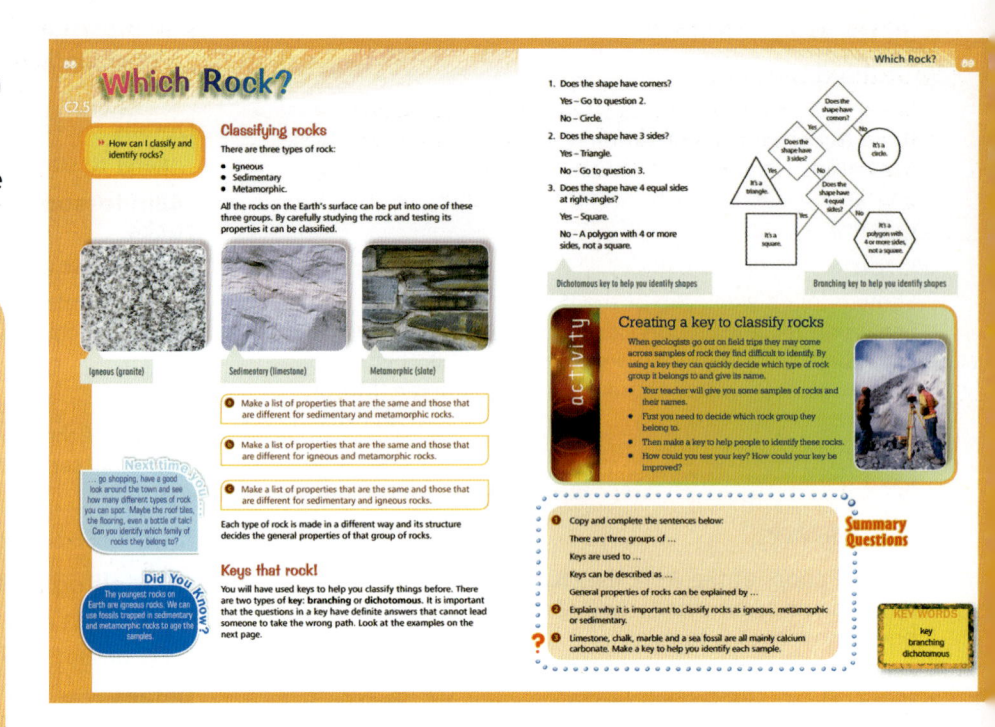

Functional Skills Link-up
English
- Present information on complex subjects concisely and clearly (level 2).

Learning Styles
Visual: The key could be image-based, rather than text-based.

Interpersonal: Checking the keys prepared by others and providing feedback.

Answers to in-text questions

a Same: layers, may have fossils. Different: sedimentary tend to be non-interlocking structure and porous, with no crystals, but metamorphic tend to be interlocking crystals and non-porous.

b Same: has crystals, interlocking structure, non-porous. Different: metamorphic rocks have veins of minerals and igneous do not. Igneous cannot have fossils, metamorphic might; metamorphic forms layers, but igneous do not.

c Same: none. Different: igneous have crystals, are interlocking, non-porous, don't have fossils. Sedimentary don't have crystals, are non-interlocking, porous and can have fossils.

The Lesson

Starter Suggestions

What is it?
Show pupils a picture of a piece of rock (any sort). Ask them to decide whether they think it is igneous, sedimentary or metamorphic, giving reasons. (5 mins)

Word up
Ask pupils to come up with as many words as they can from igneous, sedimentary and metamorphic. Longest list wins. To make it harder, only allow words over a certain length. (10 mins)

Main Lesson

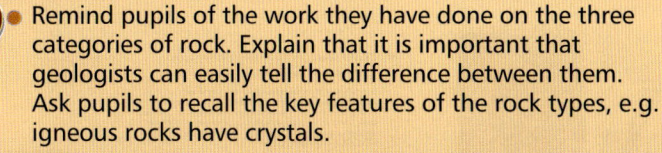

- Remind pupils of the work they have done on the three categories of rock. Explain that it is important that geologists can easily tell the difference between them. Ask pupils to recall the key features of the rock types, e.g. igneous rocks have crystals.
- Explain to pupils what an identification key is. There is an example in the pupil book. You could, at this point get pupils to prepare a simple one of their own. For example, to identify sports equipment the first question might be: 'Is it round?' or 'Does it have strings?'
- Ask pupils to carry out 'Creating a key to identify rocks' as described in the pupil book. You will need to make named rock samples available.
- Ask pupils to check each other's keys once they have been prepared. Get them to suggest corrections for any errors and, perhaps, to score each others' work out of 10 for, say, usability.

Plenary Suggestions

Ancient history
Ask pupils to think about what they have learned about rocks to explain why fossils are usually only found in sedimentary rock. [The process of formation of igneous and most metamorphic rock destroys any fossil record.] (5 mins)

Sort it out
Give pupils a description of the three rock types and ask them to match the correct name to each: igneous, sedimentary or metamorphic. They should also try to give an example of each. (10 mins)

Practical Support

Creating a key to identify rocks

Equipment and materials required
Per group: selection of named rock samples from the last three lessons, hand lenses.

Details
Refer to pupil book. A good starter question for pupils who are struggling would be: 'Does it have crystals?'

Safety
Normal laboratory rules.

Differentiation

SEN
Allow pupils to build up to the task of preparing the rock key by giving them some rock samples which they should sort into three groups, each corresponding to the three rock types. Allow them to build from there. Instead of preparing a key which identifies particular rock samples, help lower attaining pupils create a key which just differentiates between igneous, sedimentary and metamorphic.

Extension
Insist that the key prepared by higher attaining pupils doesn't just differentiate by the appearance of the rocks. They should include detail that, for example, identifies igneous rock as intrusive or extrusive. [Intrusive: large crystals, cooled slowly; extrusive: small crystals, fast cooling.]

Homework Suggestion

Pupils could find out about the work of Alfred Wegener in relation to geology. [Wegener was the first man to propose the idea of drifting continents in 1915.]

Answers to Summary questions

1. There are three groups of rock: igneous, metamorphic and sedimentary.
   Keys are used to help classify and identify items.
   Keys can be described as couplets or flow charts.
   General properties of rocks can be explained by looking at their structure.

2. It helps us study rocks, predict the properties of a rock and suggest uses.

3. Pupil's own key.

C2.6 Weathering

NC links for the lesson
- Geological events are a combination of chemical and physical processes.
- Human activity and natural processes can lead to changes in the environment.
- Use a range of scientific methods and techniques to develop and test ideas and explanations.

Learning Objectives

Pupils should learn:
- What weathering is.
- How plants and animals can change rocks.
- How to plan an investigation.

Learning Outcomes
- All pupils should be able to recognise when a rock has been weathered.
- Most pupils should be able to recall the three main types of weathering and identify key variables in an investigation.
- Some pupils should also be able explain biological weathering and plan a detailed investigation into its effects.

How Science Works
- Describe and identify key variables in an investigation and assign appropriate values to these (1.2b).

Functional Skills Link-up

ICT
- Obtain, insert, size, crop and position images that are fit for purposes (level 2) – see question 3 in summary questions.

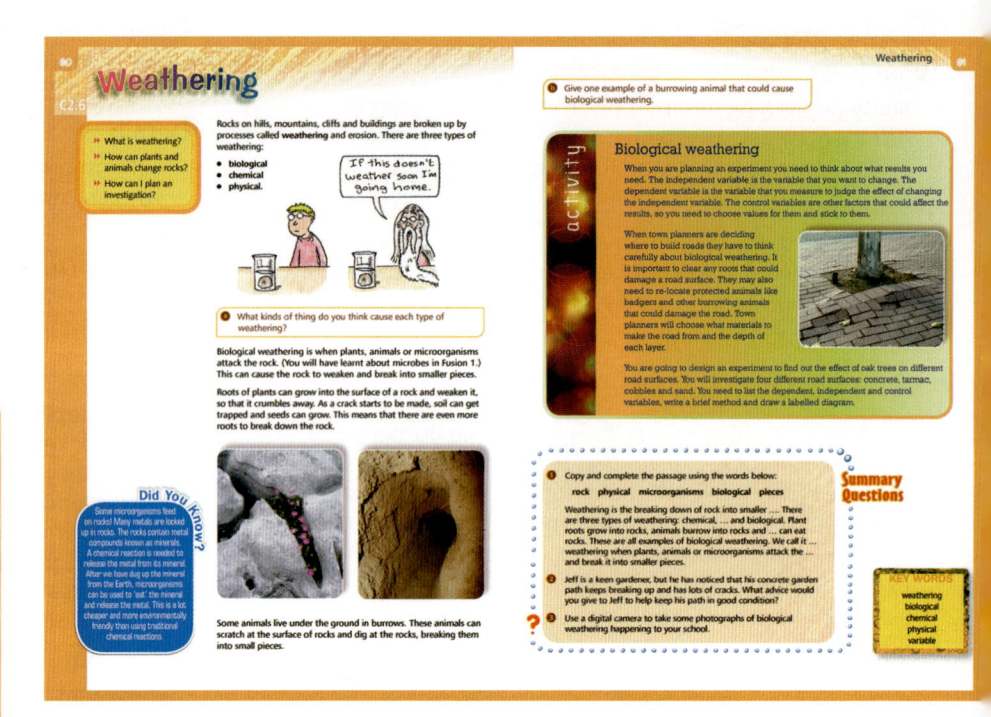

Learning Styles

Visual: Observing examples of biological weathering.
Auditory: Describing how rocks might be weathered.
Intrapersonal: Considering how to plan a fair investigation into weathering.

Answers to Summary questions

1. Weathering is the breaking down of rock into smaller **pieces**. There are three types of weathering: chemical, **physical** and biological. Plant roots grow into rocks, animals burrow into rocks and **micro-organisms** can eat rocks. These are all examples of biological weathering. We call it **biological** weathering when plants, animals or micro-organisms attack the **rock** and break it into smaller pieces.

2. Put weed killer on the cracks to stop plants growing in the cracks and increasing their size. Do not plant up to the path. Remove any burrowing animals.

3. Pupil's own digital camera work.

Answers to in-text questions

a. The breaking down of rocks into smaller pieces.

b. Any burrowing animal, e.g. a rat.

Weathering

The Lesson

Starter Suggestions

What's happening?
Show pupils a photograph of tree roots disrupting a pavement. Ask them to explain what is happening. (5 mins)

Name that rock
Begin to describe one of the three rock types, out loud. Be vague to start with and then give more clues. Pupils have to guess which one you are describing and the first to guess wins. You could get pupils to play this in small groups and include some specific types of rock. (10 mins)

Main Lesson
- Remind pupils that sedimentary rock is made from grains of other rocks. Ask pupils to suggest how that may happen. Establish that, somehow, other rocks get broken down over time.
- Ask pupils to think about how this may happen, allowing very broad responses.
- Collate responses into groups on the board, placing them into one of three groups: biological (caused by plants and animals), physical (caused by weather and other physical processes) and chemical (caused by chemical reaction). Take care here over the difference between 'weathering' and 'erosion'. Weathering is the breakdown of rock *in situ* whereas erosion is the wearing way of rock by contact with abrasive material (usually transported pieces of weathered rock).
- Ask pupils to plan the 'Biological weathering' investigation. They will not be able to carry out the plan as it takes too long, but they need to consider how to make their investigation as fair as possible.

Plenary Suggestions

Txt spk
Ask pupils to explain, as if they were writing a text message to their friend, what weathering of rocks is. You could make them stay within the limit of a normal text message of 160 characters, including spaces. (5 mins)

Plant power
Plant bean seeds in a jar of sand, with the seed next to the glass. The pupils will be able to observe the roots pushing through the sand as they grow. A suggested opportunity to look at these again is in the starter for lesson C2.10. (10 mins)

Practical Support

Biological weathering

Equipment and materials required
For teacher: acorn, photo of a fully grown oak tree, photo of a damaged road.

Details
Refer to pupil book. Pupils need to use their imagination for this. They must consider how they could set the investigation up fairly. The independent variable will be the road material, while the dependent variable is the amount of damage. Pupils will need to think of a way to measure this, such as the height the road surface is raised by the root. They must also plan how to get reliable results by carefully considering the controlled variables, e.g. set each road surface up more than once, give each plant the same amount of water.

Safety
Normal laboratory rules.

Plenary: Plant power

Equipment and materials required
Per group: jam jar or beaker, sand – enough to fill the jar, access to cold water, bean seed.

Details
Half-fill the jar with sand. Place the bean seed against the glass and gently press it into the sand. Fill the jar up with sand and gently moisten the sand. Leave the seeds to germinate, watering as necessary. Observe the roots pushing the sand out of the way as they grow (soaking seeds first will speed up germination).

Safety
Normal laboratory rules.

Differentiation

SEN
Give pupils a planning grid to help them plan the experiment.

Extension
Ask pupils to go out into the school site with a digital camera to record examples of biological weathering taking place. In each case they should try to explain what is happening.

Homework Suggestion
Pupils could look for examples of biological weathering caused by plants and animals around the town.

C2.7 Chemical Weathering

NC links for the lesson
- Geological events are a combination of chemical and physical processes.
- Human activity and natural processes can lead to changes in the environment.
- Use a range of scientific methods and techniques to develop and test ideas and explanations.
- Carry out practical and investigative activities, both individually and in groups.

Learning Objectives
Pupils should learn:
- What chemical weathering is.
- How chemical weathering changes rocks.

Learning Outcomes
- All pupils should be able to recognise chemical weathering.
- Most pupils should be able to explain what chemical weathering is.
- Some pupils should also be able to represent chemical weathering in word equations.

How Science Works
- Explain how the observation and recording methods are appropriate to the task (1.2d).

Functional Skills Link up
ICT
- Bring together and organise components of images and text (level 2).

Answers to in-text questions
a) Alkali, base.
b) A chemical reaction in which a base (alkali) reacts with an acid.
c) When oxygen reacts with a chemical.

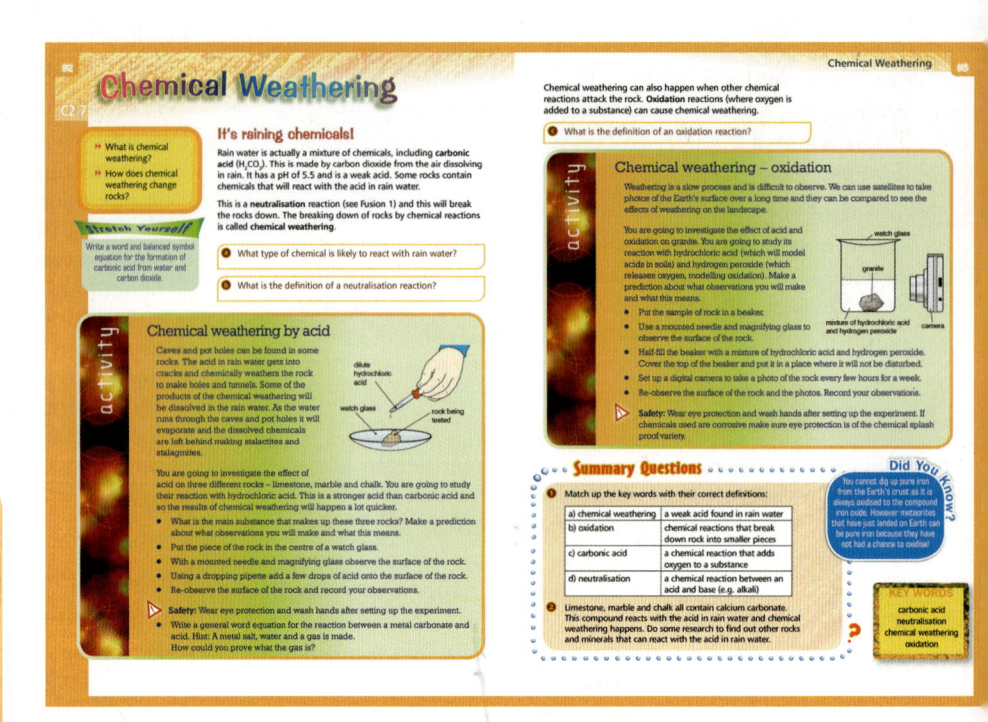

The Lesson

Starter Suggestions

Word up
Ask pupils to make as many words as they can using the letters in 'chemical weathering'. Longest list wins. (5 mins)

Acid test
Give pupils a blank pH scale and ask them to add labels and indicate where some common substances should fit along the scale. (10 mins)

Learning Styles
Visual: Observing the action of acid on rocks.
Auditory: Sharing the key things they have learnt this lesson.
Kinaesthetic: Investigating the action of acid and oxygen on rocks.
Interpersonal: Sharing ideas in groups with other pupils.
Intrapersonal: Understanding that chemical weathering of rock is often a very slow process.

Answers to Summary questions

1.
   a) Chemical weathering: chemical reactions that break down rock into smaller pieces.
   b) Oxidation: a chemical reaction that adds oxygen to a substance.
   c) Carbonic acid: a weak acid found in rain water.
   d) Neutralisation: a chemical reaction between an acid and a base (e.g. alkali).

2. Research.

Chemical Weathering

Main Lesson

- Remind pupils of the work they did in the last lesson into different sorts of weathering. Review what they can remember about biological weathering (caused by animals and plants). If you set up the bean plants as a plenary in the previous lesson, it may be worth checking these, depending upon how long ago that lesson was.
- Explain to pupils that rocks can also be weathered by the action of other chemicals upon them.
- Explain that there are many acidic substances present in nature and that these can damage some rocks by reacting with minerals in the rock. Ask pupils to carry out the 'chemical weathering by acid' investigation as described in the pupil book. You may wish to mention the concept of acid rain here, but it is dealt with in detail next lesson.
- Suggest that oxygen in the air also causes substances to degrade by oxidising them. You could use examples such as the rusting of iron or wine turning to vinegar, before suggesting that the same thing may happen to rocks, albeit much more slowly.
- Ask pupils to set up the 'Chemical weathering – oxidation' investigation described in the pupil book.

Plenary Suggestions

It's a gas
Pupils may have identified that when the acid reacted with the carbonate rock in 'Chemical weathering by acid', that a gas was produced. Ask them to suggest what this gas was. Establish that it was carbon dioxide before asking them to remember the test for carbon dioxide. Demonstrate the test. (5 mins)

Share – pair, square
Ask pupils to work in pairs to list the five most important things they have learned in this lesson. Then get them to share their ideas with another pair to refine their five points. If you have time, you could continue to broaden the groups until the class agrees on a list of five points. (10 mins)

Practical Support

Chemical weathering by acid

Equipment and materials required

Per group: 3 watch glasses, a small piece each of limestone, chalk and marble, 10 cm^3 of 1 mol/dm^3 hydrochloric acid, dropping pipette, magnifying glass, mounted needle.

Details

Refer to pupil book. All the rocks are principally made of calcium carbonate and will react with acid in the same way as any other carbonate, releasing carbon dioxide. Pupils should use the mounted needle and magnifying glass to assess the texture and hardness of the rocks. The softer the rock, the more easily it will be damaged by acid.

Safety

Clear up acid spillages immediately, hydrochloric acid: CLEAPSS Hazcard 47A.

Eye protection must be worn.

Ensure pupils do not misuse pipettes.

Chemical weathering – oxidation

Equipment and materials required

Per group: 250 cm^3 beaker, walnut-sized piece of granite, 50 cm^3 1 mol/dm^3 hydrochloric acid, 50 cm^3 20 vol. hydrogen peroxide, mounted needle, magnifying glass, watch glass or cling-film to cover beaker, digital camera with time-lapse facility.

Details

Refer to pupil book. If a digital camera (still or video) is available which has a time-lapse facility, it will make collecting the results much easier. Time-lapse is a function which records an image at fixed intervals. If such a camera is not available, pupils will need to make visual observations of their experiment as often as possible; once or twice per day would be adequate, but more often if possible.

Safety

Wear eye protection.

Clean up spills immediately.

Hydrochloric acid: CLEAPSS Hazcard 47A.

Hydrogen peroxide is an irritant: CLEAPSS Hazcard 50.

Plenary: It's a gas

Equipment and materials required

For teacher: 2 boiling tubes filled with carbon dioxide and stoppered, 5 cm^3 of limewater, eye protection.

Details

Remove the stopper from the carbon-dioxide-filled boiling tube and pour in a small amount of limewater. Replace the stopper and shake the tube. Observe the limewater becoming milky. Use the second tube if required.

Safety

Wear eye protection.

Limewater is an irritant: CLEAPSS Hazcard 18.

Differentiation

SEN
Focus on the acid experiment rather than the oxidation investigation. The former provides instant and concrete results.

Extension
Ask pupils to devise a method of collecting the gas from the 'Chemical weathering by acid' experiment. [Pupils could carry out the experiment in a boiling tube with a delivery tube attached, leading to another test tube.]

Ask pupils to write word equations for the reaction between calcium carbonate and hydrochloric acid.

Homework Suggestion

Pupils could find some examples of weathered limestone and marble buildings, such as old cathedrals.

C2.8 Acid Rain

NC links for the lesson
- Geological events are a combination of chemical and physical processes.
- Human activity and natural processes can lead to changes in the environment.
- Use a range of scientific methods and techniques to develop and test ideas and explanations.

Learning Objectives
Pupils should learn:
- What acid rain is.
- What causes acid rain.
- What the effects of acid rain are.
- Ways we could reduce acid rain.

Learning Outcomes
- All pupils should be able to describe what causes acid rain.
- Most pupils should be able to explain the difference between 'normal' and acid rain.
- Some pupils should also be able to explain methods of reducing the effect of acid rain on the environment.

How Science Works
- Explain some issues, benefits and drawbacks of scientific developments with which they are familiar (1.1b).

Functional Skills Link-up
English
- Present information and ideas clearly and persuasively to others (level 2).

Learning Styles
Visual: Observing the pH of rain water samples.
Auditory: Taking part in the class debate.
Interpersonal: Allowing others to have their say during the class debate.

The Lesson

Starter Suggestions

Acid test
Show pupils pictures or bottles of some common substances. Ask them to decide whether they are acids or not. Common acid substances include lemon juice, vinegar, milk, battery electrolyte and several stock reagents with acid in their name. (5 mins)

Acid from the sky
Give pupils some 'samples' of rain water to test the pH of. Each one will have different amounts of gases dissolved in it. They should test the pH using universal indicator and decide how acidic each one is. (10 mins)

Main Lesson
- Remind pupils of the work they did in the previous lesson about chemical weathering. Explain to them that one of the key sources of acid, which they have seen can damage rock, is the rain. Or, more specifically, it is gases dissolved in the rain which make it acidic. In general, any non-metal oxide dissolved in water will form an acid. Environmentally, the worst offender is sulfur dioxide, formed when the sulfur often present in fossils fuels,

Answers to Summary questions

1. Acid rain contains strong acids.
   Acid rain can be neutralised with weak alkalis.
   Sulfur is an impurity in fossil fuels and can go on to cause acid rain.
   Nitrogen in car engines combusts to form nitrogen oxide which can make acid rain.

2. sulfur + oxygen ⟶ sulfur dioxide
   sulfur dioxide + oxygen + water ⟶ sulfuric acid

3. nitrogen + oxygen ⟶ nitrogen oxides
   nitrogen oxides + oxygen + water ⟶ nitric acid

4. Pupil's own poster.

Acid Rain

especially coal, burns. Nitrogen oxides are also a problem. Although nitrogen, which accounts for 80% of the air, does not normally react with oxygen, it will in the high temperature and pressure environment in a combustion engine. Carbon dioxide does reduce the pH of rain but not enough to cause much damage.

- If pupils did not undertake 'Acid from the sky' as a starter, it may be worth demonstrating it now. If you did use the 'Acid from the Sky' starter, ask pupils to set up a longer term investigation into the effects of acid rain. They could grow cress seeds watered with various forms of 'acid rain' to see what effects the rain has on plant growth. Please refer to 'Investigating the effects of acid rain' described in the 'Practical support' section.
- Use the materials in the pupil book to give pupils a greater understanding of what causes acid rain and prompt them to think about what could be done about it.
- After giving the class a short time to prepare, hold a class debate on what people could do to reduce the damage caused by acid rain. You could extend this to include the 'Great Debates' described in the pupil book. Variations on a straightforward debate are suggested in the differentiation section. [Ultimately, the solution is to reduce fossil fuel usage. However, oil companies are going to great lengths to remove sulfur from fuels and catalytic converters on vehicles break down nitrogen oxides so only nitrogen reaches the end of the exhaust. Talk about the pressure to balance the damage caused by acid rain against demand for energy.]

Plenary Suggestions

Acid burn
Ask pupils to list 10 things which can be damaged by acid rain, based on what they can remember from the lesson. (5 mins)

Dear sir…
Ask pupils to write a letter to their local MP asking them to put forward their ideas to Parliament about ways to reduce acid rain. The letter should state some suggestions for reducing acid rain. (10 mins)

Practical Support

Starter: Acid from the sky
Equipment and materials required
Per group: $5\,cm^3$ of $0.1\,mol/dm^3$ sulfuric acid, labelled 'sulfur dioxide in rain water'; $5\,cm^3$ of $0.1\,mol/dm^3$ nitric acid, labelled 'nitrogen oxide in rain water'; $5\,cm^3$ of sparkling water, labelled 'carbon dioxide in rain water'; 3 test tubes, test tube rack, universal indicator, solution or paper, eye protection.

Details
Pour a small amount of each type of 'rain water' into a separate test tube. Test the pH and establish which is the most strongly acidic. [Sulfuric acid should be the most acidic, then nitric acid, then carbonic acid.]

Safety
Nitric acid is an irritant: CLEAPSS Hazcard 67.
Universal indicator is flammable.
Wear eye protection.

Main lesson: Investigating the effects of acid rain
Equipment and materials required
Per group: cress seeds, 4 Petri dishes, filter paper or cotton wool to line Petri dishes, $0.1\,mol/dm^3$ sulfuric acid, labelled 'sulfur dioxide in rain water'; $0.1\,mol/dm^3$ nitric acid, labelled 'nitrogen oxide in rain water'; sparkling water, labelled 'carbon dioxide in rain water'; distilled water, 4 measuring cylinders.

Details
This is a good opportunity to allow pupils to plan the details of this experiment, if time allows. In particular, ask them to consider the control variables: for example, same number of seeds, same amount of cotton wool, same volume of 'rain' added at each watering, plants positioned in same light/ temperature conditions. It is likely that about 20 cress seeds per Petri dish would be suitable and about $5\,cm^3$ of water added every 1–2 days. The level of watering required will depend upon the placement of the dishes. The plants would need regular monitoring: depending on the class, pupils might be persuaded to drop in to care for their plants or it may need to be done by teachers/ technicians in between lessons. Pupils should observe how well the plants grow, either by comparison or by taking measurements such as stem length or number of seeds germinated. They should record their observations regularly during the experiment.

Safety
Nitric acid is an irritant: CLEAPSS Hazcard 67.

Differentiation

SEN
During the debate, team lower attaining pupils up with higher attaining ones where you can, so that they may develop ideas together. If this is not possible, you could try using the 'opinion line'. Set up a rope or line across the room with the words 'Completely agree' at one end and 'Completely disagree' at the other. Read out statements such as, 'We could stop using fossil fuels tomorrow.' or, 'Most acid rain is caused by other countries so we don't have to do anything.' and get pupils to stand next to the rope in a position which reflects their opinion. You can then ask them to explain why they stood there.

Extension
There is an ideal opportunity for higher attaining pupils to lead the class debate. They could be set up as 'experts' in a particular area or to play a particular role; they could argue the case for building a new coal-fired power station or they could be in charge of a group of pupils posing as environmentalists who do not want it to be built.

Homework Suggestion
Give pupils some pieces of universal indicator paper and ask them to collect and test the pH of rain water where they live. They will need to ensure the container they use is not contaminated before the collect the rain. (**Safety:** Universal indicator is flammable.)

Answers to in-text questions

a Similarities: both mixtures, both solutions, both contain acids, both react with bases. Differences: rain water only contains a weak acid; acid rain contains a strong acid. Acid rain has a lower pH than rain water.

b Sulfuric acid and nitric acid.

C2.9 Physical Weathering

NC links for the lesson
- Geological events are a combination of chemical and physical processes.
- Human activity and natural processes can lead to changes in the environment.
- Use a range of scientific methods and techniques to develop and test ideas and explanations.
- Carry out practical and investigative activities, both individually and in groups.

Learning Objectives

Pupils should learn:
- What physical weathering is.
- How physical weathering changes rocks.

Learning Outcomes
- All pupils should be able to recognise onion-skin and freeze-thaw weathering.
- Most pupils should be able to list the processes involved in onion-skin and freeze-thaw weathering.
- Some pupils should be able to explain onion-skin and freeze–thaw weathering in terms of particles.

How Science Works
- Explain how the observation and recording methods are appropriate to the task (1.2d).

Answers to in-text questions

a) No new chemicals have been made, so it is a physical change.

b) The volume of solid water is greater than the volume of liquid water – the only chemical to do this.

The Lesson

Starter Suggestions

Expanding milk
Show pupils a picture of a frozen milk bottle, showing the cap being forced off. Ask them to think about how it happened. [Water, the main substance in milk, expands when it freezes, overfilling the bottle and pushing the top off.] (5 mins)

Particles party
Ask pupils to recall from Year 7 work, and to sketch, the arrangement of particles in a solid [regularly arranged and all touching], a liquid [mostly touching but not regularly arranged] and a gas [not touching, randomly arranged]. (10 mins)

Main Lesson
- Discuss with pupils the different ways of weathering rocks they have met so far: biological weathering and chemical weathering. Explain to them

Learning Styles

Visual: Observing the ways that rocks can be weathered.
Auditory: Describing how weathering processes occur.
Kinaesthetic: Investigating physical weathering.
Interpersonal: Working with others during practicals.
Intrapersonal: Understanding that the weathering processes are very slow.

Functional Skills Link-up

English
- Present information on complex subjects concisely and clearly (level 2).

Physical Weathering

that rocks can also be weathered by physical processes such as changes in temperature and by movement.
- Get the class to set up 'Investigating freeze–thaw weathering' described in the pupil book. You may wish to have a frozen cylinder which you prepared earlier. [The volume of ice is greater than the volume of liquid water which formed it, owing to the way the molecules align in the solid. You could link this to particle arrangements in matter. The expansion in volume forces rocks to split.]
- The instructions for 'Demonstrating onion-skin weathering' are given in the pupil book. Pupils must be very careful about broken glass during this experiment as the glass rod will break and may shatter. For this reason, you may wish to demonstrate rather than allow the pupils to carry it out. [The surface and the centre of the rod expand when the rod is heated and contract when it is cooled in the water. However, these processes happen much more quickly on the surface and the two parts do not move at the same rate.]

Plenary Suggestions

Sort it out?
Give pupils statements which describe how freeze–thaw weathering takes place, but in the wrong order. Ask them to place the sentences into the correct order. (5 mins)

A tall tale?
Ask pupils if the following statement is true or false: The mountains of Snowdonia, North Wales were once taller than many in the Alps. [True; although the highest point in Snowdonia is now only 1085 m above sea level while many mountains in the Alps tower at over 3000 m, the Alps are new in geological terms and still growing, raised up by the action of tectonic plates in the Mediterranean. Snowdonia is much older and the mountains we see today are merely the harder, metamorphic rock which used to lie under a huge mass of limestone. This limestone has been weathered and transported away.] (10 mins)

Practical Support

Investigating freeze–thaw weathering
Equipment and materials required
Per group: 100 cm^3 measuring cylinder, 100 cm^3 water, access to a freezer in which the cylinder can sit upright.

Details
Refer to pupil book. It may be best to have placed a replica of the pupil experiment into the freezer the night before, as pupils will otherwise have to wait until a later lesson to see the outcome.

Safety
Normal laboratory rules.

Demonstrating onion-skin weathering
Equipment and materials required
Per group (or for teacher): glass stirring rod (which will get broken), Bunsen burner, heat mat, matches, 250 cm^3 beaker, 150 cm^3 cold water, eye protection.

Details
Refer to pupil book.

Safety
Pupils must be very careful not to burn themselves or each other and to look out for glass shards flying off glass rod when reheated.

Wear eye protection.

Differentiation

SEN
In 'Investigating freeze–thaw weathering' lower attaining pupils should concentrate on the qualitative results, rather than measuring the pieces. They could draw sketches of the pieces.

Extension
Ask pupils to research why broken rock in mountains is usually sharp-edged, unlike beach pebbles. [The rock in mountains has not rubbed against other rock to round it and is more likely to have been broken by freeze–thaw and fallen to its resting place.]

Answers to Summary questions

1
  a) Physical weathering is caused by physical changes in rocks.
  b) Large changes in temperature can cause rocks to peel.
  c) Trapped rain water in rocks can freeze and expand, causing the crack to get bigger.
  d) When rocks get hot, they expand, and when they get cold they contract.

2

Information	Biological	Chemical	Physical
Definition	Rocks break down into smaller pieces	Rocks broken down into new chemicals	Rocks broken down into smaller pieces
Type of change	Physical change	Chemical change	Physical change
Human impact	Can kill/control animals and plants and eliminate this	Can be speeded up by pollution (e.g. acid rain)	Physical change

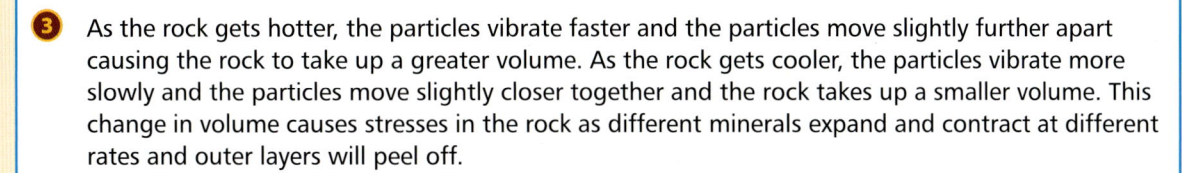

3 As the rock gets hotter, the particles vibrate faster and the particles move slightly further apart causing the rock to take up a greater volume. As the rock gets cooler, the particles vibrate more slowly and the particles move slightly closer together and the rock takes up a smaller volume. This change in volume causes stresses in the rock as different minerals expand and contract at different rates and outer layers will peel off.

C2.10 Erosion

NC links for the lesson
- Geological events are a combination of chemical and physical processes.
- Human activity and natural processes can lead to changes in the environment.
- Carry out practical and investigative activities, both individually and in groups.

Learning Objectives
Pupils should learn:
- What erosion is.
- What happens to weathered rock.

Learning Outcomes
- All pupils should be able to recall a definition for erosion.
- Most pupils should be able to explain the size of particles in a river in terms of energy flow.
- Some pupils should also be able to predict where different sizes of particle will be found in a river and to explain why.

How Science Works
- Describe how the use of a particular model or analogy supports an explanation (1.1a1).

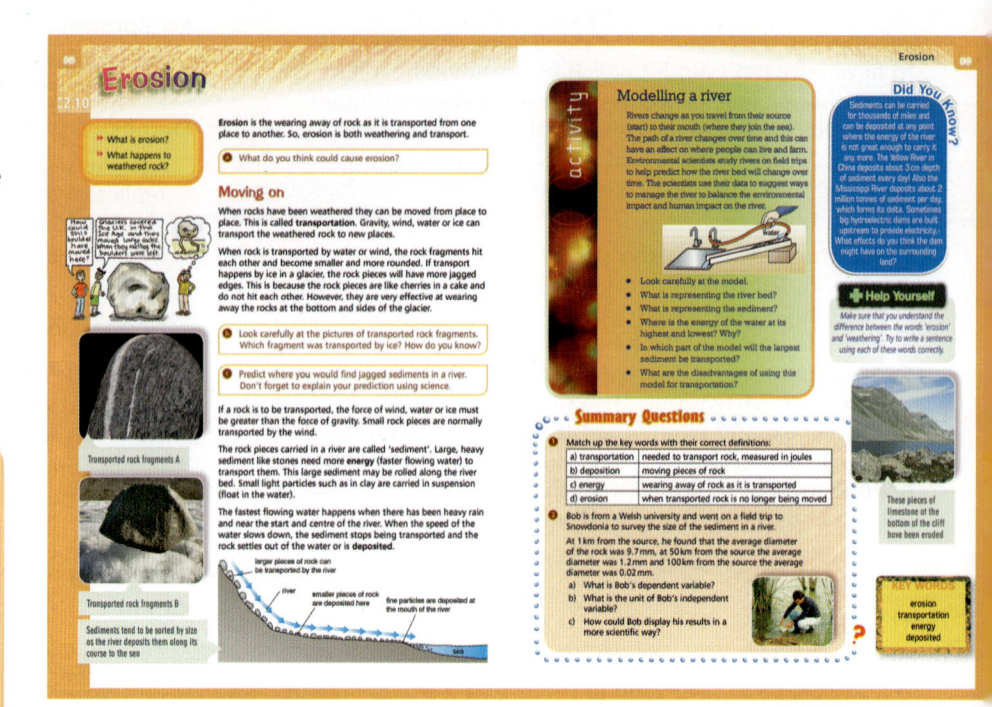

Learning Styles
Visual: Observing the movement of rock fragments in the transportation investigation.
Auditory: Sharing their observations with each other.
Kinaesthetic: Investigating transportation.
Interpersonal: Working with others during the practical.

Answers to Summary questions

1.
   a) Transportation: moving pieces of rock.
   b) Deposition: when transported rock is no longer being moved.
   c) Energy: needed to transport rock, measured in joules.
   d) Erosion: wearing away of rock as it is transported.

2.
   a) Average diameter of rock.
   b) km
   c) Table – not a line graph as there are not at least five data points.

Erosion

The Lesson

Starter Suggestions

Tread carefully
Show pupils a photograph of a badly eroded footpath and ask them to suggest how it has happened. (5 mins)

Plant power (Part 2)
Ask pupils to look again at the bean plants they may have planted in lesson C2.6. Study the way the roots have damaged the sand and pushed it aside. (10 mins)

Main Lesson

- Ask pupils to recall the ways in which rocks can be weathered that they have studied over the past few lessons. Remind them too of how sedimentary rocks form from sediments which settle in the sea. Ask pupils to suggest how pieces of rock from mountains might be found by the sea. They may suggest that water can transport them.

- Ask pupils to carry out the 'Modelling a river' investigation described in the pupil book. They will need to set it up carefully and to observe closely what happens to the 'sediment' in the river. The water flow rate must not be too great or all the sediment will wash down at once.

- Ask pupils to work in small groups to come up with a description of what they saw happening. They should then share their ideas with another group, before the whole class comes together to decide how they think rocks are transported by rivers. [Small pieces are transported more easily. When the river slows the bigger pieces are 'dropped' first.]

- Ensure pupils are clear about the difference between 'weathering' and 'erosion'. [The former refers to breaking up of the original rock mass, where it was formed. The latter refers to the breaking down of fragments of rock as they are transported. Together, weathering and erosion lead to 'denudation' of the landscape.]

Plenary Suggestions

Waterfall
Show pupils a picture of a waterfall. Ask them to explain why waterfalls move upstream over time. [The foot of the waterfall is continuously eroded and the cliff breaks off, moving the waterfall upstream.] (5 mins)

How did it happen?
Show pupils a picture of an oxbow lake. Ask them to try to explain how it formed. [The 'bow' was once part of the main river channel. However, the flow of the water cut through the banks at the start of the bow, eventually creating a short-cut.] (10 mins)

Practical Support

Modelling a river

Equipment and materials required
Per group: 80–100 cm length of square guttering, water trough or sink, 20 cm^3 ink, length of rubber tubing, access to a tap, rock fragments of different sizes – stony soil would work well.

Details
Refer to pupil book. Pupils should run water down the guttering first, without any stones, dripping some ink in to observe the flow rate better at different points. After putting in the rock fragments they should gently wash them with water, observing the different flow rates depending upon the size of the pieces. You may wish to fit traps to the sinks to prevent soil and stones being washed down them. A fine sieve could be attached to the end of the guttering.

Safety
Normal laboratory rules.

Differentiation

SEN
Lower attaining pupils may need assistance in setting up the investigation successfully. It is important that the flow rate is neither too slow (nothing moves) or too fast (all the rock moves). In either case it will be impossible to observe what happens in nature. Give pupils a series of small diagrams showing rocks of different sizes. Ask pupils to place the images in order of the ease with which they are moved by the water, from fastest to slowest.

Extension
Ask pupils to find out how lapidary is carried out using grits and stones of different sizes to work and polish rocks.

Homework Suggestion

Pupils could find out what National Park authorities are doing to limit footpath erosion on popular routes such as the Pennine Way. [Much of it is being laid with rock slabs which wear away much more slowly. However, some believe that this is damaging to the environment both because of the helicopters which are often used to transport the stone and because of the vastly altered appearance of the landscape.]

Answers to in-text questions

a Wind, water (rain or rivers), ice.

b B, it has jagged edges.

c Where the rock has just been weathered into the river. This is before the rock has had the chance to be transported and the other rocks have not had the chance to erode the surface.

C2.11 Rock Cycle

NC links for the lesson
- Geological events are a combination of chemical and physical processes.
- Human activity and natural processes can lead to changes in the environment.
- Use a range of scientific methods and techniques to develop and test ideas and explanations.
- Assess risk and work safely in the laboratory, field and workplace.
- Carry out practical and investigative activities, both individually and in groups.

Learning Objectives
Pupils should learn:
- How new rocks are made from old ones.
- What the rock cycle is.

Learning Outcomes
- All pupils should be able to describe that igneous, sedimentary and metamorphic rocks are connected by a series of processes.
- Most pupils should be able to recall the main parts of the rock cycle.
- Some pupils should also be able to explain how new rocks are formed from old.

Learning Styles
Visual: Completing the diagram of the rock cycle.
Auditory: Describing sections of the rock cycle to the group.
Intrapersonal: Understanding that the processes in the rock cycle take millions of years to occur.

Answers to in-text questions
(a) Igneous, sedimentary, metamorphic.
(b) Erosion → deposition → compaction → cementation.

Rock Cycle

The Lesson

Starter Suggestions

Word Up
Give pupils anagrams of the key words from this unit, such as igneous, metamorphic, sedimentary, weathering, transportation and erosion. They must unravel the words. (5 mins)

Recycled rocks
Ask pupils to sketch a flow chart to show how they think igneous rocks can become sedimentary rocks. (10 mins)

Main Lesson

- Remind pupils of the work they have done in this unit, from the different types of rock to the work done on weathering and erosion.
- Explain to the class that the minerals on Earth are recycled naturally over millions of years. The weathered fragments of igneous rock can be transported by rivers and eroded, eventually becoming sediments in the sea. These sediments can be compressed and cemented, forming sedimentary rock over time. Both igneous and sedimentary rock can be changed by heat and pressure inside the Earth into metamorphic rock.
- Pupils could make a model of the rock cycle using wax crayons or candles. They could use these to demonstrate each process within the rock cycle and label a flow diagram.
- Give pupils an outline diagram of the rock cycle and ask them to annotate and complete it. They should add the names of any missing rock types and processes such as weathering and transportation. They should also, if they can, add details to summarise how each step takes place, such as how sedimentary rocks are formed.
- To complete the activity you could ask individual pupils to explain a section of the cycle.

Plenary Suggestions

Have I been asleep?
Ask pupils to imagine what Britain might look like after 100 million years of the rock cycle have taken place. (5 mins)

Poet's corner
Ask pupils to create a rhyme or phrase to help them remember the order of the main sequence in the rock cycle. For example: Igneous, Weathering, Transportation, Sedimentary, Metamorphic, Igneous … could be remembered as 'Ian went to Skegness, made ice'. (10 mins)

Differentiation

SEN
You may wish to give pupils pre-written labels to add to their rock cycle, rather than leaving them to write their own. They would need to decide where to put the labels, rather than write their own text.

Extension
Ask pupils to research a recent earthquake and to find out how severe it was. They may need to research the Richter scale first and they should also find out what causes earthquakes. [There are many earthquakes every day around the world, though most are very minor. Quakes occur along the boundaries of tectonic plates where, owing to the sliding of two plates, stresses occur in the rocks. These stresses can release suddenly, shaking the ground. Common earthquake zones include the western coast of the USA and South America, Japan and Southern Europe. Developed in 1935 by Charles Richter, the Richter scale describes, from 1 to 10, the severity of an earthquake. It is not, however, a linear scale.]

Homework Suggestion

Ask pupils to write a story about the life of a crystal in igneous rock. The story should give details of what happens to the rock after it has been weathered.

Answers to Summary questions

1. Igneous rocks can become other types of rock, when they have been eroded.
   Metamorphic rocks are made when heat and/or pressure changes other types of rock.
   The Earth is a closed system.
   Rocks are constantly changing and being recycled.

2. Differences: Intrusive rock is formed surrounded by other rocks, having large crystals. Extrusive rock is formed on or near the surface of the Earth and is made of small crystals.

   Similarities: They are both made from cooled magma. Neither will contain fossils and both will usually contain crystals.

3. Discussion.

C2.12 Rocks in the Universe

NC links for the lesson
- Geological events are a combination of chemical and physical processes.
- Obtain, record and analyse data from a wide range of primary and secondary sources, including ICT sources, and use their findings to provide evidence for scientific explanations.

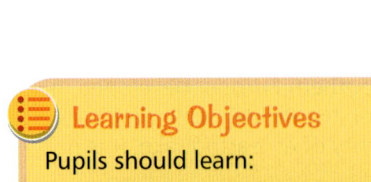

Learning Objectives

Pupils should learn:
- That igneous, sedimentary and metamorphic rocks are found elsewhere in the universe.
- That other planets have rock cycles.

Learning Outcomes

- All pupils should be able to recall that rocks are found elsewhere in the universe.
- Most pupils should be able to explain that other planets have rock cycles.
- Some pupils should also be able to explain how evidence for what is happening in other parts of the universe is gathered.

How Science Works

- Describe what needs to be considered in the collection and manipulation of secondary evidence to evaluate the conclusion or interpretation made (1.2f).
- Recognise that the selection, ordering or rejection of secondary data could lead to different conclusions (1.2f).

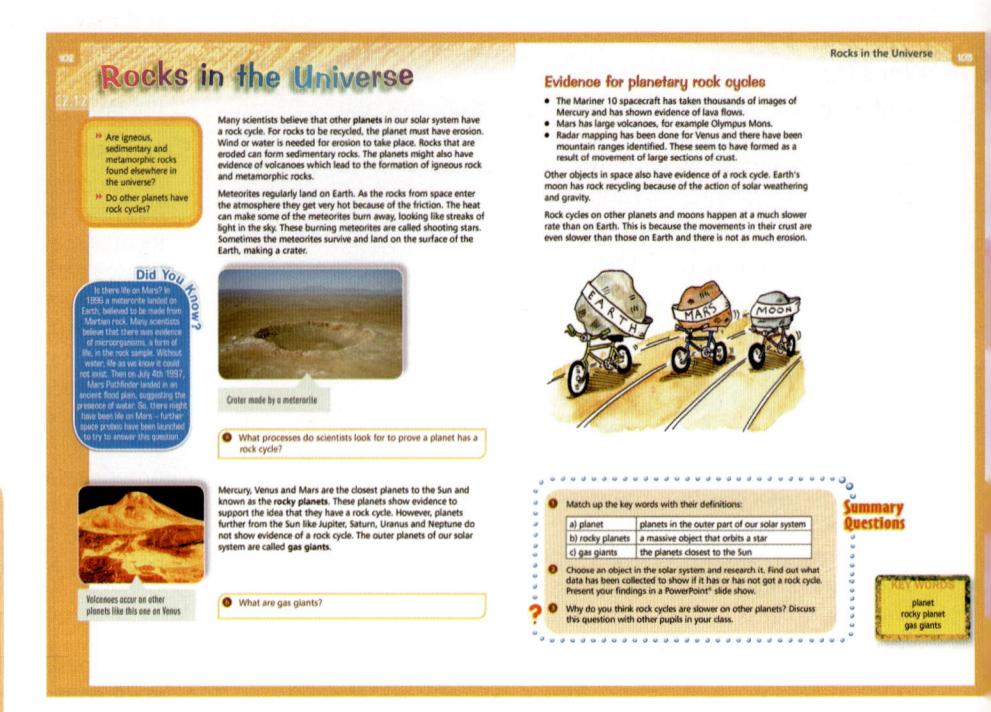

Learning Styles

Auditory: Describing their research into other planets.
Kinaesthetic: Investigating meteorites.
Intrapersonal: Understanding that other planets may have a rock cycle.

Functional Skills Link-up

Literacy
- Writing a report about rock cycles on other planets and the newspaper report.

ICT
- Researching information about other planets.

Answers to in-text questions

a) Erosion and volcanic activity.

b) The outer planets of our solar system, e.g. Jupiter, Saturn, Uranus and Neptune.

Rocks in the Universe

The Lesson

Starter Suggestions

Solar system
Ask pupils to name the planets in our solar system, in order, starting from the Sun if possible [Mercury, Venus, Earth, Mars, Jupiter, Saturn, Neptune, Uranus and Pluto. However, there is an ongoing debate about whether Pluto is too small to be classed as a planet.] (5 mins)

Rock on!
Ask pupils to recall the key elements of the rock cycle. (10 mins)

Main Lesson

- Remind pupils about the rock cycle. Suggest that it might be possible for other planets to have a rock cycle too. Ask pupils whether they think this might be possible.
- Gather suggestions as to what scientists might look for when trying to ascertain whether other planets have a rock cycle and how they might obtain this evidence. [Evidence might include: the presence of volcanoes (as on Mars), images of lava flows (which may be visible on Venus) or the existence of mountain ranges which are often brought about by the movement of tectonic plates. Evidence could be obtained by satellite pictures or from data sent back to Earth by probes.]
- If you have the resources available, give pupils some pieces of meteorite to study. Explain that meteorites are pieces of rock which were not formed on Earth, but in other parts of space. Ask pupils to decide whether the meteorite samples could be classified as one of the rock types found on Earth. If they can it would be further evidence of rock cycles existing on other planets.
- Give pupils the opportunity to research the possibility of rock cycles on other planets. The best way to do this is probably via the Internet, using search terms which include the name of a planet and terms such as 'tectonic' or 'volcano'. Good websites to begin research include: http://solarsystem.nasa.gov/planets and http://bbc.co.uk/science/space/solarsystem/earth
- Ask members of the class to report back their findings. They could do this as a short PowerPoint display.

Plenary Suggestions

Sort it out
Give pupils the key words from this topic and ask them to match them to definitions. (5 mins)

Read all about it!
Ask pupils to write a newspaper report about a volcano eruption on Mars, as seen by a satellite above the Earth. (10 mins)

Practical Support

Main lesson: Studying meteorites

Equipment and materials required
Per group: access to several pieces of different meteorites. Samples may be loaned from the Schools and Education section of the Science and Technology Facilities Council website (www.stfc.ac.uk), hand lens, mounted needle.

Details
Study the meteorite samples and decide whether they can be classified as igneous, sedimentary, metamorphic or none of these.

Safety
Mounted needles are sharp. Care must be taken when carrying or using them.

Differentiation

SEN
Lower attaining pupils will need extra support for the research task. It may be best to concentrate on just Mars and Venus where there is plenty of evidence of a rock cycle and to find a reliable webpage before the lesson. The content on the Internet changes too fast for it to be worth including an address here.

Extension
The key opportunity here is in the depth and quality of the research carried out. Pupils could be encouraged to look for common patterns in the geology of all the planets in the solar system, e.g. whether Earth's minerals are found elsewhere. Pupils could also consider the reliability of 'evidence' found on meteorites, for example could the bacteria which have been found on some actually have come from contamination on Earth?

Answers to Summary questions

1.
   a) Planet: a massive object that orbits a star.
   b) Rocky planets: the planets closest to the Sun.
   c) Gas giants: planets in the outer part of our solar system.

2. Research and presentation.

3. Discussion.

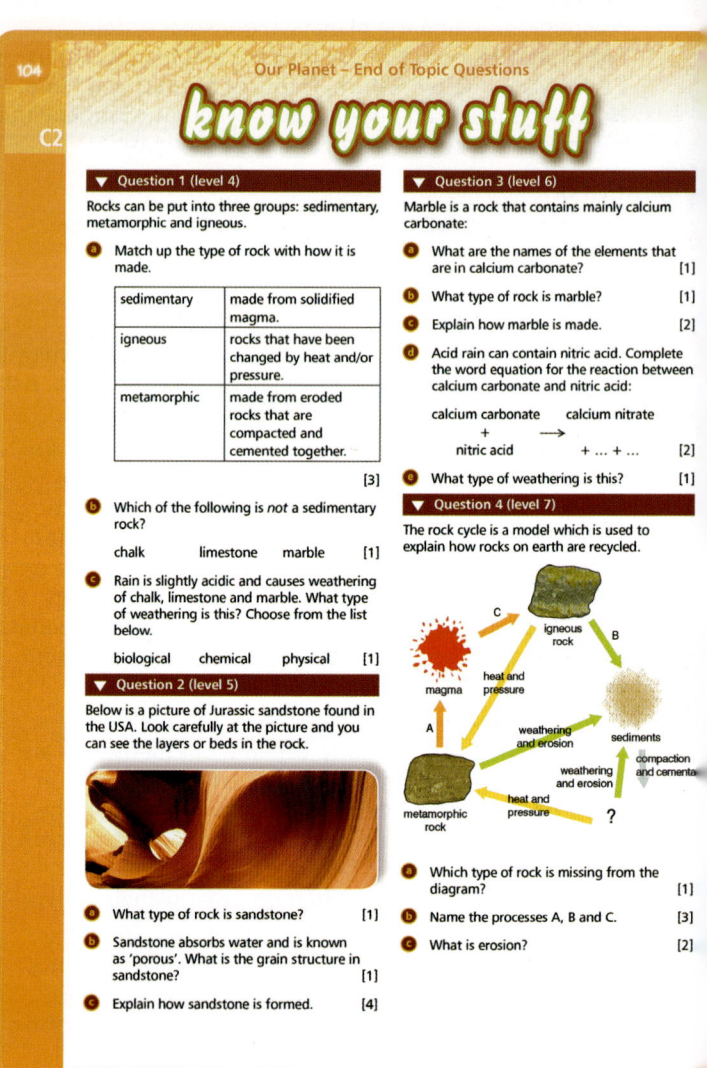

Answers to Our Planet – End of Topic Questions

Answers to know your stuff questions

1.
   a. Sedimentary: made from eroded rocks that are compacted and cemented together. Igneous: made from solidified magma. Metamorphic: rocks that have been changed by heat and/or pressure. [3]
   b. marble. [1]
   c. chemical. [1]

2.
   a. Sedimentary. [1]
   b. Non-interlocking. [1]
   c. Rock is weathered and transported/eroded. [1]
   Sediment is deposited/dropped. [1]
   Sediment is compacted/squashed. [1]
   Sediment is cemented/stuck together with minerals. [1]

3.
   a. Calcium, carbon and oxygen. [1]
   b. Metamorphic. [1]
   c. Sedimentary rock containing calcium carbonate/limestone/chalk [1]
   is changed by heat and/or pressure. [1]
   d. calcium carbonate + nitric acid → calcium nitrate + **carbon dioxide + water** [2]
   e. Chemical. [1]

4.
   a. Sedimentary. [1]
   b. A: melting. [1]
   B: Erosion/weathering and transport. [1]
   C: solidifying/freezing. [1]
   c. Weathering/breaking down rocks. [1]
   Transport/moving sediment. [1]

Our Planet – End of Topic Questions

How Science Works

Question 1 (level 4)

Doug and Mohammed wanted to investigate if temperature affected the speed of chemical weathering. They measured the time it took for a piece of marble to produce 20cm³ of gas when it was in acid at 0°C, 10°C, 20°C, 30°C and 40°C.

a What are the control variables in Doug and Mohammed's experiment? These are the variables they kept constant to make sure this was a fair test. [2]

b Explain how Doug and Mohammed could cool acid down to 0°C. [1]

c Which of the following pieces of equipment would be the most sensitive way to measure the volume of acid? Choose one from the list below.

beaker   measuring jug
measuring cylinder   balance [1]

d What piece of equipment would Doug and Mohammed use to measure the independent variable (the variable they chose to investigate)?

thermometer   ruler   stopwatch   balance [1]

Question 2 (level 5)

Louise decided to investigate how temperature affects the crystal size in an igneous rock. She used liquid salol to model magma. Louise dropped a small amount of salol on warmed or cooled microscope slides and let it solidify. She then measured the diameter of three crystals on each slide.

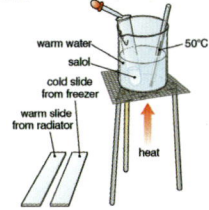

a Why did Louise have to use a model to investigate the crystal size in rocks? [1]

b What is the independent variable in Louise's experiment? (The independent variable is the one she chose to investigate.) [1]

c What is the dependent variable in Louise's experiment? (The dependent variable is the one she measured to see the effect of changing the independent variable.) [1]

d How could Louise make her measurements more precise? [1]

Question 3 (level 6)

Dan and Charlie went on a field trip and collected information about the average sediment size in a river. They found out that at 0km from the source of the river, the rocks had an average diameter of 10.1mm, at 5km it was 9.3mm, at 15km it was 5.1mm, at 10km it was 8mm and at 20km it was 4.4mm.

a Draw a table of Dan and Charlie's results. [4]

b Which is the least precise measurement of diameter? [1]

c Explain why a line graph could be drawn from this data. [2]

Answers to How Science Works questions

1 a Any two: concentration of acid/volume of acid/mass of marble/surface area of marble. [2]

b Use an ice bath. [1]

c measuring cylinder. [1]

d thermometer. [1]

2 a We cannot get to high enough temperatures to use molten rock in a school lab. [1]

b Temperature. [1]

c Diameter of crystal. [1]

d Use a different measuring instrument with finer scale divisions. [1]

3 a

Distance from source (km)	Average diameter (mm)
0	10.1
5	9.3
10	8
15	5.1
20	4.4

Correct column headings. [1]
Units included in column headings. [1]
Data put into the table. [1]
Data put in the table in order of distance from the source. [1]

b 8mm [1]

c Both the independent and dependent variable are continuous. [1]

There are five data points, which are the minimum needed to draw a line graph. [1]

P1.1 Light and Space

NC links for the topic
- Energy, electricity and forces: energy can be transferred usefully, stored, or dissipated, but cannot be created or destroyed (light). Forces are interactions between objects and can affect their shape and motion.
- The environment, Earth and universe: astronomy and space science provide insight into the nature and observed motions of the Sun, Moon, stars, planets and other celestial bodies.
- Key concepts: Using scientific ideas and models to explain phenomena and developing them creatively to generate and test theories. Critically analysing and evaluating evidence from observations and experiments. Use a range of scientific methods and techniques to develop and test ideas and explanations. Assess risk and work safely in the laboratory, field and workplace. Carry out practical and investigative activities, both individually and in groups.

Level descriptors for the topic
- **AT4 level 4:** Pupils describe some processes and phenomena related to energy, forces and space, drawing on scientific knowledge and understanding and using appropriate terminology, for example the observed position of the Sun in the sky over the course of a day.
- **AT4 level 5:** Pupils explain processes and phenomena, in more than one step or using a model, such as the length of a day or a year. They recognise that both evidence and creative thinking contribute to the development of scientific ideas, such as objects being seen when light from them enters the eye.
- **AT4 level 6:** Pupils describe processes and phenomena related to energy, forces and space, using abstract ideas and appropriate terminology. They take account of a number of factors in their explanations of processes and phenomena, for example in the relative brightness of stars and planets. They also use abstract ideas or models, for example the refraction of light. They apply and use knowledge and understanding in unfamiliar contexts. They describe some evidence for some accepted scientific ideas, such as the transfer of energy by light, sound or electricity, and the refraction and dispersion of light.
- **AT4 level 7:** Pupils apply and use more abstract knowledge and understanding in a range of contexts, such as the appearance of objects in different colours of light. They explain how evidence supports some accepted scientific ideas.

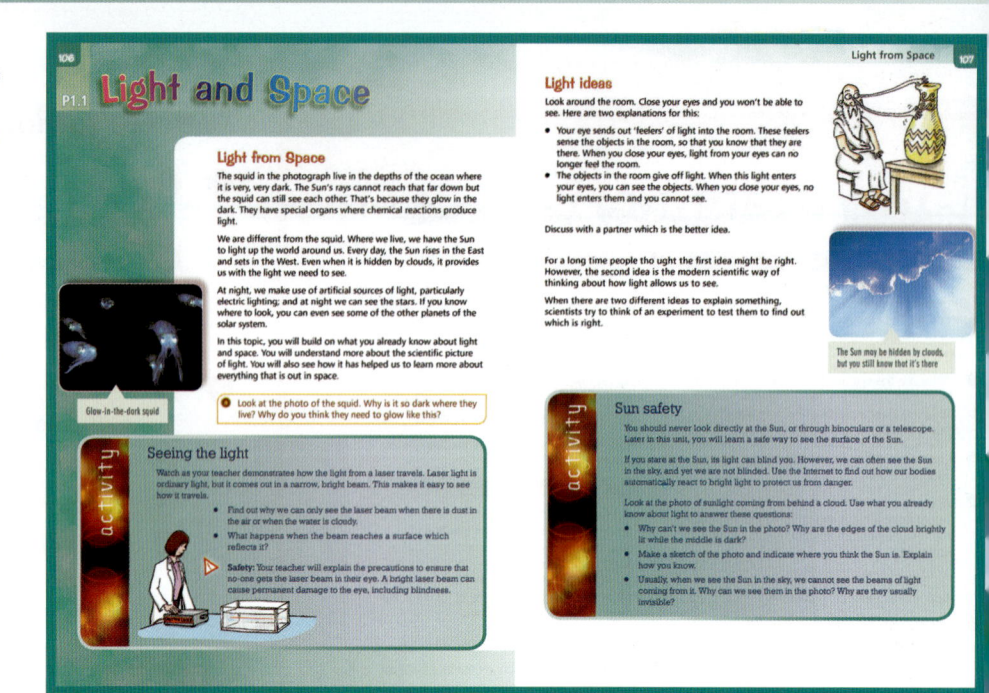

Learning Styles
Visual: Watching demonstrations of light travelling.

Auditory: Discussing the effect of light on our eye.

Kinaesthetic: Drawing ray diagrams.

Interpersonal: Discussing the history of the study of light.

Intrapersonal: Making observations about the behaviour of light.

Learning Objectives
Pupils should learn:
- That light rays travel in straight lines.
- That we see objects when light rays are reflected off them and enter our eyes.

Learning Outcomes
- All pupils should be able to state that light travels in straight lines.
- Most pupils should be able explain, using a simple ray diagram, that we see objects when light travels from them into our eyes.
- Some pupils should also be able to explain why it is not possible that we see by emitting energy from our eyes.

How Science Works
- Describe more than one model to explain the same phenomenon and discuss the strengths and weaknesses of each model (1.1a1).

Answers to in-text questions
a The water above them absorbs the energy of the light so it does not reach them. They glow so that they can detect each other more easily; this helps them stay together.

Light from Space

The Lesson

Starter Suggestions

Making light work

Ask the pupils to make a list of ways and objects that produce light. This will include the Sun, electric lights, candles and some chemical reactions. Discuss what most of them have in common. [Most are very hot.] If you have time, then demonstrate a few. (5 mins)

Under the sea

Show the pupils a slideshow of creatures that live deep in the ocean. Use images of species that produce their own light along with some that are completely blind. A scene in *Finding Nemo* from Pixar Studios shows a (slightly exaggerated) fish that is worth watching. (5–10 mins).

Main Lesson

- Start the lesson by looking into the depths with the 'Under the sea' starter. The pupils will begin to understand the importance of light to the sensing of our environment.
- Use the 'Seeing the light' demonstration to get across the concept of a ray; this is vital for understanding much of the next few lessons. Show the pupils the hazard symbol for laser light and discuss what it means including the potential damage to the retina.
- The ray should look very straight and sharp. Use this to emphasise that a ruler must always be used when drawing rays to ensure accuracy. Ask the pupils to draw a simple diagram of a light ray to check that they do this.
- Some pupils may want to know why light spreads out from a source, such as a lamp, if it only travels in straight lines. You can spend some time here describing the way that sources produce a very large number rays that spread out to clear this issue up early. This also explains why the light appears dimmer as you move further away (fewer of the rays enter your eye). With higher attaining pupils you could mention that light can be modelled in another way, the wave model, and this is better at explaining the way light spreads.
- The ideas concerning how we see objects were debated by the ancient Greeks. The Greek philosophers (with the notable exception of Euclid) tended towards the idea that light was sent out from the eye so that we could see things. There were obvious problems concerning why we could not see as well at night or in a cave, but various God-related explanations for this were proposed. This is an excellent opportunity to discuss the key concept of development of scientific ideas through creative thought.
- The Muslim scientist Ibn al-Haytham seems to have settled the matter in detail with his *Book of Optics* in the early 1000s. This covered quite a lot of what we now know of as optical theory. This links in well with the key concept of cultural understanding where science has its roots in different societies.
- Early comic book characters with X-ray vision tended to emit rays from their eyes so that they could see through materials. More modern variations have updated this after criticism of the mechanisms as unrealistic! You may be able to find images on the Internet showing these ideas and discuss why they are wrong.
- Be careful with the idea that we see objects when they give out light; most objects simply reflect light from the actual sources of light. Mention the ideas of a light *source* at this stage if it has not already come up.

- The warning given about the laser beam cannot be emphasised strongly enough. The eye has a natural reflex to look away from bright light sources, but this can be partly overcome and damage to the retina is permanent.

Plenary Suggestions

Shiny happy people

Many people love sunlight. Discuss, or ask the pupils to write about, whether sitting out in the Sun is good or bad for us. Most will know that sunlight can damage the skin, but do any know of any benefits? (5–10 mins)

Bright light! Bright light!

The pupils may have seen a warning symbol for laser light, but can they design one warning people not to look at the Sun? The symbol must not contain words as it has to be international. (5–10 mins)

Practical Support

Demonstration: Seeing the light

Equipment and materials required

A low power laser light source (a laser pointer pen is suitable if it is clamped in position; some modern 'spirit levels' use low power laser light and these are also suitable), chalk dust or talc to show the beam path.

Details

This is a simple demonstration of laser light intended to show the idea of rays. Shine the laser light onto a dark matt surface so that the students can see the laser spot; they will not be able to see the beam itself. Use chalk dust to show the ray itself, explaining that the beam is visible because parts of it are now reflecting off the very small particles.

Safety

Laser light can be damaging to the eyes, even at the level from a low power laser. The laser must be pointed away from all pupils onto a matt surface to avoid the possibility of an intense beam of reflected light reaching the pupils' eyes. Domestic lasers are not always calibrated or categorised correctly. Store securely. More info on CLEAPSS CD-Rom/handbook section 12.12 and PS52. The teacher must do a risk assessment and make their own decision based upon the class.

Differentiation

SEN

Provide the pupils with cartoons showing the two possible explanations about how we see things. Ask them to add notes to these explaining which is most likely to be correct.

Extension

The pupils could look into how the idea that light travels in straight lines was developed. There is a rather interesting history of the optical theory starting with Ibn al-Haytham (sometimes referred to as 'Alhacen') and leading up to Newton, Huygens and even Einstein, where the whole idea of 'straight lines' becomes a bit stranger as space itself becomes curved by gravity.

Homework Suggestion

Either one of the two differentiation activities is suitable for homework.

P1.2 Straight-line Light

NC links for the lesson
- Energy, electricity and forces: energy can be transferred usefully, stored, or dissipated, but cannot be created or destroyed (light).

Learning Objectives
Pupils should learn:
- That light (and infra-red) rays travel in straight lines.
- That light travels at the fastest possible speed.

Learning Outcomes
- All pupils should be able to describe a method to show that light travels in straight lines.
- Most pupils should be able to describe an experiment that can be used to test whether or not infra-red rays also travel in straight lines.
- Some pupils should also be able to state that light travelling in a vacuum travels at the fastest speed possible but travels at lower speeds in other materials.

How Science Works
- Describe an appropriate aproach to answer a scientific question using sources of evidence and, where appropriate, making relevant observations using appropriate apparatus (1.2a).

Functional Skills Link-up
Mathematics
- Carry out calculations with numbers of any size (level 2).

Answers to Summary questions
1. A ruler has a straight edge and light travels in a straight line.
2. Between 1 and 10 seconds (1.33 seconds).

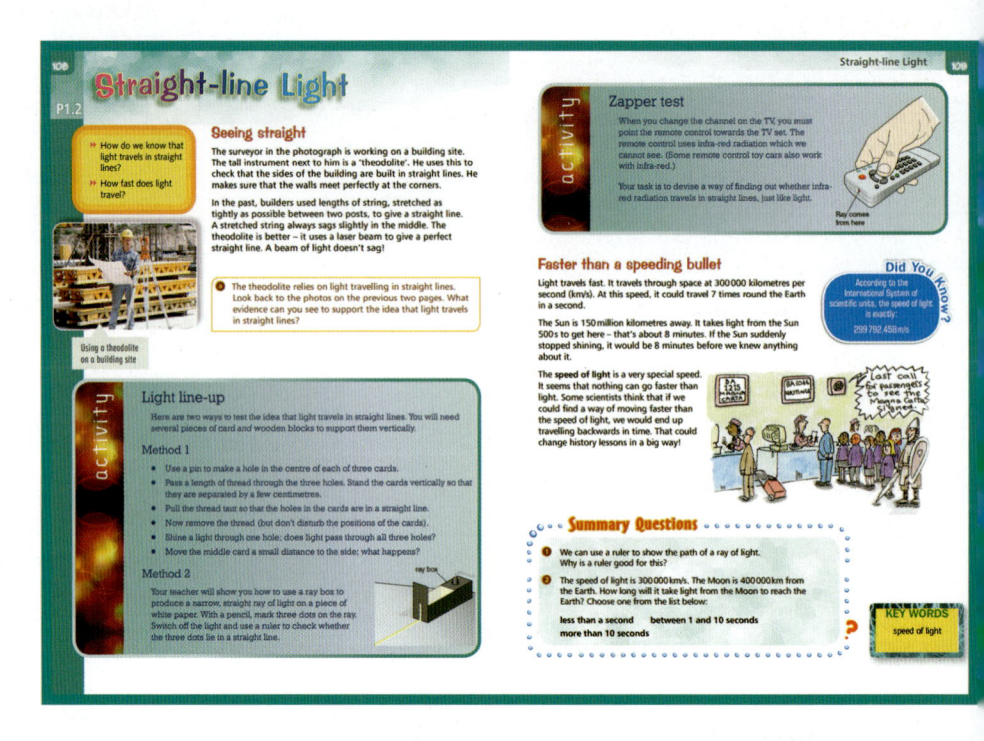

Learning Styles
Visual: Observing ray paths.
Auditory: Discussing the significance of the speed of light.
Kinaesthetic: Careful manipulation of equipment in practical task.
Interpersonal: Working in groups to plan an experiment.
Intrapersonal: Thinking about and evaluating the ray model for light.

Answers to in-text questions
a. The laser beam travels in a straight line.

Did You Know?
The speed of light is known exactly because length measurements are based on it and not the other way around. If we improve our measurement of the speed then the definition of a metre would have to change to make sure that the speed of light definition is left the same. The **current** definition of a meter is the distance travelled in a vacuum by light in 1/299 792 458 of a second. Of course, this means that we have to define exactly what a second is ...

The Lesson

Starter Suggestions

Straight to the point
Show the pupils a map showing the whole of Europe. Ask one to draw the shortest route from London to Rome. Everybody will probably agree that it's a straight line. Now show the pupils a globe. Is the shortest route still a straight line? (5–10 mins)

A level playing field
How can the pupils show that their desks are level? The pupils should come up with as many ways as possible to check this using simple equipment. The discussion can then be extended to larger objects or areas (snooker tables, football pitches) if you wish. (10–15 mins).

Main Lesson

- Demonstrate the problem with dipping string by hanging a piece across the length of the classroom. There will be a noticeable dip in the middle even when it is fairly taut. You could also demonstrate the path of a laser (using the technique from the previous lesson) across the room but make sure the beam does not come near any of the pupils.

- The first method in the 'Light line-up' activity is straightforward but can be a bit challenging to get just right. It is worth trying this method before the second, more traditional one, as it shows the three-dimensional nature of light travelling which is not usually clear in optical experiments.

- The second method is much simpler and introduces the techniques required to use ray boxes successfully. The pupils will need to be careful in order to get the crosses in the centre of the rays as these spread out a little as they get further from the source.

- Once the pupils are convinced that light is travelling in straight lines, you can move on to testing infra-red with the 'Zapper test' activity. This is primarily designed to let the pupils plan the experiment, but you can go further if time permits. This develops skills in investigatory work to an appropriate level.

- If you decide to test these out, the results will often show that the rays don't have to travel in straight lines. This is because the LED on the remote control spreads infra-red radiation in a wide beam, so doesn't have to be pointing at the sensor (which accepts IR from a wide angle too). To overcome this, you should add narrow cardboard tubes to both the transmitter and receiver.

- Getting the speed of light across to the pupils is rather difficult, especially if they have never travelled very large distances. Ask if anybody has been to New Zealand (or Australia) and how long it took. This will be about 20 hours. Click your fingers. In the length of time that the 'click' lasted, light would have reached New Zealand and got back.

- A speeding bullet travels at 1 km/s (three times faster than sound). Light is 300 000 times faster than this. The fastest a human has ever travelled (in Apollo 10) is only 11 km/s. That's nothing compared to light.

- Travelling at the speed of light is a bit difficult. To get even the tiniest particle up to that speed would require infinite energy.

- There are plenty of time travel movies to mention at the end of the lesson. Very few involve moving faster than light; instead they use other, equally impossible, techniques. However, in the film *Superman* the eponymous hero nips back in time by travelling at high speed to save Lois Lane from being crushed to death. Use this idea to lead into the 'Excellent adventure' plenary.

Plenary Suggestions

Speed-o-meter
Give the pupils a set of cards with a range of moving objects depicted on them: a snail, bicycle, car, plane, sound wave, light and some others. Can they put them in order of slowest to fastest? (5 mins)

Excellent adventure
Where would the students visit on a time travelling history field trip? What would they like to see and do? They can write down or discuss their ideas with you. (5–10 mins)

Practical Support

Light line-up (Method 1)

Equipment and materials required
For each group: three pieces of card, cotton on a large needle, three retort stands and boss and clamps, light source.

Details
The pupil book describes the technique. You may want to use the stands to hold the cards steady.

Safety
Needles (if used) will be very sharp.

Light line-up (Method 2)

Equipment and materials required
For each group: ray box with suitable power supply, blanking plates and a single slit, A4 white paper, pencil and ruler.

Details
The pupils follow the technique described in the pupil book.

Safety
The filament lamps in ray boxes can become very hot and should be handled with care especially when they are being put away.

Differentiation

SEN
Provide the pupils with some 'ideas cards' that give them clues about how to design the 'Zapper test' experiment.

Extension
The pupils can look into the International System of Units (SI) to find out why the speed of light is known exactly whereas other speeds are not. The pupils could also look at some of the other fundamental units used in physics: kilogram, second, ampere etc.

Homework Suggestion

The pupils could try the 'Excellent Adventure' plenary at home and write a bit more about their visit. Perhaps a pupil has *already* brought this homework in.

P1.3 Materials and Light

NC links for the lesson
- Energy, electricity and forces: energy can be transferred usefully, stored, or dissipated, but cannot be created or destroyed (light).

Learning Objectives
Pupils should learn:
- That materials can be described as transparent, opaque or translucent depending on how light passes through them.
- That light energy can be absorbed or transmitted by materials.
- How to measure the intensity (brightness) of a light source.

Learning Outcomes
- All pupils should be able to place materials into the categories transparent, opaque and translucent.
- Most pupils should be able to measure the intensity of a light source and compare the transparency of materials.
- Some pupils should also be able to evaluate an investigation into measuring the transparency of different materials.

How Science Works
- Describe and identify key variables in an investigation and assign appropriate values to these (1.2b).

Learning Styles
Visual: Observing the effect of different materials on light.
Auditory: Discussing the uses of various materials.
Kinaesthetic: Measuring light intensity.
Interpersonal: Discussing the uses of various materials.
Intrapersonal: Thinking about the interactions light has with materials.

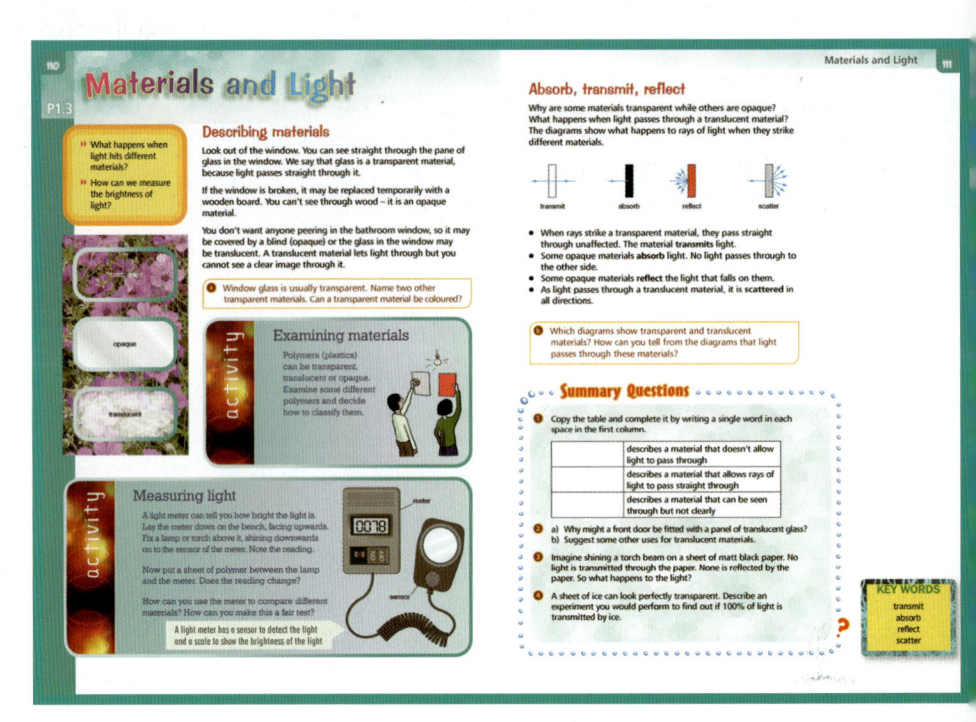

The Lesson

Starter Suggestions

Material choices
Give the pupils a range of materials (see the choices in the 'Examining materials' activity). They have to come up with one use for each of the materials. They don't have to use the correct scientific terms in their uses yet. [For example, a translucent plastic or glass for bathroom windows because it blurs the light.] (5 mins).

Group theory
Let groups of pupils examine the materials that they will be using during the lesson and a few extra ones. They have to sort the materials into three (and only three) groups and then explain what the groups are to you. Once they have done this they have to sort the materials into three entirely different groups and explain their decisions again. (5–10 mins)

Main Lesson
- This lesson contains quite a bit of scientific vocabulary that has to be used correctly. The pupils should be making a list of this vocabulary so that they can refer back to it when they are unsure. This is suggested as one of the plenary tasks 'Illuminate me'.

Answers to Summary questions

1. Opaque. Transparent. Translucent.
2. a) So that light can enter but there is some privacy.
   b) Bathroom windows, lights and lampshades, illuminated signs and anywhere privacy is required.
3. The paper takes in all of the energy from the light.
4. The experiment should involve measuring the intensity of the light before it enters the ice and then after it leaves. If the two measurements are the same then the block is perfectly transparent.

Materials and Light

- Start by letting the pupils handle the materials that will be used during the practical tasks. The 'Material choices' starter is a good option. This leads directly into a discussion of how we can describe the materials themselves.
- The pupil can then categorise the materials using the 'Examining materials' activity. This should be based on the categories: transparent, opaque and translucent. Make sure that all pupils understand these terms; they should be familiar with them from Key Stage 2, but reinforcement of key words is always useful.
- There may be some discussion about whether the coloured plastics are transparent or translucent. They are transparent (but only to certain colours) because they don't cause the image to be blurry.
- To perform the 'Measuring light' activity, the pupils will need access to a set of light sensors or meters. These are fairly cheap and worth investing in if your department hasn't already got a set. The focus should be on taking numerical measurements so that a true comparison can be made. The practical can be performed as a demonstration but isn't nearly as effective.
- When showing how to operate the light sensors you may want to show the intensity of sunlight compared to artificial light sources. On a reasonable day you should find that the Sun is many times brighter than a typical bulb. This does not seem correct when checked with the human eye (don't look directly at the Sun!) because the eye adapts to the brightness level and so can't make a fair comparison of brightness. This is a good investigatory point to discuss with the pupils; we can't trust our eyes so we use measuring instruments instead; good experiments yield measurements not opinions.
- The pupils should concentrate on making the test fair. This is rarely possible as, even if the light source is uniform and the distance to it is kept the same, the materials should be the same thickness and they usually aren't. Use this point to lead the pupils to evaluate and improve the design.
- The final part of the lesson focuses on three more key words: absorb, transmit and reflect. If anything these are more important than the first set. Make sure that all students can use them by getting them to describe a light journey from a source, through a transparent material (that transmits it), then a translucent one (that scatters it), onto a reflective material and finally onto an opaque material that absorbs the light. A diagram can help a lot.
- There are a number of software packages that simulate light ray journeys, including reflection and absorption that can be of help during this lesson. Not very many cover translucency though.

Plenary Suggestions

Taboo
The students can play 'taboo' with the words from this and other lessons from the light unit. Use a set of cards with the key words used so far (absorb, etc.) and words they cannot use in the description ('takes in', 'stops'); the pupils must get others in their group to guess the key word on the card. (5–10 mins)

Illuminate me
The pupils make a list of all of the scientific terms (transparent, opaque, translucent, absorb, transmit, reflect and scatter) and give definitions for them. Check these carefully. (5–10 mins)

Practical Support

Examining materials

Equipment and materials required
Each group needs access to some of the following materials: glass (a block), Perspex, polythene: thicker sheets or strips, paper, tracing paper, wood, wax (thin is best), sheets of plastic filters (red, green, blue) and black plastic bin liners. Other materials can also be used.

Details
The pupils just need to examine the materials and decide which categories they belong in. The materials are used in the following practical task too.

Safety
If glass materials are used then they need to be handled with care. Check for sharp edges; tape or file them if necessary.

Measuring light

Equipment and materials required
The pupils need access to some of the materials used in the previous experiments along with light sensors, rulers and lamps. Some sensors need to be connected to data-logging equipment to operate and so this equipment may be required.

Details
The exact details will depend on the design of the light sensors and the methods the pupils design. In general the material should be placed over the sensor and the luminosity recorded when the lamp is a set distance away from the sensor.

Safety
The lamps may become hot with prolonged use. The pupils should not stare directly into the light.

Differentiation

SEN
Provide diagrams showing a light ray being transmitted, reflected, absorbed etc. and allow the pupils to label these with the correct scientific terms.

Extension
The pupils can find out about how the eye operates and, in particular, how it adapts to different light levels. Just how sensitised is a 'dark-adapted eye' and how does it detect light? Warn pupils not to look directly at the Sun.

Homework Suggestion

The pupils can design improvements for the 'Measuring light' experiment based on their experiences.

Answers to in-text questions

a) Water, air, Perspex. A transparent material could be transparent to only certain colours, so it could be coloured.

b) The transmit diagram shows transparent material and the scatter shows opaque.

P1.4 Mirror, Mirror on the Wall …

NC links for the lesson

- Energy, electricity and forces: energy can be transferred usefully, stored, or dissipated, but cannot be created or destroyed (light).

Learning Objectives

Pupils should learn:

- That we can see images in mirrors because they reflect light.
- About the properties of these images.
- That the law of reflection is that the angle of incidence is equal to the angle of reflection.

Learning Outcomes

- All pupils should be able to state the law of reflection.
- Most pupils should be able to describe the properties of an image formed in a plane mirror.
- Some pupils should also be able to describe how an image is formed by a mirror using a ray diagram.

How Science Works

- Explain how the observation and recording methods are appropriate to the task (1.2d).

Answers to Summary questions

1. 90°
2. Pupil diagram.
3. Description of ray path.
4. Two mirrors at 60°
5. A plane mirror has a totally flat surface. The two types of curved mirrors are concave (curves inwards) and convex (curves outwards). A convex mirror can produce magnified images.

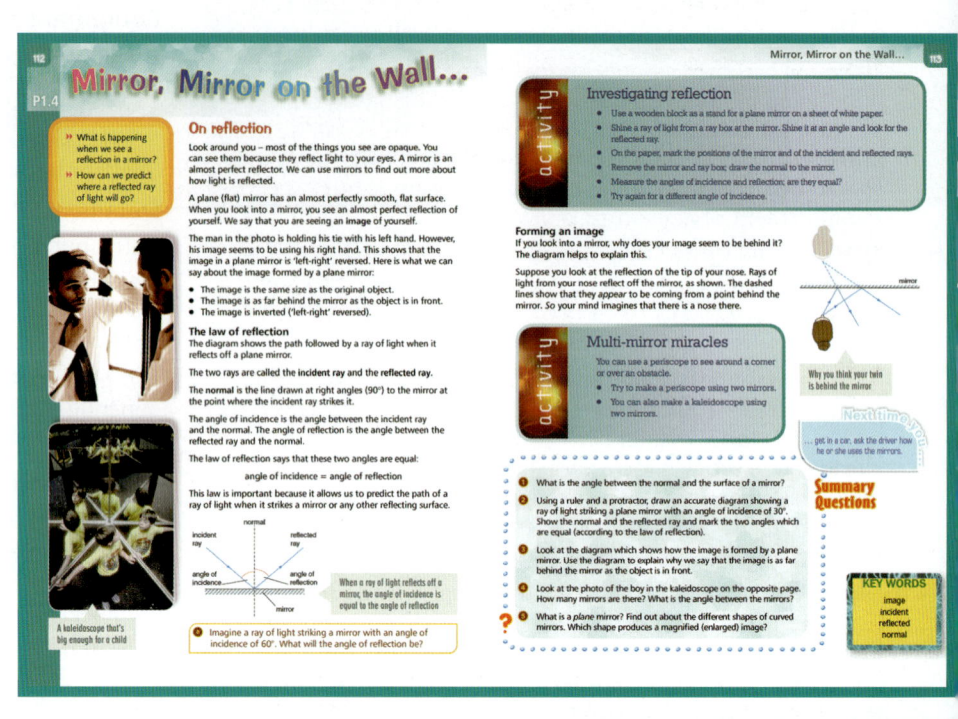

The Lesson

Starter Suggestions

Reality distortion
Show the pupils some photographs of images in distorted (fairground) mirrors. Ask them to describe the images, and see what language they use. Can they explain why the images are distorted and do they know what type of mirror doesn't distort images? (5–10 mins)

Backward
Set the pupils a few questions about light that are written in mirror text. They have to use a mirror to read the questions and then answer them. Bonus marks if they can write the answers backwards too. (10–15 mins)

Main Lesson

- This lesson is again rich in important terms: image, normal, incident and reflected. The pupils should add them to their list of definitions. Take time to ensure that the pupils can use them correctly throughout the lesson.
- During the first part of the lesson the pupils should freely examine mirrors, looking at images of themselves or writing in order to convince themselves of the properties of the image. They may come up with ways of checking the three properties mentioned in the pupil book if you ask them to. Discuss any they come up with.

Learning Styles

Visual: Observing ray paths and taking precise measurements.
Auditory: Discussing patterns in their results.
Kinaesthetic: Making precise measurements of angles.
Intrapersonal: Thinking about what an image in a mirror actually is.

Answers to in-text questions

a. 60°

Mirror, Mirror on the Wall …

- You can show that the image in a mirror is as far behind it as the object is in front by this simple technique: hold a 30 cm ruler under your nose pointing outwards. Hold a plane mirror at the end of it so you can see the image; the image you see is two ruler lengths 'away' from you so it's 30 cm behind the mirror.
- The law of reflection is a very important concept and the pupils will have to be convinced that it works. Before they try the experiment they must understand the terms used clearly especially the idea of a normal. Get them to draw a normal before they try out the experiment to make sure that they can do it.
- The angles must be measured from the normal line. The law will still work if the pupils measure from the surface of the *plane* mirror but it won't necessarily work if the mirror is not a plane one. If the angles are measured from the normal the law is *always* correct, no matter what shape the mirror (or other surface) is.
- The 'Investigating reflection' activity itself is straightforward and the results will be good if the pupils measure the reflection from the back surface of the mirror. They will be convinced that the law works after testing three or four angles of incidence. Use the task to develop the pupils' manipulative skills and ability to measure angles accurately.
- If the pupils are careless then they will only convince themselves that the law doesn't work, but won't admit to this, so it's really important to see that the pupils are actually getting the expected results.
- You can also use a reflection simulation to show that the angles are the same. This is best used as a summary after the pupils have convinced themselves it works in real life.
- Image formation is a fairly difficult concept and explaining why writing looks backwards is very difficult. Only higher attaining pupils will fully understand the ray diagrams. It's enough for most to know that the image is 'backwards'.
- Towards the end of the lesson the pupils can make a periscope or kaleidoscope with the 'Multi-mirror miracles' activity. If plastic mirrors are used then you might let the pupils keep the results.

Plenary Suggestions

Pepper's ghost
Demonstrate the magic trick called 'Pepper's ghost' using a glass plate to create the image of a flame. This shows that light can be partially reflected and partially transmitted by surfaces such as glass. (5–10 mins)

Reflecting on progress
A poor pun, but the pupils have covered some very important concepts recently so a mini-quiz can be used to check understanding. (10 mins)

Next time you …
… get in a car ask the driver how he or she uses the mirrors. 'Mirror, signal, manoeuvre.' That's the driving rule enforced during driving lessons, although some drivers speedily forget. Two types of mirror are used on cars. The rear-view mirror is a simple plane mirror and shows an object at the correct size and distance; it has a limited field of view though. The side mirrors are convex (diverging) mirrors. These collect light from more directions giving a wider field of view, but they have the disadvantage of making objects seem further away than they are; hence the 'Objects in mirror are closer than they appear' warning on some of them.

Practical Support

Investigating reflection
Equipment and materials required
Per group: a ray box, power supply, blanking plates (stops) and single slit. A sheet of white paper, pencil, ruler and protractor.

Details
The pupils set up the equipment as described in the pupil book so that a single incident ray is reflected by the mirror. The pupils should mark the position of the back of the mirror, not the front of the glass, as this is much closer to the reflecting surface and so gives more accurate results. A common problem occurs if the mirror is tilted upwards a bit; this can mean that the pupils don't see a reflected ray but it's easy to correct.

Safety
Check for chips in the glass mirrors as these can lead to minor cuts when the mirrors are handled; tape edges if necessary. Be aware of hot ray boxes.

Multi-mirror miracles
Equipment and materials required
For each pupil: card (the thicker the card the more sturdy the periscope or kaleidoscope), two (periscopes) or three (kaleidoscopes) plastic mirrors, scissors and tape (or glue). Small glass mirrors can be used, but these are heavier and can lead to cuts.

Details
The pupils cut out the general shape of the telescope. The two mirrors are mounted at each end using tape. Most plastic mirrors have a thin layer of plastic to protect the surface from smudges and scratches. This can be peeled off when the scope is finished to give a clearer picture. Assembly of the kaleidoscope is similar; the three mirrors need to be mounted inside the tube.

Safety
If glass mirrors are used then watch out for glass breakage.

Plenary: Pepper's ghost
Equipment and materials required
Glass plate, candle.

Differentiation

SEN
Use a worksheet with the mirror position, incident rays and a protractor printed onto it to make taking the readings more straightforward.

Extension
What's special about mirrors? Why can we see images in mirrors and on the surface or water or glass but not on the surface of white paper? The pupils must come up with a reason for this that includes a diagram. They could also find out about the different layers in a standard mirror or how to make a 'perfect' mirror.

Homework Suggestion
The pupils can find out about some of the uses mirrors are put to. Where are the world's largest mirrors? Are all mirrors flat? What can curved mirrors do to the image you see? As an alternative, pupils could design a device of their own that uses mirrors.

P1.5 Rays that Bend

NC links for the lesson
- Energy, electricity and forces: energy can be transferred usefully, stored, or dissipated, but cannot be created or destroyed (light).

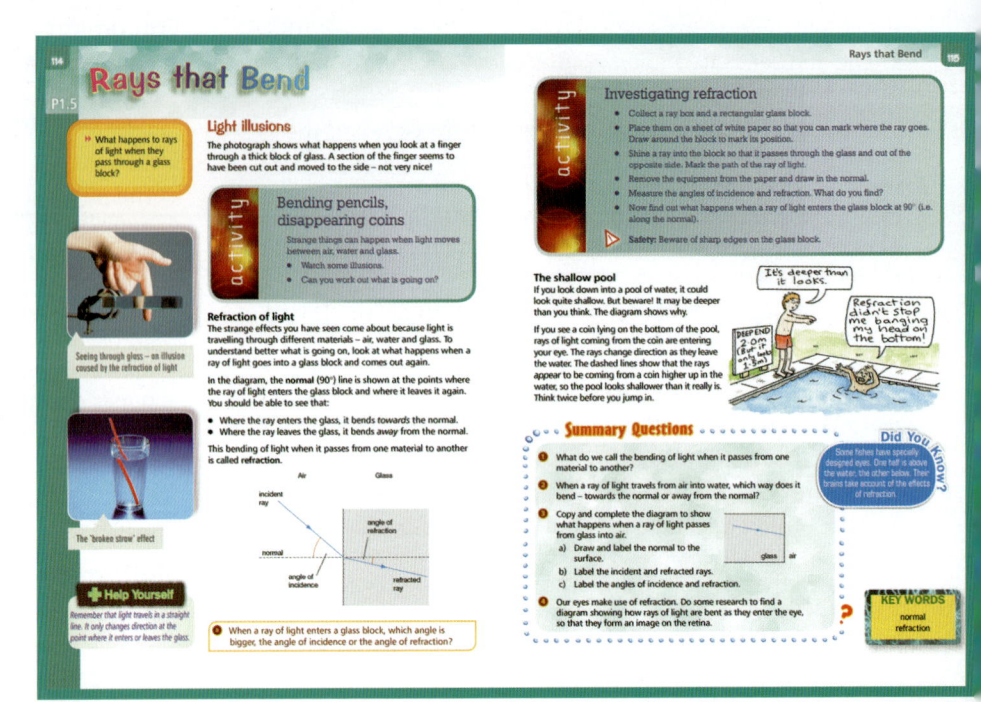

Learning Objectives
Pupils should learn:
- That light rays refract (change direction) when they move from one medium to another.
- That the amount of refraction depends on the two materials involved.

Learning Outcomes
- All pupils should be able to state that light is refracted when it moves from one material to another.
- Most pupils should be able to show, using a ray diagram, how light is refracted as it enters and leaves a glass block.
- Some pupils should also be able to explain why a pool of water appears to be shallower than it really is.

How Science Works
- Explain how the observation and recording methods are appropriate to the task (1.2d).

Functional Skills Link-up
Mathematics
- Recognise and use 2D representations of 3D objects (level 2).

Learning Styles
Visual: Observing tricks and optical phenomena.
Auditory: Discussing their ideas about how tricks work.
Kinaesthetic: Carrying out an investigation into refraction.
Interpersonal: Working in groups to obtain results.

The Lesson

Starter Suggestions

The vanishing
Show a video clip of a magic vanishing trick, there are plenty of these available on the Internet. The pupils try and work out what is really happening in the trick. This is even better if you can carry out a trick yourself. (5–10 mins)

Is it all in your mind?
There are a wide range of optical illusions, some based on static images and some based on moving ones. Show the pupils some of these and ask them to explain what they see. (10–15 mins)

Answers to Summary questions

1. Refraction.
2. Towards the normal.
3. [Diagram: ray passing from glass to air, with labels a) normal, b) incident ray, b) refracted ray, c) angle of incidence, c) angle of refraction]
4. Optical diagram of the eye.

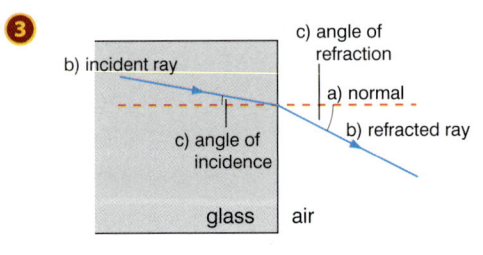

Answers to in-text questions

a. The angle of incidence is larger.

Rays that Bend

Main Lesson

- Start by demonstrating the illusions mentioned in the pupil book, see the 'bending pencils, disappearing coins' information or use 'The vanishing' starter before the scientific tricks.
- It can be difficult for all of the pupils to see the tricks, especially the coin one. If you have a data projector and video camera then use these to project the tricks onto a screen so that everybody gets a clear view.
- Explain the tricks in terms of light changing direction when it moves between two materials (media). Use the idea of bending *towards* the normal and *away* from it. Refraction occurs whenever light moves from one medium to another; limit the discussion to air, glass and water during this lesson. Higher attaining pupils can look further by examining more materials or the cause of refraction.
- Make sure that the pupils do not get the impression that the light rays are *curving* as they pass through the material. There is a sharp change of direction at the boundary between the two materials, not a gradual curve inside. Check that there are no curves on the diagrams drawn by the pupils during the following experiment.
- The main focus of the lesson is the 'Investigating refraction' activity and the results of this will show if the pupils can meet the objective of making accurate measurements with unusual apparatus: the protractor. Some pupils will attempt to use the protractor directly instead of drawing the ray path, because it's quicker than drawing the lines. This usually gives poor results so tell the pupils not to do it.
- The shallow pool effect is based on real and apparent depth. The real depth is the actual depth of water while the apparent depth is how deep it looks. The real depth of water (when viewed from air) is 1.33 times the apparent depth; this means that the water is one-third again as deep as it looks.
- You can demonstrate the effect clearly if you have a long measuring cylinder (over 30 cm) or another transparent tube. Let the pupils look down the tube when it is empty and then when it is full of water. There is an obvious difference. Placing a thick glass block on top of text also shows the effect quite quickly.

Plenary Suggestions

Fibre optic mystery

Use a loop of optical fibre to demonstrate light moving through 'curves'. Remind the pupils that light only travels in straight lines and ask them to come up with an explanation of the phenomena. Show them total internal reflection in a prism and ask them to revise their ideas. Finally show them the correct explanation using a diagram. (10 mins)

Going off the deep end

The pupils must produce a scientific warning sign to prevent people jumping into deep water accidentally. They must include the scientific reasons. (10–15 mins)

Did You Know?

There are a couple of simulations about what submerged fish can see. You could search ('fish eye surface') for these and show the pupils any useful results. Understanding what fish can see of the surface world is handy for anglers.

Practical Support

Bending pencils, disappearing coins (demonstration)

Equipment and materials required

A large transparent container (a 500 cm^3 beaker is fine), water, a pencil, a coin and bowl.

Details

Place the pencil in the beaker so that all pupils can see it. Add water slowly and the 'break' in the pencil will appear.

Place the coin at the centre of an empty bowl. The pupils have to position their heads so that they can only just see the coin. Pour water into the bowl and the coin will disappear.

Investigating refraction

Equipment and materials required

Each group: glass (or good Perspex) block, ray box, power supply, stops, single slit, protractor, A3 paper, pencil and ruler.

Details

Glass blocks work better in this experiment then Perspex, as they usually have fewer scratches (but a good Perspex block will work). The experiment works well as long as the block does not move and the pupils mark the normal lines clearly. Using A3 paper gives the pupils more space to position the block and work but A4 is satisfactory. Make sure that the pupils keep the block in position and that they are marking the normal lines. The refraction is most obvious at larger angles of incidence. Some pupils may come across the phenomena of total internal reflection and you can discuss this if appropriate. If you want to move on to this topic then have some semi-circular blocks that will show the effect more easily.

Safety

The lamps in the ray boxes will become hot during use.

Glass blocks may have sharp edges; tape if necessary.

Plenary:

Equipment and materials required

Fibre optic kit.

Differentiation

SEN

You can provide partially completed ray diagrams for the 'Investigating refraction' activity to show suitable angles for the rays to enter the block and the position of the block itself. This makes it simpler to get the expected results.

Extension

What is the cause of refraction? The pupils can find out about changes in the speed of light as it enters or leaves materials (media). What is a refractive index and what is the relationship to the speed of light (or even the angles of refraction and incidence)?

Homework Suggestion

The pupils can find out about refraction at curved surfaces; what are lenses, where are they used and how do they work?

As an alternative, the pupils could find out and learn to perform a magic trick for themselves.

P1.6 Colours of the Rainbow

NC links for the lesson
- Energy, electricity and forces: energy can be transferred usefully, stored, or dissipated, but cannot be created or destroyed (light).

Learning Objectives
Pupils should learn:
- That white light is composed of a spectrum of colours.
- That filters transmit some colours while absorbing others.
- That coloured objects can appear to be different colours from their actual colour when they are viewed through filters.

Learning Outcomes
- All pupils should be able to state the colours (ROYGBIV) of the spectrum.
- Most pupils should be able to describe how a coloured filter affects white light.
- Some pupils should also be able to explain why coloured objects appear as they do when viewed through coloured filters.

Learning Styles
Visual: Identifying shapes and flags through filters.
Auditory: Discussing the processes that are happening to light as it passes through a filter.
Kinaesthetic: Drawing out hidden messages or images.
Interpersonal: Working in groups to sort colours.
Intrapersonal: Designing a message or picture based on an understanding of filters.

Answers to in-text questions
a) Blue light is refracted more than green.
b) A blue filter transmits blue light. It absorbs the other colours of the spectrum.

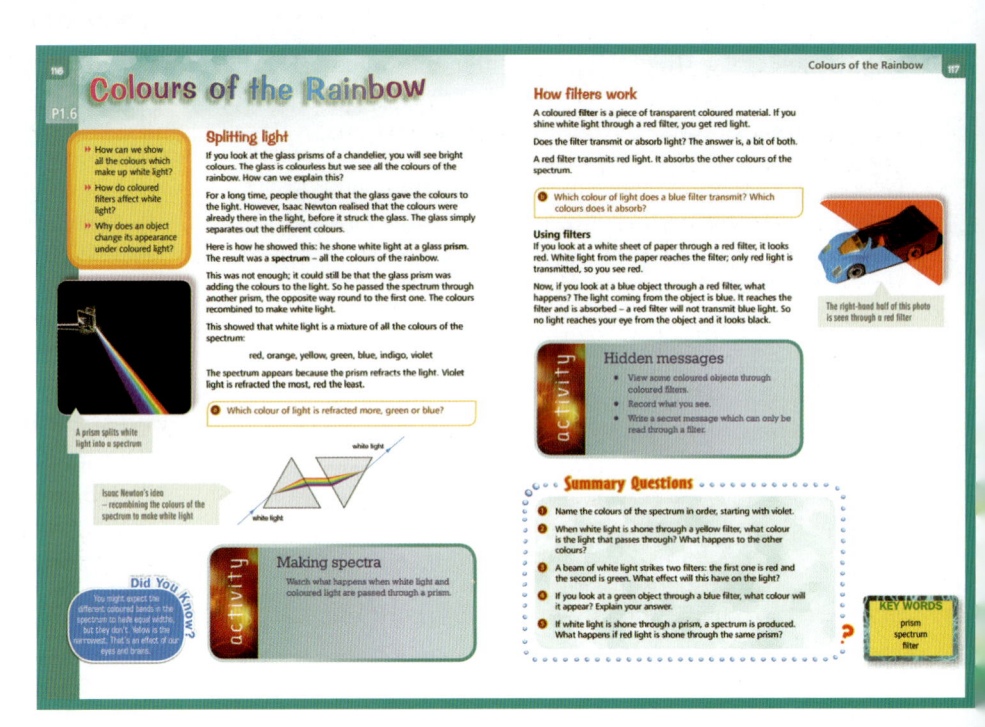

The Lesson

Starter Suggestions

Diamond
Diamond has a very high refractive index and so disperses colours strongly; this is why you can see so many colours in the gem. Show the pupils a large diamond (or pictures or video if you haven't got one) and discuss the way diamond 'shines'. Let the pupils come up with ideas about how a clear diamond can 'make' colours. (5 mins)

Colour match
Show the pupils a picture of a rainbow. Most will tell you that there are only seven colours. Now give them a few dozen colour squares cut out from a paint catalogue (there are plenty in the local DIY centre). The pupils must sort them into order. Finally challenge them to match up the names to the colours. This should show them that the seven colours are a bit arbitrary. (10–15 mins)

Main Lesson
- The brightest way of making a spectrum is to place a prism in front of a data projector or use sunlight. This should give one bright enough for the whole class to see. If your projector is ceiling-mounted then put the prism on a stick.
- The 'Making spectra' demonstration should clearly show that white light is composed of a range of colours we call the spectrum. Most of the pupils will already know the colours thanks to the ROYGBIV or 'Richard Of York Gave Battle In Vain' mnemonic. There might be one or two that think of pink or purple as spectrum colours, thanks to the *I can sing a rainbow* song. Exactly what indigo looks like is fairly tricky too.
- Filters are more of a problem for most pupils, especially if you are looking at coloured objects through them. Let the pupils look at a range of coloured objects through a sample filter and ask them to explain what is happening themselves. You can use some coloured slides as mentioned in the 'Hidden messages' activity.
- Most explanations will be along the lines of the filter 'changing the colour' of the light. This misconception needs to be challenged by showing that some colours of light are being absorbed while other colours are transmitted.
- To prove that light is being *absorbed* by the filter, as opposed to being *changed*, you should measure the light intensity before and after the filter

Colours of the Rainbow

using a sensor. There should be a clear reduction in intensity; showing that energy is absorbed by the filter. Show that every colour filter absorbs some of the energy from the light. You might like to discuss what happens to this energy [the filter heats up].

- You can also shine coloured light through a different coloured filter (e.g. red light through a blue filter) to show that all of the light is absorbed. Actually *almost* all of the light is absorbed because filters are not perfect. Then show green light passing through a green filter; hardly any of the light is absorbed (measure the intensity) because the filter is transparent to green light. You may have to repeat with another colour to reinforce the idea.
- The pupils can then try out the 'Hidden messages' activity to check their understanding of the above ideas. They should be able to describe what they are seeing in terms of absorption and transmission of different colours.
- You might want to use one of the range of light simulation packages to summarise the lesson and check understanding one last time.
- To finish off try the competitive 'Flagging' plenary showing each flag for only 10 seconds and see who gets most right.

Plenary Suggestions

Flagging
Show the pupils a set of national flags as they would be seen through a coloured filter. Can the pupils identify the country the flags belong to? (5 mins)

Using filters
The pupils should use their knowledge of filters to decide if coloured filters on car windshields would be a good idea. What colours should be used, what would the benefits and possible problems be? (5–10 mins)

Practical Support

Making spectra (demonstration)
Equipment and materials required
Two identical 60° prisms (the larger the better), a beam of bright white light (from a ray box and power supply) and a sheet of white A3 paper.

Details
Producing a spectrum is relatively simple: place the prism in the centre of the paper and in the beam of white light and rotate it until the spectrum is clear. Use a white card to show the colours more clearly.

Recombining the colours is a little more difficult to get just right. It should work by placing the second prism in contact with the first but 'upside down'; i.e. rotated by 180°. You might have to fiddle a bit and the beam may not be perfect, but it's close enough.

Safety
The pupils must not stare into the bright light.
Prisms may have sharp edges; tape if necessary.

Hidden messages
Equipment and materials required
A range of coloured filters including red, green and blue, a set of pens with very similar colours to the filters, some white and coloured paper to write on.

Details
The closer the papers, pens and filters match in colour the better the results you will get.

If you have a data projector then use it to project coloured shapes or writing onto the screen. The pupils can view these though the various filters and see the effects clearly. You may have to adjust your colour choices to match the filters to get perfect results.

Safety
Look out for sharp edges on prisms.
Do not look directly at bright light sources.

Differentiation

SEN
The pupils should draw ray diagrams showing white light passing through filters and/or reflecting off coloured objects. They can use coloured pens to show the separate colours (red, green and blue or all seven). For example when the white light passes through a red filter, the red ray would continue while the other colours would stop.

Extension
The pupils can look beyond the visible spectrum. They can find out about infra-red and ultraviolet radiation and their effects. You can demonstrate UV with a low powered UV fluorescent tube (no staring into the lamp) and a special marker pen. (**Safety:** do not look directly at the ultraviolet source.) To show infra-red use an IR sensor, or place a thermometer just beyond the red part of the spectrum you produced earlier to see a temperature rise.

Homework Suggestion

The pupils can design additional, more detailed, images to be viewed through a filter to see what they would look like. They could prepare presentations.

Did You Know?
What exactly is yellow and when does it become orange? The colour response of the eye is quite complex and the definitions of the colours are arbitrary really. Sir Isaac Newton decided that there were five colours at first (RYGBV) but added the other two colours (OI) to give seven. Other counties and languages divide up the spectrum differently: in Germany there are light-green and dark-green regions. You could divide the spectrum into millions of colours if you want, as it is continuous, just look at all of the different colours of paint!

Answers to Summary questions

1. Violet, indigo, blue, green, yellow, orange, red.
2. The yellow passes through, while the other colours are absorbed.
3. No light will pass through.
4. The object will appear black. The green object only reflects green light and this is absorbed by the filter.
5. The red light will be refracted but it won't change colour.

P1.7 Sources of Light

NC links for the lesson
- Energy, electricity and forces: energy can be transferred usefully, stored, or dissipated, but cannot be created or destroyed (light).
- Energy, electricity and forces: forces are interactions between objects and can affect their shape and motion.
- The environment, Earth and universe: astronomy and space science provide insight into the nature and observed motions of the Sun, Moon, stars, planets and other celestial bodies.

Learning Objectives
Pupils should learn:
- That stars are visible because they are sources of light.
- That planets and the Moon are visible because they reflect light from our Sun.

Learning Outcomes
- All pupils should be able to state that the Sun is the source of light in our solar system and planets reflect some of this light.
- Most pupils should be able to explain that the Sun gives out light energy because it is at a very high temperature.
- Some pupils should also be able to explain the relative brightness of the planets in terms of the size, colour and distance from them.

How Science Works
- Explain how to take action to control the risks to themselves and others, and demonstrate competence in their practical techniques (1.2c).

Learning Styles
Visual: Making observations of sunspots or discussing their images.
Auditory: Explaining why planets are illuminated only one half at a time.
Kinaesthetic: Investigating illumination via a model.
Interpersonal: Discussing the history of astronomical observations.
Intrapersonal: Considering how historical observations have helped to develop modern ideas.

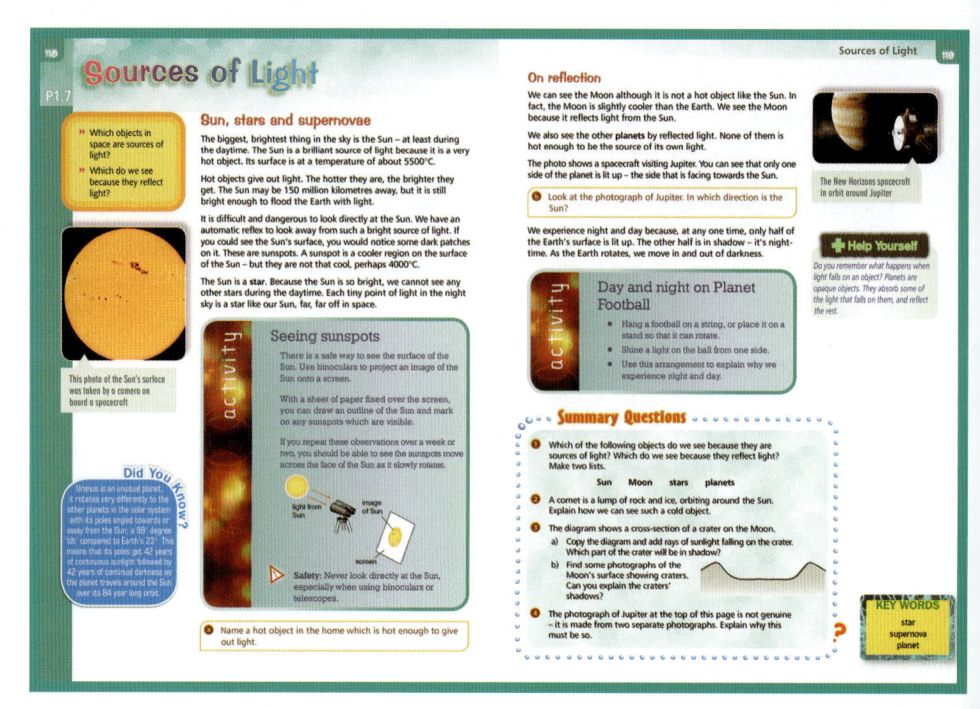

The Lesson

Starter Suggestions

Hot or not?
Show a set of photographs of light producing objects. The pupils have to decide if the object produces light because it is hot or if it is not hot. Use pictures of these hot objects: Sun, distant stars, magnesium burning, a filament lamp, a fire; and these not hot ones: a firefly, luminous squid, a glowing 'light stick', a diode and LCD monitor (or fluorescent tube). (5 mins)

Relative brightness
Give the pupils a set of cards with different light sources on them. They have to discuss the brightness (luminosity) of the source and put them in order. Use the following sources: a match, a candle, a torch, a car headlight a lighthouse, the Sun, and the pole star (a bright star). [The pole star (Polaris) is much brighter than the Sun but it is a lot further away.] (5–10 mins)

Main Lesson

- The topic is now moving on from light to an exploration of the solar system. Light is the main tool that astronomers use to gather information about the universe and this is the thread that joins the two topics together during this lesson.
- The pupils should already be familiar with the idea of hot objects producing light. As a recap use the 'Hot or not' starter to remind them.
- It's difficult to imagine a temperature of 5500°C. All of the elements would be gases at this temperature except for a few, but even these would be in liquid form. Make sure that the pupils get the impression that this is very hot indeed.
- The Sun, through the light it produces, provides most of the energy to sustain life on Earth. Green plants use this energy to produce the materials that animals need to survive, so without sunlight nothing would survive for long.
- The 'Seeing sunspots' activity can be carried out as a demonstration unless you have several sets of binoculars or telescopes. Ask the pupils to perform a basic risk assessment before you, or they, carry out the task.
- As an addition or alternative to the observations, it is fairly easy to find video clips of sunspot activity. Search for 'sunspot activity video'. You may find that these are inverted images; this makes the sunspots easier to see.

Sources of Light

- Most pupils will think of the Sun being very different from a star; it really doesn't look much like one. There are a few images of some of the close stars (search for 'Betelgeuse image') that show that they are more than just tiny twinkles. The main idea to get across is that the stars are so far away that they appear tiny. Discuss what a torch would look like if it were a few kilometres away.
- The pupils should now look at the objects in the solar system that reflect light, basically everything but the Sun. They need to understand that the amount of light reflected will depend on the colour of the planet, the size and just how far away it is from the Sun. If you have a dark room, it is easy to show that a planet (ball) near the Sun (lamp) will reflect a lot of light, while it will reflect less when it is further away. You can use different size and coloured balls to show the other factors.
- The pupils should have a good knowledge of night and day. Let them carry out the 'Day and night on Planet Football' activity to check this.
- Afterwards you can reinforce the ideas using a globe and lamp to make sure that they are clear about the details. The pupils should be asked about the flaws in the model you are using [the lamps should be much, much further from the Earth and much, much larger than it]. Computer animations can be used to support the ideas shown in a real model too.

Plenary Suggestions

Rings
Show an image of Saturn with its rings in shadow. Ask the pupils to describe how this supports the idea that the Sun is the only source of light in the solar system. A video clip of a moon moving into or out of the shadow region would be even better. (5–10 mins)

Goodbye Earth
The probe 'Galileo' took a series of images of the Earth as it passed by (search the Internet for 'Rotating Earth from Galileo). Show the pupils this, or another similar clip, and discuss the position of the Sun and whether the clip is good evidence for the points covered in the main lesson. (5–10 mins)

Answers to Summary questions

1. Light sources: Sun. Reflect light: Moon, planets.
2. Light from the Sun is reflected by the comet and reaches us on Earth.
3. a) Rays of light should be parallel; one ray grazing the top edge of the crater defines the limit of the shadow.
   b) All shadows are formed by light from the Sun. The wider the shadow, the deeper the crater.
4. The spacecraft must have been added to the photograph later as there was nothing that could take a photograph of it.

Answers to in-text questions

a) An electric lamp, torch or candle, etc.
b) To the left.

Practical Support

Seeing sunspots (demonstration)

Equipment and materials required
A pair of binoculars, retort stand, boss, clamp, solid screen and sheet of paper.

Details
Use the retort stand to hold the binoculars at an angle pointing towards the Sun; you only have to use one of the lenses. Position the screen beneath the binoculars and then adjust the distance until a clear image is seen. You should be able to get an image several centimetres across and then you can adjust the focus to get a clear image. Trace the image onto plain paper marking the outlines of any sunspots. The Sun rotates in about 28 days, so you should be able to show the movement of the sunspots over the course of a week. That's assuming that you can get a few sunny days in a row.

Safety
The Sun should never be observed directly through binoculars or telescopes at any time. Permanent eye damage will result. CLEAPSS PS17 'viewing the sun'.

Day and night on Planet Football

Equipment and materials required
A ball (on string if possible) and a lamp.

Details
The pupil book gives the general idea. If possible turn off the room lights and close any blinds so the results are more obvious.

Safety
The lamp may be hot (use a low energy bulb if intense enough). See CLEAPSS guide L194.

Differentiation

SEN
Provide a list of instructions for the 'Day and night on Planet Football' activity. These can lead the pupils to look at different sized and coloured objects.

Extension
The pupils can look at the sunspot cycle. Do the spots appear at random or is there a pattern? What does this pattern tell scientists about the Sun?

Homework Suggestion

Some pupils may want to keep records of sunspots over a period of a couple of weeks. Alternatively the pupils can find out about the length of the days on the different planets in the solar system.

Help Yourself

The amount of light that a planet reflects depends on its 'albedo'. Basically this is just the fraction of light that is reflected, although the exact definition is a little more complicated. As an example, the Earth reflects about 30% of the light that reaches it; while some asteroids have an albedo of of only 5%, meaning they are very dark. Enceladus, one of Saturn's moons, has an albedo of 99%.

P1.8 Solar System

NC links for the lesson

- Energy, electricity and forces: forces are interactions between objects and can affect their shape and motion.
- The environment, Earth and universe: astronomy and space science provide insight into the nature and observed motions of the Sun, Moon, stars, planets and other celestial bodies.

Learning Objectives

Pupils should learn:

- That scientists gather information about planets by making observations with telescopes or sending probes to the planet.
- That conditions on the other plants in the solar system are very different to those on Earth.

Learning Outcomes

- All pupils should be able to describe the basic structure of the solar system.
- Most pupils should be able to describe the methods used to explore the solar system.
- Some pupils should also be able to explain why it is difficult to investigate planets using manned exploration.

Learning Styles

Visual: Designing probes and lander vehicles.

Auditory: Discussing the conditions on different planets.

Kinaesthetic: Examining or building a telescope.

Interpersonal: Debating what a planet is (and what isn't a planet).

Intrapersonal: Thinking about the requirements of a manned exploration of the solar system.

The Lesson

Starter Suggestions

Constellation consternation

Give the pupils some diagrams of constellations, just the star positions. They have to draw what they see in the patterns. Once they are finished, show them what the ancient societies thought that the patterns were. (5–10 mins)

Lunar lander

Show the pupils the famous footage of the first steps on the Moon from the *Apollo 11* mission. This happened in 1969. The missions ended in 1972 with *Apollo 17*. The next possible mission isn't scheduled until 2020 or so. Ask the pupils why they think there is a 50 year gap between the missions. What difficulties need to be overcome to visit the Moon; what supplies need to be taken? You might want to show some other footage (http://www.hq.nasa.gov/alsj/a17/video17.html) too as the original landing isn't very high quality. (10–15 mins)

Answers to Summary questions

1. Mercury, Venus, Earth, Mars, Jupiter, Saturn, Uranus, Neptune (some resources will still include Pluto).
2. Asteroids, comets and dwarf planets (Pluto, etc.).
3. Titan will only receive a little light from the Sun as it is very far away.
4. Research. Pupils might want to visit the site http://www.badastronomy.com to find out more.

Answers to in-text questions

a. There are eight planets (there were nine once).

Solar System

Main Lesson

- Most pupils show a great deal of interest in the solar system and either of the starter activities will lead to some interesting discussions.
- The focus of the lesson is how the solar system has been explored, how the evidence has been gathered and how it has changed in light of new ideas.
- Show the pupils a simple convex (converging) lens. One with a focal length of 10 cm shows the curved shape clearly and they should be able to see that it can be used to magnify the text in their books by holding it above the words.
- Now show the pupils a real telescope if you have one available. They should be able to see that the aperture is considerably larger than a pupil of the eye. This means that more light is gathered and fainter objects can be seen. The image is also magnified, meaning that more detail is available; typical amateur telescopes magnify over 150 times.
- If you don't have a telescope, or want a practical task, the pupils can build a small astronomical telescope. See the 'Telescope building' activity in 'Practical support'. You could ask them to improve this basic design.
- The pupils can then discuss what they already know about the solar system. The simplest mnemonic for remembering the order of the planets is **M**y **V**ery **E**asy **M**ethod **J**ust **S**peeds **U**p **N**aming (Planets). The pupils can think up their own method, possibly including the asteroids.
- Poor old Pluto. It was discovered in 1930 and survived as a planet until 2006 when it was demoted to a mere 'dwarf planet'. Use this to start a discussion about how our knowledge of Pluto has changed, it's a lot smaller than first thought, and how this led to astronomers having to come up with a better description of what a planet is. Our picture of the solar system has changed radically and a whole lesson, if one is available, could be set aside for the pupils to look at the changes in ideas.
- The 'Planetary explorer' activity will take up the major part of this lesson. You will need to suggest a few web-based resources if you are using the Internet as there are literally millions of pages dedicated to the planets. The main goal of the activity is to compare conditions to those on Earth. Temperature, length of year and day are the most important aspects to look at, but the pupils are sure to want to include a lot more detail.
- Once the pupils have chosen a planet, they can design the mission to explore it. Remind them that any probe sent must be able to survive the conditions on the planet. This part of the activity could be set as a homework task, as some pupils will want to spend quite a bit of time on their design.

Plenary Suggestions

Tiny planets
The pupils have to describe all of the planets clearly in the fewest words possible. [For example, 'red rocky mini moons' for Mars.] (5–10 mins)

Pluto strikes back
The pupils could write a letter to the International Astronomical Union demanding that Pluto regains its status as a planet. They should try to come up with their own definition of what a planet is and then use a scientific argument to get the IAU to change their minds. (10–15 mins)

Practical Support

Planetary explorer

Equipment and materials required
Access to textbooks and the Internet.

Details
This is primarily a research project and the pupils will need access to the Internet or textbooks that contain the data. Bookmark a few appropriate sites and give the pupils a list that they must stick to.

The design of a robotic rover module is the more difficult part of the task and some will struggle with it. They should find a list of suitable equipment by looking at the Viking Landers, Spirit rovers or Galileo probe.

Main lesson: Telescope building

Equipment and materials required
For each group: a 50 cm ruler, two converging lenses (5 cm and 30 cm) and some Plasticine.

Details
Use the Plasticine to attach the pair of lenses to the ruler along its flat edge. Place the 5 cm focal length lens 5 cm from the end of the ruler; this is the eyepiece. Now place a 30 cm lens at the 35 cm point; this is the objective. Hold the telescope near the eye and view an object though the eyepiece. This should give a small magnified image, by a factor of six, which is inverted.

Safety
The pupils must not use the telescope to observe the Sun.
Glass lenses may have sharp edges.

Differentiation

SEN
Provide the pupils with a range of specially chosen websites to use for the research project, so that they do not get swamped with the information available. You may want to set just one website backed up with a few textbooks.

Extension
The pupils can investigate the patterns in the whole solar system. What happens to the surface temperature and length of the year as you move further away from the Sun, etc.?

Alternatively the pupils could look at the variety of planets that have been discovered in other solar systems.

Homework Suggestion

The pupils can develop their ideas and designs for planetary exploration (see Main lesson).

Did You Know?

The evidence for humans being abducted by aliens is fairly insubstantial; they cover their tracks well. Most alien abduction seems to be carried out by aliens called 'Greys' that have a strange interest in human anatomy but don't seem to harm the victims much. Before alien abductions started to be reported, there were similar events attributed to angels or demons.

P1.9 Phases of the Moon

NC links for the lesson
- Energy, electricity and forces: forces are interactions between objects and can affect their shape and motion.
- The environment, Earth and universe: astronomy and space science provide insight into the nature and observed motions of the Sun, Moon, stars, planets and other celestial bodies.

Learning Objectives
Pupils should learn:
- That the phases of the Moon are caused by different parts of the Moon being illuminated by the Sun at different times.
- That all objects in the solar system are only lit over half of their surfaces; the half pointing towards the Sun.

Learning Outcomes
- All pupils should be able to state that the phases of the Moon are caused by the different ways it is lit by the Sun.
- Some pupils should be able to describe how the phases are caused in detail.
- Some pupils should also be able to expand these ideas to explain how all of the objects in the solar system are illuminated and how this causes their appearance to vary when viewed from the Earth.

How Science Works
- Describe how the use of a particular model or analogy supports an explanation (1.1a1).

Learning Styles
Visual: Describing diagrams showing the phases of the Moon.
Auditory: Discussing the evidence for phases of the Earth.
Kinaesthetic: Manipulation of the Earth–Moon model.
Interpersonal: Working in teams to make the best model of the phases.

The Lesson

Starter Suggestions

Obscure angles
Show the pupils a set of photographs of objects that are taken from an obscure angle, or lit up in unusual ways, and ask them to work out what they are. These could be familiar objects from around your laboratory, for example a Bunsen burner from underneath, a pencil strongly lit from above, and so on. (5 mins)

Utter lunacy!
Get the pupils to list all of the non-scientific ideas about the Moon they have heard: 'it's made of cheese', 'it turns people into werewolves', and so on. Discuss why the ideas are not scientific. They may come up with a couple of scientific ones that they don't believe, so watch out. (10 mins)

Main Lesson
- Either starter works well as an introduction, although the 'Utter lunacy!' brings up more interesting conversations.
- The pupils should all recognise the phases from experience, but there are numerous animations made from sets of photographs available online which show the sequence of the phases of the Moon. Use these to show

Answers to Summary questions

1. A straight ray from the Sun strikes the Moon's surface and is reflected towards the Earth. [Pupil diagram.]

2. Diagrams matching full, first and third quarter.

3. a) The new Moon is shown at the start and end of the sequence.
   b) Approx. 14.
   c) Approx. 28 or 29.
   d) A 'gibbous moon' is what you see when there is more than half of the Moon visible but less than a full moon.

Phases of the Moon

- the change in appearance and to show that the change is gradual; there aren't just a few fixed shapes.
- The website www.inconstantmoon.com allows you to view the surface of the Moon in any of the phases and has a fairly detailed map of the surface that can be panned and clicked. It can also produce an image of what the Moon would look like if it were viewed at that moment.
- The pupils can then carry out the 'Modelling the Moon' activity to check their understanding. It can be helpful for them to mark their position on the Earth with a cross or some other marker. They shouldn't worry about the rotation of the Earth during this process; it only complicates matters. Watch out for the Earth blocking the light to the Moon and causing eclipses. These are dealt with in P1.11.
- They should eventually be convinced that they would see the same shapes as the phase pictures they have seen. Let one of the groups demonstrate their techniques to the others to consolidate. It is important that the pupils discuss how effective their models are for this, and then experiment. Are they realistic enough to reach valid conclusions?
- The Moon was thought to be a perfectly smooth object at first. It was only with the advent of the telescope that scientists began to make detailed observations and notice the details on its surface. Early pioneers in moon mapping include Galileo and, soon afterwards, the pairing of Giovanni Battista Riccioli and Francesco Maria Grimaldi who named most of the features.
- In 'The Earth from the Moon' the pupils again test out their understanding. They should find that any lunar colonists would see phases just like those found by observing the Moon. In fact the Earth will look a bit more spectacular as it's a touch more colourful and the atmosphere will cause some nice effects around the edges.
- There aren't as many pictures showing the phases of the Earth as there are showing the Moon. Take the opportunity to ask the pupils why they think this is. Where would you need to be to take the pictures and how many people have been able to do this? To find some example images search for the term 'earthrise' using the Internet and you will see a few variations of the image used in the pupil book.

Plenary Suggestions

Inconstant Moon
The pupils should write a short poem or piece of prose that incorporates the ever-changing phases of the Moon. Can they beat Shakespeare? (5–10 mins)

Life in the sea of tranquillity
The pupils can describe what they think it would be like to live on the Moon. They need to include as many scientific facts as they can in their daily routine. (10–15 mins)

Answers to in-text questions

a) Second row, right hand side.
b) Upwards.

Practical Support

Modelling the Moon

Equipment and materials required
An angle-poise lamp, a ping-pong ball (Moon) and a ball around the size of a small football (Earth). (A round balloon can work as an alternative Earth.) The balls can be attached to cotton or supported on sticks so that the pupils can move them about. See CLEAPSS Guide L194.

Details
The pupils have to work out how to demonstrate the phases of the Moon. This involves working out a point on the Earth from which to view the Moon and imagining what the Moon would look like from that point. It is best to hold the Moon slightly 'above' (north of the Equator) the Earth to prevent the Earth blocking the light completely and eliminating the possibility of a full moon.

One problem will be to get the scale suitable. The lamp should be placed at the same height as the Earth and then the Moon moved around the Earth so that different parts are lit. The room needs to be quite dim to see the effect clearly. To be accurate, the pupils should make sure that the same face of the Moon is pointed towards the Earth at all times, although this doesn't make a difference to the phases.

Safety
The lamps will become hot with use (using a low energy bulb will keep the temperature down).

The Earth from the Moon

Equipment and materials required
As above.

Details
This is very similar to the 'Modelling the Moon' experiment, except that the pupils are imagining what the Earth would look like. The patterns would be the same. The simplest place to imagine you are would be the far side of the Moon. You would never see the Earth from there.

Safety
The lamps will become hot with use (using a low energy bulb will keep the temperature down).

Differentiation

SEN
Give the pupils some instructions about how to set up their Earth and Moon models and provide them with a set of circles they can colour in to show their observations.

Extension
What do the phases of the Moon look like from the southern hemisphere? Would they be exactly the same? The pupils can try to model this by putting the Moon below the Equator in their models. They should find that the Moon 'appears' from the opposite side.

Homework Suggestion

The pupils can find out about the history of lunar exploration. This can be from the very earliest of maps, through the manned landing and even towards a possible future expedition.

P1.10 The Seasons

NC links for the lesson
- Energy, electricity and forces: forces are interactions between objects and can affect their shape and motion.
- The environment, Earth and universe: astronomy and space science provide insight into the nature and observed motions of the Sun, Moon, stars, planets and other celestial bodies.

Learning Objectives
Pupils should learn:
- That weather patterns change during the course of a year due to the Earth's axial tilt.
- That the changes in day length and temperature are more extreme further from the Equator.
- That different cultures describe seasons differently.

Learning Outcomes
- All pupils should be able to describe the length of the year in term of the Earth's orbit and the length of the day in terms of the Earth's rotation.
- Most pupils should be able to describe the relationship between the length of a day, height of the Sun and the season.
- Some pupils should also be able to explain the differences in the seasons in terms of the axial tilt of the Earth.

Functional Skills link-up
ICT
- Use appropriate techniques and design queries to locate and select relevant information (level 2).

Answers to in-text questions
a Sunrise is later and sunset is earlier. The Sun does not rise as high above the horizon.

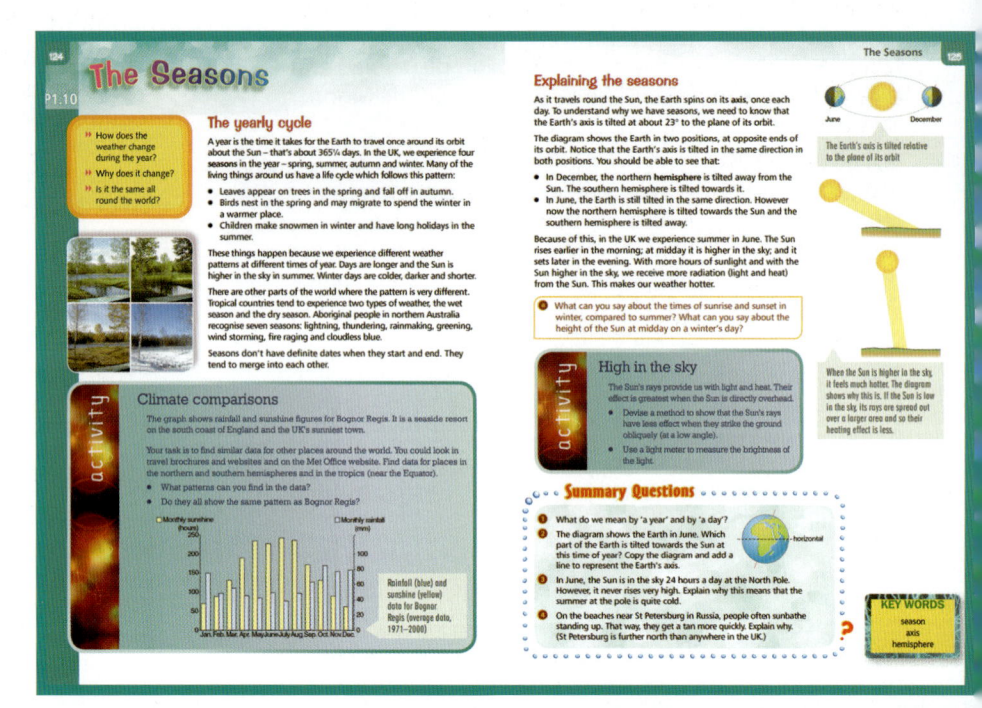

The Lesson

Starter Suggestions

Spot the season
Show the pupils a set of photographs and let them decide which seasons they were taken in. Start with obvious ones, e.g. falling leaves in autumn, but get a bit trickier, e.g. Santa in Australia. Finally move on to locations that the pupils will be unfamiliar with, e.g. wet and dry seasons in the tropics. (5–10 mins)

A year in the life
Ask the pupils to look out of the windows, or an imaginary view. They must draw a comic strip showing the changes that will happen over the next 12 months. (10–15 mins)

Answers to Summary questions

1. A year is the time it takes the Earth to complete an orbit around the Sun; a day is the time it takes for the Earth to rotate once.

2. The Northern hemisphere. The Earth's axis passes through the N and S poles, and is tilted so the northern hemisphere is tipped towards the Sun. [Pupil diagram.]

3. Not much light or thermal energy can reach the surface.

4. In northern areas, the Sun is never high in the sky. Because of this, a person standing intercepts more rays of sunlight than a person lying down. (Imagine the Sun close to the horizon; if you lie down with your feet to the Sun, only your feet will be lit up.)

Learning Styles
Visual: Watching demonstrations and simulations of the seasons.
Auditory: Describing how the tilt of the Earth affects the seasons.
Kinaesthetic: Researching weather information.
Interpersonal: Consolidating information from different groups.
Intrapersonal: Interpreting information to find patterns.

The Seasons

Main Lesson

- The best starting point is to use the 'Spot the season' starter. This will allow you to judge the prior knowledge the pupils have. As you move through the pictures, you will find out just how much they know about the variation across the globe.
- The 'Spot the season' starter also allows you to discuss other cultures and how they are affected by the changes in weather patterns. Once the pupils understand that, you can start to focus on the patterns in the UK.
- To explain the cause of seasons you will have to use a globe; two or more identical ones would be better. Remind the pupils about the day and night cycle; they should be familiar with this by now. Show them that the Earth rotates but it is tilted significantly.
- Place a lamp with no cover on a desk and the globe to one side of it with the pole angles towards the lamp direction. Make sure that the centre of the lamp is at the same height as the centre of the globe. If you have a second globe, position it directly opposite the first one. The first globe will be in the 'summer in the northern hemisphere' position, and the second in the 'winter in the northern hemisphere' position.
- Rotate the first globe and show that the pole has sunlight for 24 hours each day while the South Pole is in permanent darkness. Describe how the length of the day varies with latitude, mentioning your current location. The pupils will all know the conventional descriptions of the seasons, but quite a few are unfamiliar with the differences that occur at different latitudes; so it is important to get this concept across during the demonstrations. Refer back to the images used in the 'Spot the season' starter if you used them.
- Discuss the second globe now, reminding the pupils that the globe has travelled for six months to get to this side of the Sun. You can also show the globes at other positions and discuss the day length.
- Computer simulations can fail to impress the ideas upon the pupils but they are very useful to support the above demonstration. If you have a simulation then use it to recap what you have just shown.
- The 'Climate comparisons' activity will allow the pupils to find patterns in the weather conditions around the globe and should result in a greater understanding of the variation. It can take quite a lot of time unless you limit the number of sites or books the pupils can use.
- Now move on to look at the path the Sun takes across the sky during different seasons. It's important to remind the pupils that the Sun isn't moving; it only appears to be doing so. The final 'High in the sky' activity is meant to be a planning activity, but it can be carried out if time is available.

Plenary Suggestions

Seasonal eating?

Can the pupils match pictures of various locally produced foods with the seasons they are ready in? What do they think about the idea of flying in fresh food from around the world? Are there any problems with having 'seasonal' food available all year round? (5–10 mins)

Sun worshiper

The pupils can describe a plan so that they can always depend on the weather being warm without having to live in a desert. They have unlimited funds to spend on their lifestyle so 'the sky's the limit'. Winter lovers can plan the reverse. (5–10 mins)

Practical Support

Climate comparisons

Equipment and materials required

Access to the Internet and a spreadsheet.

Details

The pupils need to gather data on sunshine and rainfall locations from around the world. This data should be relatively easy to find using search terms such as 'rainfall figures Berlin' or similar, but the sheer volume of figures may confuse a number of pupils. Try to find a few sites beforehand that will give the statistic that you want. One site that is fairly easy to navigate is www.theweathernetwork.com and their statistics section. It's wise to provide the pupils with a list of six or seven suitable cities and a map of their locations, so that they can find the pattern that you want them to see. Make sure that the pupils know that 'precipitation' means rainfall.

You can provide a spreadsheet template with the appropriate city names and columns for the rainfall and or sunlight hours for the 12 months but without the data. This could automatically produce a graph for the pupils to print out and use to look for patterns, saving them a lot of time.

High in the sky

Equipment and materials required

Per group: a lamp, protractor, light sensor and possibly a ball to represent the Earth.

Details

The pupils don't actually have to use a globe to carry out this test. All they need to do is shine a light sensor at a range of angles and measure the intensity. They should then compare the angle to the intensity and see if there is a pattern.

Many pupils will want to use a globe. This will make the measurements of angle more difficult but not impossible. If everybody decides to do this method, then you should show them the simpler idea and discuss which technique is most suitable.

Safety

The lamps will become hot (using a low energy bulb will keep the temperature down).

Main Lesson

Lamp, 2 globes.

Differentiation

SEN

Provide a completed spreadsheet of weather statistics for the pupils to analyse. They should concentrate on looking for patterns and matching the data to locations on a map.

Extension

The pupils could look at more detailed weather statistics to see if they can find any evidence of changes in the weather patterns. They need to find rainfall figures for the past 50 years for a few chosen locations and see if it increasing, decreasing or staying the same. Do they have enough evidence to say that weather patterns are changing due to global warming?

Homework Suggestion

The research into changes in weather patterns can be done out of school hours.

P1.11 Eclipses

NC links for the lesson
- Energy, electricity and forces: forces are interactions between objects and can affect their shape and motion.
- The environment, Earth and universe: astronomy and space science provide insight into the nature and observed motions of the Sun, Moon, stars, planets and other celestial bodies.

Learning Objectives
Pupils should learn:
- That a solar eclipse occurs when the Moon blocks out light from the Sun causing a region of the Earth to be in shadow.
- That a lunar eclipse occurs when the Earth blocks the path of light to the Moon causing it to be in shadow.
- How to use a model to explain observations.

Learning Outcomes
- All pupils should be able to state that an eclipse of the Sun occurs when the Moon obscures it and an eclipse of the Moon occurs when the Earth obscures the Sun.
- Most pupils should be able to draw a simple diagram showing how a shadow is formed on the Earth during a total eclipse of the Sun.
- Some pupils should also be able to explain why, during eclipses, the whole surface of the Moon can be in eclipse while only a small part of the Earth is in total shadow.

How Science Works
- Describe how the use of a particular model or analogy supports an explanation (1.1a1).

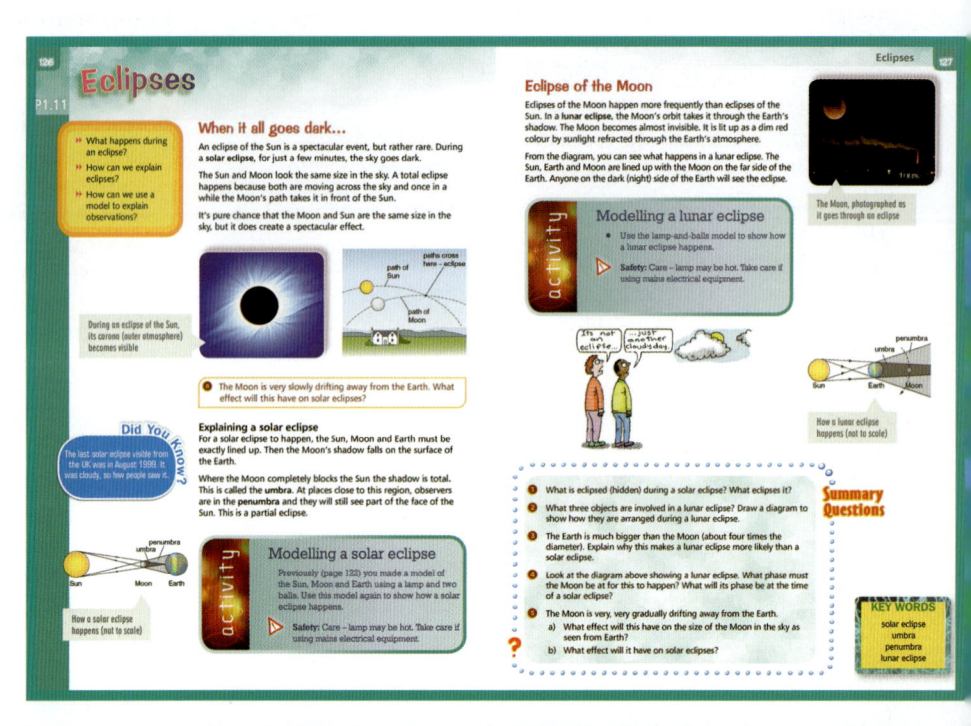

The Lesson

Starter Suggestions

Total eclipse
The next best thing to being present at a total eclipse of the Sun is watching a video clip. Show the pupils a clip and discuss what is happening. Follow up with a series of photographs showing a little more detail. (5 mins)

Shadow
The pupils have to give a detailed description of how shadows form. This must include a ray diagram. What happens if the light source is large? [You get a partial shadow, 'penumbra' around the edge.] (10 mins)

Answers to Summary questions

1. The Sun is eclipsed by the Moon.
2. The Sun, Earth and Moon are lined up with the Moon on the far side of the Earth. [Pupil diagram.]
3. It is more likely that the Earth will get 'in the way' of the light from the Sun and stop it reaching the Moon.
4. There must be a full Moon during a lunar eclipse and a new Moon every solar eclipse.
5. a) The Moon will look smaller and smaller.
   b) Solar eclipses won't be total as the Moon won't be large enough to block out all of the sunlight.

Answers to in-text questions

a) The Moon will look smaller and smaller. Solar eclipses won't be total as the Moon won't be large enough to block out all of the sunlight. The final total eclipse will be somewhere around 600 million years from now.

Eclipses

Main Lesson

- It is unlikely that the pupils have ever experienced a total solar eclipse but ask anyway. If not, ask them to imagine and describe what they think the event would be like. There are a few things they might not think of; birds return quietly to their roosts, flowers close up and it grows quite cold. It's no wonder ancient civilisations were impressed by these rare events.
- One of the best sources of information on the timing of eclipses is http://sunearth.gsfc.nasa.gov/eclipse/eclipse.html . This can tell you when there will be a total eclipse for the next thousand years or so. The website also has pages to find the times of eclipses in most major cities. You can use it to find out the chances that the pupils will see an eclipse locally over the next hundred years or so. It finds total and partial eclipses.
- Discuss the diagram showing how a solar eclipse happens and then let the pupils carry out the 'Modelling a solar eclipse' activity to confirm their ideas. Make sure that they are looking at the shadow on the surface of the Earth.
- You should discuss why only part of the surface of the Earth is ever in shadow even during a total eclipse of the Sun. This will require some understanding of the scale involved as mentioned in the next point. However the pupils should be able to cast a shadow, as long as the lamp they are using is around a metre from their models and pointing towards them.
- Getting a realistic sense of scale for the Sun, Earth and Moon system is difficult in a classroom. Using a typical globe or football-sized object for the Earth (30 cm diameter) would mean that the Moon would have a diameter a bit smaller than a tennis ball (7 cm) and would orbit it at a distance of nearly 9 m away. On this scale, the Sun would have be nearly 3.5 km away. Placing the Moon too close, the usual mistake, actually makes the shadow larger and easier to see.
- The pupils then move on to looking at a lunar eclipse in the 'Modelling a lunar eclipse' activity. As with the 'Total eclipse' starter, try to find some video or time lapse footage of this event happening. It is much easier to appreciate the shadow of the Earth falling on the Moon if you can see the curved edge moving across the lunar surface. You can also see the development of a characteristic red tint as totality is reached.
- Discuss the diagram from the pupil book and allow them to check the ideas with their simple models. This should be easy as the pupils tend to place the Moon quite close to the Earth and so it easily falls into shadow.
- Get one of the groups to show the rest of the class what they have found so that you can check their understanding before wrapping up with one of the plenary suggestions.

Plenary Suggestions

Seek me out
Give the pupils a word search with the key words from the topic. Don't provide a word list; instead give them a set of questions as clues to the hidden words. (5–10 mins)

The final frontier
The pupils have now finished their flyby of the solar system. They should consolidate all that they have learned in a mind map or similar summary diagram. (10–15 mins)

Practical Support

Modelling a solar eclipse

Equipment and materials required

An angle-poise lamp, ping-pong ball (Moon) and a ball around the size of a small football (Earth). (A round balloon can work as an alternative Earth.) The balls can be attached to cotton or supported on sticks so that the pupils can move them about.

See CLEAPSS Guide L194 for light sources, etc. and PS17 for information on viewing eclipses.

Details

This is very similar to the earlier experiments. The main difficulty will be in getting the lamp distance correct and the room dark enough to see a strong shadow on the surface of the Earth.

Safety

Hot lamps (using a low energy bulb will keep the temperature down).

Modelling a lunar eclipse

Equipment and materials required

As above.

Details

This time, the pupils will have an easy time getting the Moon to move into shadow. If they try a more realistic scale, the Moon being a few metres away from the Earth, they will have a bit more difficulty.

Safety

Hot lamps (using a low energy bulb will keep the temperature down).

Differentiation

SEN
Provide some hint diagrams to hep the pupils set up their models.

Extension
The arrangement of the Sun, Earth and Moon is not as simple as the models used in this topic may suggest. If everything was in line, then there would be a total eclipse every month but we only get around three each year. The pupils can try to find a more detailed model or simulation that takes into account the details of the arrangement and the tilt of the Moon's orbit.

Homework Suggestion

The pupils can find out where and when the next solar and lunar eclipses are. They can even work out how much it would cost to go and see them.

Learning Styles

Visual: Observing the changing phases of the Moon.

Auditory: Describing the behaviour of the Earth and Moon.

Kinaesthetic: Modelling the movement of the Moon around the Earth.

Interpersonal: Working in teams to model eclipses.

Intrapersonal: Evaluating their models.

Answers to Light and Space End of Topic Questions

Answers to know your stuff questions

1
  a C. [1]
  b The normal (at the point of incidence). [1]
  c [diagram showing incident ray A, reflected ray B to C, D, with normal X] [2]
  d Two equal angles marked, either angles of incidence and reflection, or 90 minus these. [1]

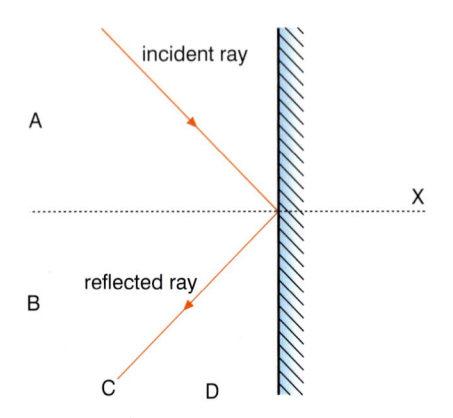

2 A, D: incorrect; B, C: correct. [4]

3
  a D; is in Earth's shadow. [2]
  b B; rays of sunlight are closest to perpendicular to Earth's surface. [2]
  c C, D; their hemisphere is tilted away from Sun. [3]

4
  a It is the source of its own light. [1]
  b Any star, supernova, etc. [1]
  c On diagram: ray from Sun to Moon, reflected to Earth. [2]

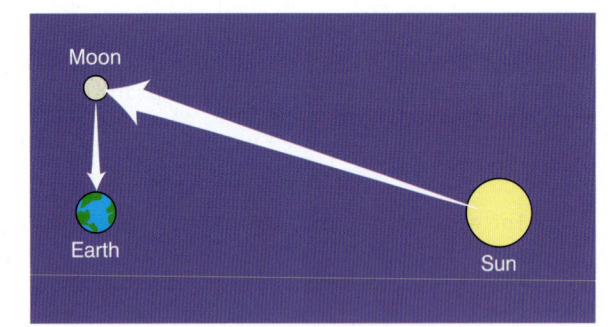

  [diagram showing Moon, Earth, Sun with rays]

  d On diagram: position of Moon shown on opposite side of Earth to Sun. [1]

  [diagram showing Moon, Earth, Sun in line]

  Moon must go round 90 degrees to the left, so that it lies in a line with the Earth and the Sun. It must remain at the same distance from the Earth.

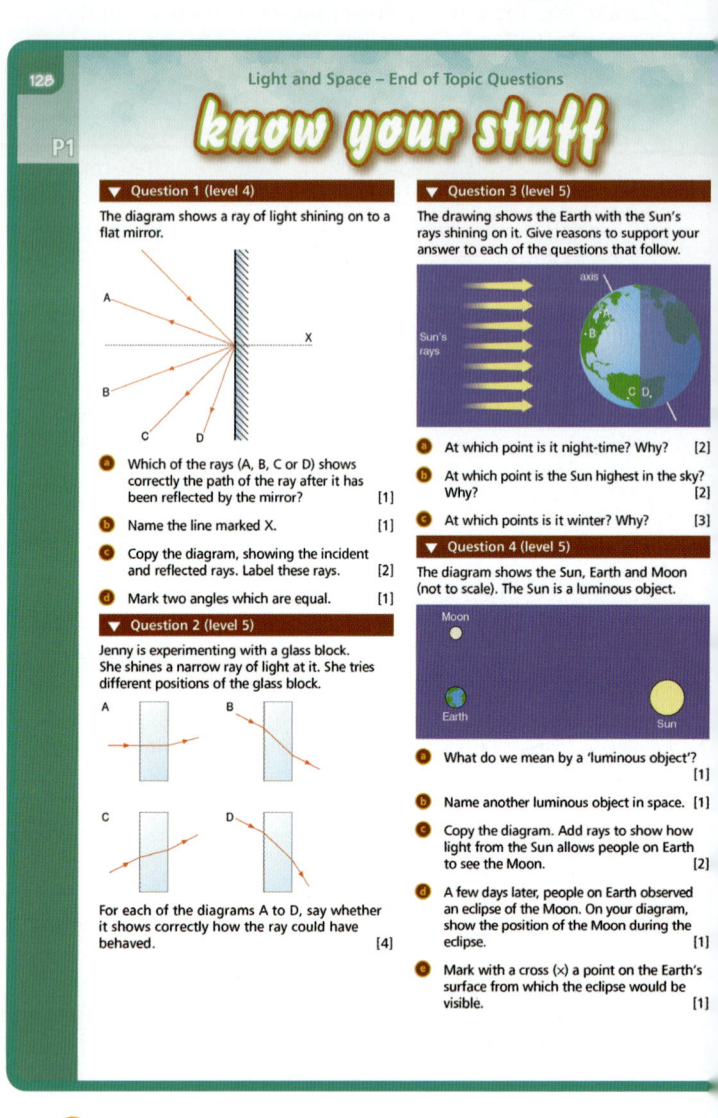

  e On diagram: position × marked on left-hand half of Earth. [1]

  [diagram showing Moon, Earth with ×, Sun]

Light and Space – End of Topic Questions

How Science Works

▼ Question 1 (level 6)

Jake was investigating how light is refracted as it passes through a glass block. He used a ray box to produce a narrow ray of light.

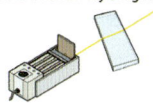

Jake recorded the path of the ray and the position of the glass so that he could draw a diagram and measure the angles of incidence and refraction.

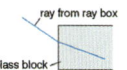

a Copy the diagram of the glass block and ray of light; mark and label these angles:
(i) angle of incidence
(ii) angle of refraction. [2]

Jake did this experiment three times. The table shows his results.

Angle of incidence	Angle of refraction
32°	21°
38°	24°
44°	28°

b Which *two* of the following are reasonable conclusions to draw from Jake's results? Give the letters.
A The angle of incidence is greater than the angle of refraction.
B The angle of refraction is greater than the angle of incidence.
C The ray always bends away from the normal when it enters glass.
D The ray always bends towards the normal when it enters glass. [2]

c Jake's experiment would have been better if he had used a greater *range* of values for the angle of incidence. Give *two* additional values of the angle of incidence, each of which would have increased the range. [2]

▼ Question 2 (level 7)

Astronomers have detected a planet orbiting around a distant star. Its orbit has a different shape from the Earth's orbit around the Sun; it is an elongated ellipse, as shown in the drawing.

Janet is investigating how the light falling on the planet will change as it orbits a star. She sets up a bright lamp to represent the star and moves a light meter around it to represent the planet.

a Why is it important that Janet works in a darkened room? [1]

b In each position of the 'planet' around its orbit, Janet adjusts the light meter, tilting it around until it gives the maximum reading. Why does she do this? [1]

Janet measures the distance between the 'planet' and the 'star' and records the meter reading each time. The table shows her results.

Distance between star and planet (m)	Light meter reading
1.20	0.6
0.90	1.6
0.60	3.8
0.30	14.9

c Draw a graph to represent Janet's results. [2]

d Janet felt that she might have made a mistake in the final reading (light meter = 14.9) and that it did not fit the pattern of the other results. Suggest *two* things she could do to check this idea. [2]

Answers to How Science Works questions

1 a

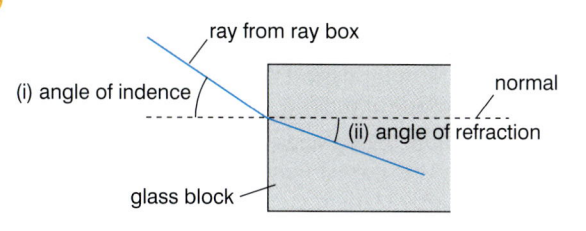

(i) angle of incidence
(ii) angle of refraction
ray from ray box
normal
glass block
[2]

b A, D. [2]

c One angle less than 32°, another greater than 44°. [2]

2 a Any other light would add to the reading on the light meter. [1]

b If meter is tilted, reading will be low. (Maximum reading when meter perpendicular to rays.) [1]

c

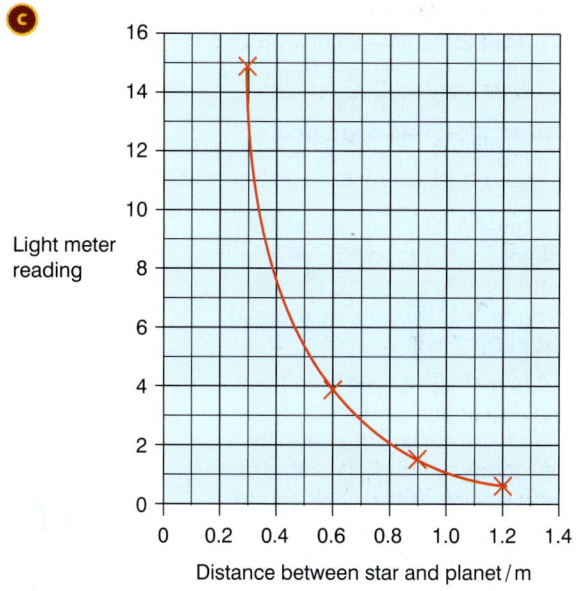

Light meter reading vs Distance between star and planet / m

[2]

d Repeat the reading at 0.30 m; take a measurement between 0.30 m and 0.60 m. [2]

P2.1 Heat and Sound

NC links for the topic
- Energy, electricity and forces: energy can be transferred usefully, stored, or dissipated, but cannot be created or destroyed.
- Chemical and material behaviour: the particle model provides explanations for the different physical properties and behaviour of matter.
- Key concepts: using scientific ideas and models to explain phenomena and developing them creatively to generate and test theories. Critically analysing and evaluating evidence from observations and experiments.
- Key processes: use a range of scientific methods and techniques to develop and test ideas and explanations, assess risk and work safely in the laboratory, field and workplace, carry out practical and investigative activities, both individually and in groups.

Level descriptors for the topic
- **AT3 level 6:** Pupils describe processes and phenomena related to materials, their properties and the Earth, using abstract ideas and appropriate terminology, for example the particle model applied to solids.
- **AT4 level 4:** They recognise that evidence can support or refute scientific ideas, such as sounds being heard through a variety of materials.
- **AT4 level 5:** They apply and use knowledge and understanding in familiar contexts. They describe applications and implications of science, such as the ways sound can be produced and controlled, for example in musical instruments.
- **AT4 level 6:** Pupils describe processes and phenomena related to energy, forces and space, using abstract ideas and appropriate terminology. They also use abstract ideas or models.
- **AT4 level 7:** They explain, using abstract ideas where appropriate, the importance of some applications and implications of science, such as the uses of electromagnets (controlling sound levels). They describe a wide range of processes and phenomena related to energy, forces and space, using abstract ideas and appropriate terminology and sequencing a number of points, for example how energy is transferred by radiation or by conduction.
- **AT4 level 8:** Pupils demonstrate extensive knowledge and understanding related to energy, forces and space, for example the passage of sound waves through a medium.

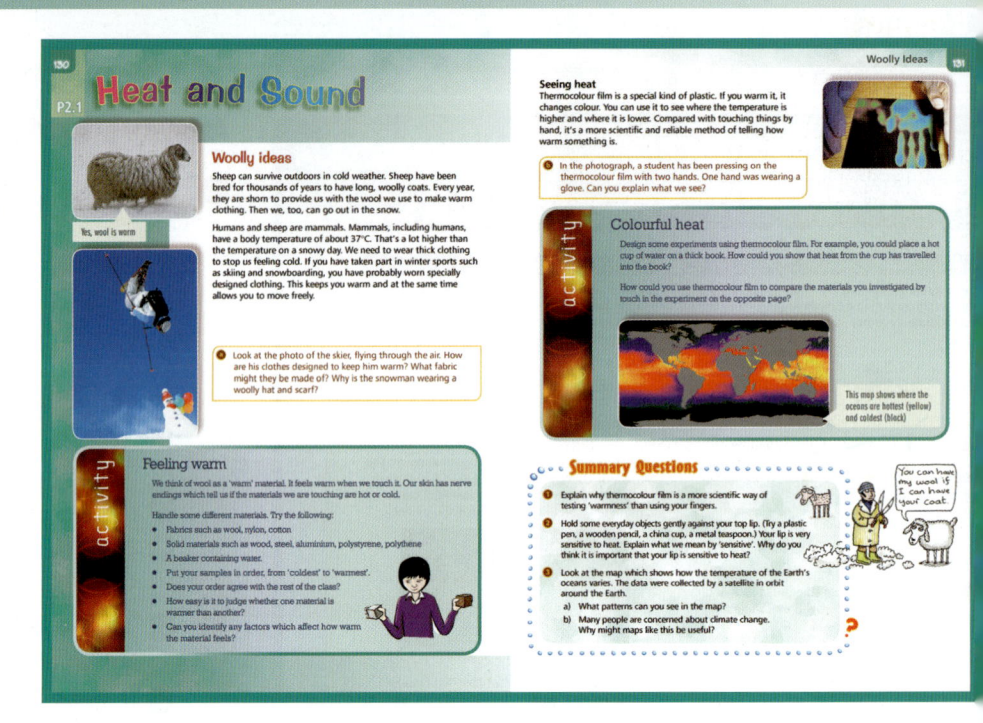

Answers to in-text questions

a The fabric will be a fluffy man-made fibre and the clothing will be in many layers. The snowman is wearing the hat and scarf for fashion reasons; keeping warm is a bad move for a snowman but the hat and scarf will help in a small way to keep him cold!

b The hand with the glove was insulated.

Learning Styles
Visual: Observing thermocolour film to detect temperature differences.

Auditory: Describing how an object feels.

Kinaesthetic: Feeling and sorting materials.

Interpersonal: Discussing how thermocolour films can be used in an experiment.

Intrapersonal: Thinking about what we mean by the words 'warm' and 'cold'.

Learning Objectives
Pupils should learn:
- That materials can feel warm or cool because of their physical properties as well as their actual temperature.
- That temperature is a measure of how hot an object is.

Learning Outcomes
- All pupils should be able to arrange a set of materials in order from coolest to warmest.
- Most pupils should be able to use thermocolour film to place objects in order of temperature.
- Some pupils should also be able to explain why it is inappropriate to describe objects as 'warm' or 'cool' when making a scientific measurement.

The Lesson

Starter Suggestions

It's cold out
How can you tell that it's cold outside by watching through a window? What are the signs? The pupils may come up with ideas like snow, ice, frosty breath, warm clothing and so on. What are the signs that it's warm outside? (5–10 mins)

Clear out the woolly thinking
Check the pupils' prior learning by asking them to draw a mind-map or similar diagram showing what they know about heating and cooling. This should include their ideas about how thermal energy travels between and through objects. Use the maps to identify misconceptions that you need to clear up through the topic. (10–15 mins)

Main Lesson

- The pupils should already be aware that some materials keep them warmer than others. Use the idea of different clothing to find out if the pupils think that the material itself is warming you up or if it works in another way. Some will be aware of the idea of insulation.
- The pupils can move on to the first activity, 'Feeling warm'. This is a straightforward sorting task and the pupils should have no real difficulty in concluding that 'fluffy' materials feel warm whereas the metals feel cold.
- It will be fairly common for pupils to use phrases like 'wool *is* warm' and 'metal *is* cold'. The goal of the first few lessons is to clear up these misconceptions and to give a clearer idea of what temperature represents. In this lesson you will start to challenge them at the end, so it is important to point out that the materials only *feel* warm; most of them will be at room temperature.
- If you want to show a larger difference in the temperature that objects seem to be then take a polythene block and a steel block out of a refrigerator and let the pupils compare these. The steel will seem much colder than the plastic even though they are at the same temperature.
- Thermocolour film is readily available and it provides and excellent way of 'visualising temperature' far beyond what thermometers can show. Demonstrate how it operates by placing your hand onto the film and showing the colour changes. Try to work out which colour represents the warmest area.
- Now let the pupils think up ideas for using the film with the 'Colourful heat' activity. Have some basic equipment available to allow them to test out their ideas.
- Finish off by showing the pupils the objects they used in the 'Feeling warm' activity again and demonstrating that they are all at the same temperature. Tell them that we need a better way of deciding if one object is hotter than another.

Plenary Suggestions

Product placement
The pupils can think up commercial uses for the thermocolour film technology or similar. What products could it be used in and how would they market them? What about paints that change colour depending on the weather? (5–10 mins)

Warm words
Give the pupils a set of words used to describe temperature (or ask them to think of some) including: freezing, cold, icy, arctic, warm, hot, boiling, roasting, scorching. In small groups, the pupils must discuss the words and agree an order to put them in from coldest to hottest. The groups then see if they all agree. (5–10 mins)

Practical Support

Feeling warm

Equipment and materials required
For each group: a range of materials as shown in the pupil book.

Details
The pupils try to sort the materials into order depending on how hot they feel. One interesting thing to try is comparing how the water feels through the glass as opposed to touching the water itself. The pupils should find that the fluffy materials seem warmest while the metals feel coldest.

Safety
Take care with hot water.

Colourful heat

Equipment and materials required
For each group: thermocolour film and apparatus as requested.

Details
The pupils need to think up ideas about using the film. These could include:

measuring body temperature (placing a small strip on the forehead);

showing that thermal energy passes into a book (place a sheet inside the book and a hot object on top);

placing the material on the outside of a mug to measure the temperature of the contents;

seeing if sunlight will heat up the film.

Differentiation

Extension
The pupils can look at microscope slides and electron micrographs of natural and man-made fibres (search the Internet). Can they see which fibres are the 'fluffiest' and does this match how warm the material feels?

Homework Suggestion

Humans have to maintain a body temperature very near to 37°C. The pupils can find out what the body does to try to keep in this narrow temperature range and what happens if we get too hot (hyperthermia) or too cold (hypothermia).

Answers to Summary questions

1. It gives a fair result. The colours will match a certain temperature.

2. 'Sensitive' means that it can detect small changes. It is important to sense the temperature of food so that it does not burn us when we place it in our mouths.

3. a) The sea near the equator is warmest.
   b) To monitor changes in temperature.

P2.2 Taking Temperatures

NC links for the lesson
- Energy, electricity and forces: energy can be transferred usefully, stored, or dissipated, but cannot be created or destroyed.

Learning Objectives
Pupils should learn:
- That the temperature of an object can be measured using a thermometer.
- That there are a range of different types of thermometer and each type is suitable for differing types of measurement.

Learning Outcomes
- All pupils should be able to use a liquid-in-glass thermometer to measure the temperature of a liquid.
- Most pupils should be able to use a range of thermometers to measure the temperature of a material.
- Some pupils should also be able to select a thermometer for a particular measuring task taking into account the range and precision of the thermometer.

How Science Works
- Use a range of scientific vocabulary and terminology consistently in discussions and written work (1.1c).

Functional Skills Link-up
Mathematics
- Understand and use positive and negative numbers of any size in practical contexts (level 2).

Answers to in-text questions
a) They are testing the temperature with a very sensitive part of the body: the elbow. Hands may not be as sensitive and you could place the baby into water that it too hot for it.

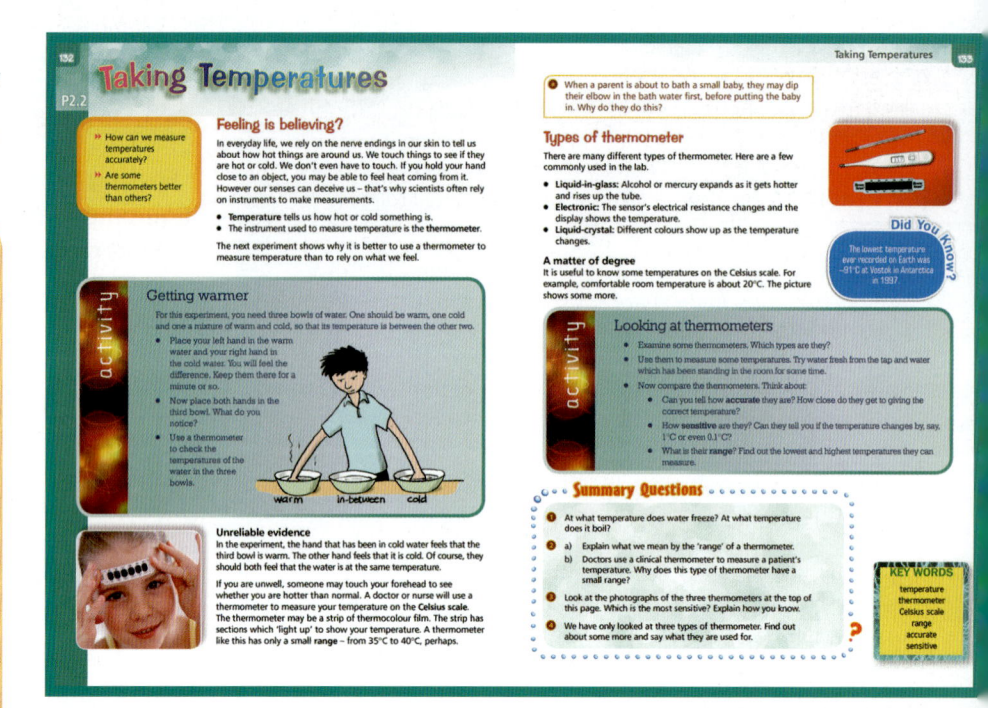

The Lesson

Starter Suggestions

Instrumental
Give the pupils a worksheet showing various scientific measuring instruments. They must describe the property the instrument measures, the range of the instrument and the precision. For example, a ruler measures length with a range of 300 mm and a precision of 1 mm. (5–10 mins)

Heating
How many different ways are there to heat something up? The pupils make a list and describe how they think that the processes work. Examples include flames (energy from chemical reactions), electrical heating (energy from moving charges), rubbing (frictional force) and so on. Each situation should show that energy enters the object. (10 mins)

Main Lesson
- Start with a brief recap of the problem from last lesson. Human senses are not good enough to use to make measurements, so we need measuring instruments.
- The 'Getting warmer' activity will show the pupils that we are fairly unreliable judges of temperature. The sensation felt from the third bowl can be slightly confusing if both hands are placed in at exactly the same time. Have the pupils place their left hand in first and quickly describe what they feel [it should feel cold] before placing their right hand in, giving an impression that the water is warm.

Learning Styles
Visual: Taking precise readings from thermometers.
Auditory: Listening to explanation of the difference between range, sensitivity and accuracy.
Kinaesthetic: Measuring the temperature of water.
Interpersonal: Discussing which thermometer is most appropriate for a particular type of measurement.
Intrapersonal: Thinking about what a 'good' scientific measurement is.

Taking Temperatures

- The pupils should know that thermometers are used to measure temperature. Remind them of the Celsius scale and show them how a liquid-in-glass thermometer works.
- You can then show some other types of thermometer, as mentioned in the pupil book, so that the pupils understand that there are a few different technologies that work.
- The focus of the 'Looking at thermometers' activity should be to discuss what is meant by 'accuracy', 'sensitivity' and 'range' of scientific instruments. Many pupils struggle with these terms, so take some time over them.
- An *accurate* instrument gives a reading that is close to the true value. When the pupils examine the thermometers they will find that most of them agree on room temperature, but they may find one or two that are quite a way out.
- A *sensitive* instrument can detect small changes. Most school thermometers will only be sensitive to changes of 1°C or 0.5°C, but you should have a few more sensitive than this. They pupils should be able to see that a small change in temperature (placing the bulb of a thermometer in their hand) will have a noticeable effect on a sensitive thermometer.
- The *range* of the thermometer is the difference between the highest and lowest temperature it can read. Simple thermometers have ranges of −10°C to 110°C which is good enough for water. The pupils should also see clinical thermometers with a very small range (but high sensitivity) and very large range thermometers (with lower sensitivity). Discuss why these are so.
- The pupils could draw up a table showing the accuracy, sensitivity and range of a few of the thermometers so that you can check that they clearly know the difference between the terms.
- Finish off by discussing some common temperatures, using the diagram of the thermometer in the pupil book and perhaps following up with the 'Temperature sorting' plenary.

Plenary Suggestions

Read it right
Give the pupils some diagrams of thermometers and ask them to read off the temperature. The thermometers should have different ranges and sensitivities. Show a set of thermometers all at once and ask the pupils to spot the inaccurate one. (5–10 mins)

Temperature sorting
Give the pupils a set of cards containing temperature readings. They have to match these to the objects at that temperature. (5–10 mins)

Answers to Summary questions

1. Water freezes at 0°C and boils at 100°C.
2. a) The range tells us the highest and lowest possible temperature it can measure.
   b) A living human can only have a narrow range of temperatures. By having a thermometer with a small range, the sensitivity can be very high.
3. The digital thermometer, it can measure a change of 0.1°C
4. Research.

Practical Support

Getting warmer
Equipment and materials required
Three bowls of water: one cold, one room temperature and one warm. A towel to dry hands.

Details
To achieve noticeable results the cold water should be a few degrees above freezing, while the warm water should be hot but not uncomfortably so. Use a thermometer to test it.

Safety
Test the temperature of the water carefully and make sure that the pupils do not leave their hands in for too long; one minute should do.

Looking at thermometers
Equipment and materials required
As wide a range of thermometers as possible; try to include a clinical thermometer and high temperature thermometer. Each group will also require a beaker for the water.

Details
The pupils need to examine the thermometers and determine their range and sensitivity. They also need to decide if the thermometer is accurate. To do this they will need to know room temperature. As an alternative you can give them some iced distilled water and tell them that this should be at 0°C.

Try to make sure that you have some thermometers that are entirely unsuitable for measuring cool water. Some only operate from 100°C and above. You could discuss what these are used for if there is time.

Safety
Watch out for breakages. Mercury-based thermometers will leak mercury if broken so a clean up kit is required. See CLEAPSS handbook/CD-Rom sections 12.13 and 7.7.

Differentiation

SEN
You may want to limit the range of thermometers a little. Some pupils will find digital thermometers far easier to read than liquid-in-glass.

Extension
A clinical thermometer has a few features designed to make it useful for measuring a person's temperature. What properties should the thermometer have? The pupils should come up with precision, limited range, robust (so it does not break), and responsive, so you don't have to wait a long time to get a reading. What other technologies are used to measure a patient's temperature?

Homework Suggestion

The pupils can find out about some temperature records and values. For example, the highest and lowest recorded temperatures in the UK. What temperature do ovens operate at and so on?

As an alternative they can find out about the origins of the Celsius scale or even the Fahrenheit scale. Are there any other temperature scales in use?

P2.3 Warming up, Cooling down

NC links for the lesson
- Energy, electricity and forces: energy can be transferred usefully, stored, or dissipated, but cannot be created or destroyed.

Learning Objectives
Pupils should learn:
- That an object warms up when it gains thermal energy from its surroundings and cools down when it loses energy to its surroundings.
- That the temperature of an object is a measure of the average thermal energy of a particle in the object and the total thermal energy depends on this and the size of the object.

Learning Outcomes
- All pupils should be able to explain cooling in terms of energy loss to the surroundings.
- Most pupils should be able to carry out an experiment to measure the rate of cooling of a liquid.
- Some pupils should also be able to describe the difference between temperature and thermal energy.

How Science Works
- Describe ways in which the presentation of experimental results through the routine use of tables and line graphs makes it easier to see patterns and trends (1.2d).

Functional Skills Link-up
Mathematics
- Collect and represent continuous data, using ICT where appropriate (level 2).

Answers to in-text questions
a) The energy would leave the drink more quickly because the temperate difference is greater.

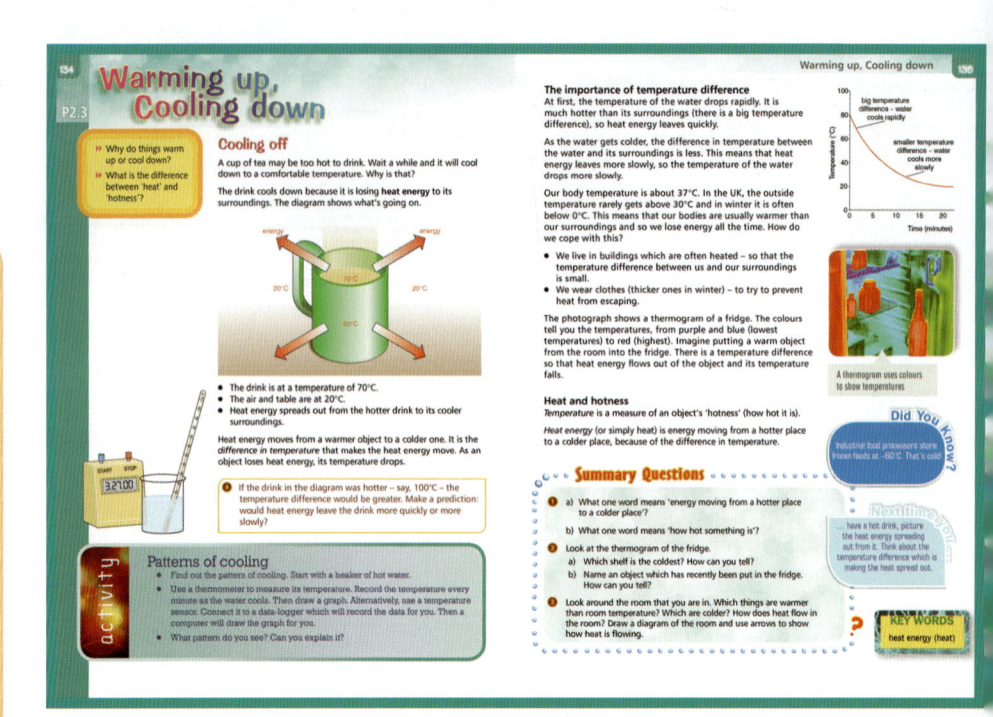

The Lesson

Starter Suggestions

Yuck, it's gone cold
Bring a cold cup of tea to the lab. Ask the pupil to explain why it has 'gone cold'. What processes have happened? Do the pupils know of any way you could have kept your tea warm for longer? (5–10 mins)

Constructive criticism
Give the pupils a set of graphs that all show the same data but all are flawed. For example, how the temperature of the room increases over time when the heating is switched on. The graphs can have problems such as one with uneven sales, one where the points are joined 'dot to dot' and anomalous results are not ignored, and one where the graph only takes up a tiny proportion of the available space and so on. The pupils have to explain the problems with the graphs and construct an improved graph from the raw data. (10–15 mins)

Answers to Summary questions

1. a) Cooling.   b) Temperature.
2. a) Top shelf is coldest as there are more purple and blue colours.
   b) The bottle has recently been added, as it's red with yellow.
3. Pupil diagram.

Learning Styles
Visual: Drawing accurate graphs.
Auditory: Discussing patterns in results.
Kinaesthetic: Recording measurements.
Interpersonal: Working in groups during experiments.
Intrapersonal: Imagining the flow of energy from one object to another.

Warming up, Cooling down

Main Lesson

- Start by finding out what the pupils already know about cooling. Make sure that none of them are thinking about 'cold' moving into objects. Emphasise that hot objects have more thermal energy than cold ones.
- Once this is clear move on to the 'Patterns of cooling' activity. You can give detailed instruction or allow the pupils some flexibility to demonstrate their skills in How Science Works. For example you might allow the pupils to choose their own thermometer from a range provided, choose the volume of water and the time interval between readings. They may want to share results with other groups to get an average cooling graph.
- During the practical task the pupils should focus on making systematic measurements that are as precise as the thermometer and stop-clock allow. Make sure that they are taking the readings every minute or, better still, every 30 seconds.
- Ideally the thermometer or temperature probe should not touch the glass of the beaker as this will reduce accuracy. Discuss this problem with the pupils to see if they can come up with a way of suspending the thermometer in the water; a retort stand is satisfactory but they must make sure that they can still read the scale.
- The pupils should design their own graph where possible, choosing the appropriate scales. Ideally this should be a line graph and the pupils should draw a clear curve through their data points. This will show rapid cooling at the start, slowing down at the end.
- Discuss why the rate of cooling changed, making sure that the pupils understand that it is the difference between the temperature of the water and the room that is important. They should appreciate that the cooling will stop when the water has reached room temperature; the curve becomes flat.
- Make sure that the pupils have a good grasp of the idea of thermal energy. When an object loses thermal energy it cools; when it gains energy it heats up. Check for the 'cold' moving misconception again to make sure. You might want to talk about thermal energy exchange in more detail with higher attaining pupils at this point.
- Mammals use quite a bit of energy keeping warm, reptiles are cooler and often rely on sunlight to warm them up before they become active. We can be active in darkness. Because we are warmer than the surroundings, we can easily be spotted in the dark using a thermal camera. Show some infra-red images taken in complete darkness; it is easy to spot humans.
- Some pupils now need to understand the difference between temperature and the total thermal energy of an object. Temperature is actually related to the kinetic energy of one of the particles in a substance, whereas the thermal energy has to take into account all of the particles; the mass. This means that more massive objects have more thermal energy than small ones, when they are at the same temperature. There are other complications that don't need to be mentioned.

Plenary Suggestions

Spotting anomalous results

Show the pupils a table with a large set of data including several repeat measurements. They have to spot the anomalous results and calculate the average readings. (5–10 mins)

Comparing cooling

Give the pupils sets of data generated from the cooling of water in three different containers. These could be different colours or different surface areas. The pupils must plot the data on a set of axes and make a comparison of the cooling patterns. (10–15 mins)

Did You Know?

The technology for cooling food rapidly was initially developed by Clarence Birdseye (not a captain), who realised that the faster the food was frozen the better the preservation was (while working in a chilly laboratory). The rapid cooling prevents damage to the cells that would occur because of the slow growth of ice crystals.

Practical Support

Patterns of cooling

Equipment and materials required

Kettles to heat the water. Per group: a 250 cm³ beaker, a thermometer (0–100°C with 0.5° sensitivity).

Data-logging equipment can also be used; a retort stand, boss and clamp, can be useful to hold the sensor in place, use pieces of rubber or polystyrene to protect thermometers when clamping.

The pupils will also need graph drawing equipment.

Details

The pupils pour hot water into their beaker and monitor its cooling over a period of 10 minutes. The higher the starting temperature the more marked the cooling pattern will be; a starting temperature between 70–80°C works very well, resulting in a clear cooling curve.

The data-logging equipment is very useful. If only a limited number of sets are available, then one or two groups can use it and discuss the advantages at the end. You could also attach one set to a data projector to show the whole class a set of results.

Safety

The starting water does not have to be boiling, but take care; 70–80°C should be adequate to show a cooling pattern.

Differentiation

SEN

Provide supportive instruction for the cooling water task. This can include a table for the results and some pre-prepared axes for the graph plotting if required.

Extension

Discuss thermal energy in more depth with these pupils. An object reaches *thermal equilibrium* with its surroundings when the energy it is emitting is matched by the energy that it is absorbing from the surroundings.

Homework Suggestion

If one of either the 'Constructive criticism' starter or 'Comparing cooling' plenary were not used, the pupils can try out the tasks as a homework activity to enhance their graphical skills.

P2.4 Thermal Conduction and Insulation

NC links for the lesson

- Energy, electricity and forces: energy can be transferred usefully, stored, or dissipated, but cannot be created or destroyed.
- Chemical and material behaviour: the particle model provides explanations for the different physical properties and behaviour of matter.

Learning Objectives

Pupils should learn:

- That a thermal conductor is a material that transfers thermal energy quickly and metals are good thermal conductors.
- That a thermal insulator is a material that transfers thermal energy slowly and that examples include wool, plastics and wood.

Learning Outcomes

- All pupils should be able to give examples of thermal conductors and thermal insulators.
- Most pupils should be able to describe an experiment to compare a range of thermal conductors.
- Some pupils should also be able to explain why materials at the same temperature can feel warm or cool in terms of their thermal conductivity.

How Science Works

- Describe and identify key variables in an investigation and assign appropriate values to these (1.2b).

Learning Styles

Visual: Watching the 'Comparing metals' demonstration.

Auditory: Listening to definitions of insulators and conductors.

Kinaesthetic: Handling and describing different materials.

Interpersonal: Discussing what we mean by the terms 'hot' and 'cold' in relation to materials.

Intrapersonal: Imagining the flow of energy from our body.

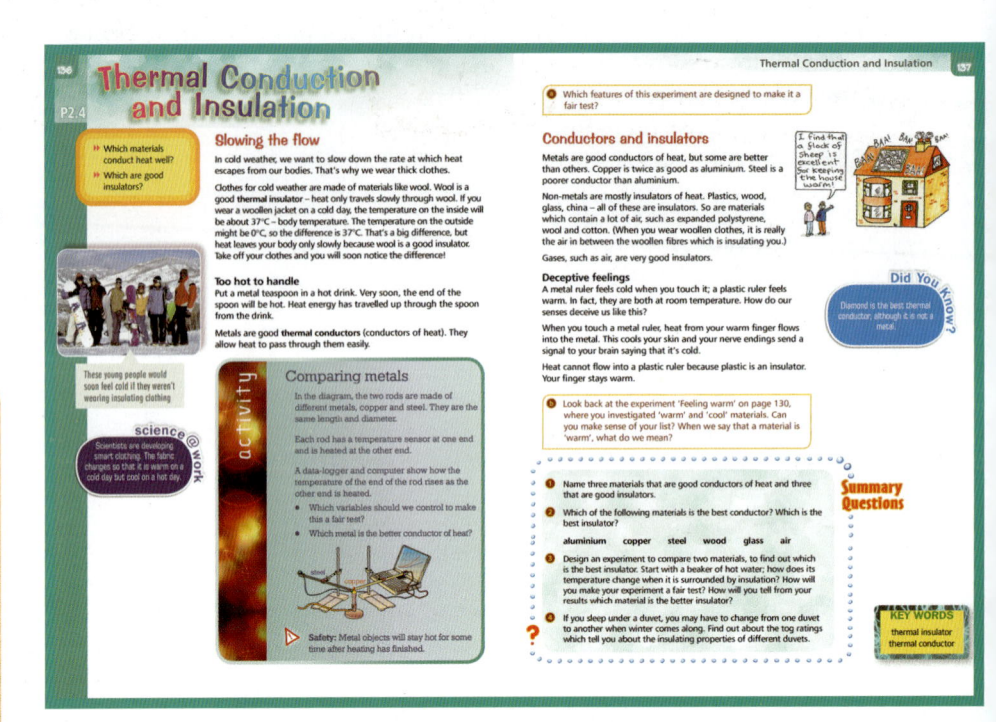

The Lesson

Starter Suggestions

Chilly, isn't it?

Show some video footage of animals that live in extremely cold conditions. These could include polar bears, Emperor penguins, sea lions and so on. Discuss with the pupils how these manage to survive in temperatures that are far below 0°C without special clothing. The discussion should include fur, feathers and fat. (5–10 mins)

Siberian survival

The pupils have unfortunately become stranded in coldest Siberia during a badly planned field trip. Give them a list of materials that are available and ask them to design clothing and a shelter. (10–15 mins)

Main Lesson

- Begin with the 'Chilly isn't it' starter; this leads naturally on to the clothing used to protect us from cold conditions. The pupils will have little trouble understanding that some materials are better insulators than others.
- Demonstrate the 'Comparing metals' experiment to show the flow of energy through a material. The pupils should note that the temperature changes gradually; it takes some time for the energy to travel through all of the material.
- There are various alternatives to the 'Comparing metals' demonstration that you could consider. The best of these includes using metal bars that have thermocolour film attached. The bars can be dipped in hot water and the film changes colour as the bars heat up. This helps to visualise the energy passing through the bars. If you have this equipment than you should use it to reinforce the ideas from the demonstration.
- Use the same materials as you did for P2.1 again. The pupils should sort them into the same order as they did last time. The metals should all be in the 'cold' area while the plastic, wood and wool in the 'warm' area.
- You can discuss the properties of these materials paying particular attention to the trapped air in the wool and other fibres. As before, detailed images of the material structure can be useful. You could see if the pupils know anything special about metals; they should know that they are good electrical conductors too. Can they explain why metals conduct electricity? Is there a connection between electrical conduction and thermal conduction?

Thermal Conduction and Insulation

- Bring out a metal ruler and a similar plastic one from a refrigerator (as you may have in an earlier lesson). The metal ruler will feel very cold compared to the plastic ruler, but placing them both on thermocolour film or using a temperature sensor should show that they are the same temperature.
- Use this to discuss why one feels cold; it is the loss of energy from our bodies that our senses detect. A material that feels warm is simply not allowing thermal energy to pass through.
- The pupils should now have a solid grasp of the difference between a thermal conductor and insulator. They will move on to explaining the behaviour in the next lesson.

Plenary Suggestions

Heat resistant?
Just how heat resistant is a heat resistant mat? Set up two Bunsens with tripods, one with a metal sheet on top and one with a small heat-resistant mat. Try to melt an ice cube through each and time how long it takes. Is this a good way to test materials? How could the pupils test the insulation properties of plastic? (5–10 mins)

Natural or artificial
The pupils can design a test to see which material is the best thermal insulator, a natural fibre like wool or an artificial one like nylon. They should focus on making the test as fair as possible. (10–15 mins)

science @ work

One research group looking into the potential of smart clothes can be found at www.artschool.newport.ac.uk/smartclothes. Some smart clothes may end up even smarter; they are being designed to include health monitoring sensors (sensitive to sweat and blood) to monitor how patients are recovering from injuries.

Answers to in-text questions

a The rods are both the same length and diameter. They are placed in the same part of the flame.

b Materials that are 'warm' are poor conductors of thermal energy (heat).

Answers to Summary questions

1. Any three insulators and conductors.
2. Copper is the best conductor, air is the best insulator.
3. Pupil's detailed plan.
4. Pupils tog rating research. The higher the tog rating, the better the insulation. A summer duvet has a rating of around 4.5 tog, and a winter duvet is 13 tog.

Practical Support

Comparing metals (demonstration)
Equipment and materials required
Two metal rods of the same length and diameter. A Bunsen burner, two (or four) retort stands, boss and clamps, and two temperature sensors.

Details
The equipment should be set up as shown in the pupil book diagram. The most difficult aspect of this experiment is attaching the temperature sensors to the end of the metal rods without them falling off. To achieve good results the sensors need to be in close contact with the rods, so try setting up the equipment in advance to make sure that this works. You may need two more stands to hold the sensors.
Don't forget to turn the Bunsen off; the metal rods will eventually become so hot that the sensors may be damaged.

Safety
The metal bars will become very hot; allow time for them to cool before touching.

Plenary: Heat resistant
Equipment and materials required
Two Bunsen burners, two tripods, heat-resistant mat (silica or ceramic, not wood), sheet of metal, ice cubes, stop-watch or stop-clock.

Details
See above.

Safety
Make sure heat-resistant mat does not burn.
Metals will remain hot.

Differentiation

Extension
Measuring temperature by placing something in contact with the object has a few problems. The contact causes cooling and sometimes we cannot touch the object. How can we measure the temperature using just the light (or infra-red radiation) coming from the object? The pupils can find some thermal images and explain how they are made.

Homework Suggestion

The pupils can look for objects that are designed to transfer heat or reduce heat flow around their home. They can make a list of conductors and insulators from this information.
Alternatively they can research information about which materials are the best conductors and which are the best insulators.

Did You Know?

Diamond's high thermal conductivity is around four times greater then the best metals. One way of testing to see if a diamond is real is to use a very sensitive thermal probe to test the thermal conductivity, although it is worth noting that the recently developed jewellery quality silicon carbide 'Moissanite' is very similar, so check your gems carefully.

P2.5 Expansion and Contraction

NC links for the lesson

- Energy, electricity and forces: energy can be transferred usefully, stored, or dissipated, but cannot be created or destroyed.
- Chemical and material behaviour: the particle model provides explanations for the different physical properties and behaviour of matter.

Learning Objectives

Pupils should learn:

- That when materials are heated the particles in the material gain energy and move further apart.
- That thermal energy can be transferred through a material by conduction processes.

Learning Outcomes

- All pupils should be able to state that materials expand when they are heated.
- Most pupils should be able to describe expansion in terms of a particle model.
- Some pupils should also be able to describe thermal conduction in terms of a particle model.

How Science Works

- Describe how the use of a particular model or analogy supports an explanation (1.1a1).

Functional Skills Link-up

English

- Present information on complex subjects concisely and clearly (level 2).

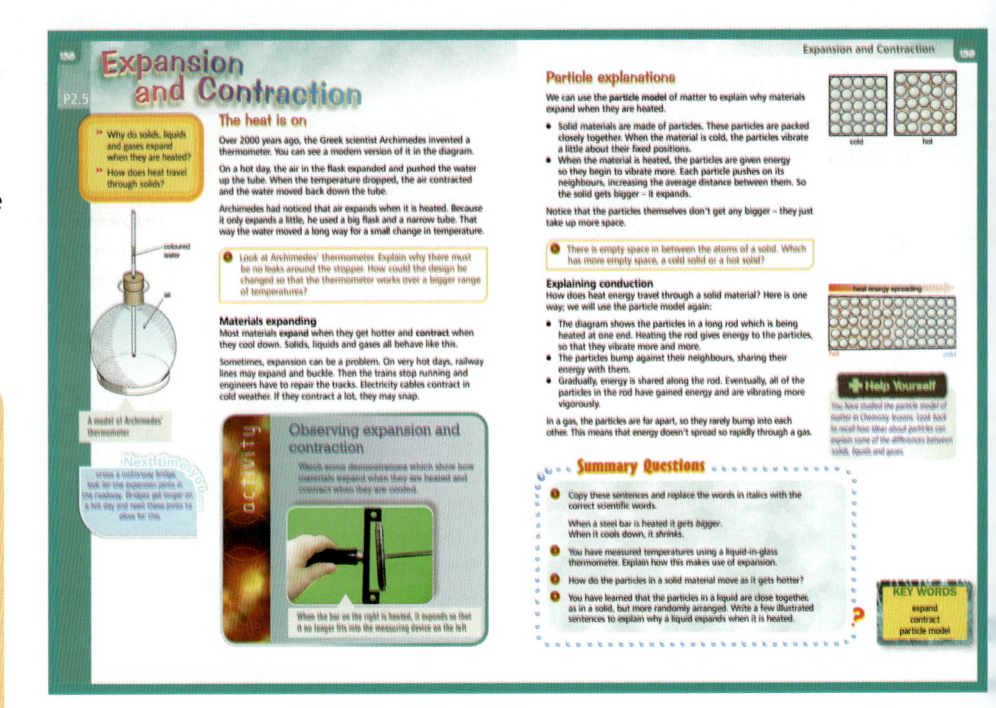

The Lesson

Starter Suggestions

Safety first

The pupils should draw up a table to note down the hazards and safety precautions that are taken through the lesson. They should start by noting any unnecessary risks already present in the laboratory; for example trip hazards. At the end they will give you a safety rating for your work today. (5–10 mins)

The particle model of matter

Ask the pupils what they already know about how solids, liquids and gases behave and how their properties are explained by these models. They can draw a brief summary diagram of each state and you can show them the expected diagrams and explanations. It's worth checking the liquid's diagrams; many pupils draw the particles in little groups separated by a fairly large distance. Take the opportunity to explain that the particles are actually all very close together but they can move about relative to each other, unlike particles in a solid which can only vibrate about their fixed positions. (10–15 mins)

Learning Styles

Visual: Drawing diagrams of the particle model.
Auditory: Describing the behaviour of particles in detail.
Kinaesthetic: Examining the apparatus before use.
Interpersonal: Discussing what can be concluded from the demonstrations.
Intrapersonal: Imagining the behaviour of particles in a material.

Answers to in-text questions

a No air should be allowed into the thermometer or liquid escape. The glass tube could be longer to measure a greater range of temperatures.

b A hot solid.

Expansion and Contraction

Main Lesson

- In this lesson the pupils really get to grips with the particle model of matter, particularly solids. They need to use it to explain expansion and thermal conduction. This is a fairly high level concept and some pupils will struggle with it.
- The pupils will be watching demonstrations through the lesson; you could ask them to note any hazards and the precautions taken to avoid them. At the end of the lesson they could give suggestions about how you could improve your safety practice and discuss whether it would be safe for them to carry out the demonstrations that you did.
- The demonstrations for the 'Observing expansion and contraction' activity are described in the 'Practical support' section. There are a range of similar activities you could try here too, depending on the equipment available in your department.
- The pupils can now discuss the consequences of expansion in hot weather; bridge design, and so on.
- Discuss the demonstrations again and ask the pupils what they think is happening inside the materials; why do they expand when they get hotter? This should lead to two main ideas: the particles expand or they move further apart.
- It is very important to make sure that the pupils do not become fixed on the idea that the particles themselves are expanding. The particles are moving further apart as the material heats up. Show the pupils a set of diagrams showing the correct idea. With higher attaining pupils you might want to explain why the particles are further apart.
- There are a number of useful simulations of particle behaviour you can use to reinforce the idea of expansion. Use one if you have it. The pupils should be able to see that the particles vibrate more as the material heats up and so they take up more space.
- You now need to move on to using the particle model to explain thermal conduction. The description should explain why it takes some time for energy to be passed through a material. The key idea is that energy is passed from one particle to its near neighbours. The energy is transferred slowly because of this. If you have a simulation of the conduction process you should use it as reinforcement.
- At the end of the lesson recap the particle models used. The pupils should be able to imagine the behaviour of the tiny particles during both expansion and conduction at this stage.

Plenary Suggestions

Cartoon conductor

The pupils must draw a short cartoon showing clearly what happens to the particles in a metal rod when it is heated at one end. No words are allowed in the cartoon. (5–10 mins)

Modelling conduction or expansion

Can the pupils think up any models that are similar to the way conduction or expansion in solids work? They should try to think up ideas to explain the concepts to Year 6 pupils. A typical one for conduction involves packing pupils together and pushing one, creating a sort of 'chain reaction' of energy that is passed on. (5–10 mins)

Practical Support

Observing expansion and contraction

Equipment and materials required

A bimetallic strip, model Archimedes' thermometer (round-bottomed flask filled with coloured liquid as shown in the pupil book), ball and ring expansion apparatus, bar and gauge apparatus.

Details

There are a range of demonstrations that show expansion and contraction.

Archimedes' thermometer: hold the flask in both hands and the liquid level should rise as it warms. The liquid is expanding. For a greater effect you can cool it down by placing it in a bowl of crushed ice or heat it in warm water.

Ball and ring: Show the pupils that the ball fits through the ring easily. Heat the ball strongly with the Bunsen for about a minute and then try to fit it through the ring; it will not fit. You will need to use tongs to put the ball on top of the ring. Demonstrate the ball contracting by holding the ball on the ring under a slow tap behind a safety screen, there will be a lot of steam and the ball will fall through the loop.

Bimetallic strip: Show the pupils the strip and explain that the two metals expand at different rates. Heat the strip and it will curl. Ask the pupils to explain why this has happened.

Safety

All of the metal objects will become very hot, do not allow pupils to touch them. Use safety screens and eye protection.

Differentiation

SEN

Provide the pupils with a set of diagrams showing the particle behaviour during expansion and conduction so that they can concentrate on adding brief notes.

Extension

Why are metals particularly good thermal conductors? The pupils can find out about the role that electrons play in the conduction process. How is expansion and contraction taken into account when designing large structures such as bridges?

Homework Suggestion

The 'Modelling conduction or expansion' plenary task could be set for homework.

Answers to Summary questions

1. When a steel bar is heated it **expands**. When it cools down it **contracts**.
2. The liquid expands when it is heated and so it moves up the length of the thermometer giving a bigger reading.
3. The atoms vibrate more and more and occupy more space.
4. The particles vibrate more and more and take up more space. The liquid expands. [Pupil diagram.]

P2.6 Radiation and Convection

NC links for the lesson
- Energy, electricity and forces: energy can be transferred usefully, stored, or dissipated, but cannot be created or destroyed.
- Chemical and material behaviour: the particle model provides explanations for the different physical properties and behaviour of matter.

Learning Objectives
Pupils should learn:
- That thermal energy can be transferred by radiation and this is the only way thermal energy can travel through a vacuum.
- That convection currents carry thermal energy through fluids owing to changes in density.

Learning Outcomes
- All pupils should be able to state that heat can only pass through a vacuum by radiation and that fluids (liquids and gases) can transfer energy by convection.
- Most pupils should be able to describe how infra-red radiation can be detected.
- Some pupils should also be able to describe a convection current in terms of particle behaviour and density changes.

How Science Works
- Describe how the use of a particular model or analogy supports an explanation (1.1a1).

Functional Skills Link-up
English
- Present information on complex subjects consisely and clearly (level 2).

The Lesson

Starter Suggestions

Night vision
Show the pupils some video footage shot through an infra-red camera or a set of stills. Ask them to identify what is happening. They should be able to spot hot objects quite clearly. (5–10 mins)

Light refreshment
What are the properties of light? The pupils have five minutes to make a summary diagram of what they remember from P1 earlier. See if any remember that you also examined infra-red radiation. (10 mins)

Learning Styles
Visual: Watching the action of a convection current.
Auditory: Listening to or describing a convection current in detail.
Kinaesthetic: Carrying out practical activity.
Interpersonal: Carrying out group work.
Intrapersonal: Recalling previous work.

Answers to Summary questions

1. a) Conduction. b) Radiation. c) Convection.

2. A hot air balloon is carried along by convection currents. A balloon can only move in the direction of the convection current. If hot air is rising, the balloon will be carried upwards. If cold air is sinking, it will descend.

3. Diagram showing the smoke being carried up the chimney by a warm air current.

4. The Earth radiates away energy so its surface is cool at night. It is coldest just before dawn as it has cooled all night.

Radiation and Convection

Main Lesson

- The pupils should be asked to pay particular attention to risk assessment during this lesson. There are no particularly dangerous activities but they should be developing this skill.
- The pupils have touched on infra-red radiation before and this is strongly linked to visible light. Ask them to recap the properties they already know. They should remember that light can travel in a vacuum from the Sun.
- A Leslie's cube filled with freshly boiled water can be used to let the pupils feel the radiation being emitted by a hot object. The pupils don't have to know about how different surfaces emit infra-red radiation, so just use the matt black side. The pupils must not touch the surface!
- Once you have established that infra-red radiation exists you can try to detect it with a camera using 'Seeing infra-red radiation'.
- If you do not have any cameras suitable for looking at IR objects, then you should be able to find a very wide range of IR images using the Internet. You can discuss what these images show before moving to convection.
- Convection currents are fairly easy to demonstrate. Allow the pupils to carry out the 'A model convection current' experiment. Give the pupils a hazard card for the potassium manganate (VII) before they start and ask them to note down two hazards and how they will be avoided. These should include fire hazards and a mention of what an 'oxidising agent' is. Larger scale apparatus is available for a teacher-led demonstration if necessary.
- Convection currents in gases can be shown by using a smoke chimney. The smoke particles are dragged downwards from one chimney and then back up another. This can be used to explain draughts in houses; when hot air escapes towards the top of a house new, colder, air enters near the bottom. Explain that this is why it is important to insulate loft spaces.
- It is again important that the particle model is used to explain these changes. The pupils will need to picture the material expanding when it is heated; link back to the last lesson. The pupils will have to be reminded of their work on density (see pages 138–139) to explain why the warmer material rises upwards. As the material cools down it contracts, becomes denser and sinks again.
- The whole of this sequence gives us convection currents. The pupils should be able to sketch a diagram of convection current and put simple labels on it, e.g. material heated ⟶ expands ⟶ less dense ⟶ floats then material cools ⟶ contracts ⟶ more dense ⟶ sinks
- Watch out for pupils using the phrase 'heat rises', it is very common. Make sure that they are describing warmer *material* rising upwards and thus transferring energy.

Plenary Suggestions

Risk management
Ask the pupils to match up a set of risks with the action or action taken to control the risk. This could be a worksheet, set of match-up cards and an inter-activity on the whiteboard. (5–10 mins)

Hot topic
The pupils should make a table summarising the three methods of thermal energy transfer: conduction, convection and radiation. They should mention particle behaviour and how rapid the process is. (5–10 mins)

Practical Support

Seeing infra-red radiation

Equipment and materials required
Video camera sensitive to infra-red radiation.

Details
Many cameras are sensitive to IR as well as visible light. Video, digital stills, web cameras and mobile phone cameras will show a bright light from an infra-red LED on a TV remote control when a button is pressed, even though no visible light is emitted. Try out a few to see if they can be used to detect IR in a darkened room. If not, there are some specially designed ones available from science equipment suppliers. The pupils can use the cameras to look at Bunsen flames (compare yellow and blue), radiant heaters.

Safety
The pupils must not be able to touch the hot objects.

A model convection current

Equipment and materials required
For each group: a large beaker (at least 500 cm^3), Bunsen burner, heat-resistant mat, tripod, gauze, forceps, water and a small potassium manganate (VII) crystal.

Details
The pupils drop the crystal into the water off-centre and then light and position the Bunsen so that it will heat the beaker directly under the crystal. The pupils should watch the pattern of flow, the hot water rises and spreads across the surface before cooling and sinking on the other side of the beaker.

Safety
Potassium manganate (VII) is an oxidising agent and harmful. Handle crystals with forceps or tweezers. See CLEAPSS Hazcard 81. The pink solution is low hazard.

The pupils do not need to boil the water so the Bunsen should be turned off once the concept has been demonstrated.

Differentiation

SEN
Provide a diagram of a convection current for the pupils to label with key phrases.

Extension
You may wish to use the term 'electromagnetic radiation' when discussing light and infra-red radiation. The pupils could look at other parts of the electromagnetic spectrum. Alternatively they could make a plan to see which surfaces are the best absorbers or emitters of IR radiation.

Homework Suggestion

Knowledge of thermal energy transfer is essential in fire fighting. The pupils could produce a report showing how fire fighters need to understand radiation and convection currents. Areas that could be covered include shiny suits, flashover, backdrafts and so on.

Answers to in-text questions

a) The top of the cup does not contain any of the hot liquid so it stays cooler. The person gives out infra-red radiation as they are warm from their body heat; the tips of the fingers are coolest as there is less blood-flow there.

P2.7 Seeing Sounds

NC links for the lesson
- Energy, electricity and forces: energy can be transferred usefully, stored, or dissipated, but cannot be created or destroyed.
- Chemical and material behaviour: the particle model provides explanations for the different physical properties and behaviour of matter.

Learning Objectives

Pupils should learn:
- That the amplitude of a sound is its loudness.
- That the pitch of a sound wave is related to its frequency; the number of vibrations each second.

Learning Outcomes
- All pupils should be able to state that the larger the amplitude a sound wave has the louder it will be.
- Most pupils should be able to compare oscilloscope traces to determine which sound has the highest amplitude and frequency.
- Some pupils should also be able to describe the patterns they find in waveforms produced in musical instruments.

Learning Styles

Visual: Making detailed observations about waves.

Auditory: Listening to musical instruments.

Kinaesthetic: Drawing waveforms.

Interpersonal: Collaborating in collection of sounds.

Intrapersonal: Relating sound wave patterns to the actual sounds.

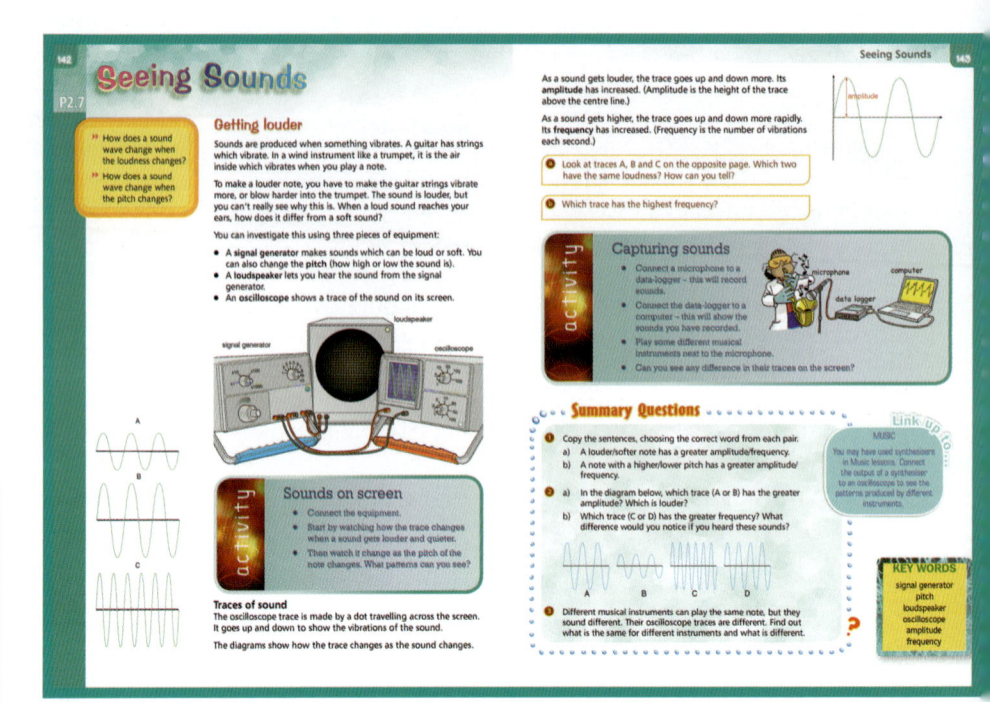

The Lesson

Starter Suggestions

Just waving

Ask the pupils what a wave is. How many examples of waves can they give? They may only come up with water waves but ask them what waves actually *do*. Show them an example of wave motion using a video clip or simulation or demonstrate the most basic of musical instruments: a wobble board (see the 'Wobble' practical in 'Practical support'). (5–10 mins)

Music maestro please

Borrow a range of instruments from the music department, e.g. guitar, drum, flute and so on. Play a note on each of them and ask the pupils to describe what is happening. Lead them to the idea that a part of the instrument is vibrating. Ask how a louder note can be played and what this does to the vibration. If you have pupils gifted at music, ask them to carry out the demonstration for you and describe what they are doing. (10 mins)

Main Lesson

- In this lesson the pupils start to link sound to wave behaviour and look at frequency and amplitude. They will move on to the details of particle behaviour in the next lesson.
- Showing actual vibrations in instruments makes certain that the pupils will link sound to vibrations. The 'Music maestro please' starter is very effective, especially if pupils take part. They can *gently* feel their own throats while talking to notice the vibrations that are produced while speaking.

Answers to Summary questions

1. a) A **louder** note has a greater **amplitude**.
   b) A note with **higher** pitch has a **greater** frequency.
2. a) Trace A has greater amplitude and so is louder.
   b) Trace C has greater frequency. Trace C would be higher pitched.
3. Pupil research.

Seeing Sounds

- Demonstrating sound waves with an oscilloscope can present some problems (see the 'Sounds on screen' activity) but it is essential that the pupils get to see the waveforms produced by a signal generator. They will need to be able to compare these in terms of frequency and amplitude.
- The pupils must understand the relationship between the pitch and the frequency (vibration per second) and also amplitude and volume, so show plenty of example waves to get this across.
- Be careful to make sure that the pupils understand that the amplitude is measured from the central point of the wave to the peak; many will mistakenly think that it is measured from the top to the bottom of the waveform.
- The pupils can then attempt to capture the waveforms from some sounds in the 'Capturing sounds' activity. They should find that simple instruments can produce fairly simple patterns, but a voice is very complex in its waveform. They can sketch these waves and see if they can make a link between the shapes and the way instruments sound.
- You can also provide some tuning forks for the pupils to use; these should be struck gently to prevent damage to them. They should give a simple waveform.
- After the experiments you can discuss the findings. Try to find some images of traces in advance, just in case the pupils do not have clear ones.

Plenary Suggestions

Noted
Can the pupils match up the waveforms with the instrument that created it? Show a set of six instruments and six waves and get the pupils to match them up. (5–10 mins)

Sketching sound waves
Give the pupils a diagram of a sound wave. Ask them to sketch the following three wave traces based on it: one with twice the frequency but the same amplitude; one with twice the frequency but half the amplitude; one with half the frequency and twice the amplitude. They should explain in what ways the sounds would sound different from each other. (5–10 mins)

Practical Support

Sounds on screen

Equipment and materials required
Signal generator, cathode ray oscilloscope and loudspeaker.

Details
It is unlikely that you will have sufficient equipment for the pupils to carry out this experiment for themselves. You may need to allow the pupils to use it in small groups while other pupils are carrying out the 'Capturing sounds' task. Alternatively it can be demonstrated, but it is unlikely that all pupils will be able to see the oscilloscope screen clearly.

Some oscilloscopes can be connected directly to a computer and there are devices that can use a computer as the display. These have the great advantage as the display is considerably larger and can even be projected via a data projector so that the entire class can see it easily.

Connect the signal generator to both the oscilloscope and the loudspeaker. Set the signal generator to generate a clearly audible note (1 kHz) and then adjust the oscilloscope control until a clear trace is shown with at least two complete waves across the screen. Adjusting the signal generator will adjust the frequency (pitch) and the wave displayed will change accordingly.

If the pupils are carrying out this task, then it is wise to mark the controls on the signal generator and oscilloscope in some way so that the pupils can start from a setting that is known to work well.

Safety
Do not let the pupils listen to loud noises for too long.

Capturing sounds

Equipment and materials required
Data-logging software, computer and microphone.

Details
The exact details will depend on the data-logging software being used, so check the manual. Most software has a simple sound capture mode that the pupils can use.

Some computer operating systems have built in sound recording software too. For example Macintosh computers have 'Garageband' that can be used to capture voice 'instruments'. Again, the detail will have to be found in the appropriate manual.

Safety
No problems.

Main lesson: Wobble

Equipment and materials required
A rectangular sheet of flexible material measuring approximately 80 cm by 50 cm. Thin hardboard (high density fibreboard) works best.

Details
Hold the board horizontally in the palms of your hand and wobble up and down. The wave shape is shown clearly and a 'wobble' sound can be heard. The instrument was popularised by Rolf Harris, and you may be able to find video clips of people playing the instrument if you cannot make one.

Safety
Make sure the edges are not sharp.

Differentiation

Extension
The pupils can find out more about the connection between music and the waveforms instruments produce. Is there are connection between the frequency and the scales used in music?

Homework Suggestion
The pupils can find out about how various musical instruments operate, from the obvious drum and piano to the Theremin.

Answers to in-text questions
a) Sounds B and C, they have the same amplitude.
b) Trace C has the highest frequency.

P2.8 How Sound Travels

NC links for the lesson
- Energy, electricity and forces: energy can be transferred usefully, stored, or dissipated, but cannot be created or destroyed.
- Chemical and material behaviour: the particle model provides explanations for the different physical properties and behaviour of matter.

Learning Objectives
Pupils should learn:
- That sound will travel through all materials but it cannot travel through a vacuum.
- That sound travels as a wave of compressions through a medium.
- That sound travels more quickly through dense materials as the particles are closer together.

Learning Outcomes
- All pupils should be able to state that sound requires a medium (material) to travel through.
- Most pupils should be able to describe how sound travels as a wave through materials.
- Some pupils should also be able to explain why sound travels faster through solid materials than gases in terms of particle movement.

How Science Works
- Describe and identify key variables in an investigation and assign values to these (1.2b).
- Describe and suggest, with reasons, how planning and implementation could be improved (1.2e).

The Lesson

Starter Suggestions

Run silent, run deep
Show the pupils a tense clip from an underwater war film where sonar is being used to hunt a submarine. Ask the pupils to explain how they think this works. Alternatively you could show clips of dolphins moving quickly in dark water, or a bat flying in the dark. (5 mins)

Moving through solids
The pupils need to explain, or draw a set of diagrams showing how thermal energy is conducted through a solid material. (5–10 mins)

Main Lesson
- In this lesson the pupils return to the particle model to explain how sound travels though materials. Understanding and explaining the details of this is a high level skill, so some pupils are bound to struggle.
- The 'Run silent, run deep' starter should give you an idea of how they think sound moves; misconception will be dealt with during the lesson.
- The 'In space no-one can hear the doorbell' demonstration can be a bit fussy; sometimes the jar has a small leak and so the air cannot be evacuated

Stretch Yourself
In air, light travels nearly one million times faster than sound. This means that over reasonable distances light appears instantaneous; while there can be a noticeable delay in the sound arriving. The sound from a lightning flash one kilometre away will take three seconds longer than the light to arrive. If the light and sound are arriving almost simultaneously it is time to hide indoors.

Learning Styles
Visual: Watching simulations or demonstrations of wave movement.
Auditory: Listening to sound waves through materials.
Kinaesthetic: Measuring sound levels with a sensor.
Interpersonal: Working in groups and discussing plans of action.
Intrapersonal: Understanding how sound travels through a medium.

Answers to in-text questions
a. Light can travel through a vacuum as it doesn't need particles (it is an electromagnetic wave) but sound needs particles.
b. Stand behind a window, the air cannot pass through the glass but you can still hear.

How Sound Travels

well enough. Test it out in advance to make sure there is a noticeable effect.

- You now need to discuss the wave nature of sound. This is a bit difficult as the waves cannot be seen and, worse still, longitudinal wave motion is hard to describe as it is difficult to imagine what is waving. The pupils need to be able to imagine the behaviour of the particles in the material. These oscillate and push other particles and so on.
- Traditionally you can use a 'Slinky' spring. Stretch this out a bit and place a sticker on one of the coils half way along. If you move one end in and out you will produce a longitudinal wave and the pupils will be able to see the compressions. They should also note that while the sticker 'waves' back and forth it doesn't actually go anywhere; this shows that while energy is being transferred there is no material transferred.
- As an alternative or extra reinforcement, you can use a computer simulation of longitudinal wave motion. You should be able to find a web-based one fairly easily by searching for 'longitudinal wave motion' with any search engine, including the term 'java' will give more advanced simulations.
- Once the pupils have a firm grasp of the movement of sound you can move on to the 'Sound and solids' activity. This will take up quite a bit of time, as it is important to allow the pupils to make the design decisions whenever possible in order to develop their How Science Works skills.
- The pupils have to consider how to make the experiment fair. This should include some way of ensuring the sound is at a constant volume; this can be difficult when background sounds are taken into account. The materials tested should also be the same thickness; this tends to be a problem and can be discussed as part of the evaluation of the task.
- Pupils often find evaluation of their experiment and results rather difficult. Let them think about whether the results that have been obtained are reliable enough and how the quality could be improved. They could also evaluate the plan and results of an imaginary group in the 'Evaluation time' plenary.

Plenary Suggestions

The speed of sound
Give the pupils a set of data showing the speed of sound in a variety of materials. Ask them to present this information graphically. They could have a discussion about what type of data it is and which graph would represent it best. (10 mins)

Evaluation time
Give the pupils a plan for comparing the insulation properties of three materials along with the results produced. The pupils must work in pairs, spot problems and suggest improvements. (10 mins)

Practical Support

In space, no-one can hear the doorbell (demonstration)

Equipment and materials required
An electric bell in a bell jar, a vacuum pump and power supply.

Details
The bell is suspended inside the sealed jar with leads to connect it to a power supply. The pump is attached to a tube to remove air from the jar.

Let the pupils hear the bell ringing inside the jar before starting, then turn on the pump while explaining what it does. As the air is evacuated the sound will diminish. You may not be able to remove enough air for the bell to become completely inaudible but you should get a noticeable effect. Let the air back into the jar slowly to show that the sound can be heard again.

Safety
Use safety screens and keep pupils well back. Risk of implosion and flying glass.

Sound and solids

Equipment and materials required
A sound source, this could be a loudspeaker connected to a signal generator or any other source that can produce a reasonably constant loudness. A decibel meter or other sound meter.

A range of test materials: expanded polystyrene, metal sheets, cotton wool, wool, plywood and so on.

Details
The pupils need to design a test to see which material is the best conductor of sound (or best insulator). To do this they must use a sound source that produces a constant loudness, and position a sensor a fixed distance away from the source. They could then place materials between the source and detector and measure the reduction in loudness.

Safety
Avoid loud sounds.

Differentiation

SEN
Pupils can be provided with a plan for the 'Sound and solids' task so that they can focus on gathering and analysing results.

Extension
With some pupils you might want to describe the sound wave in more detail using terms like longitudinal wave, compression and rarefaction. You could mention the idea of pressure and emphasise that particles in gases are already moving randomly; the sound wave is super-imposed on top of this random movement.

Homework Suggestion

Summary question 5 works well as a homework task.

Answers to Summary questions

1. Vibrate and wave.
2. Bang one end of the rod and detect sound at the other end with a sensor.
3. A snail, a motorcyclist, sound waves in air, sound waves in steel, light.
4. Pupils describe wave motion in a 'Slinky'.
5. Sound generally travels fastest in solids (except for mercury).

P2.9 Noise Annoys

NC links for the lesson
- Energy, electricity and forces: energy can be transferred usefully, stored, or dissipated, but cannot be created or destroyed.
- Chemical and material behaviour: the particle model provides explanations for the different physical properties and behaviour of matter.

Learning Objectives

Pupils should learn:

- That the ear can detect only a limited range of frequencies and can be damaged by loud sounds.
- That sound intensity is measured in decibels.
- That sound levels can be reduced by insulation.

Learning Outcomes

- All pupils should be able to state that humans can only detect a limited range of frequencies and other animals can detect different ranges.
- Most pupils should be able to explain how the loudness of sound is measured and describe measures to reduce noise pollution.
- Some pupils should also be able to describe how the ear detects sound.

How Science Works

- Recognise that decisions about the use and application of science and technology are influenced by society and individuals, and how these could impact on people and the environment (1.1b).
- Describe an appropriate approach to answer a scientific question (1.2a).

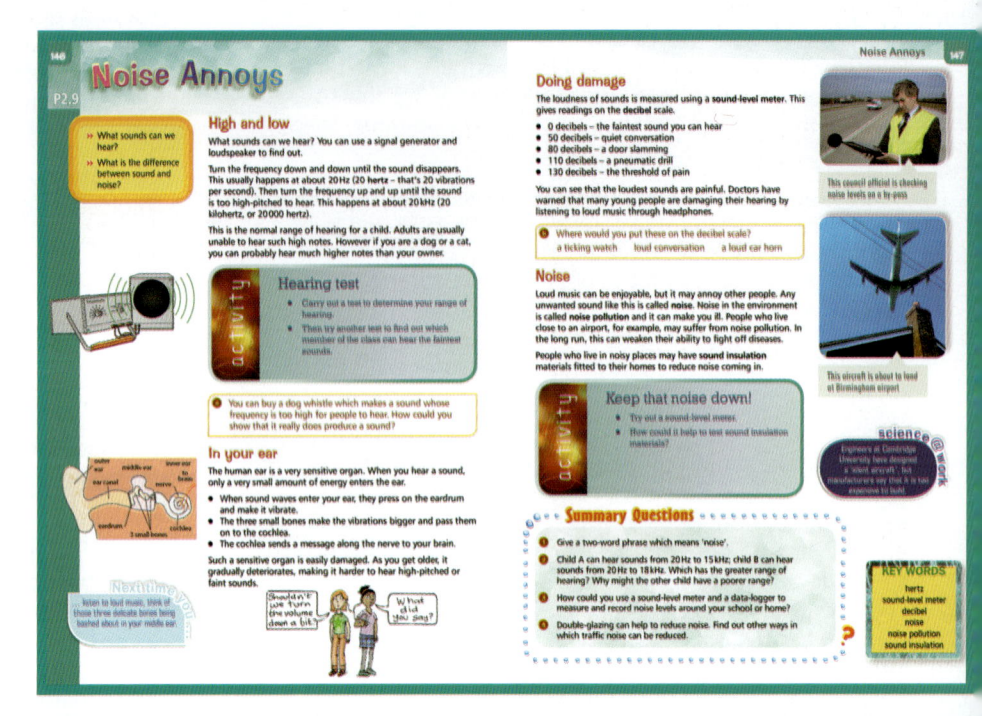

The Lesson

Starter Suggestions

A matter of taste

What is the difference between sound and noise? Give the pupils a list of sounds and let them sort them in order of 'pleasantness'. Which sounds could they listen to all day and which for only a few minutes. This is a good time to play the annoying sounds mentioned in the main lesson; try concentrating while listening to a dental drill! (5–10 mins)

Stop, children what's that sound?

Let the pupils take part in a mystery noise quiz. Play ten sample noises and get them to write down what they think the noise is. Show them the answers at the end. The game must be played in complete silence. (10–15 mins)

Learning Styles

Visual: Looking at the parts of a model ear.
Auditory: Taking part in a range of listening activities.
Kinaesthetic: Operating a sound meter.
Interpersonal: Discussing the importance of noise reduction.
Intrapersonal: Thinking about the effects of hearing loss.

Answers to in-text questions

a Use a sound meter or a microphone connected to an oscilloscope.

b A ticking watch 10 dB, loud conversation 60 dB, a loud car horn 100 dB.

Noise Annoys

Main Lesson

- The 'Stop, what's that sound?' starter is a very interesting way of beginning. You can use a very loud sound as the final example to focus the pupils' attention on loudness.
- Remind the pupils that the frequency of a sound is the number of vibrations each second and the loudness is related to how much energy the sound wave carries.
- Move on to the 'Hearing test' activity. Take part yourself; your hearing range should be a bit more limited than that of the pupils. Some pupils may not want to take part in the hearing test so don't make it compulsory. You might find a few pupils can still hear the sound even with the equipment turned off!
- You can then move on to explain how we actually hear the sound. A large model ear or diagram is essential. You may be able to find a computer animation to support the learning too. Point out how sensitive and fragile the parts of the ear are and give some ideas about how they can be damaged.
- The pupils will generally be able to put sounds in order of loudness. You may not want to use the dB abbreviation for decibel with the pupils.
- The decibel scale is not linear; it's logarithmic. An increase from 10 dB to 20 dB is not the same as an increase from 20 dB to 30 dB. That's why the table in 'doing damage' seems a little odd. The way that the ear actually determines sound difference is well beyond Key Stage 3.
- To show how annoying noise can be, you can play a background noise while the pupils are trying to concentrate. This can be a single annoying note from a signal generator or a recording of traffic noise or an aircraft landing (see 'silent flight' in 'science@work' below for a suitable one). Only play this for a few minutes though.
- The pupils can have a look at a sound meter again with 'Keep that noise down'. They should notice that the readings can be erratic, and that to get an accurate picture of noise levels they would need to take a series of measurements over a period of time.

Plenary Suggestions

Sound off
Finish off the unit with a range of verbal questions focussing on how the particle model can be used to explain thermal energy transfer and sound. (5–10 mins)

Keep it down
The pupils can design a booklet or poster explaining how to reduce noise pollution in a school, office or other building. (10–15 mins)

Practical Support

Hearing test
Equipment and materials required
Signal generator and loudspeaker.

Details
Test the pupils hearing over a range of frequencies. They should be between 20 Hz and 18 kHz.

The simplest way is to ask the pupils to put their hands up when they start to hear the sound and put them back down when the frequency gets too high. This avoids the pupils having to talk over the sound. You may find some pupils claim to hear the sound at frequencies above 20 kHz; this may be buzzing from the loudspeaker caused by interference.

Safety
Do not use overly loud sounds, particularly at frequencies the ear is most sensitive to.

Keep that noise down!
Equipment and materials required
A sound-level meter.

Details
The pupils can test out the sound levels of a range of noises from quiet talking to bangs.

Safety
Do not use very loud sounds.

Differentiation

SEN
Provide the pupils with a help sheet showing the parts of the ear for them to label.

Extension
The pupils could plan and carry out a full investigation into which materials provide the best sound insulation for a particular job. This could be focussed on how many layers of glass it is economical to use for windows, or which material is the best for reducing echoes from walls in sound studios.

Homework Suggestion

Does listening to music on personal music players and mobile phones cause ear damage? The pupils can find recent articles or newspaper stories and write a short report on the issue.

Answers to Summary questions

1. Noise pollution.
2. Child B has a greater range of hearing. Child A has lost some high frequency range, possibly from listening to loud music.
3. Set the data-logger to record the sound levels over a long period and analyse the results later.
4. Pupil research.

science@work

You can find out detailed information about the Silent Aircraft Initiative on the website www.silentaircraft.org. The site contains some diagrams of the design, some samples of how aircraft landing sound, how the new craft would sound, efficiency estimates and some video simulation clips.

Answers to – Heat and Sound End of Topic Questions

Answers to know your stuff questions

1.
   a. A thermometer. [1]
   b. Conduction; convection. [2]
   c. The water will not get any colder; it is at the same temperature as its surroundings, so no heat will flow. [2]

2.
   a. Increases. [1]
   b. Decreases. [1]
   c. Increases. [1]
   d. Increases. [1]
   e. Cold air flows in to replace it (forming a convection current). [1]

3.
   a. C. [1]
   b. B. [1]
   c. Pupils to add to graph A: wave with greater amplitude but same frequency. [1]
   d. Louder but same pitch. [2]

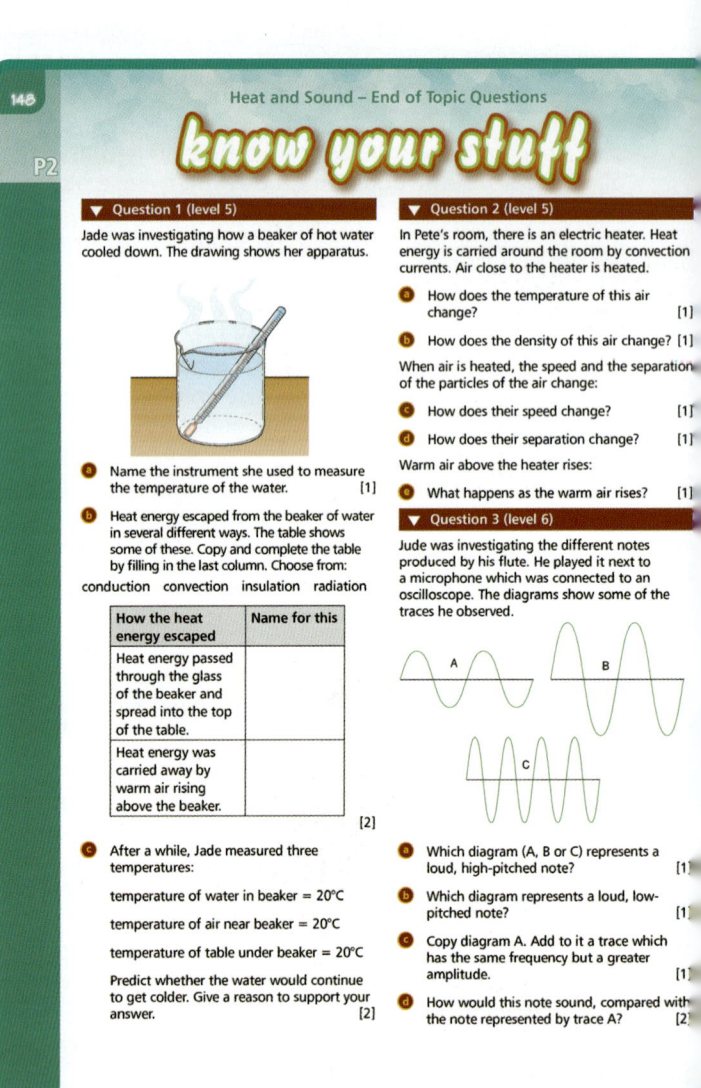

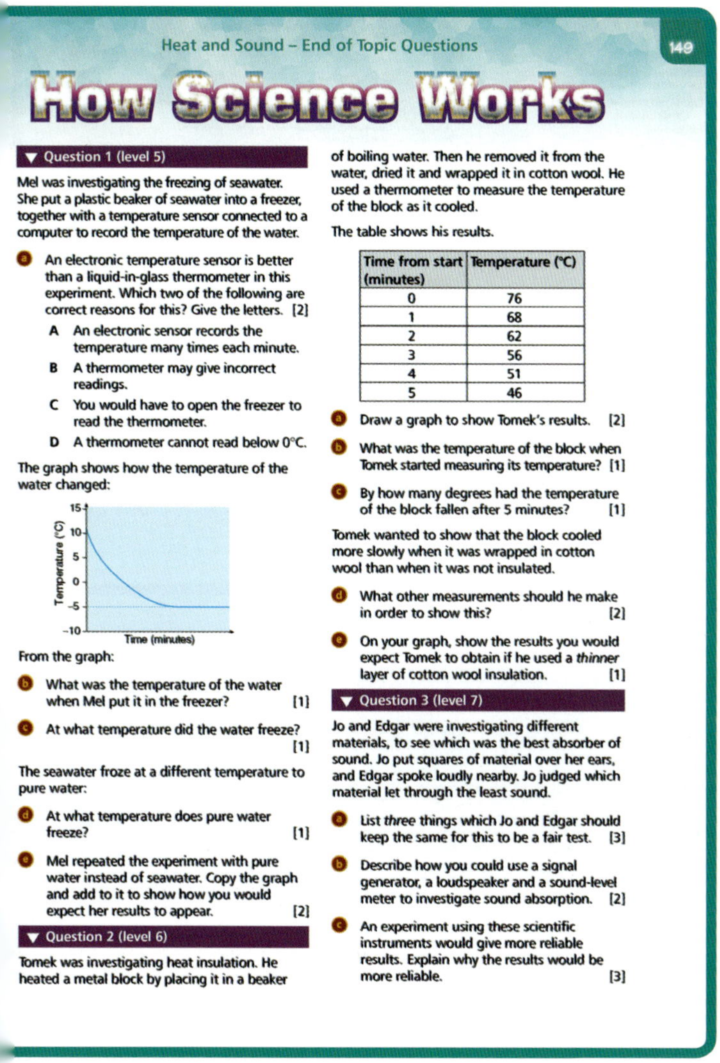

How Science Works

Heat and Sound – End of Topic Questions

▼ Question 1 (level 5)

Mel was investigating the freezing of seawater. She put a plastic beaker of seawater into a freezer, together with a temperature sensor connected to a computer to record the temperature of the water.

a An electronic temperature sensor is better than a liquid-in-glass thermometer in this experiment. Which two of the following are correct reasons for this? Give the letters. [2]

  A An electronic sensor records the temperature many times each minute.
  B A thermometer may give incorrect readings.
  C You would have to open the freezer to read the thermometer.
  D A thermometer cannot read below 0°C.

The graph shows how the temperature of the water changed:

From the graph:

b What was the temperature of the water when Mel put it in the freezer? [1]

c At what temperature did the water freeze? [1]

The seawater froze at a different temperature to pure water:

d At what temperature does pure water freeze? [1]

e Mel repeated the experiment with pure water instead of seawater. Copy the graph and add to it to show how you would expect her results to appear. [2]

▼ Question 2 (level 6)

Tomek was investigating heat insulation. He heated a metal block by placing it in a beaker of boiling water. Then he removed it from the water, dried it and wrapped it in cotton wool. He used a thermometer to measure the temperature of the block as it cooled.

The table shows his results.

Time from start (minutes)	Temperature (°C)
0	76
1	68
2	62
3	56
4	51
5	46

a Draw a graph to show Tomek's results. [2]

b What was the temperature of the block when Tomek started measuring its temperature? [1]

c By how many degrees had the temperature of the block fallen after 5 minutes? [1]

Tomek wanted to show that the block cooled more slowly when it was wrapped in cotton wool than when it was not insulated.

d What other measurements should he make in order to show this? [2]

e On your graph, show the results you would expect Tomek to obtain if he used a *thinner* layer of cotton wool insulation. [1]

▼ Question 3 (level 7)

Jo and Edgar were investigating different materials, to see which was the best absorber of sound. Jo put squares of material over her ears, and Edgar spoke loudly nearby. Jo judged which material let through the least sound.

a List *three* things which Jo and Edgar should keep the same for this to be a fair test. [3]

b Describe how you could use a signal generator, a loudspeaker and a sound-level meter to investigate sound absorption. [2]

c An experiment using these scientific instruments would give more reliable results. Explain why the results would be more reliable. [3]

Answers to How Science Works questions

1
  a A, C. [2]
  b 11°C [1]
  c −5°C [1]
  d 0°C [1]
  e [2]

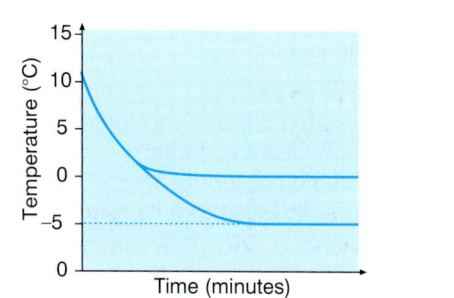

2
  a [2]
  b 76°C [1]
  c 30°C [1]
  d Repeat experiment with no cotton wool. [2]
  e See graph 2a. See blue line. [1]

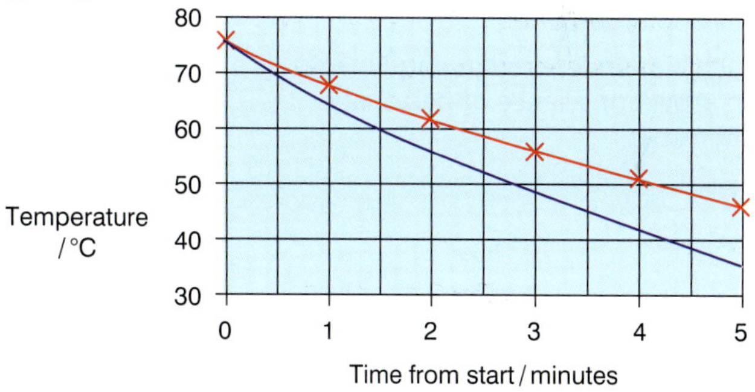

3
  a Loudness of speaking, distance from ear, thickness of insulating material. [3]
  b Connect loudspeaker to signal generator to produce sound. Place sound-level meter nearby, with insulation over sensor. [2]
  c Can be sure that sound level doesn't vary; distance between loudspeaker and meter is fixed; meter gives numerical readings not based on judgement. [3]

HSW: Carrying out Project Work

NC links for the lesson

2 Key processes
- 2.1 Practical and enquiry skills
- Pupils should be able to:
- Use a range of scientific methods and techniques to develop and test ideas and explanations.
- Plan and carry out practical and investigative activities, both individually and in groups.
- 2.3 Communication
- Pupils should be able to:
- Use appropriate methods, including ICT, to communicate scientific information and contribute to presentations and discussions about scientific issues.

4 Curriculum opportunities
- The curriculum should provide opportunities for pupils to:
- Research, experiment, discuss and develop arguments.
- Pursue an independent enquiry into an aspect of science of personal interest.

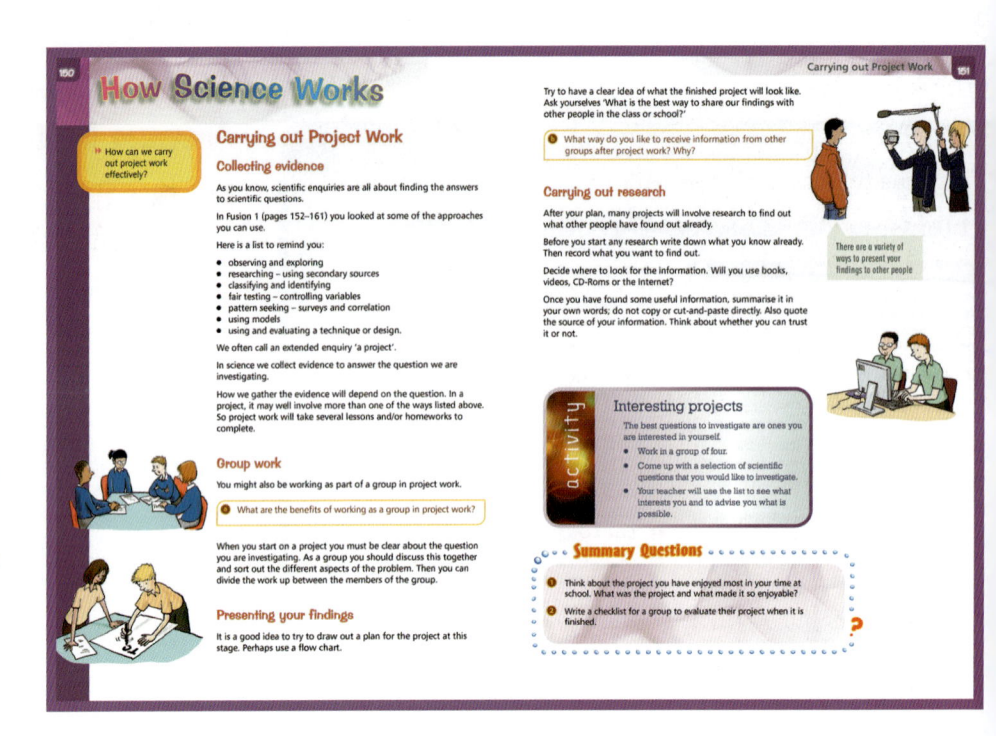

Learning Styles

Auditory: Discussing questions that would be interesting to investigate.

Interpersonal: Working in groups to identify the benefits of group work.

Intrapersonal: Reflecting on the nature of scientific enquiry and how to find the answers to scientific questions.

Functional Skills Link-up

English
- Write documents, including extended writing pieces, communicating information, ideas and opinions, effectively and persuasively (level 2).
- Make a range of contributions to discussions and make effective presentations in a wide range of contexts (level 2).

Learning Objectives

Pupils should learn:
- How to carry out extended project work effectively.

Learning Outcomes
- All pupils should be able to frame a variety of scientific questions.
- Most pupils should be able to plan the major steps needed in project work.
- Some pupils should also be able to identify opportunities and plan in detail how to tackle a scientific project.

How Science Works
- Adapt the stylisic conventions of a range of genres for different audiences and purposes in scientific writing (1.1c).
- Describe an appropriate approach to answer a scientific question using sources of evidence and, where appropriate, making relevant observations or measurements using appropriate apparatus (1.2a).
- Recognise that the selection, ordering or rejection of secondary data could lead to different conclusions (1.2f).

Carrying out Project Work

The Lesson

Starter Suggestions

What, where, why, when, how?
Ask pupils to write five scientific questions about a topic, for example the Sun, starting with each of the words in the title of the starter. Share questions with the whole group. (5 mins)

Scientific enquiry
With the pupil book closed, ask the class to work in groups to think of different methods we use in science to gather evidence in order to answer questions. After 5 minutes, they can open the pupil book and check their ideas against the list given under 'Collecting evidence'. (10 mins)

Main Lesson

- Pupils can use this opportunity to go over the wide variety of methods that scientists use to gather data to answer questions.
- Stress the creativity involved in problem solving in science – not all investigations are merely a fair test.
- Lead into the need for extended enquiries, i.e. what we tend to call 'projects' in schools. Encourage pupils to talk about projects they have done which were memorable or enjoyable, as well as ones they have not got much out of. Why? From the discussion draw out some key points for a successful project, for example, achievable objectives, defined and agreed roles for members of a team in group work, checkpoints, clear vision of end product.
- Reinforce different forms of presentation available for sharing the results of their project work. Discuss advantages and disadvantages of different methods.
- Go over the essentials of carrying out effective research before asking pupils to generate some possible questions to investigate in the activity 'Interesting projects'.
- Keep the outcomes of this activity as a basis for future project work (which might be an individual or group work project). Weed out the questions that you feel will be unsuitable or unproductive. The pupils will feel ownership of the project if they know the options you give them to investigate were originally their own ideas.

Plenary Suggestions

Sharing projects
Ask groups to join with a neighbouring group to discuss their ideas from the 'Interesting projects' activity. Try to come up with a joint list of the five most promising questions to investigate. (10 mins)

'No 'I' in TEAM'
Form groups to review their answers to the in-text question a) 'What are the benefits of working as a group in project work?' Decide on the three most important benefits. (5 mins)

Differentiation

SEN
For lower attaining pupils, you may wish to model how to fill in a research help sheet using a specific example.

Extension
Higher attaining pupils can take one question and classify the different modes of working required to conduct an extended enquiry to answer that question.

Answers to in-text questions

a For example, it enables larger projects to be tackled as the task can be divided up; it can make the most of particular strengths of team members; it gives people responsibility for setting and achieving targets.

b Pupils' personal preferences with reasons.

Answers to Summary questions

1 Pupils discuss previous project work.

2 For example:
- Did you discuss what the task required before starting?
- Were the roles shared out fairly between the team in group work?
- Did you collect enough data to draw a firm conclusion?
- Did the finished project effectively communicate your findings to other people?

HSW: Communicating New Science

NC links for the lesson

1 Key concepts
- Applications and implications of science
- Exploring how the creative application of scientific ideas can bring about technological developments and consequent changes in the way people think and behave.

4 Curriculum opportunities
The curriculum should provide opportunities for pupils to:
- Use real-life examples as a basis for finding out about science.
- Explore contemporary and historical scientific developments and how they have been communicated.

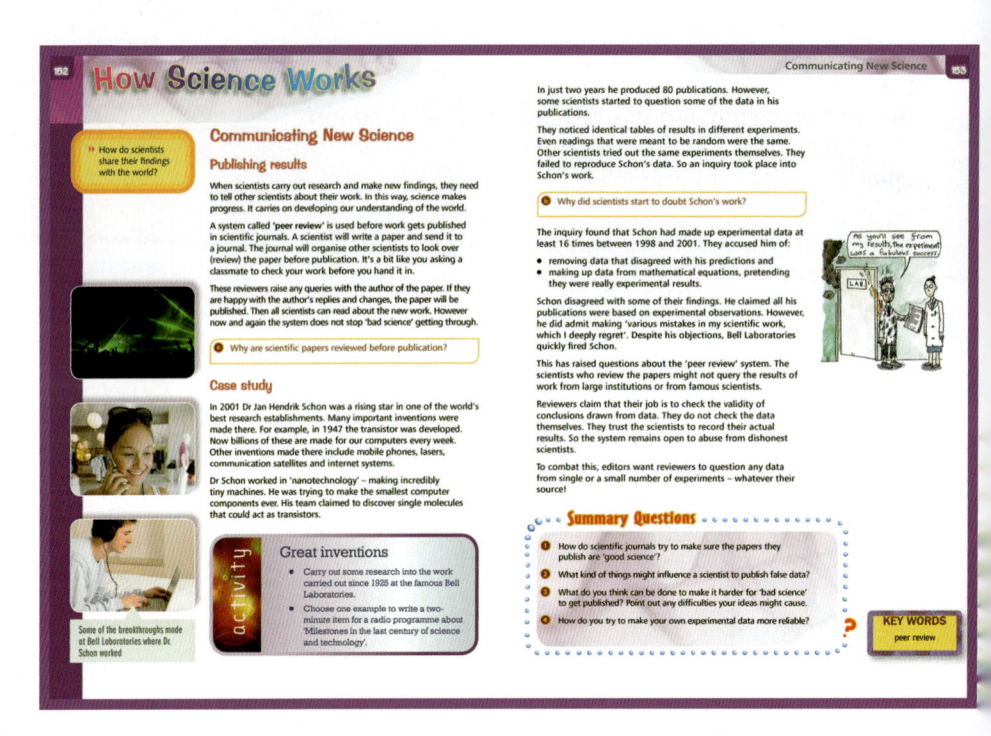

Learning Objectives

Pupils should learn:
- How scientists add to the body of scientific knowledge by communicating through journals.
- How scientific papers are subjected to peer review and that occasionally this can be abused.

Leaning Outcomes
- All pupils should be able to list some important scientific inventions.
- Most pupils should be able to describe how science makes an important contribution to everyday life and how new scientific papers undergo peer review.
- Some pupils should also be able to explain why a particular scientist might falsify data in a scientific paper.

How Science Works
- Recognise that science is a communal, and therefore fallible, human activity and that different explanations can arrive from individual bias (1.1a2).
- Describe how scientific evidence from different sources carries different weight in supporting or disproving theories (1.1a3).

Learning Styles

Visual: Looking at complex data in a scientific journal.

Auditory: Listening to a partner reviewing a piece of their practical work.

Interpersonal: Discussing peer review.

Intrapersonal: Reflecting on the ethics of why a scientist might falsify data.

Answers to in-text questions

a) To check that the science described in the paper is rigorous and the findings are fit for publication.

b) They noticed that identical tables of results in different experiments and readings that were meant to be random were the same. Also other scientists couldn't reproduce his results.

The Lesson

Starter Suggestions

Application of science
Ask pupils to come up with a list of inventions that have been introduced in their lifetimes. (5 mins)

Reliability
Can we trust data? Ask pupils to discuss data presented in the media. Can we generalise? Would you view data in an advert in the same way as data in the evening news on TV? (10 mins)

Main Lesson

- Pupils can be asked how they think scientists communicate their new findings to each other (and hence to the media).
- Have some copies of scientific journals for pupils to look at. Show some from the web if possible. Choose an article with experimental data in it.
- Discuss the 'peer review' system used to vet scientific papers before publication.
- Ask pupils to consider the complex experimental data in a paper. Why would it be difficult for a reviewer to check all the data? What things might make a reviewer suspicious of a set of data?
- Go over the case of Dr Schon outlined in the pupil book. Discuss the pressures there might be on young scientists to falsify evidence.
- The research activity 'Great inventions' can be undertaken after a complete discussion of the peer review system or after introducing the work of Dr Schon as a research scientist at Bell Laboratories.

Plenary Suggestions

'Bad science'
Discuss the consequences of falsifying data for Dr Schon. You might mention other controversial cases, such as cold fusion in the 1980s or more recently Andrew Wakefield's work on autism and the MMR jab. A good source site is found at http://en.wikipedia.org/wiki/Scientific_misconduct. (10–15 mins)

Peer review
In pairs ask pupils to swap exercise books with somebody they do not normally work with and choose an experiment to review for their new partner. They should each ask three questions related to the data gathered in the experiment. (10 mins)

Differentiation

SEN
Help can be provided for pupils in producing the radio item in 'Great inventions' by providing information, for example on the first mobile phones, so they can concentrate on making the recording.

Extension
Pupils can find out about nanotechnology or transistors and report back to the class.

Answers to Summary questions

1. Papers are sent to fellow scientists to check and question – a system called 'peer review'.

2. E.g. the desire to prove his/her ideas are correct/fame or recognition in the scientific community and beyond/monetary gain.

3. E.g. Every experiment could be reproduced and each data point checked before publication. This would take a lot of time and would be very expensive. There would not be enough well qualified reviewers willing to do this work. This could result in long delays in publication.

4. You repeat readings, discard anomalous results and take averages. You check your results against other groups doing the same experiment.

HSW: The Application of Science

NC links for the lesson

1 Key concepts
- Applications and implications of science:
- Exploring how the creative application of scientific ideas can bring about technological developments and consequent changes in the way people think and behave.
- Examining the ethical and moral implications of using and applying science.

4 Curriculum opportunities
The curriculum should provide opportunities for pupils to:
- Use real-life examples as a basis for finding out about science.
- Use creativity and innovation in science, and appreciate their importance in enterprise.

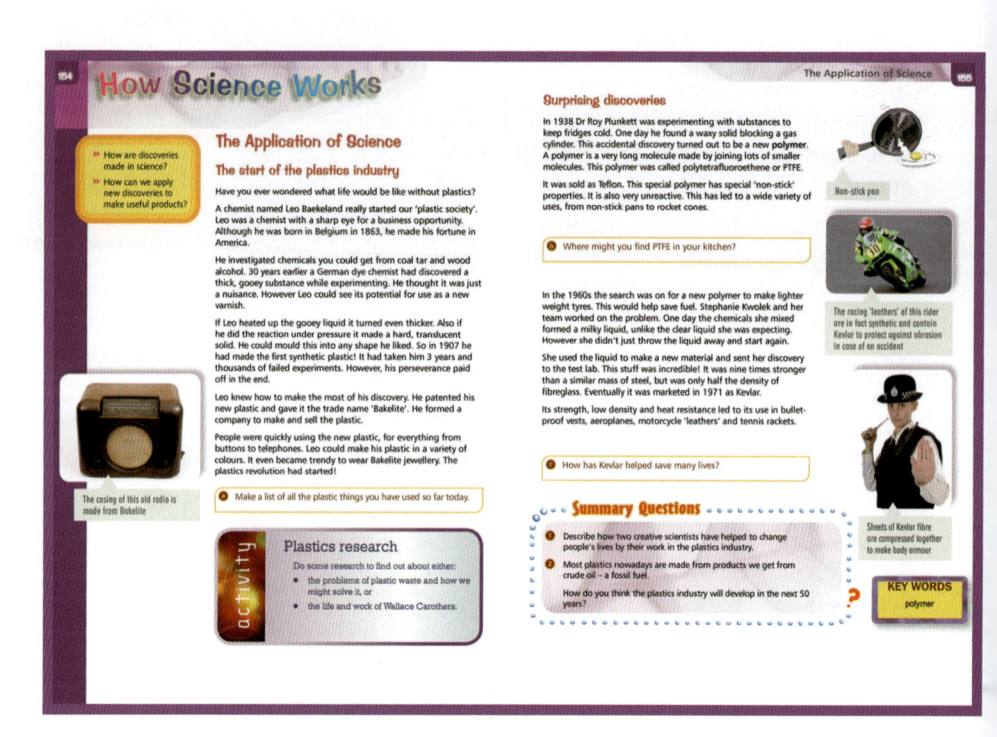

Learning Objectives
Pupils should learn:
- How new discoveries are made and exploited, changing people's lives.

Leaning Outcomes
- All pupils should be able to list two important discoveries in the field of plastics.
- Most pupils should be able to describe how the discovery of a plastic has affected people's lives.
- Some pupils should also be able to explain how creativity and innovation play a vital role in new discoveries and their application, and the effects on society.

How Science Works
- Explain some issues, benefits and drawbacks of scientific developments with which they are familiar (1.1b).

Learning Styles
Visual: Observing the joining of beads to model polymer formation.
Auditory: Listening to feedback on research into plastics.
Interpersonal: Working in groups to carry out research.
Intrapersonal: Reflecting on the future of the plastics industry.

Functional Skills Link-up
English
- Writing documents, including extended writing pieces, communicating information, ideas and opinions effectively and persuasively (level 2).

The Application of Science

The Lesson

Starter Suggestions

Where do plastics come from?
Gather pupils' ideas on where they think plastics come from. What is the raw material? [Mainly crude oil at present.] (5 mins)

Join together
You can introduce pupils to the term 'polymer' at the start of this lesson. Show them beads representing small, reactive molecules. Join them together in a chain and relate this to polymer formation. Use a different set of beads to help explain how different polymer chains (with different properties) can be made. (10 mins)

Main Lesson

- Pupils should be aware of the role science can play in developing new materials and generating wealth, as well as improving the quality of people's lives, in this case using the plastics industry as an example.
- The 'Plastics research' activity can be used to show the ethical and moral dilemmas that arise from exploiting plastics. Point out the role of scientists in trying to solve the problems associated with plastic waste.
- In discussing the examples of Bakelite, PTFE and Kevlar, explore the business implications for the discoveries made by the scientists. [Baekeland was an entrepreneur and made his own company to exploit his new plastic. Plunkett and Kwolek both worked for the giant US company, Du Pont.]
- When going over the discoveries, look at the role of hard work, luck, the ability to recognise an opportunity in the initial breakthrough and its subsequent applications.
- Any of these discoveries can be extended by further research. By dividing the class into three, more information on each plastic could be gathered, then shared.

Plenary Suggestions

Design a plastic
Explain to pupils how we now have polymers that can conduct electricity and can change colour in different conditions. Ask pupils to design plastic that could be used to advertise a designer's label on clothing. (10 mins)

In business
Ask pupils to discuss whether they would rather be an entrepreneur like Baekeland or whether they would rather work for a big company like Plunkett and Kwolek did. Make a list of advantages and disadvantages of each. (15 mins)

Differentiation

SEN
You may wish to provide beads to make chains, and then show how the chains get tangled up when polymers form plastics.

Extension
Pupils can research the latest developments in plastics, e.g. smart polymers.

Answers to In-text questions

a List of plastics used.

b Inside pans.

c Bullet-proof vests / body armour / motorbike leathers.

Answers to Summary questions

1 Description of impact of the work of Baekeland, Plunkett or Kwolek (or alternatives found in research).

2 New raw materials will need to be found, e.g. plant-based plastics.

Glossary

abdomen the lower part of the body, below the diaphragm, containing stomach, intestines, kidney, liver and, in women, the uterus

absorb when a ray of light is taken in when it strikes a surface

accurate the results are close to the truth

acid rain rain with a pH lower than that of natural rain water

aerobic respiration respiration using oxygen

alveolus air sac in the lungs where gases pass between the air and the blood

amino acid molecules that are joined together to make protein molecules

amplitude the height of a wave

amylase enzyme that breaks down starch into sugar

anaerobic respiration respiration without oxygen

artery blood vessel that carries blood away from the heart

-ate a compound that contains a non-metal and oxygen

atom the smallest particle that can exist on its own

axis the imaginary line through the North and South Poles, about which the Earth turns

balanced equation the same number and type of atom on each side of a symbol equation

bile substance produced by the liver which helps digestion, especially of fat

bioaccumulation a process in which substances such as metals or pesticides, from food, build up in the body then are passed on to the next animal in a food chain

biological weathering when a plant or animal breaks rock into smaller pieces

boiling point the temperature at which a substance turns from a liquid to a gas or from a gas to a liquid

branching a type of key

branching bronchi tube that carries air from the trachea into the lung

bronchiole smaller branch of the bronchi

capillaries smallest blood vessels, with a thin wall through which substances diffuse in and out of the blood

carbohydrate a food type used for energy; including sugars and starch

carbonic acid the natural acid found in all rain water, formed as carbon dioxide dissolves in water

cardiac muscle special muscle that the heart is made of

carnivore an animal that eats meat

Celsius scale a scale of temperature

cementation when rock particles are stuck together by minerals, to make sedimentary rock

chemical bond the force between atoms, holding them together

chemical digestion breaking down of large food molecules into smaller ones, which can be absorbed

chemical weathering when a chemical reacts with a rock to weaken the rock and make new substances

chlorophyll the green substance in plants which collects light energy

chloroplast a structure in a cell which contains chlorophyll and is the site of photosynthesis

cilia small hair-like structures on the cells lining the lungs, which brush debris from the lungs

combining power how many chemical bonds an atom can make

compaction when sediment is punched together

competition this takes place when two animals or plants need the same resource

compound more than one type of atom, chemically joined

consumer an organism that gets its food by eating other living things

contract get smaller

convection current when heat energy is carried by a moving liquid or gas

crater dent in the Moon's surface, caused by rocks from space

decibel a unit used to measure the loudness of sound

deciduous trees that lose their leaves in winter

decomposer an organism that breaks down dead animal and plant remains

density $\text{density} = \dfrac{\text{mass}}{\text{volume}}$

deoxygenated blood that has had oxygen removed from it

deposited when sediment is dropped from water or wind

diaphragm a sheet of muscle between the abdomen and thorax which helps us to breathe in and out

dichotomous a type of key

element only one type of atom and it is listed on the Periodic Table

emphysema a disease where the walls of the alveoli break down, reducing the surface area of the lungs

energy a variable, measured in joules (J)

enzyme a protein molecule that controls a chemical reaction in living organisms (including digestion of food)

erosion weathering and transportation

error a result that you can tell is wrong

excretion removal of waste chemicals, such as urea and carbon dioxide, that are produced by the body

exhale breathe out

expand get bigger

faeces indigestible remains of food, mixed with bacteria, commonly known as 'poo'

fat a food type which gives large amounts of energy and is essential in small amounts for making cell membranes

filter a piece of transparent, coloured material

food chain a diagram that shows the feeding relationships between animals and plants

Glossary

food web a series of linked food chains in a habitat

formula shows the number and type of atoms in a molecule and other compounds

freeze–thaw a type of physical weathering, where the repeated freezing and thawing of water in rocks causes them to break

frequency the number of waves or vibrations per second

gas giant a large planet made of frozen gases, e.g. the outer planets of our solar system.

gaseous exchange passage of carbon dioxide from the blood to the air in the lungs, and oxygen from the air in the lungs to the blood

glycogen a compound made of glucose molecules joined together used as a store of energy in animals

guard cell the cells around the stomata in a leaf, which make the stomata open and close

habitat the place where an animal or plant lives and reproduces

haemoglobin a protein, containing iron, used to carry oxygen in the blood

heart the organ that pumps blood around the body

heat energy (heat) energy spreading out from an object which is hotter than its surroundings

hemisphere half of the Earth's sphere

herbivore an animal that eats plants

hertz the unit of frequency; 1 Hz = 1 vibration per second

hibernate slowing down body activity to a minimum and spending winter conditions in a dormant state

homeostasis keeping body conditions, such as temperature, water content and salt concentration, constant

-ide a compound that contains a non-metal

idea a suggestion explaining something, without any evidence to prove your points

identification key a series of questions that are used to help identify an organism

igneous rocks made from cooled magma

image a picture of something, formed by light

incident describes a ray of light falling on a surface

infra-red radiation invisible rays of heat energy spreading out from an object that is hotter than its surroundings

inhale breathe in

intercostal muscles muscles between the ribs which are used in breathing in and out

key a tool to help you identify and classify things

larynx the 'voice box', used in making sounds

lava magma above the Earth's crust

lens a piece of glass shaped so that it refracts rays of light so that they come together

limiting factor a factor, such as temperature, that controls a chemical reaction

lipase an enzyme that breaks down fats

loudspeaker a device that turns electricity into sound, so that we can hear it

lunar eclipse when the Earth blocks the Sun's rays so that the Moon is in darkness

magma molten rock below the Earth's crust

material a word that scientists use to descibe what objects are made from

melting point the temperature at which a substance turns from a solid to a liquid or a liquid to a solid

metal a chemical that is shiny, malleable and a conductor; they often have high melting and boiling points and are sonorous

metamorphic rocks that have been changed by heat and/or pressure

migrate to move to another, more favourable area on a seasonal basis

mineral (biology) an element which is needed by animals and/or plants to grow

mineral (chemistry) an element or compound found in rocks

molecule more than one atom, chemically joined

mucus sticky substance produced by cells lining the respiratory surfaces; it traps bacteria and dirt

neutralisation a chemical reaction between a base (or alkali) and an acid; this makes a metal salt and water

nitrogen oxide a gas made in the engine of a car that can cause acid rain

nocturnal describes an animal which sleeps in the day and is active at night

noise unwanted sound

noise pollution unwanted sound in the environment

non-metal a chemical that is dull, brittle and an insulator; they often have low melting and boiling points

normal the line at right angles to a surface at the point where a ray of light strikes the surface

omnivore an animal that eats both plants and animals

onion-skin weathering a type of physical weathering, where the repeated heating and cooling of the rock causes its outer layer to peel off

oscillate to move back and forth

oscilloscope an electronic instrument used to show sound waves on a screen

oxidation a chemical reaction where oxygen is added

oxygen a gas that makes up about 20% of the air

oxygen debt oxygen which has to be used to break down lactic acid produced in anaerobic respiration

oxygenated blood containing oxygen

palisade cell a cell below the upper surface of a leaf where most photosynthesis takes place

parasite an animal or plant that lives on another animal, causing it some harm

particle model a way of thinking of matter as being made up of particles

peer review the checking of a scientific paper by fellow scientists before it gets published

penumbra region of partial shadow in an eclipse

Periodic Table a list of all the elements that make up the universe

peristalsis contractions of the muscles of the intestines, pushing food through the gut

pesticide a chemical that kills animals which are a pest, e.g. in gardens and farms

phases a stage in the changing appearance of the Moon, as seen from Earth

phlogiston a theory to explain combustion that has now been disproved

photosynthesis the process by which plants use light energy to convert carbon dioxide and water into glucose

physical digestion breaking down large lumps of food to smaller ones, by chewing and by contractions of the gut wall

physical factor a factor such as temperature or light which affects the organisms living in a habitat

physical weathering the breaking down of rocks due to wind, water, other rocks hitting them or the Sun

pitch how high or low a note is

pitfall trap a small trap set in the ground to catch small animals

planet a large, solid object in orbit around the Sun or another star

plasma the liquid part of the blood

platelets small cell-like fragments in the blood which help in clotting

pollution changes to the environment by humans because of noise, chemicals and heat

polymer very long molecule made by joining lots of small molecules together

pooter a suction device for catching small animals

predator an animal that catches and eats other animals

pressure a variable measured in Pascal (Pa)

prey an animal that is caught and eaten by another animal

prism a glass block with a regular shape

producer a green plant that makes food from carbon dioxide and glucose using light energy

products the end chemicals in a reaction

properties a description of how a chemical will look and behave

protease an enzyme that breaks down proteins

protein a food type used for growth and repair and found in meat, eggs, cheese and beans

pyramid of numbers a diagram that shows how many organisms there are at each stage of a food chain

quadrat a square used for collecting information about the number of plants in a habitat

radiation energy spreading out from its source

range the difference between the smallest and largest values of a quantity

reactants starting chemicals in a reaction

recycle collection and processing of used materials to make new things

red blood cells cells which carry oxygen in the blood

reflect when a ray of light bounces off a surface

reflected describes a ray of light which has bounced off a surface

reflex action rapid, automatic response by the nervous system

refraction the bending of light when it travels from one material to another

reliable every time the experiment is repeated, the results are almost the same, making them more trustworthy

rock cycle theory to explain how rocks are recycled on Earth

rocky planet a small planet made of rocky material, e.g. the four planets closest to the Sun

saliva liquid secreted into the mouth which contains amylase and also lubricates food so that it easily slides down the oesophagus

sampling a method of collecting data about the number of animals and plants in a habitat

scatter when a ray of light reflects in many different directions

scavenger an animal that eats animals which are already dead

season a division of the year

sedimentary rocks made from sediment that has been compacted and cemented together

sensitive able to detect small differences or changes

signal generator an electronic device used with a loudspeaker to produce sounds of different frequencies

solar eclipse when the Moon blocks the Sun's rays so that part of the Earth is in darkness

sound insulation material used to absorb sound

sound wave how we picture sound travelling through a material

sound-level meter a meter used to measure the loudness of sound

spectrum all the colours of light, spread out in order

speed of light the speed at which light travels in empty space; about 300 000 km/s

star a glowing mass of hot gas, e.g. the Sun

starch a type of carbohydrate found in potatoes, bread, rice and pasta

stimulus something that is detected by the senses and triggers a nerve impulse, leading to a response

stomata the small pores in a leaf that let in carbon dioxide and let out water and oxygen

sugar type of carbohydrate, found in sweet foods

sweep net a net used to catch small animals living in long grass

sulfur dioxide a gas made in the engine of a car that can cause acid rain

supernova an explosion of a massive star towards the end of its life

symbol a short, unique code for every element

symbol equation shows the symbols and formulas for the starting and ending substances in a chemical reaction

Glossary

synthesis a type of chemical reaction, where a compound is made from its elements

temperature a measure of how hot something is

theory an explanation for an observation with facts to help prove your ideas

thermal conductor a material through which heat passes easily

thermal decomposition a chemical reaction, where heat is used to break down a substance to simpler chemicals

thermal insulator a material through which heat passes only very slowly

thermometer an instrument for measuring temperature

thorax the upper part of the body containing the lungs and heart, sparated from the abdomen by the diaphragm

tissue fluid fluid formed from plasma 'leaking' from the blood and surrounding the cells of the body

trachea the windpipe, linking the larynx to the bronchi

transmit when a ray of light passes through a material

transportation moving from one place to another

tree beating a method of catching small animals by hitting a tree or shrub so they fall out onto a sheet on the ground

umbra region of full shadow in an eclipse

upthrust the upward force on an object in a liquid or a gas

urea a toxic chemical produced from waste protein

variable a quantity that can be changed, controlled or measured in an experiment

vein blood vessel that carries blood towards the heart

vibrate to move back and forth

villi small projections on the lining of the intestine which increase the surface area for absorbing food

vitamin a compound needed in very small quantities in the diet, essential for health

weathering the breaking down of rocks

white blood cells blood cells involved in fighting diseases

word equation shows the names of the starting and ending substances in a chemical reaction

Acknowledgements

Alamy 91, 112, 114.1, 120, 124, 130.2, 132, 136, 147.1, 147.2; **Andrew Lambert** 72, 74; **Bruce Coleman** 95.2; **Corbis** 44.3, 47.2, 112; **Fotolia** 35, 37, 39.1, 39.2, 42.2, 44.1, 44.2, 44.4, 44.5, 44.6, 70, 86.1, 86.2, 88.1, 88.3, 88.2, 101, 152.1, 152.2, 152.3, 154, 155.1, 155.2; **GeoScience Features Picture Library** 84.1, 84.2, 84.3; **Getty** 80, 83, 89, 90.2; **GreenGate** 54; **iStock** 21, 32, 34.1, 42.3, 42.4, 45.2, 45.3, 45.4, 45.5, 45.6, 58.1; **Mark Boulton** 133; **M Chillmaid** 117; **Nasa** 121.2, 123; **Nature picture Library** 106, 140.2, 144; **NHPA** 130.1; **OSF** 58.2; **Photolibrary** 42.1, 43.1, 43.2, 45.1, 46.1, 47.1, 47.3, 47.4; **Photo researchers** 76.2, 107, 121.1; **Science Enhancement Programme** 131; **Science Photo Library** 4, 13, 17.1, 17.2, 18, 19, 34.2, 36, 46.2, 46.3, 46.4, 57, 60.1, 60.2, 60.3, 62, 64, 76.1, 76.3, 77, 82, 84.4, 90.1, 95, 98.1, 98.2, 99.1, 100, 102.1, 102.2, 103, 104, 108, 114.2, 116, 118, 119, 122.1, 126, 127, 131, 138, 140.1; **Topfoto** 66

Picture research by GreenGate Publishing

Every effort has been made to trace all the copyright holders, but if any have been overlooked the publisher will be pleased to make the necessary arrangements at the first opportunity.

Notes

Notes